Education in
Palliative Care

Education in Palliative Care
Building a Culture of Learning

Edited by

Bee Wee, MA(Oxon), MRCGP, MRCP, PhD

Consultant and Senior Clinical Lecturer in Palliative Medicine,
Sir Michael Sobell House and Nuffield Department of Medicine;
Associate Director of Clinical Studies and
Fellow of Harris Manchester College, Oxford University, UK

and

Nic Hughes MSc, BA(Hons), PG Dip Ed, RN, DN Cert

Lecturer in Nursing and Macmillan Research Fellow,
School of Health Care, University of Leeds, UK

OXFORD
UNIVERSITY PRESS

*This book has been printed digitally and produced in a standard specification
in order to ensure its continuing availability*

OXFORD
UNIVERSITY PRESS

Great Clarendon Street, Oxford OX2 6DP
United Kingdom

Oxford University Press is a department of the University of Oxford.
It furthers the University's objective of excellence in research, scholarship,
and education by publishing worldwide.
Oxford is a registered trade mark of Oxford University Press in the UK
and in certain other countries

British Library Cataloguing in Publication Data
Data available

Library of Congress Cataloging in Publication Data
Data available

ISBN 978-0-19-856985-5

Contents

To Charlie (in memoriam), Florence, Lillian, and Richard B. W.
To Tom (in memoriam), Kate, Rosie, and Sean N. H.

Bee Wee

Born Chinese and brought up in Malaysia, she finished her schooling in Dublin and qualified in medicine from Trinity College in 1988. She trained as a general practitioner in Dublin and Trim, County Meath. She then moved to palliative medicine, first in Ireland, and then in Hong Kong. In 1995, she was appointed Consultant and Senior Lecturer in Palliative Medicine at the University of Southampton, where she became Deputy Director of Education at the Medical School and, subsequently, a member of the Head of School's Advisory Group. During this time, she completed her PhD on death rattle and, in recognition of her educational work, was awarded an Honorary Membership of the Royal College of General Practitioners (2002).

In 2003, she moved to Oxford to a joint clinical and academic post: Consultant and Senior Lecturer in Palliative Medicine, Associate Director of Clinical Studies and Fellow, and now, College Tutor for Medicine at Harris Manchester College. In addition she is the Academic Director of the Oxford International Centre for Palliative Care and Head of the WHO Collaborating Centre for Palliative Care. She continues on the Faculty of the annual national Educational Leadership course, originally a joint venture between the Association for the Study of Medical Education (ASME) and the Harvard-Macey Institute, USA. The dissertation for her MA in Education is on educational leadership. In 2005, she became a Trustee of Marie Curie Cancer Care and external examiner for the Bristol University Medical School Final Examinations and the MSc in Palliative Medicine at Bristol University. She is Honorary Professor of Palliative Medicine at Sichuan University, China, and has an adjunct appointment as Associate Professor at the Edith Cowan University, Perth, Australia. She chairs the Science Committee for the Association for Palliative Medicine of Great Britain and Ireland. In 2006, she was admitted to the Membership of the Royal College of Physicians of London in recognition of 'distinguished contributions in the field of medicine'. She has published on symptom control, specifically death rattle, and education, both medical and interprofessional.

Nic Hughes

Nic Hughes is a Macmillan Lecturer at the University of Leeds. His teaching over recent years has focused on continuing professional development for specialists in cancer and palliative care. Nic has a special interest in education for leadership and has published in the fields of education and end-of-life care.

Foreword

It could be argued that one of the most important characteristics of the health care professional (whatever the discipline) is that they are both caring and compassionate. This comment covers all specialties, but is particularly relevant in palliative care. When we consider the aim of medicine, or more broadly all caring professionals, it can be defined in simple terms as 'assisting the process of healing'. This is not just about treatment or effecting a cure but also assisting with quality of life, providing care and relieving suffering. It represents the 'wholeness' so important in palliative care. The end purpose of learning is thus to be able to provide to individuals and communities ways of improving health care and quality of life. It implies for the professional that they understand illness and disease and have a wide range of skills and expertise to deal with a multitude of problems.

Much of the educational work in palliative care has been focused on the cancer patient and I therefore welcome the discussion in this book on the care of patients with non-malignant disease. The lessons learned from the patient with cancer can often be transferred to other illnesses, but not always. Different skills are required and all can learn from each other. In a similar way the international experience set out in this book needs to be shared more widely.

So how can caring be learned? How can we become more compassionate? First being a compassionate professional cannot be divorced from the knowledge and understanding required of disease processes, methods of treatment and relieving symptoms. Being a caring professional requires knowledge of a wide range of topics without which it would not be possible to adequately care for people. This is where the curriculum becomes important in defining the breadth of knowledge and expertise required. Included within this are the skills required for caring from the management of bedsores to the complexities of pharmacology. The first prerequisite is thus an adequate knowledge base. To some this might seem to be the wrong way around, but being nice to people is no substitute for knowing what to do and how to do it.

Caring is more than just the acquisition of knowledge. It deals with emotions and feelings, of sensitivity and relationships. How can this best be learned? This is more difficult and requires a range of methods, for example experience of discussing and being involved in such issues, and of watching others tackle difficult problems, hence the particular relevance of role models. Mentoring and reflective practice all have a part to play in learning about improving one's own performance in caring for others. As described in this book, the creation of a culture of learning in the clinical team can be an important part of this; a place and a time where staff can talk openly about difficulties and learn from the experience. No matter how 'wise' we may be, we sometimes get it wrong – we all therefore need to be able to tell our stories to others and listen to their reflections on our actions.

The educational processes described in this book provide a framework for such discussions and learning. Education however is associated with more than knowledge, or the development of skills and expertise. It is more than learning the appropriate attitudes.

Education is about the transmission of values. Such values are grown and nourished in clinical communities and teams and are self-reinforcing. Being part of such a community, able to openly discuss issues and share experiences, is a powerful learning experience in which all can participate. This emphasizes the importance of teamwork and of recognizing the skills and expertise of all professions in the care of the patient. In some ways palliative care has been the model of interprofessional learning: indeed those who have been brought up in such an environment sometimes find it difficult to understand what the problem is in other clinical areas.

The issue which is at the heart of learning in palliative care is that of leadership. No particular model of leadership is advocated, nor is it assumed that it is from one particular professional group. Much of what I learned about palliative care was from vastly experienced and skilled nursing staff who helped me come to terms with the problems which we faced together. Leadership is showing by example, not only of how to do things well, but how to recognize when things have not gone well. It is about creating the culture of learning within which all can benefit and share the learning. One of my favourite books is 'I and Thou' by Martin Buber. It describes relationships between people and notes that most relationships are categorized as 'I and You'. In this we acknowledge each others presence (patient or professional) but no further. When the relationship is 'I and thou' it become much closer and Buber describes it as a 'sharing of hearts'. For the teacher and the learner the relationship begins as 'I and You' and as it develops it grows into 'I and thou'. As the pupil surpasses the master the achievement of education becomes apparent. For those who have watched others whom we have nurtured going further and higher than we ever could it is a wonderful and enriching experience. In a similar way for many patients the relationships we have may be 'I and You' type, impersonal, respectful and courteous, and recognizing their values and dignity. For others, especially in palliative care it becomes 'I and thou'; deeper and more meaningful, open and trusting, where words need not be spoken and communication is through mutual respect. To get to that level of involvement should be the end point of the learning process.

I welcome this book as a place where all concerned with learning in palliative care will find something of interest, and which will stimulate new thinking on educational issues in such an important clinical area.

Kenneth C. Calman
Durham 2006

Preface

This book is for anyone who is involved in education and training in palliative care. Books on either education or palliative care abound – volumes devoted to education in palliative care are rare. This is a gap which we attempt to fill.

Our own personal and professional experience, as practitioners and teachers, include some successes as well as our fair share of failures. In discussing these with friends and colleagues, they told the same story. So when Oxford University Press approached us to write for them, we accepted the challenge, recognizing that it would be coloured by our values, beliefs and assumptions. These inevitably shaped the decisions we made about the structure of the book and the contributions we sought from colleagues around the world.

In writing this book, we had to cross boundaries in our own thinking, through discussions with one another and with our authors. This resulted in a rich and rewarding experience for us, which we hope will come across to our readers. We hope that the authentic voice of experience will shine through in the way we have chosen and worked with our authors, from whom we have learnt a great deal. Sadly, due to the size of the book, it was inevitable that there were many other skilled, knowledgeable and well-respected teachers whom we could not include in the process. But we had to be pragmatic.

Diversity of culture and practice at every level are evident throughout the book: between palliative care practice and education in different parts of the world; between those who teach within higher education institutions and palliative care services; between teaching in small and large groups; between undergraduate and postgraduate learning and continuing professional development; between the management responsibilities of making things happen on the ground and the parallel, but different, role of leadership in pushing forward the educational boundaries. Readers may find themselves constantly challenged and pulled by the tensions which often accompany such diversity, as we were, in planning and writing this book with our various contributors around the world. We hope you will find in these pages illumination and inspiration for the important work of teaching palliative care in whichever setting you practise.

How to use this book

The book begins with an introductory chapter setting out relevant learning theories which readers may find useful. The rest of the book is divided into three parts:

Part One sets the scene for existing palliative care education around the world and is in two sections. The first discusses education for different professional groups in the UK. Section two extends this to other parts of the world. We hope that this will help readers in both the UK and elsewhere to understand and learn, as we did, from the rich cultural diversity and wide-ranging educational practice across the world.

Part Two focuses on learning, teaching and assessment in different settings. We deliberately avoid teaching on specific topics because we believe that there is no room for recipe-book teaching in palliative care education. Rather, a rigorous approach and purposeful choices are important, just as they are in the care of patients. In each chapter, the authors strive to provide bridges between mainstream education and palliative care. They balance the theory underpinning each aspect of teaching, learning and assessment with the practicalities of delivering these at the coal face.

Part Three explores ways of building and nurturing a culture of learning in palliative care, whether as an individual or as an organization.

In addition, we hope that the following will help to make this book user-friendly, particularly for a global readership:

- a clear contents list to guide readers directly to areas of interest (page *v*)
- references presented in alphabetical order at the end of the book instead of at the end of each chapter so that they can be easily found (page 311)
- a glossary (page 339) and explanation of abbreviations (page *xv*) to explain terms which may be less familiar to some readers
- useful web sites and references for those who wish to explore topics in greater depth (pages 343 and 337).

Some final thoughts

First, we leave it our readers to speculate about the future of palliative care education. For although there will be common threads, educators in different settings and countries will need to find their own opportunities and allies so that they can tackle the challenges they face.

Second, although it is obvious that not all chapters will appeal to all disciplines and professions, we urge our readers to maintain dialogue and discussion with each other, keeping open minds so that they continue to develop, learn from others and disseminate what works through writing.

Third, we make a plea for more research. For just as there is a paucity of writing on palliative care education, there is an even greater lack of educational research in palliative care. With ageing populations and rapidly growing expectations of palliative care, this is becoming urgent.

Bee Wee and Nic Hughes

Acknowledgements

We are indebted to our contributors, from whom we have learnt a great deal and who have made the process so enjoyable through their commitment, good nature and patience; to Professor Sir Kenneth Calman who has been an inspiration to palliative care teachers over many years and who has generously contributed the Foreword. We also thank our colleagues at the Oxford University Press for their encouragement and ready support, especially Catherine Barnes, Georgia Pinteau and Clare Caruana; our librarians, Sue Killoran at Harris Manchester College and Meg Roberts at Sir Michael Sobell House.

We are indebted to the many who have helped us develop our thinking over coffee breaks, informal meetings and late night chats at Harris Manchester College, Sir Michael Sobell House, the School of Healthcare at the University of Leeds and the Medical Sciences Division University of Oxford. In particular, Katy Newell-Jones helped to guide and frame the entire section on palliative care education around the world.

BW is grateful for those who stimulated her interest in education and provided role models of good teaching from early days: Gertrude Derham, Margaret Silke, Dermot Moore and George Doyle. Michael Kearney, Ilora Finlay and Richard Hillier provided later inspiration and encouragement. Michael Arthur, Chris Thompson, Chris Stephens, Lesley Millard and Barbara Clayton opened doors and provided academic opportunities in education at University of Southampton. Many others provided stimulation and intellectual challenge through collaboration and discussion about education, especially Colin Coles, Brenda Mountford, Della Fish, Jenny Field and Angela Fenwick. There has been much lively discussion about the nature of educational leadership with Elizabeth Armstrong from the Harvard-Macey Institution, Stephen Field, Anne Garden, Gillian Needham and Frank Smith from the Association for the Study of Medical Education (ASME) and Jenny King from Edgecumbe Consulting.

NH is grateful to teachers and mentors over many years who helped him learn to think and to write: David Clark, Ellis Evans, Steve Evans, Norman Howlings, Tom Kitwood, Stuart Linney, Mike McKie, Richard Neal, John O'Connell, Colin Parker, Hugh Robertson, Pauline Stafford, Gordon Sunderland, Alan Tomlinson; and to many colleagues in the School of Healthcare at the University of Leeds, in the Macmillan National Institute of Education and in the Macmillan Research Units, who have been such an important part of his working life for the last decade.

Finally we are both indebted to many of our colleagues for their patience and support during the production of this book: Michael Minton, Mary Miller, Tim Harrison and other colleagues, especially the Hospital Palliative Care Team and Study Centre Team, at Sir Michael Sobell House; Tim Lancaster, Sue Burge, Peggy Frith and Helena McNally at Oxford University Medical School; Ralph Waller, Principal of Harris Manchester College, Oxford, and the staff and Governing Body of the College; Catherine Jack, Eileen Mullard and Rachel Fawcett-Hodge at the Macmillan Education Unit, University of Leeds. It has been humbling, when starting to list acknowledgements, to discover how many people have been part of this book in one way or another and we are much indebted to all of them. And, of course, without patients, carers and students to provide us with inspiration and purpose, this book would never have been written.

Abbreviations

ABHPM	American Board of Hospice and Palliative Medicine		ELNEC	End-of-Life Nursing Education Consortium (USA)
ANZSPM	Australian and New Zealand Society of Palliative Medicine		EMQ	extended matching questions
			ENB	English National Board
APCA	African Palliative Care Association		EPEC	Education for Physicians on End-of-Life Care Project (USA)
APD	Accredited Professional Development		EU	European Union
APEL	Accreditation of Prior Experiential Learning (see also the glossary, p. 337)		FSU	former Soviet Union
			GMC	General Medical Council, UK
			GSCC	General Social Care Council
APHN	Asia-Pacific Hospice Palliative Care Network		HE	higher education
APL	Accreditation of Prior Learning (see also the glossary, p. 337)		HPC	Health Professions Council
			IAPC	Indian Association of Palliative Care
APM	Association for Palliative Medicine of Great Britain and Ireland		IASSW/IFSW	International Association of Schools of Social Work/International Federation of Social Workers
APRAC	Australian Palliative Residential Aged Care Project			
CAIPE	Institute of Community Studies for the Advancement of Interprofessional Education		IELTS	International English Language Testing System
			IQ	intelligence quotient
CAL	computer-assisted learning		IT	information technology
CAT	Credit Accumulation and Transfer (see also the Glossary)		JCHMT	Joint Committee for Higher Medical Training
CCETSW	Central Council for Education and Training in Social Work		KSF	Knowledge and Skills Framework (see also the glossary, p. 339)
CEE	Central and Eastern Europe		LEDC	less economically developed countries
CMAI	Christian Medical Association Project of India		MCQ	multiple choice question
COT	College of Occupational Therapists		MEDC	more economically developed countries
CPD	continuing professional development		MEQ	modified essay question
CPE	continuing professional education		Mini-CEX	mini clinical evaluation examination
CSP	Chartered Society of Physiotherapy		MSF	multi-source feedback
DNR	do not resuscitate		NCHPCS	National Council for Hospice and Palliative Care Services: umbrella organization for hospice and palliative care services in UK; now renamed National Council for Palliative Care (NCPC)
DOH	Department of Health, UK			
DOPS	direct observation of procedural skills			
EAPC	European Association for Palliative Care			
			NGO	non-governmental organization

NHS	National Health Service, UK
NICE	National Institute of Clinical Excellence, UK (see also the glossary, p. 339)
NMC	Nursing and Midwifery Council, UK, formerly known as the United Kingdom Central Council (UKCC), a statutory body responsible for professional regulation of nursing, midwifery and health visiting
NNHC	Neighbourhood Network in Healthcare (Kerala, India)
NVQ	National Vocational Qualification, England and Wales (see also the Glossary)
OSCE	objective structured clinical exam
OSLER	objective structured long examination record
PAHO	Pan American Health Organization
PBL	problem-based learning
PCC4U	Palliative Care Curriculum for Undergraduates Programme (Australia)
PCE	palliative care education
PEPA	Programme in Experience in the Palliative Approach (Australia)
PMETB	Postgraduate Medical and Education Training Board (Australia)
PREP	Post-Registration Education and Practice (see also the glossary, p. 339)
PRHO	Pre-registration House Officer
QAA	Quality Assurance Agency, UK (see also the Glossary)
RCT	randomized controlled trial
RITA	Record of In-Training Assessment
SHO	Senior House Officer
SNAPPS	Summarize the case, Narrow the differential diagnosis, Analyse the differential diagnosis, Probe the teacher about areas not understood, Plan the management, Select an issue for further learning.
SpRs	Specialist Registrars
STC	Specialty Training Committee
STC	Specialty Training Committees
UKCC	United Kingdom Central Council for Nursing and Midwifery
WBL	work-based learning
WHO	World Health Organization

List of Contributors

Heather Campbell
Macmillan Senior Lecturer
Macmillan Education Unit
Faculty of Health and Social Work
University of Plymouth
England

Gillian Chowns
Formerly Specialist Palliative Care Social
Worker
East Berks Macmillan Palliative Care Team
Senior Lecturer in Palliative Care
Oxford Brookes University
Oxford, UK

Margaret Colquhoun
Senior Nurse Lecturer
Programme Leader – MSc in Palliative Care
St Columba's Hospice
Edinburgh, UK

John Costello
Lecturer in Palliative Care Nursing
University of Manchester
School of Nursing, Midwifery and
Social Work
Manchester, UK

Gustavo G. De Simone
Professor of Medical Oncology (USAL)
Medical Director
Pallium Latinoamerica (NGO)
Chief of Education Department
Hospital Bonorino Udaondo
Buenos Aires, Argentina

Lorraine J. Dixon
Senior Lecturer/Field Chair in Cancer and
Palliative Care
Oxford Brookes University

Honorary Clinical Nurse Specialist in
Palliative Care
Oxford Radcliffe Hospitals NHS Trust
Oxford, UK

Tony Egan
Senior Teaching Fellow
Department of the Dean
Dunedin School of Medicine
Dunedin
New Zealand

John Ellershaw
Professor of Palliative Medicine
University of Liverpool
Director
Marie Curie Palliative Care Institute
Liverpool, UK

Gail Eva
Manager
Hospital and Community Palliative Care
Teams
Sir Michael Sobell House
Oxford, UK

Frank D. Ferris
Medical Director
Palliative Care Standards/Outcome
Measures
San Diego Hospice and Palliative Care
A primary teaching affiliate of the
University of California
San Diego, School of Medicine
USA

Marilène Filbet
Chief, Palliative Care Unit
Centre Hospitalo-Universitaire de Lyon
Hôpital de la Croix Rousse
Lyon
France, and
President
European Association for Palliative Care
Milano, Italy

Ilora Finlay
Professor of Palliative Medicine
Department of Oncology and Palliative
Medicine
Cardiff University
Velindre Hospital
Cardiff, UK

Karen Forbes
Consultant and Macmillan Professorial
Teaching Fellow
United Bristol Healthcare Trust and
University of Bristol
Bristol, UK

Barbara Gale
Clinical Services Director
St Nicholas Hospice
Bury St Edmunds, UK

Cynthia Goh
Senior Consultant and Head
Department of Palliative Medicine
National Cancer Centre Singapore
Republic of Singapore

Liz Gwyther
Senior Lecturer
Department of Family Medicine
University of Cape Town
South Africa

Bob Heath
Music Therapist
Sir Michael Sobell House
Oxford, UK, and

The Prospect Hospice
Wroughton
Wiltshire, UK

Suzanne Henwood
Managing Director
Henwood Associates (South East) Ltd
Sevenoaks, UK

Peter Hudson
Associate Professor
Deputy Director, Centre for Palliative Care
St Vincent's Health and University of
Melbourne
Victoria, Australia

Nic Hughes
Macmillan Lecturer
School of Healthcare
University of Leeds
Leeds, UK

Stephen Jones
Learning Resources Manager
Department of Oncology and Palliative
Medicine
Cardiff University School of Medicine
Cardiff, UK

Suresh Kumar
Director
Institute of Palliative Medicine
Calicut
Kerala, India

Philip J. Larkin
Lecturer in Nursing (Palliative Care)
The National University of Ireland
Galway, Ireland, and
Vice-President
European Association for Palliative Care
Milano, Italy

Rod MacLeod
District Medical Director of Palliative
Care (Waitemata DHB)
Honorary Clinical Professor in General
Practice and Primary Health Care
University of Auckland, and
Adjunct Professor in the Departments of
General Practice and Medical and Surgical
Sciences
University of Otago
Dunedin School of Medicine
New Zealand

Michelle McGannan
Macmillan Lecturer
Macmillan Education Unit
Kings College
London, UK

Mary Miller
Consultant in Palliative Medicine
Sir Michael Sobell House
Oxford, UK, and
Honorary Senior Clinical Lecturer, Oxford
University, also
Regional Specialty Advisor for Palliative
Medicine
Oxford Deanery
Oxford, UK

Kathy Munro
Acting Head of Nursing
Programme Leader – MSc in Professional
Education
School of Health Sciences – Nursing
Queen Margaret University College
Edinburgh, UK

Katy Newell-Jones
National Teaching Fellow
School of Health and Social Care
Oxford Brookes University
Oxford, UK

Gillian Percy
Clinical Specialist Physiotherapist in
Palliative Care and Lymphoedema
Countess Mountbatten House
Southampton, UK

Marilyn Relf
Head of Education
Sir Michael Sobell House
Oxford, UK

Rosalie Shaw
Consultant
Department of Palliative Medicine
National Cancer Centre Singapore
Republic of Singapore

Ruthmarijke Smeding
Founding Director of Palliative Education
Institute for Educational expertise in
Clinical, Palliative And Bereavement Care
Hanover, Germany, and
Brussels, Belgium

Odette Spruyt
Director
Pain and Palliative Care Department
Peter MacCallum Cancer Centre
East Melbourne
Victoria, Australia

Charles F. von Gunten
Director
Center for Palliative Studies
San Diego Hospice and Palliative Care
Associate Clinical Professor of Medicine
University of California
San Diego, School of Medicine
USA

Bee Wee
Consultant Physician and Senior Clinical
Lecturer in Palliative Medicine
Sir Michael Sobell House
Oxford Radcliffe Hospitals NHS Trust and
Nuffield Department of Medicine
University of Oxford

Associate Director of Clinical Studies
Medical Sciences Division
and
Fellow of Harris Manchester College
University of Oxford
Oxford, UK

Chapter 1

Introduction: learning and teaching palliative care

Bee Wee and Nic Hughes

Palliative care education is exciting, challenging and fun. Its ultimate goal is to ensure that patients with palliative care needs, and their families, receive high quality care because those involved in their care know what to do and how to do it well and are able to exercise wise judgement when doing it. The ability to teach others about palliative care and to learn from them in return is therefore crucial. Traditionally palliative care practitioners teach, but to be really effective, they should also be actively engaged in curriculum development, assessment and, because education never ends, their own lifelong learning.

In this chapter, we shall:

◆ consider how learning and teaching in palliative care differ from learning and teaching in other fields

◆ present theories, models and frameworks relevant to palliative care education and which are referred to in subsequent chapters.

How is learning and teaching in palliative care different?

Palliative care has learnt a great deal from educational practice in other fields, both within and outside health care. However, there are several issues which affect what and how we teach. First, we are dealing with dying people and their families at a fraught and uncertain time which is full of complexities. Their stories are often sensitive and emotive, and direct involvement of patients and their families in teaching requires careful preparation and support. Second, the evidence base for much of palliative care practice is slim, though rapidly growing. Up to date knowledge and skills must be taught alongside critical thinking, judgement and practical wisdom if we are to avoid being stuck in outdated practice or, equally dangerous, to succumb unthinkingly to every new bandwagon. Third, effective palliative care is best achieved through interprofessional teamworking. Palliative care education has to cater for the needs of mixed professional groups within the field as well as those in other specialties, for example primary care, oncology, gerontology, general medicine and surgery. Finally, the history of the development of palliative care means that it has to grapple with specific tensions. One is between the over-indulgent, uncritical lavishing of 'cuddly care' at one extreme and the over-simplistic, protocol-driven care at the other. Another tension is that between sticking with the traditional treatment of cancer patients only and moving into the less familiar world of all non-malignant disease. All this has implications for palliative care education.

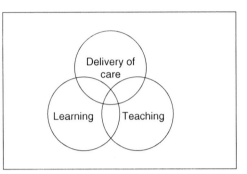

Fig. 1.1 Interlinked and inseparable components of professional practice

Our underlying assumption throughout this book is that the delivery of care, teaching and learning are interlinked and inseparable components of professional practice in health and social care (Figure 1.1). Ideally, effective health and social care professionals should remain practitioners, learners and teachers throughout their professional lives. Each aspect feeds the others to ensure that patient experience and student learning are kept fresh, relevant and grounded in the real world.

Education is the process through which learning occurs. Learning is analogous to a journey in which we end up at a different, hopefully better and more interesting, place from where we started. Motivation, energy and engagement with real experiences are necessary to fuel that journey. Training, on the other hand, is about the acquisition of knowledge or skills to deal with a particular type of event. It may be achieved through repetitive practice, whereas education is value-based and involves a process of active thinking and reflection. This is neatly summarized by Calman and Downie (1988), as cited by Calman (2000: 48): 'to be trained is to have arrived, to be educated is to continue to travel'.

Theories, models and frameworks for learning and teaching

The thought of 'learning theory' instils anxiety and anticipatory boredom in many practitioners. The literature is littered with a plethora of theories and a language and vocabulary familiar mainly to an inner circle of educational specialists. Most practitioners struggle to find the time to engage with such literature. However, they may find that doing so enables them to enhance their own teaching and learning. So, in this section, we present a selection of learning theories, models and frameworks which we have found helpful in palliative care education. These are:

- The concept of a formal, informal and hidden curriculum: Hafferty (1998)
- Two different models of experiential learning: Kolb (1984) and Race (2005)
- The iceberg as a metaphor for professional practice: Fish and Coles (1998)
- The three dimensions of learning: Illeris (2004).

Formal, informal and hidden curricula

The formal curriculum is most familiar to us all. It is the declared statement of what will be taught in a teaching session, course or programme of study. The formal curriculum is

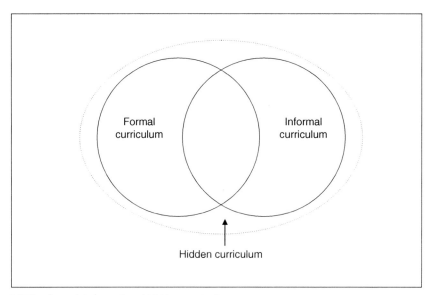

Fig. 1.2 The formal, informal and hidden curriculum

usually written and includes intended learning outcomes and teaching and assessment methods. At its simplest, this may simply be a programme which includes the aims and learning outcomes and details of the teaching activities, such as is often seen for palliative care teaching events. However, Hafferty (1998) argues that there are at least two other spheres of influence on learning: informal and hidden curriculum (see Figure 1.2).

The informal curriculum is the learning which comes from the unscripted interactions that take place between the teacher and learners and between learners themselves. This may occur during the teaching session, for example when a learner disagrees with a point that the teacher makes and a discussion ensues. Refreshment breaks also provide a rich opportunity for learning from the informal curriculum, something which most practitioners will appreciate from attendance at conferences. The hidden curriculum, depicted by the dotted circle encompassing both the formal and informal curriculum in Figure 1.2, is less tangible. It is the culture in which the learning occurs, incorporating the values, beliefs and assumptions held by the teacher and organization, and has a profound influence on the quality of learning which occurs.

Learning and teaching is most effective when there is a good match between these three types of curriculum. For example, in a communication skills course when:

1. the intended learning outcomes, the teaching methods and the assessment are realistic and well-structured, and there is good alignment between all three (*formal*),

2. the learners find that they learn in a variety of ways, not only from the teacher, but also from each other, through the feedback on their own performance and during the ample time for discussion (*informal*), and

3. the learners note the respectful and effective communication between the course teachers, the way they (the learners) are valued for their contributions and how constructive feedback leads to improvement in their own, and others' communication skills (*hidden*).

When all three types of curriculum gel together, the learning which results is rich and inspires further learning. Most of us will remember occasions when we have been invigorated and excited by the learning encounter which owed much to the informal and hidden curricula.

Experiential learning

Learning from experience is instinctive. Even very young babies learn to draw attention to their needs through incessant crying and, later, to charm adults into cuddling and playing with them by smiling and gurgling. Many educational and behavioural theorists have written about such learning but here, we shall only present two models. The first, Kolb (1984), because it is used widely in palliative care education and the second, Race (2005), because it presents a useful alternative way of thinking about experiential learning.

Listening, watching and doing, then reflecting and doing again are all part of a continuous cycle of learning (Kolb 1984). The learning styles questionnaire developed by Kolb is useful in two practical ways: first, it helps individual learners to identify their preferred learning style, i.e. the way they learn best; second, it helps teachers to recognize the diversity of preferred learning styles amongst their students and to design teaching methods which cater to a variety of needs. The individual's learning style indicates the way in which they are most comfortable learning but all effective learning requires movement through the whole cycle over and over again. A useful analogy is the favourite room in one's house, the one in which one spends most time, if permitted. For different people, that room may be favoured for a variety of reasons, for example, most relaxing, most energizing or most functional. However, at some time or other, we have to move from our favourite room to use other parts of the house, which serve us in other ways. Similarly, it is useful to be considerate of individual learners' starting points but also to design activities that take them through other parts of the learning cycle, recognizing that it takes more energy and effort for them to learn in those other areas. Honey and Mumford's (2000) learning style questionnaire is also widely used in teaching and learning. An example of how the Kolb experiential learning cycle may be used to structure a teaching session in palliative care is shown in Figure 1.3.

An alternative model for experiential learning is the 'ripple effect on a pond' (Race 2005). The learning process is conceptualized as four layers of ripples (see Figure 1.4). At the centre, driving and motivating learning, is the need or 'want' to learn. This may be for personal interest or professional advancement. Whatever the reason, learning can only occur if this central catalyst exists. The learner also has to do something, i.e. actively engage with a real experience. Then there needs to be 'downtime': time for review and reflection so that the lessons can be considered, interpreted and absorbed. The final element in this model is feedback: opportunity for self-feedback and feedback from peers and the teacher.

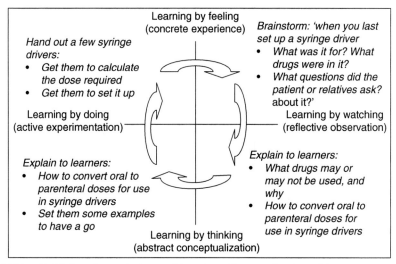

Fig. 1.3 Using Kolb's learning cycle for teaching about the use of syringe drivers

Consider the example where you are helping less experienced teachers to teach better. They may need to do so because their clinical job demands that they teach effectively (*need*). They may also want to improve their teaching ability for their own satisfaction (*want*). Observed by you, they do some teaching (*doing*). After the teaching, they spend a little time reflecting on what happened (*downtime*). Finally, the teacher in the 'hot seat' is invited to share his/her reflections on the teaching; then feedback is given by others, including you (*feedback*). It is important that feedback is structured and constructive, and that there has been prior agreement about the nature of this feedback.

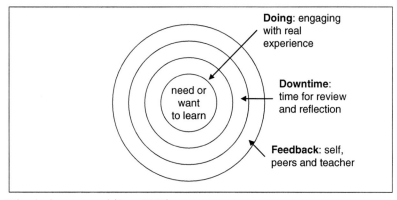

Fig. 1.4 The ripple on a pond (Race 2005)

The iceberg as a metaphor for professional practice

Fish and Coles (1998) use the iceberg as metaphor for professional practice (see Figure 1.5). The part of the iceberg above the waterline represents the performance aspects of practice which are visible to the professionals themselves and others; for example, carrying out a clinical procedure or the act of teaching itself. Such actions are explicit and measurable. The part of the iceberg below the waterline is not easily viewed, but is a continuous part of that iceberg and responsible for its stability. Similarly, underlying the observable performance of a professional and hidden from view are the individual's feelings, expectations, assumptions, attitudes, beliefs and values. Increasing professionals' awareness of these hidden aspects enables them to better understand how these influence their practice, whether clinical or educational. Some of these are easier to expose, for example feelings and expectations; others lie at the core of that individual and are more difficult to access and, consequently, more powerful when individuals are supported in exploring and challenging them.

For example, the iceberg metaphor may be used when teaching around critical incidents. First, the incident is outlined and the professionals describe what they did. They may explain how they based their decisions on their knowledge and experience. They are then asked to explore their underlying feelings and what expectations they had of themselves, others and the situation at the time. This is likely to engender some discussion in which individual assumptions and attitudes may be exposed. If not, the facilitator may encourage by asking 'why' questions or inviting these professionals to explain how their beliefs and

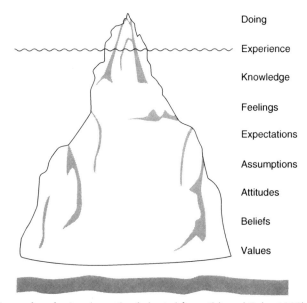

Doing

Experience

Knowledge

Feelings

Expectations

Assumptions

Attitudes

Beliefs

Values

Fig. 1.5 The iceberg of professional practice (adapted from Fish and Coles 1998). Reprinted from Fish D and Coles C (1998). *Developing professional judgement in health care: learning through the critical appreciation of practice*, p 306. Oxford: Butterworth-Heinemann, with permission from Elsevier

values influenced their actions. At this level professionals can feel quite exposed: it is important that clear ground rules have been set from the start of the session and that the facilitator keeps charge of the process. Exploration of critical incidents is often threatening but provides opportunity for powerful learning.

Three dimensions of learning

The final framework we wish to introduce is Illeris' (2004) three dimensions of learning (see Figure 1.6). All learning occurs at two levels:

1. internal: where new knowledge is acquired by the learner and then connected with their existing knowledge and understanding
2. external: because the learner does not exist in isolation; they must interact with the surrounding social, cultural and physical environment.

Moreover, there are three dimensions to any learning: cognitive, emotional and social. The cognitive dimension consists of knowledge and skills. Typically, this is the dominant dimension when teaching about symptom control or wound care. The emotional dimension includes feelings and motivation, for example teaching about death and dying. The social dimension encompasses cooperation and communication. We rarely place teaching only in that dimension. Illeris (2004) emphasizes that all learning and teaching take place within a specific cultural or societal context. This is evident in the chapters in this book describing palliative care education around the world and in different settings.

When planning palliative care teaching, teachers should bear in mind the three dimensions of learning. For example, a balanced teaching session on wound care needs to include

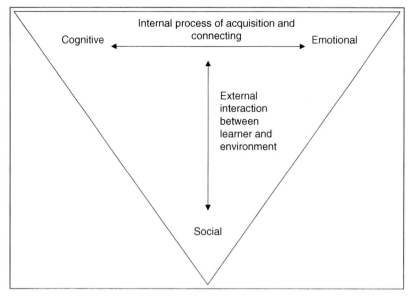

Figure 1.6 The three dimensions of learning (Illeris 2004)

knowledge about damaged and infected tissues and assessment and dressing skills (*cognitive dimension*). It could include reflection and discussion about fears and emotional responses that the learners themselves experience when managing smelly or disfiguring wounds, leading to a discussion on how this might be for patients (*emotional dimension*). Learners could jointly develop some strategies for supporting patients and their families and friends in dealing with the impact of an altered body image (*social dimension*).

Conclusion

Earlier in this chapter, we presented a number of theories, models and frameworks for learning and teaching. Our selection was based on those suitable for palliative care but this was by no means comprehensive. We hope that palliative care teachers will read more widely and in greater depth about different learning philosophies for themselves.

We firmly believe that teaching should be a thoughtful process, with teachers making careful, critical decisions about what and how they teach and why they make the choices they do. The diversity and influence of culture at every level are evident throughout this book: between palliative care practice and education in different parts of the world; between those who teach within higher education institutions and palliative care services; between small and large group teaching; between teaching and reflective learning; between the different professionals which make up the health and social care teams; between undergraduate, postgraduate and continuing professional development; between the managerial aspects of making things happen on the ground and the leadership challenge of pushing forward boundaries. We hope that readers will find themselves constantly challenged and pulled by these tensions as we were, in planning and writing this book with our various contributors around the world.

Part I

The Current State of Palliative Care Education

Section One: In the United Kingdom

Chapter 2

Medical education

Mary Miller and Bee Wee

Introduction

Medical education in the UK is undergoing radical change. Against a background of similar changes in the National Health Service (NHS) and in the public perception of professionals, we shall try to provide a snapshot of this rapidly changing landscape in medical education.

In the UK, palliative medicine was established as a medical specialty within the Royal College of Physicians in 1987. Since 1993, under the reforms brought in by the then Chief Medical Officer, Sir Kenneth Calman, to comply with European regulations, those aiming to become specialist physicians in palliative medicine must undergo four years of higher specialist training. Successful completion of this programme enables their names to be entered on the General Medical Council (GMC) Specialist Register for Palliative Medicine. It is illegal for any doctor to be appointed as Consultant in Palliative Medicine unless his or her name is on this Specialist Register.

The aim of this chapter is to provide readers who may be less familiar with medical education with a basic understanding of:

◆ how doctors are currently trained in the UK

◆ the pathway from trainee to specialist physician in palliative medicine

◆ key issues and recent developments in medical education in the UK.

Undergraduate and basic postgraduate medical education

In order to be eligible to apply for specialist training in palliative medicine, one has to be accepted into medical school, qualify as a doctor, undertake a period of basic postgraduate medical education and acquire a relevant postgraduate qualification. With slight national variations, this pattern holds true for medical education all over the world. In the UK, the process from medical school entrance to qualification as a specialist physician in palliative medicine currently takes at least 13 years (Figure 2.1).

Undergraduate medical education

Traditionally, students enter medical school immediately after leaving secondary education and qualify five or six years later. More recently, those who have already obtained a university degree, usually in a science subject, may be able to train as doctors through accelerated training or graduate entry programmes lasting four years.

Medical schools differ in their underlying approach to learning and teaching. Some focus on scientific training initially, followed by clinical training; some teach both scientific

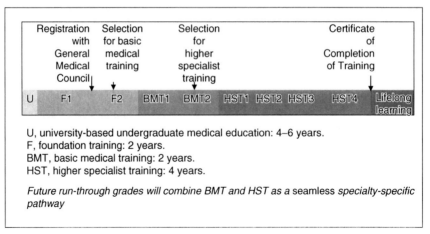

U, university-based undergraduate medical education: 4–6 years.
F, foundation training: 2 years.
BMT, basic medical training: 2 years.
HST, higher specialist training: 4 years.

Future run-through grades will combine BMT and HST as a seamless *specialty-specific* pathway

Fig. 2.1 Stages in medical education.

and clinical aspects in tandem, system by system, for example everything about the cardiovascular system, then the respiratory system, and so on; some use a problem-based approach in which students learn by working through clinical problems in facilitated groups; others use a combination of all these approaches. Despite strong claims, empirical evidence for the superiority of one approach compared to others in training the best doctors is lacking. Many medical schools now employ a range of teaching strategies, recognizing that there is a range of preferred learning styles within the student body. Rigid adherence to one approach inevitably disadvantages a proportion of students. All medical schools also include contact with patients from the first year of medical school, although this ranges from single token meetings to more extensive experiences.

The responsibility for undergraduate medical education and quality assurance of its process and outcome lie with the head or dean of the medical school and the university which awards the qualification. Thereafter, this responsibility passes to the regional Postgraduate Dean (see Box 2.1) who oversees all postgraduate medical training.

Finally, doctors are themselves responsible for continuing professional development for the rest of their careers.

Basic postgraduate medical education

Following qualification, UK doctors must practise for a year under close supervision before they are granted registration with the General Medical Council. Until recently, this was based on an apprenticeship model and these doctors were called pre-registration house officers (PRHO). This has now been superseded by a two year Foundation Programme, with registration awarded at the half-way point. The aim of the Foundation Programme is to provide experience of different specialties so that these doctors (now called F1s and F2s) are exposed to a broad range of career options, acquire the generic skills required of any good doctor and can safely manage acutely ill patients. Most Foundation Programmes are made up of six four-month blocks, including care in the community. A key difference between the old PRHO training and the new Foundation

Box 2.1 Postgraduate Deanery

There are 21 deaneries in the UK, each responsible for the delivery of postgraduate training for doctors and dentists in the National Health Service within a specific region. Each deanery is led by a Postgraduate Dean but, for any one specialty, there is a national lead Dean who takes overall responsibility for workforce planning and specialist registrar numbers across the country.

Postgraduate Deans appoint specialty-specific Programme Directors to coordinate training. Within each deanery, there are Specialty Training Committees (STC) to advise the Dean about postgraduate training for that specialty in that region. Membership of this Committee includes the Regional Specialty Advisor (appointed by the relevant Royal College), Programme Director, consultant trainers and specialist registrar representative.

Programme is the latter's emphasis on formal teaching, reflective learning and structured assessments. Pilot programmes indicate positive feedback from these doctors (Beard *et al.* 2005) but it is too early to evaluate the impact on clinical services and on the doctors' practice as Foundation Programmes have only been fully implemented since August 2005. The focus of the Foundation Programme on generic skills provides an excellent opportunity for palliative care teachers to become involved in formal teaching programmes and to offer short attachments for these doctors, wherever possible.

After the Foundation Programme, doctors spend two years in Basic Medical Training (see Figure 2.1), acquiring further experience and undertaking postgraduate examinations in order to gain entry into the Royal College of the specialty they wish to pursue. Readers may be familiar with the old system whereby the PRHO year was followed by several years as Senior House Officer (SHO). Under the new system, the title SHO is being phased out to Basic Medical Trainees, BMTs (Modernising Medical Careers UK Strategy Group 2004). Plans to amalgamate basic medical and higher specialist training as 'run-through' grades, to be introduced from August 2007, will force doctors to select their destination specialties before the end of their Foundation Programme training (Modernising Medical Careers UK Strategy Group 2004; Al-Wakeel and Handa 2006). It is not yet clear how palliative medicine will be affected by this change. The current plan is to recruit doctors to the specialist training programme who already have at least two additional years of training in general medicine following their Foundation Programme years. Up to now, doctors in many general practice training schemes and some general medicine training programmes have had the opportunity to spend three to six months in palliative care as SHOs. It is hoped that these opportunities will remain under the new system.

As we write, the system and its terminology are still rapidly evolving. Readers will need to check the web site (www.mmc.nhs.uk) for updates.

Issues in undergraduate and basic postgraduate medical education

Contrary to myth, entry into medical school is no longer based purely on academic grounds. The selection criteria for all UK medical schools also include aspects such as communication, teamworking and leadership skills. Those who enter medical schools are often bright, with strong academic records and have been successful in a range of extracurricular activities. They find it daunting when they move into an environment where, often for the first time, they are with other students who have had similar experiences of excelling at school. Medical students are idealistic about caring for patients and are often ill-prepared for a health care environment which is not always welcoming and sometimes even hostile. Unlike nursing and other health care students, their clinical placements are increasingly with peripatetic medical teams, so they do not have an obvious physical base or tangible task which directly contributes to patient care. This makes many medical students feel awkward and surplus to need. On hospital wards, these students often feel physically 'in the way' and are wary about being perceived to be a nuisance, especially by nurses and ward clerks. Some of them respond by trying to melt into the background even if this compromises their learning; others try to meet the situation head on and seek learning opportunities for themselves but may become labelled as pushy in the process. In the rare environment where the interprofessional team takes ownership for looking after these students, their learning and contribution to the team are both rich and rewarding.

When should learning about palliative care begin? Hillier and Wee (2001) suggested that this should start in the early undergraduate years but that learning needs to be commensurate with the student's experience, preferably being taught as a thread throughout undergraduate and continuing into postgraduate education. Sequential surveys have demonstrated a rise in undergraduate teaching about death and dying in the UK from a mean of six teaching hours in 23 out of 27 medical schools (Field 1984) to a range of six to 100 teaching hours across all medical schools (Field and Wee 2002). More importantly, the latter found that a broader range of palliative care topics were now taught, more experiential teaching methods were being used and non-medical professionals were involved in teaching. The GMC's publication *Tomorrow's Doctors*, which provides strong guidance to medical schools about curricular reform (GMC 1993, 2002) includes clear expectations that care of the dying should be included in the core curriculum. This represents a great opportunity for palliative care teachers, especially those in new medical schools or who are involved in schools undergoing radical curricular reform.

What aspects of palliative care should be taught at this stage? Lloyd-Williams and MacLeod's (2004) systematic review showed that there is great variation in what medical students are taught and that there have been several attempts at developing a core curriculum for palliative medicine. In 1992, the Association for Palliative Medicine of Great Britian and Ireland (APM) published a curriculum (APM 1992). Building on this, a revised palliative medicine curriculum for medical students has recently been proposed based on a Delphi study carried out across the UK and Ireland (Paes and Wee 2006). However, palliative medicine teachers must work within the constraints of their local medical school curricula, particularly in the way that the overall curriculum is designed and the prevailing teaching philosophy in that school. Through our informal survey of palliative care teachers in the UK for the purposes of this chapter, we came across a range of pragmatic and creative responses to teaching palliative medicine (see examples in Table 2.1).

Table 2.1 Examples of innovative practice in undergraduate medical education (by generous permission of palliative medicine teachers)

Learning activity	Description
Goldfish bowl	Circle of 6–8 patients; students sit in outer circle to observe patients who have their backs to the students Facilitator leads 20 minute discussion with patients about hospice services and how these impact on patients' and their carers' quality of life and functioning Facilitator invites students to ask questions of the patient group as a whole Facilitator puts these questions to patients and invites answers After the session, patients are informally debriefed by facilitator Students go on to have a 'looking after yourself' session (Edmonds et al. 2004)
Rotating workshop	Students work in groups and rotate around a certain number of tables, each with a facilitator and a topic Each group works through questions, learning from each other; supported and scored by facilitator Prize awarded to the team with the highest score (Hawkins 2005)
Book club	Four-week special study module Students asked to read one of six books: contemporary literature enabling exploration of patients' perspective Group discussion Essays submitted at end of module (Lloyd-Williams 2005)
Problem-based learning day	Students work in small groups to discuss cases from general practice or medicine Problem-solving using own experience, notes on symptom control, literature search, web search and tutor support Presents responses at end of session (Woof 2005)
Longitudinal patient project	Six-month joint oncology and palliative care project Each student follows one patient for six months Monthly small group tutorials Assessment based on submitted reflection and tutors' judgement of student's commitment to project (Finlay 2005)
Engaging in reflection on worst and best case scenarios of dying	Students are invited to write for five minutes, on their own, a response to the question 'What is the worst case scenario of how I will die?', encouraging them to include lots of details such as when, where, with who, etc. They then reflect on how they are feeling, writing down a few words or phrase that would describe how they are feeling On a fresh piece of paper, the above steps are repeated, this time in response to the question 'What is the best case scenario of how I will die?' The above steps are repeated again in response to the question 'If there is one thing I need to change or do to have my best case scenario death, what would it be?' Students work in groups of three, sharing how the process went for them In plenary, ask for show of hands to several questions, e.g. how many wanted to die in hospital, die at home, die suddenly, etc.; ask how they felt and what are their insights Discuss the variety of responses – you will usually be able to draw out that the vision of a 'good death' is not the same for everybody (Spring 2005)

(Continued on following page)

Table 2.1 (continued) Examples of good practice in undergraduate medical education (by generous permission of palliative medicine teachers)

Interprofessional workshops with carers	Interprofessional workshops involving medical, nursing, physiotherapy, occupational therapy and social work students Students interview family or lay carers in small groups to find out about the carer's experience and perspective Students prepare presentation while carers are debriefed Presentation by each group followed by plenary discussion (Wee *et al.* 2001)
Informal assessment: Teacake round	Aim: check out students' understanding at the end of one week small group (25 students) attachment Each student prepares at least one question about palliative care to ask another student Each student picks up a teacake at the start of the session One student (A) volunteers to start, by throwing their teacake at another student (B) and posing their question to that student Following a correct response, student B poses a different question to student C in a similar manner, etc. By the end, every student will have answered one question and eaten a teacake Facilitator ensures fair play and checks that responses are accurate and appropriate, interrupting only when absolutely necessary to make sure that wrong knowledge is not retained. (Wee 2005, adapted from Bulstrode *et al.*)

In addition to palliative care competencies, palliative medicine provides an excellent vehicle through which to learn about interprofessional teamworking (MacLeod and Egan 2006), caring and empathy (MacLeod 2000; Lloyd-Williams and Dogra 2003), patient–doctor relationships (Coles 1996) and developing professional judgement (Fish and Coles 1998; Hillier and Wee 2001), which are all essential skills and attributes across medical practice. Some aspects of practice, such as ethics, communication skills, teamwork and carer involvement, may also be taught in other arenas of education, for example primary care and geriatric medicine. These aspects are so integral to good whole person care that it can be difficult to measure the effectiveness of palliative care teaching selectively. Student satisfaction and acquisition of knowledge are easy to quantify. Changes in attitudes and skills, leading to improved palliative care, are much harder to attribute directly to palliative care teaching. We may have to accept less direct indicators of effective palliative care education, for example:

- improvement in knowledge, skills and attitudes of junior doctors when looking after palliative care patients
- improvement in appropriate referrals from junior doctors to specialist palliative care teams
- inclusion of palliative care topics by the wider medical school teaching community
- acknowledgement of the importance of palliative care by including it in summative assessments, especially final qualifying examinations
- recognition that palliative care teachers are committed, generous and enthusiastic educators.

Many of the educational issues raised earlier in this section also relate to junior doctors in what is called basic postgraduate medical education. As these doctors become more experienced, teaching can become increasingly focused on real life situations which they have encountered. Provided the groundwork has been well laid in undergraduate education, these doctors may only require reminders and practice-based examples to reignite interest and renew and develop skills. A continuing challenge for educators is that of the reluctant, unmotivated learner. For these doctors, a range of strategies has to be adopted including careful consideration of why such negative attitudes or apathy may have arisen.

Unlike medical students, junior doctors are also employees and their learning has to be juggled with day to day practice. In the past, their learning suffered from overwork and sleep deprivation. Nowadays, the reduced training time imposed by the European Working Time Directives and other regulations means that their learning may be compromised through lack of opportunity to encounter such a wide variety of situations. There is a balance to be struck between protected study time, which enables theoretical and skill based learning to take place, and unchoreographed learning in practice, where unpredictable situations present opportunities for rich learning and development of professional judgement. At this stage of their training, many junior doctors are focused on passing their Royal College examinations and motivation for learning will be driven, at least in part, by the nature of these assessments.

Training to become a specialist physician in palliative medicine

Any doctor who wishes to train to become a specialist physician in palliative medicine must have obtained a relevant postgraduate qualification (Table 2.2) and undertaken post-registration clinical training for at least two years. This includes 18 months of on-call experience within acute hospital settings to ensure that they are competent to deal with emergencies arising in palliative care.

Appointment to training posts in palliative medicine is by competitive interview. The entry criteria are determined by a national Specialty Advisory Committee but the responsibility for selection lies with the local Specialty Training Committee (refer to Box 2.1). Each post on the training programme has to be approved by the Joint Committee

Table 2.2 Entry qualifications for specialist registrar training in palliative medicine*

Possible background for entry to palliative medicine	Membership or Fellowship of Royal College	Percentage of specialist registrars from that background
Medicine	Physicians (MRCP)	79
General practice	General practitioners (MRCGP)	20
Clinical oncology	Radiologists (FRCR)	0
Anaesthetics	Anaesthetists (FRCA)	<1

*Association for Palliative Medicine of Great Britain and Ireland census figures, 2004.

for Higher Medical Training (JCHMT) of the Royal College of Physicians, within which the specialty of palliative medicine sits. The quality of the overall training programme is assessed by formal inspection every five years. In each region, one of the palliative medicine consultants takes on the role, known as Programme Director, of coordinating this rigorous process of higher specialist training.

Once appointed, the trainees are known as Specialist Registrars (SpRs) in palliative medicine. During their four year training, they have to provide evidence of meeting the generic and specialty targets set out in the JCHMT curriculum. Each year, they undergo a formal review process (RITA: record of in-training assessment), during which they produce documented evidence of their achievements against this curriculum, and provide reports from their educational supervisors which are scrutinized. Registrars who do not achieve the minimum standards are required to undertake targeted and/or additional training.

Each training post is required to incorporate an appropriate balance of experience in different palliative care settings, adequate clinical and educational supervision, support, learning resources and protected time for the registrar's study and professional development. Palliative care services which are unable to deliver these requirements may have their accreditation for SpR training withdrawn and lose these posts. Registrars may not be legally appointed to a consultant post until a Certificate of Completion of Training has been awarded by the Postgraduate Dean and their names entered on the Specialist Register at the General Medical Council.

In 2005 a newly established independent statutory body Postgraduate Medical and Education Training Board (PMETB) became the final arbiter in approval of postgraduate medical training (Department of Health 2003b). The training curriculum for SpRs is now being updated to meet its more demanding specifications. From 2006, the Royal College of Physicians requires additional assessments to be made. These are multisource or 360° feedback, mini clinical evaluation examination (mini-CEX) and direct observation of procedural skills (DOPS), all of which are discussed in Chapter 20 (p211). For palliative medicine, the latter consists of setting up a syringe driver and performing paracentesis. Registrars also have to write at least two records per year of case-based learning from their own practice, in the form of reflective reports.

Issues in training for specialist registrars in palliative medicine

Doctors entering this stage of their training are adult learners, with diverse educational experiences and varying levels of experience in palliative medicine. They have well-established learning habits which may require modification in order to gain maximum benefit from specialist registrar training. They need to learn to balance their responsibilities as a professional with that of taking responsibility for their own learning. This can be a difficult adjustment, particularly if they had been used to receiving structured teaching organized by others. They have to learn to regard their curriculum more as a platform upon which to build further learning rather than as an end in itself.

Moreover, training posts are constrained by their history and how staff within that palliative care service view them. Setting and maintaining educational goals and direction can be a problem if the post is not a good fit for that particular registrar. In some regions, registrars move from one palliative care service to another on an annual cycle. This enables them to experience a variety of teams and services but, for some, the adjustment period may be protracted with little learning occurring until they have settled in. Registrars who work part time can find it difficult to establish their roles within the team. The majority of palliative medicine consultants are enthusiastic educators and many undertake further study on how to develop as teachers. However, the focus of such teacher-development programmes tends to be on how to deliver teaching rather than the harder task of *enabling* learning.

The relationship between registrars and their consultant trainers is somewhat unique. Consultants have multiple roles, sometimes conflicting ones, in relation to their trainee registrars: teacher, clinical supervisor, educational supervisor, assessor, mentor, colleague and line manager. Tension and difficulties may arise from such a mixed role. Consultants nurture their registrar's development and professionalism and their transformation from novice to expert as well as support them through a variety of personal and professional milestones and sometimes crises. But they also hold the responsibility for ensuring that these doctors are safe and effective palliative medicine specialists by the time they complete their training. This can be daunting for some consultant trainers, particularly if conflicts arise between them and the registrars. However, when a good relationship is established, the training of registrars is an incredibly rich and rewarding process, through which all the team benefit and learn.

One of the tensions for consultants is the shortage of consultants in palliative medicine, which leads to consultants struggling to deliver both the clinical service and registrar training. Such competing priorities means that time for training is limited. The new assessment methods and curriculum will involve even more time in training. Time pressure may force consultants and registrars to focus on achieving the minimum requirements, i.e. ticking boxes, rather than to enable learning which is both reflective and iterative. The majority of consultant trainers and programme directors undertake the bulk of this work within their own time. Employing Trusts and organizations, although charged with the duty of educating and paid to do so, often do not adequately support or fund consultants to undertake these duties. This is particularly so in the small specialty of palliative medicine where such work tends to be carried out by the same, small number of individuals. Against a target of 418 whole time equivalent consultants required nationally, there are only 235 whole time equivalent consultants in post at present (NHS Workforce Review Team 2005; Association for Palliative Medicine 2006). Moreover, the government drive to develop nurse prescribing and to train medical care practitioners, the equivalent of the North American physician assistant (Stewart and Catanzaro 2005), adds even more staff to educate and supervise without extra resources. There is an unfounded assumption that this specialist teaching can be achieved.

Conclusion

This is a time of huge change in the education of doctors in the UK so we must be vigilant and consistent, while at the same time being flexible and open to new ideas.

Health care is also changing, with a drive towards developing pathways and protocols as though the patient's journey is both predictable and straightforward. This underestimates the complexity of decision-making and the degree of professional maturing that is required before doctors can become truly effective.

Education and learning, not merely training, hold the key to the healthy development of professionalism. By starting early with medical students, staying open to collaborative teaching with other like-minded specialties and keeping our eye on the ultimate goal of improving care for all patients and their families, palliative care has much to offer the world of medical education.

Chapter 3

Nurse education

Lorraine Dixon

Introduction

Nurses represent a significant proportion of the health care workforce engaged in providing palliative care for patients with life-threatening illnesses and their families. As palliative care has developed and been acknowledged as a specialty, nurse education has been forced to be creative, resourceful and proactive in providing nurse practitioners with the skills and knowledge that they require to support patients and their families when facing a life-threatening illness. This chapter aims to:

♦ outline the trajectory of nurse education in the UK from pre-registration through to advanced nurse practitioners

♦ describe current provision of palliative care education at pre and post-registration levels

♦ consider ways in which palliative nurse education is shaped by policy

♦ explore current and future challenges facing practitioners and educators.

Two developments have particularly influenced and underpinned informal and formal teaching and curriculum development and the development of nursing practice in palliative care. First, the World Health Organization (WHO) definition of palliative care: 'the active total care of patients and their families by a multiprofessional team when the patients' disease is no longer responsive to curative treatment' (WHO 1990). Second, the five principles of the palliative care approach, promoted by the National Council for Hospice and Specialist Palliative Care Services (1996):

1. Focus on quality of life, including good symptom control;

2. The whole person approach;

3. Care encompassing both the dying person and those who matter to that person;

4. Patient autonomy and choice;

5. Emphasis on open and sensitive communication.

It should be acknowledged that nurses do not work in isolation in supporting patients and their families, but as a crucial part of the interprofessional team. This chapter should therefore be read with the chapters on medical education and education for allied health care professionals, to set the context of professional education in palliative care.

Development of palliative care as a specialty and nurse education

Health care policy development and key influential bodies have significantly influenced the role of the nurse practitioner working in palliative care in the last three decades. The Calman and Hine (1995) policy framework for commissioning cancer services explicitly stated that care for cancer patients should be seamless with access to palliative care from diagnosis. Patients, families and carers should be given clear information and assistance in a form they can understand about treatment options and outcomes available to them, at all stages of treatment from diagnosis onwards. Calman and Hine (1995) highlighted the need to develop the integration of primary and secondary care and appropriate rapid referral patterns for patients with symptoms suggesting a high risk of a malignant diagnosis. This legitimizing of the palliative care approach within mainstream health care for cancer patients from the point of diagnosis prompted a need for improved and coordinated education in palliative care for generalist and specialist nurses to enable them to have the knowledge and skills to deliver palliative care. The Manual of Cancer Services (Department of Health 2004c) sought to quality assure and support the implementation of service improvement for cancer patients in translating the recommendations of the Calman and Hine (1995) report into actions and standards for practice. The notion of competence in practice was raised, suggesting that further post-registration academic study would ensure achievement of this standard. The report outlined the expectation that nurses within cancer interprofessional teams should be able to provide evidence of meeting a minimum standard of academic study in palliative care, though it did not set out educational expectations for the wider interprofessional team.

Post-registration nurse education

Accompanying the notion of competence there was an assumption that the nurse who had undertaken a programme of study in nursing practice (accredited for at least 20 CAT points at level three), which incorporated a module(s) in specialist palliative care would be deemed to be competent to provide specialist palliative care. The standard, however, did not differentiate between practice-based and theoretical programmes of study. It assumed that nurses undertaking theoretically based programmes would be able to apply the theoretical knowledge gained into their practice. The regulation of post-registration practice became the role of the United Kingdom Central Council for Nursing and Midwifery (UKCC) in the late 1980s. Rapid changes in health care, with the development of new clinical roles for nurses, increased responsibility for nurses and the move of post-registration nurse education into universities forced a review of the post-registration framework (Nursing and Midwifery Council (NMC) 2005). The 1990s saw the introduction of Post-Registration Education and Practice (PREP) by the UKCC, requiring each nurse to undertake a minimum of five study days over a period of three years and to keep evidence to demonstrate that they had maintained their personal professional profile for registration (UKCC 2001b). This validated the need for nurses to demonstrate that they had actively engaged in continuing professional development. The parallel development

Table 3.1 Career framework for nurses*

Role	Qualification
Health Care Assistant	National Vocational Qualification, 1, 2 or 3
Registered Practitioner	Diploma or first degree In some cases a specific professional qualification
Senior Registered Practitioner	First or Masters degree and additional specialist specific professional qualification
Consultant practitioner	Masters or doctorate level, with standards proposed for recognition of a 'higher level of practice'

* Department of Health (1999).

of palliative care as a specialty saw the increase in Macmillan Nurses, clinical nurse specialists in palliative care, supported with initial funding from Macmillan Cancer Relief.

The English National Board (ENB) validated a short attendance course for nurses, 'Care of the dying patient and their family', or ENB 931. This course aimed to introduce nurses to the principles of palliative care and to explore the challenges of caring for the dying patient. The course filled a gap in the early development of nurse practitioners in palliative care. For those wanting to take their learning further a second programme, ENB 285, or the 'Continuing care of the dying patient and their family', was made available. These two programmes formed the foundations for accredited programmes today. The short ENB courses sought to share clinical practice in palliative care, surrounding what has become known as the palliative care approach, aiming to promote both physical and psychosocial well-being, with key underpinning palliative care principles such as those promoted by the NCHSPC (1996). In addition the House of Lords Select Committee on Medical Ethics (1994) expressed the view that the training of health care professionals should prepare them more fully for the weighty ethical responsibilities which they carry by giving greater priority to health care ethics, counselling and communications skills.

The Department of Health (1999) published its plans to strengthen the nursing contribution to health in its document *Making a Difference*. This document set out a new career framework for nurses and clearly stated that it would work with professional organizations, trade unions and UK Health Departments to develop clear statements of competence and identify the thresholds for each stage.

In the UK, clinical nurse specialists have been pivotal to the development of specialist palliative care services in hospice, community and hospital settings (Seymour *et al.* 2002). A study carried out by Macmillan Cancer Relief, a UK-based cancer charity which provides pump-priming funds for many palliative care clinical nurse specialist posts, showed that these nurses' roles encompassed expert clinical intervention, consultation, teaching, leadership and research in providing direct and indirect services to patients with complex palliative care needs and to their families (Skilbeck *et al.* 2002; Corner *et al.* 2003).

Preparation for this has been varied. The minimum selection criteria for a clinical nurse specialist funded by Macmillan Cancer Relief is:

- a first level nurse registration
- at least five years post-registration experience, two of which must have been in cancer or palliative care
- a degree in either palliative care or oncology (Macmillan Cancer Relief 2006).

There is a recommendation that nurses undertake specialist preparation recordable by the Nursing and Midwifery Council gaining at least a diploma in Higher Education (Macmillan Cancer Relief 2006). However, in reality, nurses are increasingly required to have completed a degree or masters programme in palliative care for the role of clinical nurse specialist in palliative care. Corner *et al.* (2002) called for further evidence that can inform the development of policy and practice in palliative nursing. A small body of literature is beginning to emerge regarding the role definition of the clinical nurse specialist in palliative care but there is little data on the clinical work they undertake (Skilbeck *et al.* 2002), the nature and scope of the role (Seymour *et al.* 2002) and impact on the patient experience.

In 2001, the Department of Health funded a large-scale District Nurse Palliative Care Education Project to increase the knowledge and skills of G grade district nurses caring for people with palliative care needs within the primary health care setting. It required district nurses to identify their own knowledge base, learning needs and level of competence in relation to palliative care, and set out a development plan with a link nurse within a specialist palliative care team. There was an expectation that competence was measured at the start of the programme and again after it was completed, once the practitioner returned to practice. This was a mutually beneficial relationship as it provided the opportunity for specialist palliative care teams to increase their network of practice, and develop the educational role of specialist nurses. It also provided the district nurses with a framework of support, which provided the opportunity for development of individual learning needs.

Pre-registration nurse education

Whilst there is a small body of growing evidence surrounding clinical nurse specialists, there is a noticeable lack of understanding of the training requirements of the generalist nurse to provide palliative care. The Nursing and Midwifery Council (NMC, formerly known as the UKCC) (Nursing and Midwifery Council 2002) published the requirements for pre-registration nursing programmes. Each programme now comprises a one-year common foundation programme followed by a two-year branch programme, with a total of 4600 learning hours over the three years: 50 per cent practice and 50 per cent theory. The minimum academic standard of pre-registration nursing programmes remains a diploma in higher education. The guiding principles for the programme relate to professional competence and fitness to practice. Palliative care education faces tough competition for space within the pre-registration curriculum and is variable between programmes. The limited formal teaching time within the pre-registration programme tends to focus on loss, bereavement and symptom management. It is often theoretically based and opportunity for students to explore the challenging nature of palliative care in small groups is minimal. The recent drive by the Department of Health to benchmark the price of pre-registration education runs the risk of increasing the number of nursing students within classrooms to enable universities to remain competitive. This change risks losing quality in the educational experience and diminishes opportunities for nursing students to feel comfortable in exploring complex and difficult issues surrounding the care of the dying on a personal and professional level.

Curriculum challenges for nurse education in palliative care

The National Council for Hospice and Specialist Palliative Care Services (NCHSPCS 1996) suggested that communication skills, ethics of palliative care, pain and symptom control, ethnic, cultural and minority issues, and religious and spiritual issues should be covered within the curriculum to improve palliative care practice. Considerable efforts have been made to develop the curriculum of both pre-registration and post-registration education for nurses by making the taught component of palliative care education for nurses explicit. This work, however, is by no means complete. Future course content for both pre-registration and post-registration will be affected by the theoretical and philosophical underpinnings of the curriculum (Lee and Zeldin 1982). It will always be directly influenced by political motivations behind the curriculum and who really sets the hidden agenda. The selection and organization of curriculum content will only be effective if it is an integral part of the curriculum process.

The NHS Executive Headquarters has stated that education, development and workforce plans should make adequate provision for the delivery of cancer and palliative care services, which reflect the need for appropriately educated, trained and supported specialist staff. Tebbit (1999) suggests that this can only be achieved with co-operation between clinical practitioners and commissioners of education, thus ensuring the integration of palliative care learning experiences within the context of practice. This is further challenged by the diversity of agencies engaged in the provision of palliative care, including the voluntary sector and social services. Rhodes (1997) suggests that with the changes in pre-registration nurse education and the move into the higher education sector, some lecturers have indicated concern about issues surrounding dying and palliative care not being dealt with in a sensitive and progressive manner due to reduced resources, which means that subjects are often taught in large groups. While this has been addressed in some areas with the introduction of hospice placements and hospice staff's contribution to the changing curriculum, it is important to emphasize the necessity for strong links to be maintained between education and practice at all levels. This has become increasingly difficult, as financial reward is not always given in return for the time the practitioner spends in educational activity. Moreover, as educational delivery often falls to practitioners, situated within different organizations to the educational establishment, managers are not consistently sympathetic to practitioners' involvement in curriculum development or delivery.

Post-registration palliative care education for nurses faces some tough challenges within the current climate of tight resources and increased expectation. To survive the current demands and continue producing competent practitioners for the future, institutions of higher education and clinical practice have to work closely together, moving away from a content-driven curriculum for palliative care to create more opportunity for 'scaffolding' the development of palliative care practice. Scaffolding is the concept of assisting learners to reach their potential by providing a framework to help them build their learning and development (Vygotsky 1978). The opportunity to capitalize on work undertaken in practice, that supports continual professional learning and creatively utilizes the mechanisms for academic achievement, would enhance the development of practice. Schön (1987) suggests that a student cannot be taught what they need to know but that they can be coached. Higher education ably provides the framework to ensure quality of the learning experience and to support the accreditation of continuing professional development. Communities of practice in palliative care have the clinical expertise and ability to translate theory into practice. There is the potential for a powerful partnership of practice and education in the development of future practitioners in palliative care.

The place in which palliative care education for nurses operates is also a key factor to be considered in the development of curriculum. Hall *et al.* (1996) state the necessity of being aware of current trends and responding with marketing strategies accordingly. The need for clinical practice to raise its profile and involvement in formal education has at last been acknowledged (Bines and Watson 1992). We have witnessed the emergence of practice-led curricula using tools such as reflective practice to enable students to learn through reflecting on their practical experiences in relation to the theoretical underpinnings of nursing theory (Palmer *et al.* 1994). Curriculum designers have had to be responsive to this development within nursing, by adapting the organisation and integration of learning experiences and context with respect to the teaching and learning process in the classroom. This has had a positive effect in producing more critical thinkers within the nursing profession who are able to challenge current practice.

The NHS is constantly facing financial constraints with an ever-expanding population and raised expectations within the public domain, and has difficulty in releasing staff to attend formal accredited study. It is therefore crucial that creative attempts are made to adapt the curriculum to meet these financial realities. The emergence of work-based learning, blended learning and distance learning may assist with the difficulty of releasing students from work for study. Work-based learning also has the value of recognizing students' learning opportunity within their own practice, but there is danger that, in losing the face-to-face contact in the classroom, students may not develop and benefit from the broader community and network of practice around them, nor develop the more personal approaches that are so effectively achieved within group teaching with the support of peers.

Informal nurse education

Palliative care in the early days was synonymous with terminal care and care of the dying patient. The hospice movement bred centres of excellence in supporting dying patients and their families, providing a resource of practitioners to share their expertise informally, through role modelling and learning through exposure to practice. As hospices grew into centres of excellence a range of formal study programmes were established, meeting the needs of practitioners in sharing examples of good practice and debating challenging case studies. The content of the study days was largely focused on symptom management in caring for the dying patient, following a traditionally medical approach. This has matured to meet the needs of a broader community of interprofessional practitioners and to complement the more formal education provided in educational establishments. Nurses have had the opportunity to share examples of best practice with colleagues from a range of different professions working in palliative care. This has been of significant value in the light of the role-blurring which often occurs in palliative care and provides an opportunity for developing increased awareness of the interpretation of palliative care principles within other health care professions working in palliative care.

The importance of learning on the job should also be acknowledged. A range of practitioners working in palliative care services are involved in teaching both students on clinical placements and junior colleagues. They provide a valuable source of knowledge in palliative care, offering the opportunity for learning from role models.

Interface between education, research and practice for palliative care professionals

There is a distinct lack of comprehensive research that explores the impact of palliative care nurse education on the patient experience. A future challenge for education and practice is to evaluate the impact of the move to define competence in practice. The Framework for Nurses Working in Specialist Palliative Care (Royal College of Nursing 2004) defines four levels of practice which correlate with the current grading system. The framework suggests it can be used as a tool to develop nurses' knowledge and skills in the form of:

- appraisal to assess competence and identify training needs
- a plan for team training to assess team competence and consider skill mix
- a mechanism to help individuals develop their career pathway
- enabling the development of a comprehensive induction programme for new staff.

This framework may be used alongside the Knowledge and Skills framework (Department of Health 2003a), which explicitly outlines the expectation that the individual will apply knowledge and skills in a number of dimensions to achieve the specific expectations of their job. The challenge now is to translate the formal and informal education support into mechanisms for developing the skills and competence of nurses working in palliative care, within these frameworks. The other challenge is to evaluate the impact that education has on patient care and the experience of individual patients and their families when facing the challenge of a life-threatening illness.

Conclusion

This chapter has attempted to capture and describe the major developments in palliative care nurse education today, through summarizing some of the key underpinning policies which have prompted service developments in palliative care. It has considered how these policies have shaped palliative care nurse education and influenced current provision. These changes pose some exciting, if daunting, challenges for practitioners, stakeholders, educators and higher education institutions. Nurse education in palliative care cannot be considered in isolation but must be explored in the context of education of, and with, others within the interprofessional and global community of palliative care practitioners.

Chapter 4

Occupational therapy, physiotherapy and social work education

Gail Eva, Gillian Percy and Gillian Chowns

Introduction

Collaborative working is a well established principle of palliative care practice and inter-professional education in palliative care is gaining ground. Those who work in specialist palliative care are often called upon to teach members of other professional groups. While multidisciplinary teamwork has many benefits for patient care, the role-blurring it entails can cause some uncertainty over the way in which each professional group differs in its knowledge and skill base. This chapter has the following aims:

- to clarify interactions between occupational therapists, physiotherapists and social workers, identifying their overlapping and distinctive roles
- to outline the pre-qualifying education provided for occupational therapists, physio-therapists and social workers
- to describe the issues in palliative care education and training for occupational thera-pists, physiotherapists and social workers, both at pre-qualifying and post-qualifying levels, relating these to the impact of the National Institute for Clinical Excellence (NICE) Guidance on Supportive and Palliative Care (NICE 2004).

We hope the chapter will be useful to providers of post-qualifying specialist palliative care education, both formal and informal courses, where course participants would include occupational therapists, physiotherapists and social workers, as well as to providers of pre-qualifying occupational therapy, physiotherapy and social work educa-tion, clinicians who supervise and train these students on their practical placements, and education policy-makers.

Interprofessional working in palliative care

Professional roles overlap in many specialties, and collaborative working is an important feature of palliative care. Tookman *et al.* (2004) describe the continuum between multidis-ciplinary teamwork, where professional individuals and groups work with consideration of one another but retain autonomy in decision-making in their own areas, and interdis-ciplinary teamwork, where there is collaboration with the aim of achieving consensus on goals for patient care. It is generally agreed that shared and overlapping roles are desir-able for achieving good outcomes for patients and their carers in palliative care

(Dharmasena and Forbes 2001; Levorato *et al.* 2001; Cowley *et al.* 2002; Lee 2002); but, at the same time, the role-blurring that this entails can present a challenge to team members. To understand one another's roles sufficiently to foster the trust and respect required to enable co-operation and compromise (and to avoid arrogant or defensive behaviour) requires confidence in one's own expertise and skills, and clarity about boundaries. Figure 4.1 gives an indication of the way that physiotherapy, social work and occupational therapy both interlink and retain their own individual areas of practice (Robinson 2000; Oliviere 2001; Jolliffe and Bury 2002; Bray and Cooper 2004; College of Occupational Therapists 2004; Doyle *et al.* 2004; Monroe 2004).

Pre-qualifying occupational therapy education

Occupational therapists address the occupational dysfunction that people experience when illness or disability disrupt their daily lives. Occupational therapy encompasses all of the activities that contribute to a person's identity, integrating physical, cognitive, psychological, social, environmental, economic, creative and spiritual aspects. It is concerned with enhancing the daily life skills of individuals with physical or mental health problems,

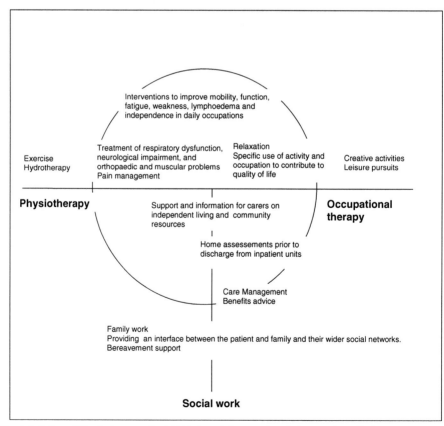

Fig. 4.1 Roles of Physiotherapy, Social Work and Occupational Therapy in Palliative Care

or social needs. Occupation is used to acquire, restore, or maintain balanced life roles through the development of skills in the areas of self-care, productivity and leisure (Quality Assurance Agency for Higher Education 2001a). Pre-qualifying curricula include subjects drawn from occupational science, ergonomics, psychology, sociology, social policy, physiology, anatomy and pathology. The profession-specific skills of the occupational therapist include:

- knowledge and understanding of occupation as it relates to health and well-being
- appropriate selection, adaptation, use and evaluation of occupations as therapeutic media, using occupation both as the means of an intervention (for example, practising wheelchair mobility to use public transport) and as its required outcome (for example, a person who is paraplegic being able to manage the weekly family grocery shopping independently)
- the impact of occupational dysfunction/deprivation on individuals, families, groups and communities and the importance of restoring occupational opportunities.

Pre-registration occupational therapy programmes are offered in a variety of ways: full-time programmes lasting three or four years leading to a Bachelor's degree (some with honours); part-time or in-service programmes for students who combine employment with study; accelerated programmes lasting two years for those with a previous degree and experience in social and health care. Pre-registration programmes must have a minimum of 1000 hours dedicated to supervised practice placements, and most programmes spread these out over the course, providing students with experience in a range of settings.

Pre-qualifying physiotherapy education

Physiotherapists are primarily concerned with human function and movement. They use physical approaches to promote, maintain and restore physical, psychological and social well-being. Physiotherapists treat a wide range of physical conditions, particularly those associated with the neuromuscular, musculoskeletal, cardiovascular and respiratory systems, across all ages and those presenting with varying health status, relating both to physical and mental health. They take into account the impact of cultural, social and environmental factors on individuals' functional ability and give careful consideration to the needs of patients' carers (Chartered Society of Physiotherapy 2002a). Pre-qualifying curricula include subjects drawn from anatomy, physiology, human development, anthropometrics, ergonomics, pathology, physics, exercise science, psychology and sociology. The profession-specific skills of the physiotherapist include:

- therapeutic exercise – planning, delivering and evaluating exercise programmes for individuals and groups
- manual therapy (for example, the application of mobilization, respiratory physiotherapy, neurotherapeutic handling and massage techniques) to facilitate and restore movement and function
- electrotherapeutic modalities – a range of modalities based on the utilization of electrical, thermal, light, sonic and magnetic energy which bring about physiological and

therapeutic effects to alleviate symptoms, especially pain, and restore function (Quality Assurance Agency for Higher Education 2001b).

Pre-qualifying physiotherapy programmes are offered at honours degree and post-graduate levels. Study may be full time or part time, and all programmes include a mandatory practice component of at least 1000 hours (Chartered Society of Physiotherapy 2002b).

Pre-qualifying social work education

The International Association of Schools of Social Work/International Federation of Social Workers (IASSW/IFSW) have adopted the following definition of social work:

> The social work profession promotes social change, problem solving in human relationships and the empowerment and liberation of people to enhance well-being. Utilising theories of human behaviour and social systems, social work intervenes at the points where people interact with their environments. Principles of human rights and social justice are fundamental to social work.
>
> Sewpaul and Jones (2005: 218)

Social work interventions range from primarily person-focused psychosocial processes to involvement in social policy, planning and development. Pre-qualifying curricula include subjects drawn from sociology, psychology, political studies, social policy, criminal justice, law and human development as applied to social work and social work practice. The profession-specific skills of the social worker include:

- engaging in problem-solving, facilitative and supportive activities with individuals, families, groups and communities
- assisting and educating people to obtain services and resources in their communities
- assessing the degree and nature of risk to which vulnerable individuals are exposed
- facilitating the inclusion of marginalized, socially excluded, dispossessed, vulnerable and at risk groups of people, by addressing and challenging the barriers, inequalities and injustices that exist in society (Quality Assurance Agency for Higher Education 2000).

Together with the recent changes in the requirements for registration of social workers by the General Social Care Council (GSCC), there has been a radical overhaul of social work training. Since September 2003, the previous Diploma in Social Work awarded by the professional body (then the Central Council for Education and Training in Social Work – CCETSW – since replaced by the GSCC), has been superseded by an honours degree awarded by accredited universities (Parker 2005). There is a requirement for 200 days of supervised and assessed practice as an integral part of the degree (Department of Health 2002).

Pre-qualifying palliative care education

A number of organizations are involved in regulating the training of occupational therapists, physiotherapists and social workers. These include the College of Occupational Therapists (COT), the Chartered Society of Physiotherapy (CSP), the Health Professions Council (HPC), the General Social Care Council (GSCC), and the Quality Assurance

Agency for Higher Education. For each of the three professional groups, there exists a detailed template for the knowledge and skills that are required to be taught at pre-qualifying levels, but these do not specify the content for particular areas of practice, such as palliative care. The amount of palliative care education provided to students varies widely between institutions, and is dependent, to a great extent, on the interests and experience of lecturers. Specific content on palliative care could range from nothing at all, to a series of lectures, workshops, seminars and tutorials. Some institutions offer optional modules. Where a palliative care module is offered, this provides students with the opportunity to study the subject in some depth. It is, however, possible that a student could qualify without any specific teaching on palliative care in their pre-qualifying training, although it is likely that palliative care issues, such as loss, would have been incorporated into other topics. For social workers, in particular, loss and bereavement are prominent themes in their understanding of relationship breakdown and the loss of social roles (Parker 2005). For all three professions, an understanding of loss is integral to working with people who have health problems or are encountering disability. In the same way, the general principles underpinning training – the ability to identify and assess health and social care needs, to plan care, to evaluate outcomes and to work collaboratively with other professionals – will be transferable to any practice situation, including palliative care. At pre-qualifying levels, all students will gain an understanding of holistic care. Although this may come in different packages and with different terminology in the different professional groups, such as patient-centred care (Gibson *et al.* 2005), client-centred practice (Law *et al.* 1995) or relationship-based practice (Howe 1998), students will have an appreciation of the way in which effective practice relies on negotiated relationships and respect for individuals.

At various times over the past decade, a number of different palliative care programmes have been initiated in pre-qualifying courses, some of which continue in varying forms while others have been replaced by new priorities. Examples include a one year pathway at Middlesex University where social work students had the opportunity to undertake their practical placement and research project in palliative care, with active support and supervision provided (Oliviere 2001), and an in-depth 'experiential' course incorporated into the pre-qualifying social work course at the University of Hull (Parker 2005).

The virtual absence of a recognized career structure between practice and education is a problem for all three professions (Department for Education and Skills and Department of Health 2003). Very few appointments exist jointly between service-delivery employers and academic institutions, and this shortage considerably reduces career flexibility for staff, forcing a choice between practice and teaching. The scarcity of joint appointments contributes to a situation where academic staff may lack practice credibility, and experienced practitioners are without the track record, in terms of research output and publications history, required by higher education institutions. Many occupational therapy, physiotherapy and social work posts in specialist palliative care are part-time (Field 2000; Hall 2004) and the predominant organisational expectation of post-holders is that they will be strongly practice-focused, thereby significantly reducing opportunities for involvement in policy-making, education and research.

Pre-qualifying or pre-registration practical experience

Like their medical and nursing colleagues, occupational therapists, physiotherapists and social workers practise in a very wide range of settings – in primary, secondary and tertiary care across health and social care services, and in the voluntary sector. Practice is becoming more complex, and it is recognized that pre-qualifying programmes, even with the stipulation of large practice components, can provide only a limited range of practice experiences. Because practice placement opportunities in specialist palliative care are relatively few and far between – given the small number of specialist palliative care services that employ occupational therapists, physiotherapists and social workers with sufficient staffing levels to enable them to take students – only a small minority of students will have had any pre-qualifying palliative care experience. In general, it is those students who have a specific interest in palliative care and who actively request these placements that will gain palliative care experience. Specialist palliative care organizations employing occupational therapists, physiotherapists and social workers have a responsibility to contribute to student training in these professions, not only by providing placements but, just as importantly, by supporting staff who supervise placements. Increasingly, practice educators are expected to have undergone training in student supervision. The role of the practice supervisor or educator is an extremely important one, and requires adequate time and resources to ensure that it is properly carried out.

Formal and informal post-qualifying education in palliative care

There are a number of universities that offer post-qualifying programmes in palliative care and these are usually open to all professional groups. Although they draw on contributions from other professionals, the courses tend to be led predominantly by nurses and doctors, with the notable exception of the masters programme at Southampton University, pioneered by the late Frances Sheldon. She was one of the six Macmillan senior lecturers in psychosocial palliative care, appointed in the mid-1990s, who have been able to raise the profile of social work and of psychosocial palliative care, and influence the curricula of multiprofessional post-qualifying programmes. These posts were pump-primed by the Macmillan Cancer Relief charity. Although only one of these posts still exists a decade on, their influence has been considerable.

Course content in formal post-qualifying programmes tends to be flexible and modular, designed to give students the ability to pursue subject areas relevant to their practice. Occupational therapists, physiotherapists and social workers working in specialist palliative care will want to develop their knowledge of core palliative care subjects such as pain and symptom control, communication skills, grief and bereavement and ethical issues. These topics tend to be well covered. In addition to the core topics, however, there is a need for courses which offer more in-depth study of profession-specific issues related to palliative care. Very few such opportunities exist. A recent survey of the training needs of occupational therapists working in palliative care identified the lack of educational opportunities relating specifically to rehabilitation in palliative care (Hall 2004). This is perhaps a consequence of the scarcity of physiotherapists and occupational therapists within programme development and curriculum planning teams.

As well as formal, accredited educational programmes, informal study days, courses and conferences play an important role in enabling occupational therapists, physiotherapists and social workers to keep up to date with developments in palliative care. For all three groups, evidence of ongoing professional development is a condition of continued professional registration, and attendance at courses is an important aspect of this. In addition to an increasingly competitive market in courses offered by palliative care organizations, the specialist sections of all three professional groups offer a variety of events for their members.

Interprofessional learning

Interprofessional learning, where two or more disciplines learn together, facilitating good relationships and interactions which enhance the practice of each discipline, is recognized as an important aspect of students' learning experiences (Fitzpatrick 1998). Palliative care, with its demands on close teamworking, has been identified as an ideal area for creating opportunities for interprofessional learning (Wee *et al.* 2001), although the development of suitable programmes is not without its challenges (MacDougall *et al.* 2001). There is the suggestion that the earlier students are involved in interprofessional education, the better the outcomes in terms of a greater appreciation of one another's roles (Singleton and Hernandez 1998). The importance of interprofessional learning both in the classroom and in practice placements is emphasized by the Quality Assurance Agency for Higher Education (2000, 2001a, b). The majority of health and social care courses include interprofessional learning opportunities in the curriculum. A recent survey found that the most common shared classroom topics between physiotherapists, nurses, occupational therapists and social workers were anatomy, physiology, psychology, sociology, research methods, communication skills, teamworking and professional practice issues (Mcclure *et al.* 2005). While a great deal of good practice exists, there is a need to integrate interprofessional learning into students' practice placements. The programme design and coordination required to enable this to happen is great, but it is proposed that interprofessional learning opportunities should be much more of an integral part of practice placements.

Impact of the NICE *Guidance in Supportive and Palliative Care*

The publication of the NICE *Guidance on Supportive and Palliative Care* (2004) provides the first formal framework in the United Kingdom for palliative care services, including social support services, psychological support services, rehabilitation services and services for families and carers. The Guidance makes a distinction between 'general' and 'specialist' palliative care services, noting that:

> Professionals involved in providing palliative care fall into two distinct categories:
>
> those providing day to day care to patients and carers ... those who specialise in palliative care... some of whom are accredited specialists.

NICE (2004: 20)

The NICE Guidance recognizes the importance of workforce development, proposing that staff meeting palliative care patients as part of a general case load, or as specialists in other conditions, will require enhanced training in 'the assessment of patients' problems, concerns and needs; in information giving; and in communication skills' (NICE 2004: 13); and the need for greater numbers of staff with specialist skills specifically related to psychological support and rehabilitation is noted. To make the distinction between general and specialist care clear with regard to rehabilitation, a four-level model has been suggested, as follows:

♦ Level 1: recognizing palliative care needs as part of general assessment and knowing how these needs can be met. Having the ability to offer simple interventions such as giving basic advice on self-management of common functional problems and conditions such as fatigue.

♦ Level 2: providing interventions which are slightly more specialist, but which are in response to routine, predictable situations, for example, post-operative physiotherapy following breast surgery.

♦ Level 3: interventions which require knowledge and experience of cancer and palliative care pathology and treatment, and a deeper understanding of the impact of life-threatening illness on patients and families.

♦ Level 4: highly specialist interventions for patients who have complex, often unpredictable, specialist needs, and who, together with families and carers, are dealing with difficult end-of-life issues.

The distinction between a specialist and a generalist, in terms of knowledge, skills and qualifications, is much less clear-cut for occupational therapists, physiotherapists and social workers than it is for doctors and nurses in palliative care. For doctors wishing to specialize in palliative care, there is a clearly defined career pathway, and the same is increasingly relevant for nurses, where a degree-level qualification in palliative care is becoming an expectation for clinical nurse specialist posts. For occupational therapists, physiotherapists and social workers coming into palliative care, making the transition between NICE levels one and two, and on to levels three and four, is more tenuous, tending to reflect local service needs and recruitment and retention issues, with remuneration and grading at local managers' discretion. In all three professions, specialist posts are recognized by the professional bodies, with the COT and the CSP having produced briefing papers and guidance on the development of clinical specialist posts for occupational therapists and physiotherapists, and the new General Social Care Council Post-Qualifying Framework for social workers making provision for awards in Higher Specialist Social Work and Advanced Social Work (Chartered Society of Physiotherapy 2001; College of Occupational Therapists 2003; General Social Care Council 2005). Although there is recognition of the benefits of a career structure for practitioners with specialist skills, these developments are in their infancy. The external drivers to gain specialist qualifications that exist for doctors and nurses in palliative care, for example appointment to posts being dependent on qualifications, do not exist for occupational therapists, physiotherapists and social workers. While it is a matter of some debate whether such a requirement would be desirable for these professions, it is the case that because the qualifications are not mandatory, there is less incentive to make available appropriate training programmes and funding, and to employ sufficient numbers of staff to enable post-holders to undertake specialist post-qualifying education, while at the same time fulfilling their clinical or practice remit.

Conclusion

This chapter has, inevitably, reviewed some of the constraints to which palliative care training for occupational therapists, physiotherapists and social workers is subject. Although issues related to palliative care – loss, holistic intervention, planning and evaluation – are among the transferable skills acquired in pre-qualifying education and in post-qualifying practice experience, the extent of training which is specific to palliative care at this level varies considerably, and the bodies responsible for registration do not demand specific content. At post-qualifying level, there is a mirror image problem: while pre-qualifying education is specific to professional disciplines but not to palliative care, post-qualifying level training opportunities in palliative care are not usually aimed at particular disciplines, being largely multiprofessional. Although interprofessional learning is to be welcomed, there is a danger that further training in profession-specific skills will be left out at the post-qualifying stage.

Underlying these patterns of provision, there is a problem relating to career structures in palliative care. While medicine and, increasingly, nursing have palliative care career pathways, the same is not true for social workers, physiotherapists and occupational therapists. The distinction between specialist and generalist is not, therefore, as clear cut in these disciplines, and clinical specialist or advanced practitioner appointments are relatively rare (and frequently part time). This is in turn means that specialists tend to be very practice-focused, with the result that the availability of practice placements for new trainees is severely limited – a situation which is compounded by the scarcity of joint appointments combining clinical work and higher education. It is clear that, in this respect at least, there is something of a vicious circle in all three disciplines: fewer specialists mean fewer training opportunities, which of course means fewer specialists. While there have been a number of encouraging initiatives, not least the recognition of these problems in the NICE Guidance, serious progress in training for palliative care will involve a concerted attempt to resolve this particular dilemma.

Section Two: In Other Continents

Introduction

Katy Newell-Jones

Palliative care, and hence palliative care education (PCE), has a presence in all continents although, as demonstrated in the following chapters, practice is both diverse and locally adapted.

This section includes case studies from Africa, Asia-Pacific, Australia and New Zealand, Europe, India, North America and South America. Each chapter draws on extensive experience within the area, providing knowledgeable insight into the historical development and current practices in PCE, together with the key challenges. These challenges are discussed in Chapter 12 (p103) in the context of the current debate around the internationalisation of education and the global dimension to learning.

Increasingly in health and education, as in other fields of study, there has been a move on the part of practitioners and academics to adopt a more international or global approach to learning and teaching, for example through drawing on practice from other countries and recognizing the importance of locally adapted curricula. There has also been a qualitative change in the ways in which different perspectives and practices from across the world are viewed. In the past, this section might have been written from the perspective of asking 'How far has PCE developed in different continents?' 'Where are developing countries in comparison to developed countries?' 'What are the implications for health care professionals from the developed world working overseas?' and even 'How might the developing world be supported in 'catching up'? Such an approach would be inappropriate in the twenty-first century as it is based on the assumption that expertise is primarily located in one part of the world and that learning should take place primarily in one direction – from 'developed' to 'developing' countries, terms which, in themselves, many find problematic. In this section, where it is appropriate to use collective terms to refer to different groups of countries, the terms more economically developed countries (MEDCs) and less economically developed countries (LEDCs) will be used, in preference to developed/developing or north/south.

This section has been approached from a specific perspective which explores the state and content of PCE across the world and also poses questions about its purpose, process and future direction as a global entity. The authors of the case studies were invited to explore:

- who is involved in palliative care education in your region?
- who is driving the agenda for palliative care education?
- in what ways does palliative care education reflect the unique characteristics of your region?
- what approaches to learning and teaching are used?
- what is the impact?
- what are the key challenges?
- who is learning from whom?
- how does palliative care education in your region interact at a global level?

Palliative care has been subject to extensive debate by the World Health Organisation (2002), the European Association for Palliative Care and others. However, PCE has not received the same attention. While recognizing that the primary purpose of PCE is to educate health and social care professionals in their development and implementation of effective palliative care practices, the underpinning driving forces, whether explicit or not, will inevitably influence the development and delivery of PCE.

The recent debate within the field of education identifies a range of driving forces for internationalization or incorporating a global dimension to learning into education programmes (Francis 1993; Currie *et al.* 2003; Newell-Jones 2003, 2005). These factors, which include fostering global understanding and transcultural learning, will be explored in Chapter 12 in the light of the chapters from different continents:

- where does PCE as a global entity fit in the debate on the internationalization of education?
- how is PCE in different countries and continents interconnected?
- what are the patterns of learning?
- what education strategies for the future development of PCE might be most appropriate?

Chapter 5

Africa

Liz Gwyther

Background

Palliative care training has been a hospice function since hospices first started in Africa with the opening of Island Hospice and Bereavement service in Harare, Zimbabwe in 1979 (Mkwananzi 2005), St Luke's Hospice, Cape Town and Highway Hospice, Durban in 1980. The initial palliative care training was for volunteers as caregivers and bereavement carers.

The Hospice Association of South Africa, now the Hospice Palliative Care Association, initiated professional palliative care education in 1989 with the Short Course in Palliative Nursing, a six-month day release programme accredited by the South African Nursing Council (Marston 2003). Undergraduate training for professionals has only recently been instituted in medical and nursing schools. Medical student training has been elective, not compulsory, until 2002. This training has been carried out at hospices by hospice personnel with palliative care training varying from a single lecture on palliative care to a two week hospice attachment. Currently, all medical schools in South Africa are integrating palliative medicine into the undergraduate curricula (Gwyther 2005). Hospice training personnel have been key in providing this education and in leading curriculum development at medical schools.

The University of Cape Town offers two postgraduate distance learning programmes for doctors – an 18-month diploma in palliative medicine and a two- to three-year distance learning MPhil in Palliative Medicine, a degree by coursework including a research component.

Palliative care has limited recognition in Africa. Palliative medicine is not yet a specialty and many medical and nursing personnel are not aware of the active clinical aspects of palliative care. In Africa, palliative care has only been available within hospices, which are non-governmental organizations (NGOs)which, until recently, have not received government funding. There has therefore not been a great deal of awareness of palliative care. Hospices have developed in communities that can support them financially and through volunteer support. This means that many poorer, rural communities do not have access to palliative care.

Palliative care is now being introduced as a compulsory part of the undergraduate medical curriculum in most African medical schools. Nursing colleges are also introducing palliative care training, although the emphasis is on palliative care in the oncology setting. There is no formal palliative care training in the undergraduate training of social care professionals.

In Zimbabwe palliative care training for medical students started in 1983. Since then it has been expanded to other health care professionals such as student nurses and pharmacists, and to non-professionals from communities that are looking after the sick at home. The Ministry of Health and Child Welfare realized the need to extend coverage in Zimbabwe and a country-wide outreach programme was commenced. The first module of palliative care was developed in 1994. Although training has been carried out, there has not been a formal curriculum developed for any health professionals. A lot of emphasis and training in palliative care is being integrated into home-based care groups who are providing services in the community in response to HIV and AIDS pandemic. A palliative care curriculum is being developed and introduced as a core course at the schools of medicine and nursing, and as a post basic diploma course, at the University of Zimbabwe (Garanganga 2003).

Driving forces in palliative care education

Professionals working in NGOs providing palliative care are the only group that has influenced and developed palliative care training programmes. These groups include the Hospice Palliative Care Association of South Africa, the Palliative Medicine Institute in Johannesburg, the Wits Palliative Care group in Soweto and Family Health International. The Education and Training Committee of the African Palliative Care Association (APCA) has based its mission on the Cape Town declaration of 2002 which stated that 'all members of the health care team and all health providers need training' and that there is a 'need to establish training programmes at all levels' (Mpanga Sebuyira *et al.* 2003; Downing 2005).

Hospice and palliative care services in Africa are strongly influenced by the UK models of hospice care but have been adapted to suit local conditions. Palliative care is primarily a domiciliary service. There are few inpatient units as this is an expensive service. With the challenge of the HIV/AIDS epidemic and the scarcity of health care professionals in many countries, hospices have recruited and trained non-professionals as caregivers. The support and supervision of these health care workers is essential for a successful palliative care programme (Fox 2002).

Specific donors and hospices themselves have funded the development of curricula. The relevant professional body awards accreditation and validates the training programmes, for example the South African Nursing Council and Health Professions Council of South Africa. The most recently developed curricula are the paediatric palliative care courses (for professionals and community careworkers) now available in South Africa, funded by the Diana, Princess of Wales, Memorial Fund and Nelson Mandela Children's Foundation.

The urgency of the HIV epidemic has also alerted health policy-makers to the need for palliative care training and service delivery. Many national departments of health are working with hospice and palliative care organizations to deliver palliative care training programmes. Examples are the close working relationship between the Ugandan government and Hospice Africa Uganda and the South African Department of Health's

Palliative Care Working Group with members from the government, Family Health International and the Hospice Palliative Care Association of South Africa. Across the borders, the APCA is working with governments, NGOs and the World Health Organisation (WHO) to develop palliative care services and train professionals and non-professionals in the discipline. The Botswana Department of Health invited the APCA to conduct palliative care training workshops in Gabarone in 2005.

Palliative care education is developed to be sensitive to the needs and unique characteristics of the region. There is emphasis on culturally sensitive care, which is a significant component in palliative care in HIV/AIDS and paediatric palliative care. Training programmes also recognize that the multidisciplinary team includes traditional healers. It is recognized that in some areas, patients will never have the opportunity to consult a Western-trained doctor and the primary health care professional will be the traditional healer. Training programmes have been developed for traditional healers as well as for other health care professionals.

There is some concern that some institutions that claim to be providing palliative care training do not have palliative care trained personnel to provide it, so that the lack of understanding or individual interpretation of palliative care is perpetuated.

Approaches to palliative care education

A variety of teaching and learning methods are used in palliative care education in Africa. At undergraduate level lectures, small group tutorials, interviews and interaction with patients, role play – particularly for learning clinical assessment and communication skills – and case-based or bedside learning are important learning and teaching methods. At postgraduate level, training is interactive. It is recognized that experienced health care professionals have identified palliative care as a gap in their knowledge and are well motivated to address this gap. Drawing on participants' experiences to illustrate and enrich case-based learning is a successful teaching method. Interactive workshops and case-based learning are effective learning experiences for learners and tutors. Personal reflection and documenting reflective learning in a portfolio of learning or a learning journal are very effective. As a tutor, it is a privilege to read these intimate and insightful reports. Role play remains an effective, if stressful, learning method for developing communication skills.

There is a great need for affordable textbooks and palliative care journals in African palliative care training sites. Some resource centres only have key texts such as the *Oxford Textbook of Palliative Medicine* and the *Oxford Textbook of Palliative Nursing*. Others also have textbooks written by a variety of international palliative care experts. In 2004, the African Palliative Care Association published the first APCA journal and this is planned to be a quarterly publication. Prior to this initiative, subscriptions to international journals, such as the *International Journal of Palliative Nursing*, had to be carefully budgeted: the cost of international journals is prohibitive for most palliative care training centres.

Assessment methods are both summative and formative. They include written assignments, written examinations, research-based assignments, a personal learning portfolio (case-based), communication skills assessment in simulated patient interviews and practical

---

Box 5.1 Example of an effective distance learning approach to palliative care training

Interdisciplinary Introduction to Palliative Care Certificate

Duration:	Six-month distance learning programme
Participants:	Doctors, professional nurses, professional counsellors (social workers, psychologists, pastoral counsellors)
Accreditation:	South African Health and Welfare Sector Education and Authority

Training

Modules:	Principles and ethics of palliative care
	Communication skills
	Grief, loss and bereavement
	Pain management
	Management of symptoms in advanced disease
	Palliative care in HIV/AIDS
	Cultural and spiritual care
	Teamwork and care for the caregiver
Teaching and learning:	Ten three-hour face-to-face interactive training sessions and workshops
	One hour per week small group learning at work sites discussing specified topics
	One hour per week self-study to complete tasks which are documented in personal learning portfolios
Assessment:	Assessment of portfolio – discussion between learner and tutor; scored assessment of tasks

---

assessment of competencies. Emphasis is placed on outcomes-based assessment that empowers and enables the learner and takes into account culture and environment.

Problems such as large rural communities, vast distances and staff shortages make distance-learning programmes a priority in Africa.

The impact of palliative care education

In general palliative care education has had a positive impact and increased the access to palliative care for patients with life-threatening illnesses. However, the urgent need to institute palliative care education has sometimes led to misinformation when non-palliative care-trained educators have developed the training course. Palliative care is not yet recognized by all health care professionals. Recognition comes mainly from oncologists who have referred patients to hospice services and experienced the benefit of working with hospice personnel in the care of their patients.

The significant international funding that has become available for palliative care from the Global Fund and the United State President's Emergency Plan for AIDS Relief has raised awareness of palliative care. However, there has been individual interpretation as to what constitutes palliative care and it has been challenging for hospice and palliative care professionals to insist that the WHO's definition of palliative care is the foundation for palliative care services. The impact of the HIV/AIDS epidemic has alerted most health care service providers to the need for palliative care. Integration of palliative care into the formal health care sector is becoming a reality, with many doctors, nurses and health care authorities requesting palliative care education.

In Africa, palliative care is primarily a nursing service. As our professional nurses are becoming equipped with knowledge, attitudes and skills of palliative care, they are influencing doctors to become more knowledgeable in patient care, for example in pain management. Nurses are challenged, in that doctors still see themselves as the authority in patient care. Palliative care-trained nurses become partners in patient care and there is a shift in the power relationship between doctors and nurses. A number of doctors have been stimulated to learn palliative care although many will simply accept the professional nurse's guidance in prescribing for the hospice patient; others will not accept any input from nursing staff.

Palliative nursing and palliative medicine are not seen as viable career options. Funding for palliative care is precarious and employment is only available in hospices. Although many hospices strive to be able to offer market-related salaries, this is often not possible and nursing staff, in particular, work in palliative care because they view this as a calling. There is no additional remuneration available for additional qualifications. Medical input is also limited. The majority of larger hospices employ doctors on a sessional or part-time basis while smaller hospices rely on voluntary support from general practitioners who may not have palliative medicine training.

The inclusion of care for the caregiver programmes in palliative care training and in hospice services helps to support palliative care personnel in their work. There is personal and professional satisfaction in the palliative care field. Although there is no documented evidence, it is likely that this has influenced professional staff to remain in palliative care or to remain in Africa despite attractive earning opportunities in the developed world.

The key challenges facing palliative care education in Africa are funding and the scarcity of trained personnel, although this is slowly improving. Successful palliative care training has only been made possible by the provision of grants or bursaries to learners.

Interaction at the global level

The initial training programmes in palliative care have been based on palliative care training from the UK, for example the Diploma in Palliative Care in Kenya presented by Oxford Brookes University and postgraduate medicine programmes at University of Cape Town developed by a South African graduate of Cardiff University, with initial support from Cardiff University staff (Gwyther 2002). Makerere University in Uganda also offers a Diploma in Palliative Care. African palliative care trainers communicate with international colleagues and use current palliative care articles to inform their teaching. The African Palliative Care Association and Hospice Palliative Care Association of South Africa have education committees to promote the development of up-to-date training materials.

At regional, national and international (African) meetings and conferences palliative care education and research topics are discussed and shared amongst colleagues. There is collaboration in developing training materials and trainers travel to other regions and other African countries to present training courses.

There are few palliative care education publications from Africa. A group of African authors are collaborating with the American authors of *A Clinical Guide to Supportive and Palliative Care in HIV/AIDS* to adapt this text to be relevant to African health care workers (O'Neill *et al.* 2003). The cost of producing this text will be covered by the National Hospice Palliative Care Organization in the U.S.A. This will include a resource list of training courses and palliative care education sites.

Conclusion

From small beginnings and individual hospice training programmes, palliative care training in Africa has developed so that it is a formal part of nursing and medical training. Further developments have included recognition and support from national governments to engage palliative care trainers in providing training to staff within hospitals and clinics. This will improve the access to palliative care for patients and families facing the diagnosis of life-threatening illness.

Chapter 6

Asia Pacific

Cynthia Goh and Rosalie Shaw

Background

The Asia Pacific is a vast region that stretches from Japan, Korea and China in the north, through Indochina, Malaysia and Singapore, to Indonesia and the Philippines, Australia and New Zealand and the islands in the Pacific. In this region there is great diversity of ethnicity, language, religion and economic development. There is also wide variation in the development of palliative care services. In the more developed economies of East Asia, such as Japan, Korea, Hong Kong, Singapore and Taiwan, hospice programmes have developed over the past two decades. Services initially started by religious groups or dedicated volunteers are now well established, cover a significant proportion of the population, and are partly or fully funded by the government. However, in many of the developing countries in South-East Asia, hospice services are still rudimentary or sporadic, caring for only a small proportion of those in need. In countries such as Laos and Cambodia some hospitals are providing care for AIDS patients but there is still very little awareness of palliative care. Myanmar has two inpatient hospices but no home care programmes. In Vietnam there are three palliative care units in hospitals in major cities but as yet no community programmes providing home care.

The Asia Pacific Hospice Palliative Care Network (APHN), a regional network of organizations and individuals working in palliative care in the region, was established in 2001 and now has more than 860 members in 28 countries. The membership includes not only countries of the Pacific rim stretching from Japan to Australia and New Zealand, but also Thailand, Myanmar, Bangladesh, Nepal, India, Pakistan and Sri Lanka. A survey of palliative care education was conducted by the APHN for the purposes of this chapter. The situation in India and in Australia and New Zealand has not been included as this has been covered elsewhere. For the rest of the region, the description has been divided into three sections, according to the degree of development of both services and palliative care education in the countries involved.

Japan, Korea, Taiwan, Hong Kong and Singapore

In the more developed economies of East Asia, the concept of hospice was introduced relatively early. The religious sisters of the Little Company of Mary started a hospice programme in Korea in 1965, and the Yodogawa Christian Hospital in Osaka, Japan, set up a team for the care of dying patients in 1973. However, palliative care services developed in all these countries in the 1980s and early 1990s. Volunteers were often involved and as the services developed, the government took a role, providing partial or full funding, and taking part in accreditation and the setting of standards for hospice care.

Japan

Japan now has over 144 services, largely hospital-based inpatient units, covering all but five of the 47 prefectures. However, because of a lack of development of home care services, coverage remains low at less than 5 per cent of cancer deaths. There are several umbrella bodies, one for hospice and palliative care service providers, one for home hospice, and several professional associations, such as the Japan Society for Palliative Medicine and the Japan Association for Clinical Research on Death and Dying. The Japan Hospice Palliative Care Foundation supports research and international exchange. Palliative medicine is not yet an accredited medical specialty in Japan, but more than three-quarters of medical schools have included palliative medicine in their undergraduate curriculum, with an average of three to five hours of teaching contact. Palliative nursing education is much better developed with unified undergraduate and postgraduate nurse training in palliative care, and accreditation of palliative nursing as a specialty in 1999. As of February 2005, there were 100 Certified Expert Nurses in Hospice Care, as compared with 157 Expert Nurses in Cancer Pain Management Nursing and 44 Certified Nurse Specialists in Cancer Nursing.

Korea

Korea has more than 100 hospice palliative care services and four umbrella hospice organizations. The Asia Pacific Hospice Conference, hosted by the Korean Society for Hospice and Palliative Care in 2005 and attended by 1200 participants, gave impetus to palliative care development in Korea. Palliative medicine is now included in the undergraduate curriculum in more than half of the medical schools, usually for two to three hours of teaching contact. Although palliative medicine is not an accredited specialty, there are postgraduate lectures and a course for family physicians. Palliative nursing is better developed and is expected to be accredited as a specialty in 2006.

Taiwan

Taiwan has about 30 accredited hospice palliative care services that are mostly inpatient units within hospitals, some with home care services. It is estimated that these services cover only about 20 per cent of cancer deaths. There are three foundations, each run by different religious groups, and two professional associations. The Taiwan Academy of Hospice Palliative Medicine is the certifying body for palliative care physicians. Palliative medicine was accredited as a medical specialty in 2001, with 351 physicians accredited by 2005. Seventy-five of these were working full time in palliative care. Palliative medicine is not included in the undergraduate medical curriculum except as part of an ethics course. The Hospice Foundation of Taiwan has had a major role in organizing three-tiered training for each of the professional groups: doctors, nurses and allied health.

Hong Kong

Eleven inpatient and home hospice services are fully funded by the government. Together they cover 60 per cent of cancer deaths in the territory. Both physicians and nurses have their own professional bodies for palliative care. The Society for the Promotion of Hospice Care promotes public education and provides training in bereavement. Palliative medicine has been recognized as a medical specialty since 1998 and there were 30 accredited specialists and 10 trainees in 2005. However, only two of these accredited specialists are practising palliative medicine full time. Palliative medicine is included in the undergraduate medical curriculum of the medical schools in the territory and in the nursing schools. Medical students get one to two hours of lectures and four to eight hours of ward rounds. Palliative medicine is included in the specialist training of related medical specialties. There are Certificate Courses in palliative care for family physicians, nurses and allied health professionals. The Diploma in Palliative Medicine from the University of Cardiff in the UK, is now a qualification which is recognized for registration with the Hong Kong Medical Council.

Singapore

Singapore has eight charities providing community based hospice home care, day care and inpatient services. Most public sector hospitals now have consultative palliative care services. Together, these cover over 75 per cent of cancer deaths or 20 per cent of total deaths. Palliative medicine was accredited as a subspecialty of various medical specialties in 2005. Until then, palliative care specialists in Singapore had relied on overseas accreditation provided by the Australasian Chapter of Palliative Medicine of the Royal Australasian College of Physicians, the American Board of Palliative Medicine and the Postgraduate Medical Education and Training Board of the UK. Palliative medicine is a compulsory part of the undergraduate medical course with eight contact hours, which include lectures, small group discussions and home visits. Palliative medicine is also included in the specialty training of other medical specialties, such as geriatric medicine, surgery and family medicine. A postgraduate course for doctors in palliative medicine is conducted every six months and is attended by both senior and junior doctors from a wide range of medical specialties, as well as overseas participants. For nurses, palliative care is included in the undergraduate curriculum and there is a one year advanced diploma course in palliative nursing. From 2006, the National Cancer Centre Singapore in conjunction with Flinders University and the APHN is offering the Flinders University Graduate Diploma in Health (Palliative Care) aimed at doctors and nurses from developing countries.

Malaysia, the Philippines, Indonesia and Thailand

This group of countries has an intermediate development in both services and education. Of these, Malaysia is the most developed. Thailand has only recently become involved in regional networking. In these countries development of the hospice movement was affected by the economic crises of the 1990s and progress has often been slow.

In Malaysia hospice programmes were established by charities in Kuala Lumpur and Penang in 1991 along the lines of the model adopted by its neighbour, Singapore, with emphasis on hospice home care. This model worked well in urban communities. Emphasis was on service, and training was usually on-the-job and at local conferences. Visiting faculties from developed countries played a role as plenary speakers at meetings and on courses. Following a pilot project at Kota Kinabalu in Sabah, the government announced in 1997 that all district hospitals were to have palliative care teams or palliative care units. By 2001 there were 11 palliative care units and 49 palliative care teams, but manpower was only seconded from other departments such as surgery. No provision had been made by the government for the training of staff. The charitable sector has attempted to make up for this deficiency by providing some training to staff in these palliative care units. In particular, many courses have been conducted in Kuala Lumpur by Hospis Malaysia, a charitable provider of hospice home care and day care. Palliative care is included in the curricula of both medical and nursing students, though this may be taught by staff with no practical experience in palliative care. In 2005 the Ministry of Health announced that palliative medicine would be recognized as a medical specialty. This will give a much needed impetus to palliative care education in Malaysia from within the public sector.

The Philippines

Hospice services blossomed around the time of the First Philippines National Hospice Conference held in Manila in 1995. However, subsequent development has been slow and fragmented. A national hospice palliative care organization was inaugurated in 2004 and this body will co-host the biennial Asia Pacific Hospice Conference in 2007 with the Philippine Cancer Society. Palliative medicine for medical undergraduates is taught in ethics and oncology modules. Postgraduate training includes seminars for family practitioners and as part of a residency training programme in Family Medicine. Palliative medicine is not accredited as a specialty in the Philippines. For nurses, palliative care is included in the undergraduate Bachelor of Nursing and postgraduate Masters in Oncology courses and in Continuing Education programmes.

Indonesia

In Indonesia palliative care programmes were started in hospitals in Surabaya, Jakarta and Bali in the 1990s, but progress has been slow with only six centres now providing palliative care in this vast country which has a population of over 238 million. In at least one medical school palliative medicine is included in undergraduate teaching and in the pre-residency programme for postgraduate students. There is only sporadic education of family physicians or others. In the mid-1990s, a group of 17 physicians from Surabaya completed the Postgraduate Diploma in Palliative Care through distance learning from Edith Cowan University. However, few of them are working full time in palliative care a decade later.

Thailand

Thailand entered the palliative care field relatively recently. Previously interested practitioners were mainly anaesthetists and pain physicians, who form a large group under the

Thai Association for the Study of Pain. More recently, radiation oncologists, paediatricians, surgeons and others have shown an interest in palliative care. Rapid progress has been made since the formation of the Thailand Palliative Care Council in 2005, with inclusion of palliative care into undergraduate curricula of many universities, and postgraduate programmes for family physicians. A certificate course in palliative nursing is available for nurses.

Myanmar, China, Vietnam, Laos, Cambodia and Mongolia

Myanmar

Myanmar has two inpatient hospices in its two largest cities, Yangon and Mandalay. However, there is as yet no formal palliative care education.

China

This vast country has a population exceeding 1.3 billion. Since two nurses from Tianjin were sent to London for oncology training in 1987, many Western groups and individuals from the USA, UK and Australia have visited to train local physicians and nurses in palliative care, but it is difficult to evaluate their impact and lasting effect. Cancer pain services have been started at various centres. In 2000, the Huaxi International Collaborating Centre was established in Chengdu, Sichuan Province, and became an international partner of the Oxford International Centre for Palliative Care (UK). Three doctors and one nurse subsequently went to Oxford for training. However, only one of these is still working in palliative care at the 24-bedded inpatient unit in the West China Fourth Hospital of Sichuan University, and little education has so far been undertaken. The Li Ka Shing Foundation based in Hong Kong and Shantou has established a network of hospice home care services in 20 major hospitals in 16 provinces and provides ongoing training for its staff. Little is known about palliative care education in most parts of China.

Vietnam

Vietnam was one of the founder sectors of the APHN and since the mid-1990s many palliative care experts have visited and taught in this country. Furthermore, a number of senior physicians and nurses were given the opportunity for attachment to palliative care programmes in Australia, the USA and Singapore. However, no services were established until 2000 when the first palliative care unit was set up in the National Cancer Hospital in Hanoi. There are now three palliative care units: in Hanoi in Northern Vietnam, in Hue in Central Vietnam and in Ho Chi Minh City, formerly Saigon, in Southern Vietnam, all of which aspire to become training centres for their region. Since 2005, the Singapore International Foundation in association with the APHN has supported a three year Training of Trainers programme in Palliative Care consisting of two one-week intensive didactic and bedside training sessions per year at two of the regional centres, taught by a team of five palliative care experts on a voluntary basis. Apart from this, other visiting experts are providing teaching in palliative care for HIV/AIDS patients.

Laos and Cambodia

Some hospitals are caring for HIV/AIDS patients. However, there is as yet little awareness of palliative care.

Mongolia

A substantial grant from the Open Society Institute of the Soros Foundation enabled the establishment of a 10-bed palliative care unit in the National Cancer Centre (NCC) in 2000. By 2005 there were 15 beds in the NCC, two free-standing inpatient units and four home care programmes in the capital, Ulaan Bataar, as well as palliative care beds in 21 regional and nine district hospitals. Training is now provided at every level. Palliative care is included in the undergraduate medical curriculum, and in postgraduate medical specialty training and training of family physicians. Nurses are taught palliative care at the undergraduate level and there are also certificate, diploma and licensing courses in palliative nursing.

Driving forces in palliative care education

The model of palliative care in the region was initially based on the Western, particularly UK, model of inpatient care, either in free-standing hospices or hospital-based units. With more exchanges within the region, through the Asia-Pacific Hospice Conferences first held in 1989, and later through the APHN, countries began to realize that service coverage is difficult to achieve without home care services. The model of hospice home care that was so successful in Singapore has been modified to suit local urban communities in many countries in the region. Other community-based models of service provision, such as the one in Northern Kerala in India, are also being studied.

In the initial stages, funding for most services was derived from charitable foundations or public fund-raising. As services became more established, they began to attract government funding, especially when governments realized that home care and hospice inpatient services could result in savings in health care costs through reduced hospitalization and fewer investigations and futile treatments. As financial support from government became available, it was necessary to find ways of accrediting services and staff working in palliative care services. In Taiwan this led to the training and accreditation of large numbers of doctors as specialists and the establishment of standards to define the hospice units eligible for funding.

In some countries, such as Korea, curriculum development was driven by the nursing profession, through academic units such as the World Health Organization Collaborating Centre for Hospice Palliative Care established in 1995 at the Catholic University of Korea College of Nursing. Traditional teaching methods through lectures are still widely used. On-site training is also common. On the whole, students are not used to class discussions and therefore didactic teaching is the norm. However, this may be changing with increasing influence from outside the region. In non-English speaking countries such as Japan, Korea and Taiwan, literature is mainly in the form of local language journals and textbooks translated from the English or written in the local language. Assessment is usually in the form of examinations.

One of the major successes of palliative care education in the region has been the incorporation of palliative care into undergraduate and postgraduate training. Palliative care has now been introduced into undergraduate education in many medical and nursing schools in the region, though often this consists of a few hours of introductory lectures. A key challenge facing palliative care education is the fact that the majority of health professionals either do not know or misunderstand what palliative care is, what the services provide, and when and to whom referrals should be made. While undergraduate medical education will reach out to future doctors and nurses, it is also necessary to include the existing practitioners in ongoing training programmes.

The concept of interdisciplinary teams overturns the traditional relationship between the more highly educated doctors and less academically trained nurses. Allied health services such as medical social work and physiotherapy did not develop in many countries of the region until the 1990s, and are still non-existent in many developing countries. Cultural norms, especially between men and women, and the respect accorded to age and seniority, also affect the functioning of the interdisciplinary team in Asian countries. Western-trained or Western-influenced members of staff may have difficulty fitting back into the more traditional societies, with subsequent unhappiness and migration of trained staff.

The introduction of palliative medicine as a specialty brings both supporters and opponents from within the medical profession. The argument that all medical practitioners should practice palliative care as part of the holistic approach to patient management militates against recognition of specialist palliative care. Fear of further fragmentation of care with increasing medical specialization is another obstacle. Yet the lack of accredited training and career path is an important obstacle in attracting physicians and nurses in training to enter the field.

In most countries there is a lack of trained manpower both in the services and for teaching. Recruitment is a major problem for most palliative care programmes. It is difficult to entice staff if there is no clear career path and few established training programmes. Consequently palliative care is sometimes seen as a soft option for those who have failed in other specialist programmes. Furthermore, there are too few doctors or nurses with the experience or expertise to teach. Most professionals working in the field are already burdened with a heavy clinical load and they are paid as service staff. This is a vicious cycle – too few trainers result in too few trained staff, which in turn means a workload that is too high for staff to train others.

Traditionally countries in the region have looked to countries such as the UK, USA and Australia for teachers and models of service and education. Lack of established courses in the region has led many practitioners to enrol in distance learning courses such as those provided by the University of Wales, Flinders University and Edith Cowan University. Workers in the field rely on these diplomas and higher degrees to give them credibility and they may also be useful when services are accredited for funding. However, these courses are very expensive for students from countries with weak currencies.

Approaches to palliative care education

The courses often provide a good theoretical basis for the practice of palliative care. They also stretch the candidate academically to consider the principles of audit, emphasize the importance of continuous self-learning and encourage research. Nevertheless, many health professionals moving into the palliative care field do not have the academic background to benefit fully from these courses. This applies particularly to nurses, most of whom do not have university degrees and are not academically orientated.

Furthermore the content of some of the courses may not be optimal. Developing countries have specific educational needs: how to make essential drugs available, how to find funding and how to start and sustain services. One encouraging aspect is that, though the region is vast and the culture and language are diverse, the problems facing palliative care are very similar. Lessons learnt in one country can be carried to another and therefore networking within the region is essential for the spread of ideas and for mutual assistance.

Another mode of training is the opportunity available for attachments to established palliative care programmes in other countries, but the matching of the needs of the trainee to the clinical setting in the host unit has to be done with care. Often this exposure is not helpful because the trainee is exposed to practices which are unavailable or inappropriate in their original countries. Even the roles of nurses and family members are very different in many countries. Much of what is considered an integral part of nursing care in developed countries, such as the feeding and cleaning of the patient, even the serving of medications, may be done by a family member, in some units designated as the family carer. There are other practices which may be culturally sensitive. For example, open disclosure of diagnosis and prognosis and the emphasis on the right of the individual to make decisions about treatment and care options may need to be handled differently in some Asian settings where the family takes a more prominent role in decision-making.

Impact of palliative care education

One of the major limitations for palliative care education in the region is language. Many doctors and most nurses in these countries are not fluent in spoken or written English, and most of the available textbooks and journals are written in this language. Local teachers may be relying on only one or two foreign texts translated into the local language. Faculties from overseas are often English-speaking and even bedside teaching must rely on interpreters.

It is desirable that each country has its own training programme appropriate to its own social and cultural contexts. It is also important to have cross-pollination of ideas. Personnel who have taken courses or done clinical attachments overseas return with new ideas and different ways of doing things. There is a need for opportunities for individuals to pursue more academic pathways, but perhaps for the majority the teaching should be practically based. Much of palliative care teaching needs to be done through mentoring, the living demonstration of the palliative care approach in the context of the patient, the family, the interdisciplinary team and the wider medical community. Bedside teaching and apprenticeship is as important as theoretical knowledge and principles, and therefore a balance needs to be achieved so that both aspects of education are available.

Until there are national policies for palliative care and the resources, both fiscal and manpower, to implement the services and the training programmes, progress in palliative care education within a country is likely to be slow. There is still a great need for courses open to doctors, nurses and health care professionals who are seeking certification in palliative care. Ideally these would be distance learning courses so that students can continue to work while they are acquiring the qualifications. In the age of information technology and with widespread availability of email, this is now feasible and highly achievable.

Conclusion

Education and training must be linked to the accreditation and funding of palliative care programmes. This requires an awareness of the need for palliative care as an essential component of health care. Only then will palliative care be seen as a requisite part of the undergraduate and postgraduate training, and continuing education of physicians, nurses and other health care professionals.

Chapter 7

Australia and New Zealand

Odette Spruyt, Rod MacLeod and Peter Hudson

Background

Palliative care in Australia and New Zealand is well established and founded on a multi-disciplinary, patient-centred model of care delivered by medical, nursing, allied health professionals and volunteers in three settings: home, hospice and hospital. Both countries have palliative care funding predominantly provided by government and with less reliance on, but continued support from, community groups, charities and religious organizations.

Palliative medicine was recognized as a medical specialty by the Medical Council of New Zealand in 2002 and by the Australian Medical Council in 2005. However, it has been a distinct academic medical discipline since 1988 with a three-year advanced training programme overseen by a dedicated Palliative Medicine Specialist Advisory Committee. The first trainees completed medical specialist training via this pathway in Australia in 1993 and in New Zealand in 1995.

Australian nurses have been caring for the dying for more than a century but, as yet, there is no credentialing or accreditation system for specialty practice. While nurse practitioner endorsement is occurring in a few states, there is no agreement on a national approach to their regulation and education (Cairns and Yates 2003). In New Zealand, palliative nursing development has seen an increased focus on therapeutic approaches including multidisciplinary team work, shared care in the community, nurse specialist in hospital consultancy and plans to recognize nurse practitioners with limited prescribing rights. Nursing competencies were incorporated into several of the main tertiary courses for hospice nurses by 2002 (Robertson 1997; Hospice New Zealand 2000).

Across all disciplines, undergraduate palliative care education competes for over-crowded curriculum time with mixed results. The Australian and New Zealand Society of Palliative Medicine (ANZSPM) developed a core curriculum in 1995 which had been accepted but not adopted by most medical schools (Ashby et al. 1997). A recent survey of the deans of 41 Australian universities, or equivalents, showed that while many topics were included in medical and nursing undergraduate curricula, few had established dedicated course time for palliative care (Yates et al. 2004; Dingle and Yates 2005). A similar situation is found in New Zealand where palliative medicine education has been undertaken in clinical schools for over 20 years but without a systematic approach. A more structured approach piloted at the Wellington School of Medicine (MacLeod and Robertson 1999) has not been sustained. Despite the recent creation of a Chair in

Palliative Medicine at the Dunedin School of Medicine, University of Otago, progress remains slow.

Nursing undergraduate education is inconsistent in both countries, with no mandate for inclusion in foundational nursing education, despite the almost universal exposure of nurses to end of life and palliative care issues. Similarly, and perhaps most markedly, allied health professionals receive little or no palliative care undergraduate education.

Therefore, most palliative care education for all clinical disciplines occurs at postgraduate level and, as such, is optional and self directed.

Driving forces in palliative care education

At government level

Modern palliative care, with its origins in the UK model, has developed considerably in Australia and New Zealand over the past 25 years. Both countries recognize an increasing need for palliative care due to ageing populations, inclusion of patients with non-malignant diseases and efforts to improve equity of access for all, in particular for rural, minority and indigenous populations.

Both countries have developed a National Palliative Care Strategy (MacLeod 2001; National Palliative Care Strategy 2005) which specifically include the fostering of education of palliative care professionals.

The New Zealand National Strategy for palliative care suggests that the ANZSPM medical undergraduate curriculum should be adopted, and that Medical and Nursing Councils provide guidelines for schools on minimum content of palliative care training. It also identified the need to ascertain the workforce and education requirements for specialist and local palliative care providers including those for Maori. The New Zealand government has increased funding for palliative care services.

The Australian government has increased its support for palliative care in recent years by funding several major education and training initiatives through the National Palliative Care Programme managed by the Department of Health and Ageing (Box 7.1).

Both countries have well-established national organizations which have an important role in establishing standards and driving education and training.

Medical leadership

A review of the establishment of palliative care postgraduate medical education and training reveals two main thrusts: clinical and university based training.

The Sydney Institute of Palliative Medicine pioneered medical registrar training in the early 1980s, adopting the apprenticeship model of the training of other specialties within the College of Physicians. The Institute is credited with training the first cohort of palliative care specialists in Australia. However, the Certificate was not recognized by the Health Insurance Commission, had no collegiate identity and no continuing medical education (Cairns and Yates 2003).

The second main thrust of education was university-based and consisted of a range of certificate and diploma courses, and more latterly, of masters and doctorate degrees.

Box 7.1 Examples of education and training initiatives: the National Palliative Care Programme funded by the Australian Government

The Programme in Experience in the Palliative Approach (PEPA)

Provides opportunity for primary care providers of all disciplines to gain clinical experience of specialist palliative care practice. Backfilling of their work commitments enabled them to leave their workplace and undertake this training. Very well received by both palliative and primary care providers. Creation of better working liaisons and relationships across the primary care and specialist zones of practice has been a particularly important outcome. This programme will run until 2006.

The Palliative Care Curriculum for Undergraduates programme (PCC4U)

Promotes the inclusion of palliative care in undergraduate curricula and ongoing education of all health professionals. Under this programme, a survey of the current status of undergraduate education in palliative care was undertaken and a range of educational resources developed for widespread use in curricula of all disciplines. The project was completed in 2005.

CareSearch (www.caresearch.com.au)

Electronic evidence-based online resource of palliative care literature not otherwise available in existing anthologies; developed for palliative care practitioners, educators and researchers (Tieman 2005). Indexed and reviewed literature includes unpublished abstracts, government- and organization-sponsored documents, theses from Australian universities and international published palliative care literature missing from standard electronic databases.

The Australian Palliative Residential Aged Care (APRAC) project

Developed Guidelines for a Palliative Approach in Residential Aged Care to improve palliative care knowledge and practice in the aged care sector. Can be viewed online on the Australian Department of Health web site (www.health.gov.au). Used to assist palliative care educators in the aged care sectors.

Many courses are interdisciplinary. Few of these courses incorporated clinical experience.

In the late 1990s, the clinical and academic training of palliative medicine specialists entered a new phase, with the establishment of the Chapter of Palliative Medicine within the Royal College of Physicians. This Chapter is charged with the responsibility for training specialists within Australia and New Zealand and, in January 2005, released the Curriculum for Specialist Training in Palliative Medicine. The curriculum is based on the

CanMED 2000 Project (Societal Working Needs Group 1996) from which the seven core roles of the doctor have been adapted and made particular to the palliative medicine doctor (Adler *et al.* 2004; Royal Australasian College of Physicians' Chapter of Palliative Medicine 2005).

A further important development by the Chapter and partner organizations has been the Clinical Diploma of Palliative Medicine, established to improve the quality of palliative medicine in the primary care setting. The diploma offers a six month supervised clinical experience in palliative care and will be piloted in limited training sites in 2006.

In New Zealand, both Auckland and Otago Universities have opportunities for multidisciplinary learning at a postgraduate level but this predominantly involves doctors and nurses.

Nursing leadership

Both Australia and New Zealand have strong nursing specialty in palliative care. Nursing postgraduate education in New Zealand has been well supported by the National Nursing Council. The 1990s saw the development of hospice standards of care, hospice education and guidelines for hospice nurses (Hospice New Zealand 2000; Robertson 2005). An important achievement has been the clinically based education and training programmes for nurses. For example, Victoria University, Wellington launched a postgraduate certificate course in clinical nursing in 2002. Multidisciplinary graduate certificates in hospice palliative care are available in Auckland, Wellington and Christchurch.

In Australia, palliative nursing has been strengthened by the appointment of chairs of palliative nursing in Brisbane, Queensland, Perth, Western Australia and Melbourne, Victoria (Dunn and Yates 2000). These personnel have championed the development of palliative education and nursing research, taking on coordination of several major educational initiatives of the National Palliative Care Programme, for example the Palliative Care Curriculum for Undergraduates (PCC4U) and the Australian Palliative Residential Aged Care (APRAC) projects (see Box 7.1). The Queensland Nursing Council is currently funding a project to develop a competency framework to guide curriculum development, role descriptions and performance appraisal for specialist nurses (Canning and Yates 2005).

Theoretically all nurses in Australia have access to postgraduate palliative care education, but practical opportunities are limited for those in rural and regional areas. There is a variety of postgraduate certificates, diplomas and masters degrees on offer from several Universities. The cost of programmes varies and, for some students, are prohibitive. Introductory courses are also on offer from the Royal College of Nursing and some palliative care service providers.

Postgraduate education for allied health professionals is difficult to find. In a recent survey of 1021 allied health professionals with a response rate of 36 per cent, reported barriers to such education were: inability to backfill positions; competing interests and clinical priorities. Communication with patients and families, teamwork and caregiver needs emerged as requested topics for further education (Dingle and Yates 2005).

There is a new trans-Tasman collaboration between the New Zealand Society of Music Therapy and the University of Melbourne which has led to the development of a programme of supervised clinical training in music therapy at Massey University, New Zealand.

The Department of Palliative Care, La Trobe University, Melbourne has a postgraduate certificate and diploma in Health Promoting Palliative Care and a two year, full-time graduate entry Bachelor of Pastoral Care. The latter is multifaith and multicultural in orientation and is open to graduates of any clinical specialty (medicine, nursing or allied health), public health, social or behavioural sciences.

Approaches to palliative care education

Given the importance of attitude and patient-centred care, many educators have utilized transformative educational experiences that encourage students to draw on their own experiences and skills. This has proved to be most effective in undergraduate teaching (MacLeod and Robertson 1999; MacLeod *et al.* 2003). An example of a comprehensive palliative medicine undergraduate curriculum is provided by the University of Adelaide, where there is specific teaching in palliative care throughout the six year curriculum. Teaching methods include lectures, demonstration interviews with patients, integration into problem-based learning, hospice tutorials and a clinical rotation to a hospice or other palliative care attachment in years four, five and six. The course has 'produced a profound shift in the understanding of the undergraduate medical students of the goals of medicine' and 'reintroduced care of the whole person' (Brooksbank 2005).

The Sydney Institute of Palliative Medicine models the apprenticeship learning method which incorporates spiral learning, iterative loops and problem-based learning, much of which is integral to medical specialist training and incorporated into the new specialist curriculum for palliative medicine specialists (Turner and Lickiss 1997). In this training curriculum, there is emphasis on the close working relationship between trainees and consultants, the daily modelling of care and expertise and comprehensive exposure to all three dimensions of palliative care. Regular case review, academic team discussion and journal or research meetings provide complementary targeted educational opportunities. The role of clinical supervision is also given particular importance in this training (Ashby 2005). Methods of teaching in paediatric palliative care are similar and are based on one-to-one supervision and mentorship (Collins 2005).

Specific training in communication skills has been introduced in some diploma courses using actors in scripted role play exercises interacting with course participants. When such exercises are carefully coordinated and conducted in a supportive and non-judgmental manner, role play has proven to be a valuable technique in our cultural context. A variety of teaching modalities are also utilized in nursing education including distance education, face to face intensives and interdisciplinary approaches. Not all courses contain a clinical component.

Other approaches include the use of pre-prepared materials such as the interactive CD-ROM developed by PCC4U (see Box 7.1) for undergraduate education in all disciplines with audiovisual resources and learning activities to stimulate reflection on the issues presented.

Web-based learning is increasingly adopted by Australian educators in recognition of the vast distances of the country, remote location of many practitioners and the accessibility of the Internet to a high proportion of Australians. The Flinders University Department of Supportive Care developed an online Graduate Diploma and Graduate Certificate in Palliative Care in Aged Care in 2004. This resource, which has attracted students from as far as Nepal, is multidisciplinary and taught by many practising clinicians from palliative medicine, nursing, psychology, gerontology, sociology and allied health teaching. The same department and the Charles Darwin University, Darwin are setting up a further online topic-Palliative Care for Indigenous Populations: Health, Culture and Society. Another example of online education is the programme developed for community pharmacists by the Monash University School of Pharmacy (Hussainy *et al.* 2005, 2006).

In addition to training of practitioners, palliative care education occurs at many other levels and is inherent to the practice of most specialist services. These include local in-service education, participation in local, state, national and international conferences and symposia, creation of annual symposia with participants from inter-state and overseas and publication of written materials. Education for non-specialists tends to be course based but the PEPA programme (see Box 7.1) has enabled non-specialists to have some clinical exposure to palliative care specialist practice.

The methods of assessment range from the traditional, with essays, short examination questions and multiple choice questions, to more complex and innovative approaches, such as communication role plays, case studies and audit projects. Specialist medical trainees are now required to develop a personal portfolio to record, reflect on and collate their training experiences. This helps them to recognize their training needs and monitor their own progress in line with expectations of adult learners.

Impact of palliative care education

Successes

Over the past 20 years, the understanding of palliative care in Australia and New Zealand has increased markedly and with that, a growing recognition of the importance of incorporating palliative care into the foundation training of all health care professionals. Many of the skills best exemplified in palliative care practice are being incorporated into training and education at many levels. In particular, the attitudinal changes seen in medical education, with more focus on patient-centred learning in problem-based learning courses, resonate well with palliative care principles. Palliative care can model doctor–patient interactions which can be translated back into the many other medical areas (Brooksbank 2005).

The Australian Medical Council, in its accreditation of the Royal Australasian College of Physicians' Chapter of Palliative Medicine, has recognized that the training programme for palliative medicine is of a high quality. More trainees are now embarking on PhDs which will result in an increase in the research capacity and capability of the field. In nursing, it is anticipated that the recently inaugurated Australian National Society of Palliative Care

Nurses will play a major role in establishing national standards for education and credentialing of senior positions. At postgraduate level, students appear to value the focus and insights of palliative care and to actively seek to develop their skills in this area in response to their perceived learning needs. However, it should be noted that the successes may be tenuous and are often dependent on individual protagonists, without whom the advances made would come under threat.

Palliative care research in New Zealand is fairly limited but has increased in volume over the last few years. Collaborations are developing. One such group is the newly formed Palliative Care Research Group at the Dunedin School of Medicine encompassing postgraduate students from a number of non-medical disciplines.

A key success of paediatric palliative care education is the evidence that more children are being supported to die at home. Education in paediatric palliative care has led to the reform and upskilling of practice for paediatric and adult palliative care (Collins 2005).

Challenges

The Royal Australasian College of Physicians submitted applications for Palliative Medicine Specialist recognition in 1993 and 1998 to the Australian National Specialist Qualification Recognition Advisory Committee, a Commonwealth Government Committee. The 1993 application was opposed by four colleges, including the Royal Australian College of General Practitioners and the College of Radiologists (Radiation Oncology). These two colleges opposed the application again in 1998. The Royal Australian College of General Practitioners was concerned that the provision of palliative care should be continued by general practitioners, especially when care was provided in the community. This conflict has now been resolved, with the Royal College of General Practitioners recognizing that palliative medicine specialists provide a consultative service and do not 'take over' care unless requested. The recognition of palliative care amongst oncology colleagues is varied in both countries. Many radiation oncologists applied for Foundation Chapter Fellowships when the Chapter of Palliative Medicine was first established in 2000. With the development of the Clinical Diploma, radiation oncology trainees may be encouraged into palliative medicine training positions for a six-month period.

Despite the many multidisciplinary courses available, there remains a need to evaluate this and other educational approaches to palliative training and education. It remains a challenge to make courses tenable to members of disciplines less able to afford the costs involved, which are often high. The emergence of non-malignant diagnoses in palliative care practice is a major challenge here as elsewhere and requires extensive development of education and services appropriate to these areas. Current resourcing of palliative care services is inadequate to meet the current and ever increasing needs.

In Australia each state has the responsibility for establishing and maintaining health services. Consequently, there are interstate variations which affect training opportunities as it is difficult to develop programmes that are organizationally achievable in each state.

Attracting medical and nursing specialists to the field is difficult, given the general shortage of skilled nursing staff and competition with other specialty areas in medicine.

Table 7.1 Medical Census data 2003

	Australia	New Zealand
Total number of Palliative Medicine Chapter Fellows	179	38
% of Chapter Fellows aged 50–59 years	26	50
No. of respondents to census	130	30
No. working full- or part-time in designated palliative medicine positions	Full-time: 61* Part-time: 46	Full- or part-time: 22
No. in teaching or research posts in palliative medicine	54	5
No. of professors in palliative medicine	11	1

*Full time in palliative medicine = 35 hours or more per week in designated palliative medicine positions. 55 of these report hours of work ranging from 36–70 hours per week.

There are few formalized rotations for medical trainees as yet. At times, trainees are required to move interstate. Coordination of a trainees' network within the Chapter of Palliative Medicine is a very recent development with a trainee representative on the education committee of the Chapter.

In New Zealand, it has been challenging to develop a sustainable medical workforce. Recently the Health Workforce Advisory Committee of the Ministry of Health has produced guidelines for the recruitment and retention of specialists in many disciplines (Health Workforce Advisory Committee 2005). This has encouraged more debate and enabled clinicians and politicians to advocate for training and workforce opportunities.

Given the youthfulness of the specialty of palliative medicine, many incumbent consultants are similarly youthful and have the role of supervising trainees older in years than themselves. The demands of providing competent supervision in this dynamic are now being considered by the Chapter and Specialist Advisory Committee.

Interaction at the global level

Australia and New Zealand have a recent history that is closely aligned to the UK. However, the post Second World War era has seen increased cultural diversity and an evolution of independence which includes the establishment of new ties with more immediate neighbours in the Asia-Pacific region. Both countries are members of the Asia Pacific Hospice Network and many palliative care practitioners of all disciplines have worked as teachers and trainers in the Asia-Pacific region and beyond. Teaching has taken many forms: bedside teaching and modeling of the palliative approach, participation in national conferences in the region, visiting and supporting new palliative care initiatives in the Asia-Pacific region, conducting or participating in courses as well as hosting palliative care visitors to Australia and New Zealand. These exchanges allow sharing of experiences which is mutually enlightening.

Conclusion

The educational challenge for palliative care was recognized in Australia a decade ago: 'More and better education in cancer pain and palliative care at undergraduate and postgraduate levels, through enhancement of existing education, introduction of new programmes, and better integration throughout Australia of disparate efforts' (Lickiss 1996: 100). Real advances have been made in several of these areas, in particular by the development of the Chapter of Palliative Medicine and the development of new programmes to enhance the palliative approach. However, we continue to be faced with many challenges. As this and other chapters demonstrate, palliative care education has been diverse and imaginative, at times highly focused and specific, at others more wideranging and all-encompassing. Creative and culturally specific responses to the challenges of education are more likely to succeed than imposed formulae and concepts.

Acknowledgements

This chapter owes much to the insights and correspondence with many colleagues in the field. In particular, thanks to Dr Mary Brooksbank, Dr Richard Chye, Ms Meg Hegarty and Ms Gaye Robertson.

Chapter 8

Europe

Marilène Filbet and Philip Larkin

Background

One of the first considerations must be to define the concept of Europe itself and the place of palliative care within it. The political and economic structure of 25 European Union (EU) member states working in partnership offers only one, albeit the most easily recognized, example of the entity Europe. In valuing the diversity of the many different countries and cultures which shape our vision of Europe, it is not feasible to suggest a single entity. Divisions such as East and West are merely arbitrary, subject to constant refinement. We note, for example, a marked distinction between those countries of Central and Eastern Europe (CEE) and the former Soviet Union (FSU), in terms of service development and access to education and training (Clark and Wright 2003). Hungary and Poland, for example, where palliative care is more firmly rooted, offer a range of formative education opportunities whereas there are limited, if any, such opportunities in resource-poor countries, such as Moldova and The Ukraine, where the political agenda and infrastructure are less stable. Although evidence suggests that palliative care practice is largely well established in Western Europe (Ten Have and Janssens 2001; Centeno *et al.* 2004), there remain major deficits within many Eastern European countries in terms of availability, financial constraints and limited access to education and training. The recent shift in the World Health Organization's (2002) definition of palliative care from *specialty* to *approach* led to debate on the extent to which palliative care should be a set of transferable principles for best practice in end-of-life care or a 'specialty' in its own right. In redefining the vision of palliative care as an approach, it would be important to sustain the agenda for Eastern Europe and not to assume that Europe can be considered as a whole in terms of opportunity, access to care, treatment and of course, education.

The European Association for Palliative Care (EAPC) was formed in 1988 as 'a focus for all of those who have an interest in the field of palliative care at the scientific, clinical and social levels' (EAPC 2005: 1). It currently represents 50,000 people drawn from 40 countries, primarily from 31 palliative care associations (termed collective members) in 20 European countries. Education forms the core of its work, through a programme which aims to 'promote the implementation of existing knowledge, train those who at any level are involved in the care of patients and families affected by incurable and advanced disease, and promote research' (EAPC 2005: 1). In 1992, the EAPC described the current state of education in different countries. Recommendations were revisited in

2000, at a meeting of palliative care experts in Lyon, France which highlighted continuing wide variance in roles, functions and training needs across Europe.

In this chapter, we propose to discuss issues which affect the implementation of palliative care education at a European level and the particular role of the EAPC in addressing education needs expressed so far, reflecting potential and practical problems faced by educators in delivering high quality education. We highlight some positive initiatives and make some recommendations for the future, based on the changing face of European palliative care. In making a case for EAPC in supporting palliative care education, we do not detract from other initiatives that may be going on within Europe under different auspices since palliative care is growing and developing at a tremendous pace. However, we argue that the EAPC mission of 'One Voice–One Vision' confronts the challenges faced by educators and offers a formally recognized structure (as a non-governmental organization of the Council of Europe) to focus the agenda for good palliative care education.

Driving forces in palliative care education

Given examples of palliative education from 40 hours of introductory courses up to Masters level across Europe, the need to offer transferable academic programmes across the European Union is an issue for a political infrastructure operating a no border policy for its citizens. There are some notable examples of EU directives enabling transferability, for example German doctors and Spanish nurses are permitted to work in France without a re-registration requirement. However, professional roles vary quite considerably and bureaucracy, matched by a lack of understanding of roles and functions, often prevents the dissemination of skills and knowledge in palliative care. For example, UK palliative social worker roles are more likely to be undertaken by a clinical psychologist in many EU countries. Paramedical roles such as physiotherapy and occupational therapy may not exist in palliative care settings. The concept of clinical nurse specialist or advanced nurse practitioner is poorly developed outside the UK and Ireland. The wide variance in basic training for nurses across Europe, particularly Eastern Europe, means a lengthy bureaucratic process in terms of re-registration for employment or training. Even then, limited career pathway opportunities inhibit developments within existing local health systems and structures. There is a constant challenge to target education to diverse uni- and multiprofessional need. Language is contentious when 230 indigenous European languages are spoken but English remains the international lingua franca of education in palliative care. This severely limits learning opportunities, particularly where exposure to English may be restricted. Even terminology causes problems as seen in the German distinction between *palliativepflege* – palliative care emphasizing nursing care–and *palliativmedizin* – palliative care in the broader context, not just medicine. The term hospice causes problems in France and Spain because of negative connotations associated with long stay elderly care, poverty and charity. Such is the context within which palliative care education in Europe is pitched.

Evidently, European organizations such as the EAPC are unable to meet the diverse needs of all European states in terms of palliative care education. As EU membership grows, there will clear challenges to balance Western philosophical concepts of palliative care with the cultural diversity of its nations. The candidacy of Turkey as a future member state, a country which bridges East and West, will pose specific challenges for palliative practice and education, requiring flexibility and sensitivity. Inevitably, such challenges enhance shared learning in the context of end of life care. The development of palliative care across the EU reflects the UK model to some degree, although the independence of hospices outside statutory health provision and the prominent role of charitable institutes are less apparent. All services, both private and public, are provided by the public health care system (as in the case of France) or a completely public health model as in Spain. Sneddon's (2004) reflection on charitable funding as the driving force behind education is a salutary lesson for European educators eager to promote palliative care. Since funding and provision of palliative care differ widely, even within countries (cantonal Switzerland being a good example of this), the degree to which palliative education is promoted will often depend on whether it is integral or supplementary to statutory health care services. In addition, there is a clear north–south divide in the development of palliative care (for example, compare Norway or Sweden with Greece and Portugal) and variation in the politics of health care and funding. Encouragingly, most countries clearly favour strategic development within their existing health systems.

Gupta's (2004) recent debate on the nature and philosophy of palliative care raises questions pertinent to European palliative care education. To whom should education be targeted? In resource-poor countries (CEE and the FSU, for example) or where palliative care is in its infancy, there may be argument for focusing education programmes towards those who may have the greatest impact on the transformation of patient care: doctors and then nurses. The effectiveness of palliative care is sometimes measured by the number of referrals, as opposed to the quality of care offered. Education has a clear role here, through focusing this debate on how we can nurture key palliative care principles to meet local resources. The issue of palliative care being a specialty or not is clearly contentious. Education initiatives need to be developed with a strong sensitivity towards respective social, cultural and political mores. Notwithstanding those countries where palliative medicine is already recognized (UK. Ireland and Norway, for example), in others, specifically France Spain and Italy, there is a move towards specialization. Academic chairs are seen as a major stepping stone towards this and efforts are directed to this end. In other countries, for example Germany, there is no such agenda and palliative care has developed from within existing clinical specialities, such as anaesthesiology and pain management, although notably, Germany does hold an academic Chair in Palliative Medicine.

In 1997, the EAPC proposed that collective member associations should each create a national education network to link with the EAPC, with the dual aim of establishing minimal training recommendations for palliative care training for doctors and nurses

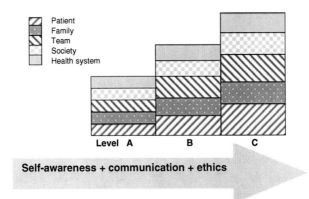

Fig. 8.1 Dimensions of the palliative care learning process. De Vlieger *et al.* (2004)

and of identifying appropriate training skills for palliative care educators (De Vlieger *et al.* 2004). Although these networks are evident at the national level, there are still European challenges, not least because of limited international agreement to date on minimum standards for curricula. The EAPC Task Force initiative has made a substantial contribution to this, through sets of recommendations for nursing and medical education. A key question is what should be taught, to whom and at what level? What has been significant has been the agreement of a three-tiered structure for education which favours a cumulative process of learning from basic through specialist enabling different countries to buy in at whatever level of clinical practice they offer (Figure 8.1). Cognisant of the needs of the new accession states, these levels of learning presuppose that every health care professional should have at least a basic (level A) understanding of the principles and philosophy of palliative care in generic training. Key individuals acting as a resource person at level B provide a bridge between general principles and the acquisition of greater knowledge for the deployment of palliative care within their own non-specialist work. Level C practice requires structured academic training at university level as well as prolonged exposure to the specialist clinical setting. In effect, level C is only possible at the specialist level. The current state of pre and postgraduate training for physicians in Europe has recently been reviewed (De Vlieger *et al.* 2004; EAPC 2004). These findings have informed a European expert group on palliative medical education, prior to a forthcoming publication of their recommendations.

Ideally, palliative care education should appear in the undergraduate curriculum of every discipline. For medicine, there are good examples of palliative care being integrated into the curriculum. France, for example, offers 16 undergraduate hours on palliative care. However, where professional training is not based within a university system, as in allied health care disciplines, an ad hoc approach is evident. Although a multidisciplinary approach to learning is a cornerstone for palliative care education (Koffman 2001), agreement on content is another matter. Even at the specialist level, teaching contact hours required to achieve an award is variable with wide-ranging definitions of the length of a teaching hour. This serves to discourage the seeking of common ground. There is agreement that at this time in Europe, efforts should be directed towards Level B training, offering direct possibilities to influence palliative care practice in the wider domains. A horizontal approach to integration means that educators respect aspects of palliative care being taught within other disciplines and work in tandem to prevent duplication. There are reports from some countries that health care professionals argue that palliative care is integral to treatment programmes and have no need for additional education. Palliative care educators must export their skills outside the arena of the discipline and consider innovative ways to encapsulate universal learning, such as ethics, communication and teamwork.

Approaches to palliative care education

Adult-based approaches (Knowles 1984; Spencer and Jordan 1999) underpin many courses, reflecting the need to incorporate prior learning through active process participation immediately applicable to practice. Course applicants often choose a specific programme of learning because of its work relevance and hence are motivated to learn new material or bridge specific gaps in their knowledge or expertise (Sneddon 2004). However, innovative approaches advocated for adult learners may challenge those whose previous exposure to learning has been predominantly through didactic lectures. In contrast, paramedical colleagues, for example social workers, often appreciate reflective small group work akin to their generic training. Problem-based learning to develop clinical reasoning skills is of increasing interest in palliative care (Keogh *et al.* 1999; Lloyd-Jones *et al.* 1998). It offers a valuable addition to the palliative care education repertoire although some questions remain over its theoretical basis (Albanese 2000; Colliver 2000). There are some excellent EU examples of innovative multidisciplinary learning (see the example in Box 8.1).

Assessments should be both formative and evaluative, involving an opportunity to disseminate knowledge, skills and attitudes within the clinical arena, as well as in the classroom. The trend towards continual assessment is not hugely evident, although it may be argued that those services which have benefited from close alignment with the UK are more likely to reflect this influence. We note many programmes now include case studies, role play, reflection and debriefing around clinical psychodynamics within their training.

In expanding the knowledge base, the need for journals in which empirical work can be disseminated has grown. There has been a proliferation of language-specific palliative care journals in recent years. The *European Journal of Palliative Care* brings together examples of best clinical practice and education. It is offered in both English and French. Germany, Italy, Spain and France all offer scientific palliative care journals in their respective languages and open the door for the majority who do not speak English. The ability to read English is quite common and journals such as *Palliative Medicine* are

Box 8.1 An example of innovative teaching practice

This example of enabling a multidisciplinary group to discuss moral dilemmas in palliative care was demonstrated by Dr Michaele Galucci and his team at the Seventh European Association for Palliative Care Congress in Palermo, Italy in April 2001.

A group of 'students' were invited to form a line across the room by the facilitator. The group were then given a moral question to consider, for example 'I believe that in all circumstances, euthanasia is morally unacceptable.' After some time to consider this, the facilitator invited those of the group who agreed with the statement to move to the other side of the room. The purpose of the exercise was for the two opposing groups to provide convincing arguments for their point of view and try and persuade members of each opposing group to transfer to their opponents' side. This required each group to work together to create a cohesive argument and develop skills in challenging emotive issues in a rational and debatable way. The facilitator ended the session with a discussion around decision-making and the choices made by professionals.

Gallucci *et al.* (2001)

readily accessible. However, limited English can preclude some professionals, particularly nurses, who do not have the proficiency to read in another language. The development of multilingual literature has been a positive development. A newsletter for Eastern Europe, sponsored through the US Open Society Institute, printed in Hungary and translated into Russian, widens the scope for dissemination of information and learning opportunities.

Impact of palliative care education

Given the arguments cited earlier about the need for an integrative and horizontal approach to education in Europe, one of the successes has been the creation of the nursing recommendations cited earlier. This EAPC consensus paper highlights a palliative learning process with resonance for other disciplines in terms of knowledge and application. Based within five domains, covering the spectrum of clinical practice, these guidelines not only identify content at the three levels discussed earlier (see Figure 8.1), but also appropriate teaching methods and clinical competency following the completion of training. These 'statements for nursing practice' demonstrate the transfer of classroom knowledge into the clinical arena. Having said that, the impact of these guidelines, and indeed those for medicine, is yet to be established.

Despite the mounting literature on palliative care education in Europe (Dowell 2002; Dowling and Broomfield 2002), and with one recent exception (Mason and Ellershaw 2004), there remains a gap in terms of assessment of the impact of training. More studies focus on the lack of available training than its potential effect. We suggest that this is an area for future development, particularly given the need to prepare professionals for practice (Sneddon 2004). For Europe, rigorous evaluation and empirical research of education will be needed to convince over-burdened health care services of its benefits to practice.

Interaction at the global level

Since 1990, the EAPC has organized nine international congresses, each based in a different European country, with the aim of bringing together the palliative care community and promoting palliative care at the highest possible level within the national system of the chosen country. Additionally, a forum which promotes palliative care research is organized every second year. Both initiatives bring together internationally recognized experts from all over the world to contribute to the development of European palliative care. More recently, these meetings have linked to local initiatives, such as national seminars, to encourage cross-fertilization of ideas. The value of education is always highly placed and parallel sessions in respective languages have been promoted wherever possible. These meetings have served as a foundation for research and education planning and international collaboration. The recently proposed 'stage' (the commonly used term for clinical placement in mainland Europe) programme is one initiative designed to look at innovative ways of sharing expert knowledge across member states. The project encourages short-term placements, avoiding permanent depletion of local palliative experts. Preliminary work has shown some good results, but further work is necessary to secure strategic EU funding.

There is good evidence of EU palliative education fostering links with the international community to develop practice. Conscious of translating palliative concepts for the world Francophone community, programmes target those countries where there is a struggle to put palliative care on the political agenda, particularly in regions of the world where AIDS has become endemic and end of life care needs to be urgently addressed. Porchet et al. (2005) report on a French initiative to create links with resource-poor countries in The Maghreb (a generic term for French-speaking Tunisia, Algeria and Morocco), using examples of European links to South America, Vietnam, Thailand, India and sub-Saharan Africa. Another notable initiative is a Swiss weekend workshop approach where a multidisciplinary group of palliative care clinicians and educators come together to look at practice guidelines for a clinical problem. Given that the workshop requires trilingual facilitation (German, French and Italian) and aims to produce best practice guidelines in a short space of time, their commitment and innovation demonstrate the possibilities of cohesive European working.

Conclusion

Sheldon and Smith (1996) argue that palliative education should mirror palliative care through integration rather than imposition of knowledge. Effective education should 'seek to enable students to reach their personal potential, as their effectiveness lies not only in the application of strategies and techniques to learning but in responding intuitively as a fellow human being' (Sneddon 2004: 639).

The European face of palliative care is ever-changing and bodies such as the EAPC have a responsibility to respond appropriately. This requires vision and conviction to meet challenges. Although the outlook for future education in Europe is positive, educators need to plan for pan-European initiatives which offer the highest possible level of learning. We must first target education towards best practice principles such as self-awareness, good communication and attention to clinical detail. Promotion of palliative care as a specialty and developing a pan-European curriculum would support this, as would integrating palliative care education as core material in all undergraduate programmes. Such initiatives as the European Summer Schools and a European masters programme in palliative care planned for the future will offer opportunity for multidisciplinary interaction, the key to successful palliative care practice. One challenge will be to support the educational needs of Eastern Europe in the face of international pressure to focus on Africa and Asia. Clinical exchange which develops theory and practice consecutively is one way to create and maintain international links. European approaches to palliative care will best develop through balancing diversity against homogeneity, respecting difference while promoting dialogue for a common vision.

Chapter 9

India

Suresh Kumar

Background

Palliative care in India is more than two decades old. Despite that, less than three per cent of patients with incurable cancer get pain relief (Stjernsward 2004) and less than two per cent of patients in need of palliative care have access to it. There is huge regional variation in the availability of services. There is practically no palliative care service in most regions in the country, where professionals are not even aware of the concept. In contrast, there are many districts in northern Kerala, the southernmost state in India, with estimated coverage of more than 50 per cent of the needy (Stjernsward and Clark 2004). Such variation makes palliative care education and training needs very different across the country.

Palliative care is not yet a recognized medical specialty in India. The government of India was a signatory to the World Health Organization's comprehensive cancer control programme and almost all the public Regional Cancer Centres have officially had pain clinics or palliative care units for more than ten years, yet most of these have been non-functional for all practical purposes. The Medical Council of India has not yet taken any steps to include palliative care in the undergraduate or postgraduate medical curriculum. The situation with the Nursing Council of India is similar. All that has been achieved so far occurred through individual initiatives by palliative care units or a handful of medical and nurse training institutions. For example, students in the Government Medical College, Kozhikode receive a total of 12 hours' exposure to palliative care as part of their undergraduate training, made possible through a project by the community medicine department. This particular institution also ensures that all junior doctors receive a week's placement in palliative care services during their housemanship. St John's Medical College, Bangalore also exposes their undergraduate students to palliative care. All the nursing schools in Malappuram district in Kerala have included a total of 20 hours of palliative nursing sessions in their undergraduate curriculum. These examples are rare exceptions at present.

In India, with its federal structure, health care comes mainly under the jurisdiction of state governments. Palliative care has not found a place in the health policy documents of central or state governments, but in regions where palliative care services operate with massive community participation, the local governments seem to have recognized the need and the presence of such services (Kumar 2004). For example, in Nilambur, Kerala where the community-owned Neighbourhood Network in Palliative Care programme is very active, all 11 Grama Panchayaths (local governments) have made it mandatory to have a representative from the palliative care team in the Panchayath Health Committee.

Driving forces in palliative care education

> The mode of being of the new intellectual can no longer consist in eloquence, which is an exterior and momentary mover of feelings and passions, but in active participation in practical life, as constructor, organizer, 'permanent persuader' and not just a simple orator.
>
> Gramsci (1996: 10)

The palliative care field in India interacts closely with the Western world, mainly the UK. A large proportion of pioneers in the field in India had their first exposure to palliative care through UK hospices. Regular participation of trainers from the Western world is also a prominent feature of palliative care training in India, all of which has led to a huge Western influence on palliative care education and training in India.

The interaction between Western palliative care institutions and health professionals in India who live and work in an entirely different socio-economic and cultural milieu has resulted in the emergence of different approaches in the delivery of palliative care in the country. The first palliative care institution in India, initiated a couple of decades ago by a cancer surgeon in Bombay, and other early hospices were developed in line with Western hospices, but there are less than ten hospices in the whole country. Free-standing or hospital based palliative care outpatient clinics emerged in the 1990s and have proved more popular (Rajagopal and Kumar 1999). Many of these clinics also offer limited home care services. There are a few programmes, like Can Support in Delhi, which offer home care services exclusively.

A further deviation from Western models occurred in the late 1990s through the emergence of Neighbourhood Networks in Palliative Care (NNPC) in the south Indian state of Kerala. The characteristics of these initiatives were ownership by the local community; a large number of trained volunteers working together with medical and nursing professionals; attention paid to socio-economic support as well as medical interventions and a heavy emphasis on home care (Graham and Clark 2005). NNPC has spread like a mass movement in certain regions in northern Kerala and programmes within its network account for more than 50 per cent of palliative care initiatives in the whole of India. This new phenomenon of active community participation in palliative care has stimulated lively discussion in Western palliative care journals about general versus specialist palliative care services (Gupta 2004; Graham and Clark 2005).

There is no central agency to coordinate or monitor palliative care initiatives in India. This has resulted in the evolution of a variety of training programmes which differ in their duration, type of participants and areas of focus. A few such programmes manage to get funding from the government although funding for training has essentially been the responsibility of the individual palliative care initiative. International agencies like Help the Hospices have played a limited but important role in this area. Individual units which run the training programmes have developed their own custom-made curricula. This extreme variation in the pattern and quality of training programmes has resulted in the formation of a task force by the Indian Association of Palliative Care (IAPC), the national association in India, to look into the issue of evaluation and accreditation of different academic and training programmes in palliative care.

On the positive side the lack of a uniform structure and curriculum at the national level has forced individual palliative care groups to evolve education and training programmes suitable for local needs. This is crucial in a country like India which has extreme regional variation in social ecology and culture. The expected interventions by the national association at this stage are likely to bring in a certain amount of uniformity to the education and training programmes without losing the local flavour.

Approaches to palliative care education

Palliative care has not yet found a place in the formal undergraduate or postgraduate curricula. A few medical and nurse training institutions include some teaching hours on palliative care, ranging from five to twenty hours. Such teaching is usually didactic, allowing minimal discussion. The one week clinical exposure to all interns at the Government Medical College in Kozhikode seems to be the only mandatory clinical exposure for junior doctors in palliative care. A few nursing institutions in northern Kerala also send their undergraduate students to the Institute of Palliative Medicine in Calicut for a two week residential foundation course in palliative nursing. At present this is the only structured course combining didactic lectures, discussions and clinical exposure for undergraduate nurses in India.

Short courses

Most palliative care training for professionals in India is delivered through short courses. These are generally in the form of continuing medical education programmes lasting a few hours, foundation courses of three to ten days and advanced or refresher courses of three to five days focused on specific areas of palliative care. Two institutions in India, Institute of Palliative Medicine, Calicut and Amritha Institute of Medical Specialties, Cochin, offer six-week residential courses in palliative medicine for doctors. These intensive courses offer a combination of lectures, clinical work, discussions, assignments and project work for the participants. Unlike the other brief courses, these two basic certificate courses also have assessment schemes involving written examination, clinical discussion and evaluation of written assignments. The Institute of Palliative Medicine also runs a similar six-week basic certificate course for practising nurses. Among the short courses, the foundation course for general practitioners run by Neighbourhood Network in Palliative Care is unique in its structure. This seven-day course involves 15 hours of interactive theory spread over three consecutive Sundays followed by clinical exposure at the local palliative care unit on four days which are convenient to the candidate.

Professionals are attracted to the short courses because of their appreciation of the humanitarian aspects of palliative care, a desire to improve clinical skills, curiosity or a combination of all these. Many palliative care institutions now offer foundation or refresher courses in the form of combinations of different modules of symptom relief and communication skills. Some of these educators believe that highlighting the training programme's potential to improve participants' clinical and communication skills works better as a marketing strategy than appealing to the goodwill or sense of responsibility of the health care professional (Paleri 2004).

Box 9.1 Starters' tips on the initiation of professionals into palliative care

- ◆ Training programmes for professionals show better attendance if done against a background of awareness programmes for the general public. The increased awareness among the public often forces professionals to seek training.
- ◆ Highlighting the potential for palliative care training programmes to improve the skills of the professional in symptom control and communication usually generates good interest.
- ◆ Always make the effort to link training programmes with plans to offer the professionals a 'space' for using the newly acquired skills and knowledge. Otherwise these might disappear without trace!

Paleri (2004)

Many palliative care units run awareness sessions for volunteers and the general public. The Neighbourhood Network in Palliative Care (NNPC), which depends on community involvement for its survival, offers a structured training programme for community volunteers with an exposure to hands-on patient care and an evaluation. This network registers only those who have successfully completed this training as community volunteers. The contents of the course include concept and philosophy of palliative care, role of the community in caring for the sick, ethical issues in palliative care, basic nursing care, communication issues and basics of cancer and HIV infection (NNPC 2004).

Most of the advanced courses and many of the foundation courses involve overseas faculty from the UK, Australia and the USA – until the late 1990s the key trainers in almost all of the professional training programmes in palliative care were external faculty.

The comparatively rapid development of palliative care services in India in the last few years has resulted in the emergence of a group of professional trainers within the country itself. Now there is a growing belief that the involvement of external faculty should be sought only after careful consideration of many delicate issues. NNPC has made a position statement on the involvement of external faculty in training programmes (see Box 9.2).

Longer courses

Until recently, advanced training in palliative care for professionals in India was dependent on foreign universities. For example, Edith Cowan University, Western Australia, has been running a one year postgraduate diploma programme in India in collaboration with the Pain and Palliative Care Society in Kozhikode. Since 2004, two Indian universities have started postgraduate courses in palliative care for doctors. Banarus Hindu University in Varanasi offers a one year Post Doctoral Certificate for Anaesthesiologists and Amrita Viswa Vidyapeedam in Kerala started a two-year postgraduate diploma in 2003.

At the moment there is one postgraduate diploma course in palliative care for nurses, the distance education programme run by the Regional Cancer Centre, Trivandrum.

> ## Box 9.2 The NNPC position statement on involvement of external faculty
>
> The Neighbourhood Network in Palliative Care (NNPC) appreciates the dedication of the external faculty, the efforts that they take and the personal sacrifices they make in coming over to teach in India. We are also aware that care that is offered to the patient should be culturally appropriate and affordable to the community. Trainers from a different socio-economic and cultural background, though well experienced in the clinical specialty, can sometimes convey wrong messages to the trainees. NNPC strongly believes that external faculty should take extra care to learn about the local culture and socio-economic situation before planning to teach. Whenever possible, the policy should be to ensure active involvement of the local faculty along with the trainers from abroad.
>
> Numpeli (2003)

In 2003, the Christian Medical Association of India (CMAI) in collaboration with the Institute of Palliative Medicine initiated a one year fellowship programme in palliative care for doctors. This distance education programme has contact sessions, clinical placements, project work and a detailed assessment with written examination and evaluation of clinical skills. In 2004, the government of India started supporting a limited number of doctors and nurses in government services for a six-month World Health Organization in-country fellowship programme in palliative care, a training period emphasizing improvement of clinical skills and organization of services at a centre of excellence recognized by the government.

As only four to five per cent of the literate population use the internet, web-based courses have not yet become very popular. The chief mechanism for passing on information in India is still through printed books and literature. Palliative care training programmes in India depend almost entirely on books and literature from abroad. The cost of such materials is one of the obstacles that trainers face but at least one overseas publisher has enabled a palliative care textbook to be made available at a cheap rate, for use as a course manual for the majority of training programmes in India.

The impact of palliative care education

Daniel Callahan observes that palliative care 'is not just a new medical subspecialty but a way of thinking about medicine's goals in a more penetrating way' (Callahan 2000: 3). The spirit of palliative care is bound to influence medical practice in the region in a positive way.

In India, training programmes in palliative care are still inadequate to generate a critical mass for a major positive change in the condition of the incurably and terminally ill patients in the country, but the limited number of courses and programmes have already started to affect the wider health care programmes. As expected, there is more impact in regions where the palliative care programmes show a more visible presence. Neighbourhood Network in Health Care (NNHC) in Kerala is an example of a programme showing such an impact (Paleri and Numpeli 2005). All health care professionals and the community volunteers in NNPC are trained in palliative care. In 2005, the Kerala state branch of the Indian Medical Association, with a membership of more than 12000 doctors, initiated palliative care training programmes to improve their members' skills in symptom relief, communication and emotional support to patients. A British consultant anaesthetist who underwent six weeks' training in palliative care at a unit with active community involvement wrote:

> Perhaps we should stop thinking that taxation should cover everything, and start to consider whether we could adopt a 'Neighbourhood Network' model adapted to our Western society, something which would belong to the community and of which the community could be proud ....And it is good to be made to think about what we are doing, and what we are trying to achieve. Sometimes a fresh look is just what is needed.

Pringle (2005: 1721)

Training programmes in palliative care have also radically altered some power relationships. A notable example is that of the communication skill training module for the national fellowship programme. This has evolved into a 20-hour stand alone training programme in communication skills for professionals and community volunteers. The faculty includes doctors, nurses and community volunteers in palliative care (Chittazhathu and Moideen 2005). This programme, which includes nurses and lay people as faculty and uses the same outline for doctors, nurses and volunteers, has become a very popular communication skills training course for doctors. In the prevailing intensely hierarchical health care system in India, such sharing would have been unthinkable back in the 1990s.

The number of people in this world who would benefit from palliative care services is huge. The majority of them are in the developing world (Murray and Lopez 1996). Most of them are too poor to access even basic human needs like proper food, drinking water and primary health care. In countries like India, palliative care is trying to find its space against a difficult background. The complexity of the situation can lead to two possible dangers. One is that of following existing models in health care and ending up providing everything for a few people. The other extreme would be to get caught in the difficult socio-economic situation, complexity and enormity of the problem, being overwhelmed and ending up making no difference to the target population in palliative care. Palliative care programmes in the developing world can make an impact only if they are sufficiently innovative. The main challenge before palliative care trainers in countries like India is to evolve training programmes facilitating the development of such innovative initiatives. This country probably needs two broad types of training programmes in palliative care. Basic training programmes should be widely available for most doctors and nurses to empower the primary health care system to address common palliative care issues (primary palliative care). There is also a need to train future trainers and professionals to support referral units (specialist palliative care).

Interaction at the global level

As already mentioned, training institutions and faculty from the West play an active role in the palliative care education and training programmes in India. For palliative care workers, these frequent interactions act as a window to the outside world. Most of these visits and training programmes occur as a result of arrangements between institutions and individuals. The Indian Association of Palliative Care (IAPC), the umbrella organization for palliative care initiatives in India, plans to make such visits by external faculty more coordinated, focused and useful (Goswami 2005). The main platform for exchange and sharing of information between individuals and initiatives within the country should be this national organisation. Since its inception, IAPC has been facilitating this process through its annual conferences, newsletters and the *Indian Journal of Palliative Care.*

Palliative care training programmes in India have also started making contributions to the development of palliative care in many other Asian countries. The six-week Basic Certificate Course in Palliative Medicine (BCCPM) and the Basic Certificate Course in Palliative Nursing (BCCPN) cater to doctors and nurses from neighbouring countries as well as locals. Palliative care initiatives in the Middle East have also identified Indian palliative care institutions as training centres (Stjernswarld *et al.* 2003). Health care professionals from Bangladesh, Nepal, and Japan have been taking these courses as entry points to the field. Doctors and nurses from Thailand, the Maldives and Bhutan have had their training in India as part of a WHO programme. The similarity in socio-economic background and culture within most of the Asian countries when compared to the West makes such initiatives particularly useful for both the trainees and trainers.

Chapter 10

North America

Frank D. Ferris and Charles F. von Gunten

Background

In North America, as elsewhere in the Western world, dying was a routine part of life until the mid-twentieth century when it became medicalized, i.e. it was primarily seen as a product of pathophysiology and the responsibility of health care professionals rather than as part of the human condition and the responsibility of family and friends (Aries 1974). Dr William Osler, a Canadian physician, reported on the first large series of dying patients (Hinohara 1993). Interestingly, he found that the moment of death was not painful or dramatic for the vast majority. The care of the dying as a special focus of activity was carried to North America by those who observed the care in France, Ireland, Scotland and England (Starr 1982; Saunders 1998).

The first evidence of specific education in North America appears in 1935 when Harvard physician Alfred Worcester published three lectures on 'The Care of the Aged, the Dying and the Dead', intending them to serve as outlines of what medical students should be taught because of the unpardonable shifting of care for the dying to nurses and sorrowing relatives (Worcester 1935). The text was circulated during the early days of the hospice movement in North America because of its thorough clinical observations and procedural recommendations and its specific injunction that younger physicians must not allow science to distract them from the art of medical practice and the 'indispensable qualifications of the physician: tact and courtesy ... sympathy and devotion ... (for) in the practice of our art it often matters little what medicine is given, but matters much that we give ourselves with our pills' (Worcester 1935: 31, 48).

At the beginning of the twentieth century, North Americans usually died of infectious diseases or trauma: by the second half of the century, they were living longer and dying primarily of atherosclerotic diseases (myocardial infarctions, stroke, congestive heart failure) and cancer. Instead of death occurring quickly, in days, there was a new period of dying that occurred over weeks to years. However, the educational paradigm of the scientific method was developed to counter the causes of deaths of the early part of the century, such as pneumococcal pneumonia and infectious diarrhoea. From this point of view, the change in patterns of death without a change in the educational model led directly to physicians perceiving death as a medical failure. Like most jokes, the following statement, which appeared in 1975, reflected an uncomfortable element of truth in medical education: 'If only patients could leave their damaged physical vessels at the hospital for repair, while taking their social and emotional selves home' (Allshouse 1993: 21).

A change in education was heralded by a lively discussion about American attitudes and practices related to death at the end of the 1960s (Mor *et al.* 1988). The publication of *On Death and Dying* by Dr Elizabeth Kubler-Ross from the University of Chicago Medical School capped this period (Kubler-Ross 1969). A remarkable feature of her work was that she interviewed real patients facing death in teaching sessions with medical students, residents and other students in a manner similar to that used in teaching other medical subjects.

Clinical palliative care programmes followed. In 1974, Florence Wald, then Dean of the School of Nursing at Yale University in New Haven, Connecticut, led the founding of The Connecticut Hospice with advice from Dr Cicely Saunders (Wald *et al.* 1980). Dr William Lamers, a psychiatrist, who pioneered much of the early interactions between hospices and medical schools, was medical director of the second hospice programme, Hospice of Marin in California. Dr Balfour Mount, a urological surgeon, founded the palliative care service at the Royal Victoria Hospital of McGill University. Finally, in New York City, a consulting team began working throughout St Luke's Hospital, a teaching hospital, in 1974 (O'Neill *et al.* 1992).

Unfortunately, these early programmes did not lead to widespread development of clinical programmes in teaching hospitals. Rather, a grassroots hospice movement started in North America resulting in the founding of a large number of hospice programmes that primarily provide care as support teams in the patient's home, far away from health professional education (National Hospice Organisation 1997).

Driving forces for palliative care education

Education of medical students, nursing students, and other health professionals about end of life care, palliative care and hospice care in North America is poor. Efforts to improve this have been stimulated by efforts to improve end of life care (SUPPORT 1995; Emanuel *et al.* 1999). This need has stimulated private and public groups to determine the core competencies that physicians and others should possess in order to provide adequate palliative care for patients and their families. This evolution culminated in the determination by the Liaison Committee for Medical Education, the accrediting body for all 126 medical schools in the USA, that all accredited medical schools must include education in palliative care and end of life care (Accreditation and the Liaison Committee on Medical Education 2001). Similar standards were established for the 17 Canadian medical schools, but such a standard has not been established for the other health professions schools.

To assist in the development of education programs for medical students, the Medical School Objectives Project identified 'knowledge . . .of the major ethical dilemmas in medicine, particularly those that arise at the beginning and end of life . . .' and 'knowledge about relieving pain and ameliorating the suffering of patients' as outcomes that all medical students should have achieved by graduation (Medical School Objectives Writing Group 1999: 4, 5, 9).

Some medical schools have described curricula on death and dying. However, descriptions of instruction in end of life or palliative care indicate that the education is provided predominately through didactic courses in death and dying during the preclinical years.

Their effectiveness is likely to be limited by the absence of immediate clinical application of the material, and therefore, no opportunity to develop the necessary skills to alleviate the suffering of the patient and their loved ones (Billings and Block 1997).

Although most medical schools offer some formal teaching of this subject, there is considerable evidence that current training is inadequate, most strikingly in the clinical years.

> Curricular offerings are not well integrated; the major teaching format is the lecture; formal teaching is predominantly preclinical; clinical experiences are mostly elective; there is little attention to home care, hospice, and nursing home care; role models are few; and students are not encouraged to examine their personal reactions to these clinical experiences.
>
> Billings and Block (1997)

These conclusions are supported by a survey of senior medical students eliciting their perceptions of the adequacy of their education on end of life issues. The majority of students felt that they were unprepared to deal with issues regarding end of life care due to lack of curricular time devoted to death and dying topics as well as lack of standardisation of training and evaluation. Although respondents did report some experience with end of life care, it is notable that only 52% of students report being present during a patient's death in a do not resuscitate (DNR) situation and 26% of students have not followed a terminally ill patient for two weeks or more (Fraser *et al.* 2001).

Although several national organizations have presented curricular and position statements on the importance of education in end of life care, no clear standards or widely adopted curricula have yet emerged for either undergraduate or postgraduate training in palliative medicine in the United States, or for clinical practice in the hospital, nursing home, or hospice, with the exception of one facet of palliative care – pain management. In Canada effort is currently underway to develop a standardized curriculum for all medical schools through the Educating Future Physicians in Palliative and End-of-Life Care Project.

Postgraduate training of physicians is little better. A survey of oncologists reported their training to be poor and that the greatest source of information about palliative care was trial and error (American Society of Clinical Oncology 1998). A national study in internal medicine found that residents, faculty and programme directors rated their palliative care training as inadequate (Billings and Block 1997). Cancer pain education research has shown that residents lack basic pain assessment skills, knowledge of opioid pharmacology and skills of pharmacological management (Committee on Care at the End of Life 1997; Block and Sullivan 1998; Foley and Gelband 2001). Internal medicine residents have poor skills in conducting advance directive discussions and discussing resuscitation orders, crucial to appropriate end of life care planning (Tulsky *et al.* 1995, 1996, 1998). In the SUPPORT trial, neither interns nor their attending faculty were consistently accurate, nor were attending physicians more accurate than interns, in assessing patient treatment preferences (Wilson *et al.* 1997).

Approaches to palliative care education

Recent initiatives have begun to address palliative care education. These efforts include development and dissemination of new end of life educational recommendations, training materials and educational training requirements at both the medical school and residency levels. The American Board of Internal Medicine added the domain of end of life care to its residency training requirements. Family medicine has since recommended this area to its residency training programmes (Weissman and Block 2002). The American Society of Clinical Oncology developed and disseminated a curriculum in pain and symptom management (Smith *et al.* 2001). Mandates and initiatives such as these have highlighted the need for study of the most appropriate and effective ways to achieve the educational objectives within the existing constraints of training. Objectives for palliative care education have also promoted high expectations for developing educational methods, sites and faculty that will inspire trainees to examine and acquire the specialized knowledge and skills required for effective end of life care.

Efforts to incorporate palliative care education within existing residency programmes face daunting obstacles. Some barriers reflect challenges unique to palliative care, including physicians' attitudes about their own mortality, assessing and treating pain and acknowledging and communicating transition from curative to palliative care. The content of a palliative care curriculum responsive to these barriers needs to include evidence-based symptom assessment and management practices, cultural and spiritual context of medical interventions and the ethical principles and communication skills that relate to interactions between and among professionals, patients and their families. A major step forward to meet this need was the development and initial dissemination of the Education for Physicians on End-of-life Care by the American Medical Association (Emanuel *et al.* 1999) that has reached more than 90,000 practising physicians (von Gunten *et al.* 2001). This curriculum has been widely adapted to teach medical students, residents, nursing students, social workers, chaplains and the public. This is largely due to the modular construction, ease of adaptability and innovative teaching methods such as trigger videotapes, all of which are provided to the teacher by the project.

The companion national effort for nursing has been the End-of-life Nursing Education Consortium (ELNEC) Project also funded by the Robert Wood Johnson Foundation to develop educational tools for undergraduate nursing faculty (ELNEC 2000). The ELNEC curriculum has been adapted for nurses in practice as well as in special circumstances: oncology, paediatrics and advanced practice. However, as in medicine, a significant shortcoming is that nurses learn best when didactic material is paired with direct clinical encounters under the supervision of expert clinical preceptors.

The impact of palliative care education

Barriers

Reform of existing curricula to include palliative care confronts challenges that pervade professional education reform in general. While the changing needs that medical education is asked to address suggest that we should be able to draw on a rich history of what works in medical education reform, the written descriptions of the outcome of such efforts suggest that we most often reaffirm the difficulty of implementing and sustaining reform.

One way to identify a domain of practice for which competence is expected is to include that domain in formal assessment. Yet the majority of residency programmes report that written evaluations by the faculty are the only means by which palliative care competence is assessed (Weissman *et al.* 2002). Even in ethics, where many programmes provide required education, very few provide supervised clinical experiences. This limits the occasions in which palliative care skills can be systematically observed and assessed. Thus, considerable burden is placed on the teaching faculty to assess the constellation of requisite knowledge (for example, drug therapy for dyspnea), attitudes (for example, fear of addiction) and clinical skills (for example, discussing treatment goals), which shape how physicians provide palliative care. The premise that programmes can simply extend existing resources to take on this burden seems unwarranted, given that programmes often reported the absence of faculty skilled in palliative care and infrequent structured performance-based assessments.

Research in palliative care education of residents is needed. Some educational interventions in single institutions have demonstrated improved pain management knowledge and skills, communication skills and ethical decision-making (Wilson *et al.* 1997; von Gunten *et al.* 1999). However, no one has demonstrated an economical approach that can be used across multiple residency programmes and will affect measures of the multiple domains in which physician knowledge, competence and confidence is required. The time and effort required from each residency programme to develop new curricula is enormous. The development and testing of an economical education curriculum that can be reproduced in multiple residency programmes will accelerate the pace of residency education reform. This, in turn, will lead to better outcomes for patients with advanced cancer and their families.

Knowledge is insufficient for change

Sadly, much of palliative care education in North America hinges on the assumption that knowledge will change practice, yet we know that education alone does not change patient and family experience. Or, to be more precise, education targeted to improve knowledge and attitudes does not change behavior. For example, in an analysis of 33 studies of educational interventions for cancer pain control, attitudes and knowledge about cancer pain could be improved – unfortunately, there was minimal change in the patient's pain (Allard *et al.* 2001).

Although the conclusions are discouraging, they should not be surprising. We have learned the same things from education about tobacco, alcohol, sex, diet, hand washing, hypertension and advance directives. Attitudes and knowledge are necessary, but insufficient, to change behaviour (Ferris *et al.* 2001).

If it is our goal to change the patient and family experience, we need to adopt a more precise way of understanding education. Dixon described a cascade of steps of education evaluation that remains helpful (Dixon 1978). We have adapted this to assist our understanding of the components or steps of education (Figure 10.1). Knowledge and attitudes precede the learning of new skills but those skills must be translated into behaviour if desired outcomes are to be seen. When enough people are experiencing the desired outcomes, there will be social improvement.

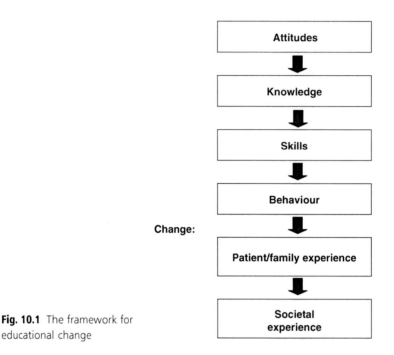

Fig. 10.1 The framework for educational change

If we use this framework to understand the necessary steps for cancer pain education, we would say that the attitude that 'it is important to control cancer pain', and the knowledge of how to control it, comes first. Then the skills of assessing pain, prescribing appropriate medications and teaching patients and families must be learned. To this end, the clinician must change his or her behaviour and implement the knowledge, attitudes and skills on a permanent basis to achieve the desired outcome. Patients must also change their attitudes, knowledge, skills and behaviour to control cancer pain. When these behaviours are exhibited by both clinicians and patients, the outcome will be improved reports of pain by patients. When all patients with cancer pain get good relief, we will have achieved a social good.

Fortunately, there is work afoot using this framework to achieve the desired ends. There are numerous projects to disseminate education about necessary attitudes and knowledge to health care professionals. The Role Model Project is a successful model for teaching pain management (Weissman and Dahl 1995). The Education for Physicians on End-of-life Care (EPEC) Project focuses on the attitudes and knowledge of physicians (Emanuel *et al.* 1999). The End-of-Life Nursing Education Consortium (ELNEC) is focusing on the attitudes and knowledge of nurses (ELNEC 2000). The Residency Education Project is focusing on the attitudes and knowledge of faculty in internal medicine, family medicine, neurology, and surgery training programs (Weissman *et al.* 2001).

There are several programmes working to change core delivery systems. The Center to Advance Palliative Care is working to influence hospital and health care systems. The new Joint Commission on Accreditation of Health Care Organizations pain guidelines will help to ensure that such measures are in place in accredited hospitals and health care systems.

Specialization

Although the specialty of palliative medicine has been formally recognized in Great Britain, Ireland and Australia for many years, it is still a developing specialty in North America (von Gunten 2002). Specialization can be seen both as a result of education and a driver of palliative care education, by creating practice standards and well-defined competencies within a specified domain of knowledge and/or practice.

The American College of Physicians and the American Board of Internal Medicine have both called for general physician competency in the care of persons with terminal illness (von Gunten *et al.* 2000; End-of-life care 2000).

Since 1996, significant strides toward meeting the requirements for formal recognition have been made (Ferris *et al.* 2002). The number of physicians seeking certification in the field is growing. The professional association is strong. Peer-reviewed research appears in seven specialized journals as well as in journals of broader interest. Formal training programmes are rapidly expanding. The devotion of an entire issue of *JAMA* solely to end of life care in 2000 signalled the interest of the wider medical community in this field (Billings 2000).

Formal fellowship programmes of at least one year in length are expanding rapidly. For the academic year 2000–2001, there were 17 active palliative medicine fellowship programmes of at least a year in length while by August 2005 (Billings *et al.* 2002), there were 55 fellowship programmes in operation or in formation, including six funded by the Veterans Administration (American Academy of Hospice and Palliative Medicine 2005).

The need for a specialty board was recognized early in the 1990s when a small working group of palliative medicine physicians was set up to plan a board that would establish and measure the level of knowledge, attitudes and skills required for certification of physicians practising hospice and palliative medicine. The American Board of Hospice and Palliative Medicine (ABHPM) swiftly established the criteria for entry into the field via an experiential track and gave its first examination in 1996 (American Academy of Hospice and Palliative Medicine 2005).

Eligibility for certification is now granted by the ABHPM via two tracks: experiential and fellowship. After ten years, over 1,700 physicians have met the qualifications. Eligibility via the experiential track requires candidates to meet criteria related to education, training, experience, competence and professional standing. The fellowship track is open to fellows who have completed a one-year fellowship in hospice and palliative medicine. The fellowship director of the training program must demonstrate that the fellowship substantially meets the voluntary standards for training in palliative medicine. As formal recognition of the specialty and its training programmes proceeds, the experiential eligibility track will be eliminated. Eventually, only fellows from accredited programmes will be allowed to enter certification through the fellowship track.

Candidates for the examination are required to have another American Board of Medical Specialties certification. Overall, 55 per cent reported internal medicine as their primary board while 23 per cent reported family practice, followed by anesthesiology, neurology, psychiatry, surgery and radiation oncology.

Conclusion

Palliative care education in North America still has a long way to go before it is a reliable part of the education of health professionals producing a reliable product. Nevertheless, the last 10 years have produced significant calls for reform, educational curricula and the creation of a new specialty. If other areas of health care are a guide, the creation of the specialty will provide a strong stimulus to health care education in all the disciplines.

Chapter 11

South America

Gustavo de Simone

Background

Palliative care requires attention to the wide range of symptoms affecting patients with progressive diseases, emotional and cultural issues that accompany advanced illness and the needs of family members, including bereavement. The priority placed on particular needs is likely to vary from one country to another, influenced by the disease pattern, demography and age structure, cultural aspects, national health policies, availability of analgesics and training and deployment of the workforce. Palliative care training needs to take account of such diversity and individual country needs and opportunities (Maddocks 2003). The content and teaching approaches used in the developed world cannot be assumed to be relevant to South American countries.

History and demography

Until the sixteenth century, different Indian populations lived in South America. Following the downfall of the Inca Empire, the continent was ruled by the Portuguese in the east (now Brazil) and the Spanish elsewhere. Almost 75 per cent of people have Spanish or Italian roots. Other immigrants came from Germany, France, England, Switzerland, Austria, East Europe and Japan, and more recently, Asia. Nowadays, the population in the region is a mixture of European and American Indian descendents. Spanish remains the predominant language in the region, but Portuguese is the official language for Brazil.

Geographically, South America is divided into three areas: the Andean area (Bolivia, Colombia, Ecuador, Peru and Venezuela), Southern Cone (Argentina, Chile, Paraguay and Uruguay) and Brazil. Almost half the continent's population lives in Brazil. Despite the improvement of the health situation in South America since the 1990s, there remain huge regional variations. The worst situation relates to communicable diseases associated with deficient living conditions, poverty and progressive environmental degradation. Social inequalities persist and globalization continues to be a mixed blessing. The ease of restrictions on trade and international financial transactions (Pan American Health Organization [PAHO] 2002) has made society more permeable to external forces of change, governments less in control of events and increased the dissemination of international health risks. In addition to the well established relationship between health and economy, health inequalities in the South Americas are further influenced by the degree of equity in the distribution of that income. Gains in life expectancy, infant and maternal mortality and survival, and per capita health expenditure have been systematically greater in those countries with more equitable income distribution. The healthier societies in South America are not necessarily those that are wealthier, but those most equitable in their distribution of income.

By the beginning of the twenty-first century, mortality rates had declined in virtually every country. Two contrasting mortality patterns currently coexist: one typical of poor societal living conditions (infectious and parasitic) and the other of more developed societies (chronic and degenerative), combined with high mortality from accidents and violence. This polarization serves to emphasize the persistence of significant health gaps between different social groups and geographical areas within countries. The risk of illness and premature death correlates with inequities in the distribution of resources. These regional and national inequalities in health are replicated with greater intensity at the subnational and local levels (PAHO 2002). The HIV/AIDS epidemic continues to spread in the Americas, particularly among women, the poor and those living in rural areas where access to health services and information is limited.

On the other hand, with life expectancy increasing in parts of the region, cardiovascular and malignant diseases have become manifest. Today, more than two-thirds of all reported deaths are due to chronic diseases and external causes. The rise in the incidence of neoplasms is also significant (PAHO 2002). The incidence of cervical cancer in South American cities is among the highest worldwide, probably due to a high frequency of risk factors and/or a low screening coverage for cervical cancer (Eluf-Neto and Nascimento 2001).

The health care system in some South American countries is complex. For example, the Argentinean health service is made up of three sectors: public health service, health plans and a medical health system. The annual public health service expenditure represents 54 per cent of the total expenditure. These services are free or involve minimum payment and exist under federal, provincial or municipal jurisdiction. In contrast, approximately 300 health plans are managed by trade unions, financially dependent on employers' and employees' dues. The medical health systems comprise some 200 institutions and paid membership is voluntary. Nearly 60 per cent of the population in this country has some type of health insurance through health plans or the medical health system (PAHO 1998). Argentina has more physician specialists than general practitioners, and more doctors than nurses, with just one registered nurse for every three doctors. Problems in the health care system may be attributed to: fragmentation of the system; unsuitable treatment prioritization; inequalities in health care provision; outsourcing of management responsibilities; an inadequate legal framework; inadequate policies for the provision of drugs; limited public health care promotion and disease prevention policies; lack of universal health care insurance coverage and inadequate quality control policies (Scopinaro and Casak 2002). Most of these problems can also be seen in other South American countries.

Cultural and social perspectives

South America is a region with a strong Latin culture that influences several aspects of palliative care. Paternalism is strong. Doctors and nurses do not receive communication skills training. Relatives frequently block patients receiving information about cancer diagnosis and prognosis, and doctors join this conspiracy of silence. Studies in Argentina suggest that early palliative care consultation, interfacing curative and palliative approaches, facilitates disclosure of diagnosis and prognosis, and that counselling enables patients to adjust their expectations (De Simone *et al.* 1990; Bertolino *et al.* 1996; Eisenchlas and De Simone 2002).

Most people in the mountain range, in keeping with their Inca inheritance, are stoic in the face of painful experiences. In villages far from large cities folk medicine and quackery exert a strong influence, and these beliefs and practices hinder some dying persons from accepting medical treatments such as pain and symptom control (Junin 2001). The majority of patients now die in hospitals, for a variety of social, economic and medical reasons (Junin 2001).

Driving forces in palliative care education

Prior to the mid 1980s, both public and private programmes in health care aimed to reduce mortality rates but did not include palliative care and pain relief. The development of palliative care has been driven primarily by the motivation of local practitioners, influenced and supported by the British hospice movement, the World Health Organization Collaborating Centres in Oxford, New York and Wisconsin and leading centres in Edmonton, Texas, Catalonia, Las Palmas and Milan.

The diversity of health care resources in different regions necessitates different ways of providing palliative care. Most teams have more doctors than nurses and psychosocial professionals. Most teams consist of part time paid or voluntary palliative care professionals (Cullen and Vera 2001; Junin 2001). Many teams teach at their institutions and beyond. In June 2005, a new programme of postgraduate multiprofessional and interdisciplinary residence training began in Buenos Aires, sponsored by the local government and coordinated by teams from the Femeba-Tornu Programme and Hospital Udaondo-Pallium. National associations exist in some countries. The Latin American Association assumes a leading role for the region (Colleau 2002).

The most important factor driving the demand for palliative care training is the existence of a large and rapidly expanding population of patients dying with unrelieved suffering. The World Health Organization has challenged training institutions to ensure that palliative care is compulsory in courses, leading to a basic professional qualification, and that it is assessed and recognized by universities and professional bodies as an appropriate subject for postgraduate training programmes (World Health Organization 1990).

Approaches to, and impact of, palliative care education

The content of palliative care education in South America has focused primarily on the relief of suffering and improving quality of life in uncurable conditions. It includes a call for a change in the organization of health systems, development of primary care, investment of resources in response to the needs of society and equitable use of these resources. A new reflexive literature on the role of medicine within society is emerging from Canada: trainees should be prepared for different roles, including scientific expert, communicator, collaborator, manager, health advocate and professional (Societal Working Needs Group 1996). This literature calls for social contracts with the communities we serve and espouses a philosophy attuned to palliative care.

In teaching palliative care there is a need to address attitudes, knowledge and skills. From the above review of the challenges which palliative care faces throughout South America, it is apparent that attitude change is key to further development of the discipline. Educationalists in Latin America have stressed the importance of implementing educational programmes which transform various domains, for example social and economic matters, health care and industry production.

Educational theory is widely used in health education for professionals and the public. There are three main pedagogical trends in South America: traditional, conditioning-based and empowerment (Pereira 2003):

1. *Traditional pedagogy* is based on ideas and knowledge being the most relevant aspects of education. Students are receptors of knowledge and teachers are the transmitters. This approach has been predominant in South America.

2. *Conditioning-based pedagogy* focuses on the behavioural outcome of the educational process, with students responding to teacher expectations. Many medical programmes are based upon this philosophy, which is more useful in training for technical skills than the problem-solving required in end of life care.

3. *Empowerment (problematization) pedagogy* regards students as key agents who identify real problems and develop creative solutions. The importance of knowledge and behaviour is acknowledged but the main skill required is the ability to formulate relevant questions in order to understand problems. The ability to understand what is happening, identify resources and hurdles and implement actions at individual, organizational and social levels to solve the defined problems are paramount. This pedagogy was developed by the Brazilian Paulo Freire (1921–1997) who is considered one of the most influential educationalists in the late twentieth century. He was concerned with developing dialogue that is respectful, action that is informed and value based, consciousness that has the power to transform reality and educational activity that should be situated in the lived experience of participants (Taylor 1993).

An increasing number of health professionals involved in educational programmes in South America and other underdeveloped regions of the world contend that the empowerment pedagogy can produce better results than the others by liberating and allowing students active participation in the learning process, fostering continuous development of human skills amongst health workers and those who use the service (Nutbeam 2000; Kickbush 2001; Sonobe *et al.* 2001; Pereira 2003). A Latin American programme of teaching the teachers has now been implemented, led by a non-governmental organization, Pallium Latinoamerica. This was adapted from similar workshops developed by Dutch educational psychologists (Smeding and Oderkerk 1997).

Early initiatives in palliative care in South America depended largely on charitable initiatives. The pioneers in the region established small models of care to form the focus for educational initiatives so that palliative care practice could then disseminate widely. Education was part of the original programmes in Argentina, Brazil, Uruguay and other countries, simultaneously promoting changes in government policies and opioid availability. With widely different backgrounds, those pioneers provided a good understanding of meeting the needs and the magnitude of the task of delivering the service. It was also a challenge in terms of understanding each other as doctors from different specialties, psychologists, nurses, social workers, ethicists, and ministers of different faiths all had to learn to work together (De Simone 2002).

Although there was no systematic palliative care education in medical or nursing schools for many years, a fundamental change is now occurring (Cullen and Vera 2001; Junin 2001). A variety of training programmes have been implemented, including university and non-university courses, single discipline and interdisciplinary courses, distance learning education systems and programmes with a marked emphasis on clinical activities, for example the two-year residence in Buenos Aires. An increasing number of medical schools in Buenos Aires, Montevideo, Rosario, Santiago, São Paulo and other capital districts now include palliative care in their curricula. Apart from Buenos Aires, systematic palliative care undergraduate education remains absent from most South American nursing schools but the need to incorporate palliative care subjects in their university training curricula has been recognized (Junin 2001).

At the postgraduate level, palliative care education programmes are provided by the major centres including Pallium Latinoamerica, the Tournu-Femeba Programme, the education department of Buenos Aires city and Rosario city governments in Argentina, the national chapters of the International Association for the Study of Pain in Peru, the national cancer programmes in Chile and Brazil and many charitable Christian organizations in the region.

Liaison with established overseas services is still essential, with visiting experts who can lecture appropriately, provide clinical demonstration and encourage learning opportunities. Meeting such visitors and hearing their messages provides continuing inspiration and enhances the vision, charisma and commitment of local pioneers. However, the best learning happens when students identify difficulties and devise good responses to such problems, recognizing and working within local gaps and difficulties while exploring ways through them (Maddocks 2003).

Palliative care education in South America embraces a range of educational opportunities, including half day demonstration programmes, short attachments to clinical units, workshops over several days, certificate courses accrediting basic competence, fellowships allowing longer attachments and academic award courses suitable for preparation for specialist roles. Distance study packages in the Spanish language are available and there are education opportunities for health service administrators, supported by the World Health Organization and PAHO. Some initiatives target the public through open days, simple brochures and volunteer training. Courses for volunteers and lay people are run at public hospitals, with advanced development stage teams in Buenos Aires (De Simone 2003; D'Urbano and Salguiero 2003). The educational needs of religious ministers are met by some of the programmes mentioned above or by specific Catholic congregations, for example the Camilians in Argentina, Colombia, Ecuador, Paraguay and Peru.

Palliative care education is progressively included in the curricula of other specialties such as medical oncology and geratology. The first School and Superior Career of Medical Oncology in the region, belonging to the Universidad del Salvador in Buenos Aires, changed its curriculum in 2001 to include palliative care as a core subject for oncologists in training. This leads to a special award from the Universities' Commission for Accreditation, facilitating career paths in palliative care (De Simone 2003).

Systematic education is also provided to nurses in the public hospitals of Buenos Aires, following a survey which demonstrated the need for training in communication skills, dealing with emotions, pain and symptom relief, and family matters (Junin 2001).

Interaction at the global level

Pallium Latinoamerica began as a non-profit-making organization of individuals and centres of palliative care in the Buenos Aires and La Plata, Argentina. Pallium works toward high quality palliative care provision and education in Latin America. The original centres in 1990 were Bonorino Udaondo Gastroenterology Hospital in Buenos Aires and the Jose Maria Mainetti Foundation – Comprehensive Cancer Centre in La Plata. In 1995 other centres joined in: palliative care teams from Angel Roffo Cancer Institute, Buenos Aires University, the Psycho-Oncology Section of Hematology Research Institute from National Academy of Medicine in Buenos Aires, Hospital de Clinicas in Montevideo and the Erasmo Gaertner Cancer Hospital in Curitiba, Brazil.

Pallium developed the first library on palliative care in the region, with most of the international journals and key books on palliative care and related topics. This library serves as an information service for the community. In order to consolidate a regional task force of clinical teachers in palliative care, members of Pallium were sent on training courses, focusing both on scientific aspects and educator development. These included diploma and masters programmes at the University of Wales and training for teachers workshops through the Stichting Pallium Foundation in the Netherlands. More than 50 clinical teachers in Argentina, Brazil, Colombia, Peru, Paraguay and Uruguay attended international seminars on training for teachers, developed in Cuzco (Peru) and Patagonia (Argentina) under the international direction of educationalist Dr Smeding.

The Pallium Latinoamerica organizes a variety of educational activities, aimed at different audiences (Figure 11.1).

Since 1993, one of the major annual training activities has been the student-centred, problem-based Diploma Course on Palliative Care, certified by Universidad del Salvador, Buenos Aires, with the academic support of the Oxford International Centre for Palliative Care. This is a one-year multiprofessional, interdisciplinary distance learning postgraduate course with residential modules. The teaching team is multiprofessional, consisting of medical, nursing, psychology and social work professionals, all clinically active and trained in education, working with the support of local and international experts in education. Educational materials include specially written articles on each topic, audio cassettes with local and international experts on clinical, ethical and health policy matters and videotapes of communication scenarios. There are two cycles: an introductory level, from June to August, and the advanced level, from August to the following May (see Box 11.1).

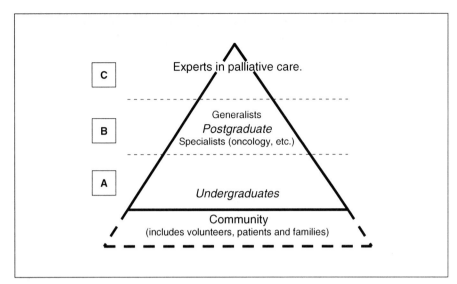

Fig. 11.1 Pallium Latinoamerica's education activities: levels of teaching

Box 11.1 Pallium Latinoamerica: the Diploma course on Palliative Care

Introductory Course

- Two three-day weekends in Buenos Aires or the city where the course is based, at the start and end of the course.
- Content designed to fill the gap created by the lack of palliative care education in most professionals' undergraduate curricula.
- Students introduced to the methodology of problematization and active multiprofessional discussion.

Advanced Course

- Consists of nine modules: three weeks each, with two to four main topics per week
- Three long weekends in the city where the course is based
- Content of written material specific to students' professional background
- Objectives for each topic are formulated at four levels:
    - (i) operational
    - (ii) specific
    - (iii) circumstances
    - (iv) minimum.

Box 11.1 *(continued)* Pallium Latinoamerica: the Diploma course on Palliative Care

This helps students to identify the most crucial competencies to be achieved and facilitates evaluation of the learning process.

- Learning methods: regular written assignments, case studies, portfolios and audits on patients within students' own practice
- Group work within residential weekends based on problematization, promoting active discussion among students
- Role-playing exercises are highly valued by most students as a useful way of learning and feedback focused on technical aspects as well as emotions and feelings
- The teacher's role is focused both on knowledge transmission and skills training, as well as helping students to put learning in their own clinical context and to identify students' own emotional reactions towards different parts of the programme. Ethical argumentation in the decision-making process, emotional involvement and highly interactive work are relevant parts of the learning experience (Smeding and Oderkerk, 1997).

Assessment

- In-course assessments: 24 weekly written assignments, for example case studies, clinical vignettes and designing brochures, as well as two portfolios and role-playing exercises.
- Final written and oral examinations and role playing in a consulting room undertaken by students who had completed at least 80 per cent of their coursework.

Evaluation

- Carried out at the end of each residential module and overall course
- Students evaluate the contents and methodology of the course and the personal and professional benefits they consider they have received. The atmosphere facilitates highly valued comments and critique, in terms of benefits, satisfaction and suggestions for improvement.

The first course started in 1993. By May 2005, more than 350 professionals had completed the advanced level course. Students came from Argentina, Brazil, Chile, Colombia, Costa Rica, Ecuador, Paraguay, Uruguay and Venezuela. More than 700 students completed the introductory course held in Buenos Aires, La Plata, Bahia Blanca, Cordoba and Jujuy, in Argentina, and in Curitiba and Londrina, Brazil.

A survey conducted in 2000 demonstrated that morphine prescription by doctors had increased fivefold and involvement in education and research work in palliative care increased threefold among those who had completed the course, compared to their practice prior to the course. Ninety per cent of the course attendees reported increased satisfaction and improved quality in their practices as a result of the course (Garrigue *et al.* 2001). More than 70 per cent of the students are working in palliative care teams at public or private hospitals and some of them are involved in building programmes at their local level.

Conclusion

There are enormous needs and many opportunities for palliative care education in South America. The priority given to the care of those with advanced and terminal diseases is low because of competing needs. Most ambitious medical graduates are attracted to curative procedures while nurses often lack the status to advocate for their patients with effect. It is not easy to identify outcomes for these education initiatives, as most of them lack proper audit measures. There is insufficient collaboration and coordination among different programmes. Despite these limitations, it is highly probable that most of the positive changes observed at clinical practice and policies have their origins in the educational effort of a few health workers who deserve strong encouragement and much practical support.

Chapter 12

Implications for global education

Katy Newell-Jones

Palliative care education (PCE) has developed a wealth of approaches at the local, national and regional levels to meet different needs. Previous chapters have identified key challenges and tensions relevant to different continents. This chapter begins with an introduction to the current debate in education around the purpose and nature of learning from a global perspective. This is followed by exploring PCE under four headings:

1. embracing diversity

2. identity and sustainability

3. power and authority

4. patterns of learning.

The chapter concludes with recommendations arising from the discussion.

Exploring palliative care education through a global education lens

There are a number of initiatives currently under way exploring standards for palliative care at global and regional levels. The focus of this chapter is not to discuss standards but to explore some of the factors influencing the approaches to learning within which palliative care education activities take place, and standards are met. This debate is reflected, in part, in the current discussion between the concepts of palliative medicine or nursing as a specialty and palliative care as an approach. Since 2002, the World Health Organization has defined palliative care as an approach, whereas the strength of feeling in both Europe and North America favours viewing palliative care as a specialty (World Health Organization 2002).

Sterling's (2001) four functions or roles of education, together with the definitions of the purposes of education from Francis (1993), Currie *et al.* (2003) and Newell-Jones (2003) will be used to provide a framework within which to explore some of the key challenges and issues in palliative care education.

Sterling (2001: 25) in *Sustainable Education: Revisioning Learning and Change*, identifies four functions of education (see Table 12.1). Where the primary function of education is on the development of the individual, this might be vocational, focusing on training people for employment, or more liberal in nature, developing individual potential. Where the primary function is on society, this might be to encourage citizenship and extending aspects of society already established, or to challenge and change attitudes, towards a better society. Sterling stresses that these functions are not mutually exclusive but represent

Table 12.1 Functions or roles of education

	Focus on the individual	**Focus on society**
Product-led	Vocational	Socialization
Operating within, or adapting existing structures	Primary function – to train people for employment	Primary function – to replicate aspects of society and culture and promote citizenship
Process-led	Liberal	Transformative
Challenging existing structures and/or establishing new frameworks	Primary function – to develop the individual and his/her potential	Primary function – to encourage change towards a fairer society… and a better world

Adapted from Sterling (2001: 25).

different elements which are frequently in tension with each other. Exploring the balance of these functions in different continents might shed light on the tensions within the debate of the concept of palliative care. Where palliative care represents a radical change to existing societal norms and is reliant on a community-based workforce, greater emphasis might be placed on the transformative function. However, where palliative care is located less in communities and more in institutions the function might be more vocational in nature.

The vocational function to PCE, which has a tendency to favour the view of palliative care as a specialty as opposed to an approach, appears most deeply embedded in North America, and perhaps parts of Europe. In this book Ferris and von Gunten discuss how in North America there is a greater emphasis on the vocational than the other three functions of PCE (Chapter 10). PCE is highly academicized with a primary focus on palliative medicine and training for employment. There is an additional goal of the establishment of palliative care as a specialty, which might be seen as having a higher professional status and be regarded by some as an essential prerequisite for 'security' within academic institutions, and hence enhanced funding. They also emphasize the need for increased awareness of and extended accessibility to palliative care, both of which are more societal in nature and might need a more transformative approach.

The predominantly vocational model might be most appropriate in more economically developed countries. However, Becker (2004: 192–3) reminds us that 'it is important to remember that the well-developed, university validated, academic, formal model of education based on western ethical values does not hold the moral high ground'.

A stark contrast is seen in approach between Ferris and von Gunten's discussion of PCE in North America and that of de Simone (Chapter 11) in South America. De Simone takes a transformative approach to PCE, recognizing the need to respect and sometimes challenge social norms, such as the paternalistic attitudes which frequently reduce the flow of information and inhibit patient involvement in decision-making around their treatment options, or issues such as living wills. The traditional role of family members as caregivers, combined with the reliance on a voluntary community-based workforce, places a greater emphasis on the need for palliative care education to be embedded in an approach to caring for the dying. However, alongside this, there are those who are being trained in the specialty of palliative care. De Simone recognizes a tension in South America, where the approach to teaching and learning tends to be transmissive, which does not fit comfortably alongside a transformative model of education which he advocates.

The strength of Sterling's four functions is the recognition that no single function is correct or most appropriate, but that there is usually a balance of functions. By making the functions more explicit, advantages and disadvantages can be explored and choices can be made.

Francis describes the internationalization of higher education in British Columbia as

> a process that prepares ... for successful participation in an increasingly interdependent world... fostering global understanding and developing skills for effective living and working in a diverse world.
>
> Francis (1993: 4)

By stressing the increasing interdependence in the world and the value of enhanced global understanding, Francis is explicitly valuing curricula which are global in their outlook. Within this definition the concept of learning being multidirectional is implied, which would favour more collaborative and participative, as opposed to transmissive, approaches to learning.

Since the destruction of the Twin Towers in New York on 11 September 2001 definitions of the purpose of education tend to be more explicit about creating a climate for a more peaceful and tolerant world. Currie *et al.* (2003) recognize the value of

> a positive exchange of ideas and people contributing to a more tolerant world. Ideally, internationalisation should lead to a world where neither one culture nor economic system dominates, but rather where a plurality of cultures and ethnic diversity are recognised and valued.
>
> (2003: 10)

This definition focuses more on the social role of education and training than the development or transfer of knowledge or the acquisition of skills. This is further reflected by Newell-Jones (2003: 5) who sees the role of the educator to encourage learners to:

> be actively asking questions about global issues and looking at traditional information and materials from a new perspective, which takes into account... social justice, sustainable development and interconnectedness.
>
> Newell-Jones (2003: 5)

Within PCE, the plurality of cultures and ethnic diversity is readily recognized. The greater challenge posed by Currie *et al.* (2003), that of neither one culture nor economic system dominating, is far more difficult to achieve where less economically developed countries continue to be dependent on international funding. However, the acceptance of this as an intention might lead to ensuring decision-making bodies within PCE increasingly questioning the composition of consultation bodies, possibly the location of international gatherings and the decision-making processes adopted.

It is easy to agree wholeheartedly with the definitions posed above and not see the radical perspective behind them or engage with the challenge of incorporating such perspectives into practical approaches to education and training programmes. Higher education institutions, particularly in North America, Europe, Australia and New Zealand operate increasingly in a financially accountable, market-driven climate (Currie *et al.* 2003). Currie *et al.* (2003: 10) cite Van der Wende (2001) who states that 'Anglo-Saxon countries have chosen an explicit (and sometimes even aggressive) *competitive* approach to internationalization of Higher Education.

The discussion so far highlights some of the challenges facing palliative care education, and other fields, in developing a global approach to education and training. Balancing market-driven, vocationally focused goals with valuing diversity, social justice and interdependence is an immensely challenging task.

Embracing diversity

Currie *et al.*'s (2003) focus on diversity is echoed in each of the chapters on palliative care education in other continents. De Simone, writing about South America (Chapter 11), highlights the way in which the considerable inequalities in the distribution of wealth and income between countries and between communities are mirrored as inequalities in health and availability of health services. Filbet and Larkin (Chapter 8) emphasize the significant differences between income, wealth and health between different European countries. The marked differences between health and education in urban and rural communities are recognized in India by Kumar (Chapter 9). Goh and Shaw (Chapter 6) highlight the diversity in language, religion, economic development and ethnicity across the Asia-Pacific region and the considerable differences in palliative care services available across the region. One size will not fit all at the national, regional or global level. Clearly in the face of such diversity, there is a need for a variety of different approaches and models for PCE which do not just accommodate diverse needs but actively draw on the diversity as a resource and strength. One of the major challenges facing PCE is how to develop globally applicable core principles and concepts for PCE while recognizing the need to adopt approaches which meet diverse needs and contexts. One of the keys is to accept that diversity is present at all levels. Even within a single group of learners there will be a wealth of opinions and views, which can be an obstacle to achieving consensus, or a valuable learning resource to explore.

Identity and sustainability

Although palliative care has been formally recognized for a considerable period of time, for example over a century in New Zealand (Spruyt *et al.*, Chapter 7) and more than 30 years in Africa (Gwyther, Chapter 5), the global impression of PCE is of an area of practice striving to establish a secure identity and sustainable future, alongside more traditional areas of nursing and medicine. The struggle to clarify the values and priorities of PCE and to ensure it is embedded in core education and training programmes is manifested in different ways, sometimes with agreement across continents and sometimes with intense polarization of perspectives. The change in definition of palliative care by the

World Health Organization from a specialty to an approach (World Health Organization 2002) reflects this tension in identity at a global level.

Efforts are evident in all continents to replace the historical reliance of palliative care on charitable donations and a volunteer workforce with more reliable, consistent and sustainable sources of funding, professionalization of the workforce and the positioning of PCE within the core compulsory curriculum for education and training for health and social care professionals.

Equally universal is the recognition of the need to strengthen the position of PCE and to extend its accessibility. The challenge of ensuring widespread recognition is evident, for example, in India, where currently only two to three per cent of the population are estimated to have access to palliative care (Kumar, Chapter 9) and in Africa, where Gwyther (Chapter 5) describes palliative care nursing and medicine as having low status and limited resources, which results in palliative care frequently not being seen as a viable career option. The need to strengthen the position of PCE is also evident in New Zealand, where although PCE is well established, sustainability is not guaranteed. Spruyt *et al.* (Chapter 7) report that PCE remains strongly dependent on champions and promoters, leaving its future dependent on the continued emergence of such individuals. In North America and Europe the debate around identity centres around the perception of palliative care as a specialty, which would enable it to be accommodated more readily into existing formal accreditation frameworks and career pathways, alongside other more established professions within health and social care (Chapters 11 and 8). This debate has the combined intentions of extending the accessibility of palliative care and hence improving patient care, but also increasing the security of PCE within high-status institutions and establishing it as a core element of medical and nursing curricula.

Less economically developed countries face the additional challenge of throwing off the mantle of being perceived primarily as beneficiaries and actively adapting the PCE curriculum to suit the local context. The challenge of adapting both curriculum content and approaches to learning and teaching to local contexts is rooted in the historical origins of formal PCE in the UK and other more economically developed countries. This is compounded by less economically developed countries remaining, in part at least, dependent on international funding. The need for locally adapted programmes is highlighted by Kumar (Chapter 9) who explores the current tension in India between existing PCE models and emergent approaches which are more in tune with local cultures. In Chapter 11 De Simone argues strongly that in South America Western approaches are not applicable in either content or approach. Goh and Shaw (Chapter 6) report on the dangers in Asia-Pacific countries of Western-trained staff being less able to integrate into traditional communities and consequently challenging traditional roles and leading to tensions at the family and community levels.

Power and authority

Historically, the power and authority in palliative care lay primarily within those countries whose provision was more strongly developed and resourced. Less economically developed countries were dependent on more economically developed countries for financial support, curriculum development, palliative care literature and medical and nursing expertise. These patterns of authority are changing, albeit slowly, in a number of ways. Perhaps the most important change is the increased involvement of PCE academics and practitioners in South America, Asia-Pacific and Africa in developing PCE appropriate to their context. The support provided from more economically developed countries in establishing PCE in Asia-Pacific, India, South America and Africa is widely recognized. However, each also identifies the tensions arising from cultural inappropriateness, for example recognizing the roles of family members as carers. One of the factors driving the changes is the need to establish more community- and home-based care which is more suitable for rural and remote areas. The Asia-Pacific region is actively seeking alternative models of PCE from within its region, for example from developments in Kerala, South India (Chapter 6). The African Palliative Care Association is adapting materials to suit local contexts (Chapter 5) and in South America the non-governmental organization Pallium Latinoamerica is establishing a Latin-American resource centre and coordinating much of the PCE initiatives across the region. Interestingly, Europe is also recognizing the need to adapt its PCE curriculum to suit the East European context, thereby refocusing its attentions.

Authority is also embedded in the written word, both in terms of the availability and access to the literature and the international status of those who are published or present at international events. The palliative care literature tends to be predominantly from Europe, Australia, New Zealand and North America. There is a growing number of publications from less economically developed countries, for example De Simone (Chapter 11) reports that there are some South American publications, though still relatively few. Goh and Shaw (Chapter 6) report that in the Asia-Pacific region, excluding Australia and New Zealand, textbooks are few in number and tend to be in English or translated and the availability of journals is very limited. The community-based developments in Kerala are an exception and have been published and have attracted attention across the Asia-Pacific region but they do not currently appear to be used as a resource outside the region. Initiatives like that of Pallium Latinoamerica, who have developed the first library on palliative care in the South American region, should be supported in order to develop access to, and interest in, the literature in the region.

The adaptation of a key palliative care text from the United States to the African context is certainly a step in the right direction (Chapter 5). Hopefully, in the future, PCE practitioners and academics from Africa, South America and Asia-Pacific (excluding Australia and New Zealand) will be commissioned to write key texts from their own perspective which can then contribute to the enhanced global understanding.

Patterns of learning

Changes appear to be emerging in the patterns of learning among palliative care academics and practitioners. When discussing who is learning from whom, two kinds of responses are evident: *learning from,* where there is a clear hierarchy of expertise in the learning relationship, and *collaborative learning* based on sharing experiences and an acceptance of interdependence; the assumption of all involved that engaging in the process will extend their knowledge and understanding. The focus on interdependence by Currie *et al.* (2003), Francis (1993) and Newell-Jones (2003) would suggest that collaborative learning should form the basis of international communication and learning.

The overall picture remains one of palliative care academics and practitioners from Europe, North America, Australia and New Zealand tending to engage in collaborative learning primarily with each other. In Europe and North America the sharing of expertise with Africa, Asia-Pacific and South America is perceived as more unidirectional. However, Spruyt *et al.* (Chapter 7) report that practitioners and academics from Australia and New Zealand are engaging in collaborative learning with others across the Asia-Pacific region. Palliative care educators in less economically developed countries are also engaging in collaborative learning within their regions, but primarily learning *from* academics and practitioners in Europe, North America, Australia and New Zealand, either through courses offered by institutions in more developed countries or visiting experts from those countries. Regional and international bodies could play strong roles in encouraging more collaborative learning approaches to seminars, symposia and conferences.

The level of debate about methods of teaching and learning in palliative care is limited, although there appears to be a general recognition that participatory methods are valuable where used. Goh and Shaw (Chapter 6) explain that the methods of teaching in the Asia-Pacific region tend to be more transmissive in less economically developed countries and more participatory and discursive in more economically developed countries. This pattern appears to be reflected broadly on a global level.

Changing patterns of teaching usually require a period of exploring different teaching methods, discussing them and experimenting with new methods. In more economically developed countries courses or workshops on approaches to teaching are available to provide this level of support. Less economically developed countries usually struggle to acquire technical textbooks, so books on teaching and learning are even less likely to be readily available. Also, in less economically developed countries teaching methods tend to be more transmissive in schools. Those engaging in palliative care education are less likely to have access to workshops on approaches to teaching, hence there is a tendency to replicate their own experiences of teaching based on their formal school experiences. However, community-based learning is often more participatory and Freirean in approach than more formal learning, as is the case in South America (Chapter 11). Palliative care education might be able to draw on this expertise in introducing more participatory approaches to learning.

The current increase in the use of information technology in education programmes poses both opportunities and challenges. In Chapter 6 Goh and Shaw report an increase in demand for distance learning courses, where practitioners can remain in their home countries, continuing with their jobs while also enhancing their skills and knowledge.

Such initiatives could significantly extend the access to courses in palliative care. The challenges are to ensure that:

- the curriculum is genuinely developed to suit the local context, which will require involvement of local educational expertise as well as local palliative care expertise
- appropriate support is provided for participants to learn about distance learning and how to engage fully in the process
- the model of learning is interactive and collaborative, not transmissive.

Recommendations

Identity

1. Academics and practitioners in PCE should engage in the current educational debate around internationalization and the global dimension to learning (Currie *et al.* 2003, Francis 1993, Newell-Jones 2003). PCE would bring to this debate a field of practice which involves all levels of society and where awareness of local culture and practices is vitally important. Engaging in the debate might lead to an overarching framework of the intentions of PCE within which different countries and regions can define their specific focus and standards.

2. Establish a core set of values which reflect the global dimension of palliative care education and encourage these to be embedded into the curricula of all palliative care education.

Authority and decision-making

1. Revisit international committee structures and decision-making processes in the light of the concepts of interconnectedness, collaborative learning and valuing diversity.

2. Actively encourage and promote publications from less economically developed countries in addition to those from Australia, Europe and North America.

3. Ensure the voices of local people and minority groups are actively involved in curriculum development and review.

Approaches to learning and teaching

1. Recognize that skills in learning and teaching are essential skills for palliative care practitioners.

2. Provide more opportunities to engage in workshops, seminars and courses on approaches to learning and teaching appropriate to palliative care education as components of conferences.

3. Actively encourage and enable collaborative learning to take place at international conferences and events, for example including more round table discussions, networking sessions and panel presentations.

4. Actively encourage the development and dissemination of more participatory learning materials for example using experiential learning or problem-based learning.

5. Encourage the development of interactive distance learning programmes, with local engagement of expertise in palliative care and education.

6. Encourage local partnerships with community development programmes or other organizations experienced in participatory approaches to learning.

7. Explore learning from international students as a means of enhancing global understanding and valuing the experiences which they bring. For example, more economically developed countries report that most students do not encounter death as a normal life event as they do not nurse their relatives. Overseas students can bring a different perspective to the discussion, when facilitated sensitively.

8. Encourage publications on approaches to learning and teaching.

9. Explore ways of sharing case study materials on learning and teaching via the internet.

Part II

Learning, Teaching and Assessment

Chapter 13

Bedside teaching

Bee Wee

Introduction

At the end of the nineteenth century, William Osler, a famous Canadian physician and teacher, declared 'there should be no teaching without the patient for a text, and the best teaching is often that taught by the patient himself' (Bliss 1999: 238). He could be describing modern bedside teaching and all its variations that we employ today. Whichever model is used, bedside teaching is quintessentially patient-centred. In this chapter, I shall:

- describe how bedside teaching can affect patients, learners and teachers
- introduce selected models of bedside teaching, and
- discuss how these models might be used in teaching palliative care.

Although bedside teaching is a term that is commonly associated with medical education, it is equally important to students in health and social care, where it often takes place under different names, e.g. work-based learning. However it is described, bedside learning is particularly valid in palliative care, where the patient's tale is fundamental to everything we do. Calman describes how stories provide a framework for life by helping us to 'make sense of the world around us' (2000: 10). Who better to tell this story than the patients themselves? Where better to hear these stories than at the bedside or at home? In this chapter, the term 'bedside teaching' will encompass clinical teaching which takes place at the patient's side, usually integrated within or alongside the normal process of care.

Different perspectives

Teaching usually involves two parties: teachers and learners. In the health care context, it involves one more – the patient. Sometimes there is a fourth group: relatives or lay carers. Each group has a vested interest in the educational process and its outcome. If patients and their carers are to be active partners in education, rather than merely 'subjects' upon whom the teaching is carried out, their stories and insights must be considered fairly and equitably when planning bedside teaching. The ways in which each party is reported to benefit when patients participate in teaching have been reviewed by Wukurz and Kelly (2002) (see Table 13.1).

Table 13.1 Benefits of patient involvement

Parties	Perceived benefits of patient involvement as teacher
Students	Access to patient's personal knowledge and experience of condition Deeper understanding Received constructive feedback Anxiety reduced Confidence increased Attitudes and behaviour influenced Improved acquisition of skills Increased respect for patients Learned in context
Patients	Used their disease or condition positively Used their knowledge and experience Expertise acknowledged Empowered Had opportunity to help future patients Increased own knowledge and new insights Improved understanding of doctors and other professionals
Teachers	Additional teaching resource available Improved quality of teaching Alternative teaching opportunities Developed mutual understanding New advocates Provided value for money

Adapted from Wykurz G and Kelly D (2002). Developing the role of patients as teachers: literature review. *BMJ* 325, 818–21, reproduced with permission from BMJ Publishing Group.

Teachers

Ahmed (2002) lamented the recent decline of bedside teaching in medical education, from 75 per cent of teaching time in the 1940s to 16 per cent by the late 1970s. Yet a cross-sectional questionnaire study of clinical teachers in Australia showed that 95 per cent of teachers still regarded bedside teaching as an effective way to teach professional skills (Nair *et al.* 1998). They reported practical obstacles to bedside teaching as:

- time constraints

- noisy wards

- high workload

- not enough patients being available: not having 'good' signs, being exhausted or staying only briefly in hospital.

A focus group of American clinical teachers felt that the devaluing and erosion of the teaching ethic, decline of bedside teaching skills and concern about the aura of bedside teaching were barriers to bedside teaching (Ramani *et al.* 2003). They speculated that physicians might worry about being exposed as having less expert knowledge, particularly in areas beyond their specialties.

Students

Bedside teaching remains very popular with students. In the Australian study mentioned above, 99 per cent of students who responded felt that bedside teaching was an effective way of developing skills in physical examination, 93 per cent thought it was useful for history taking and 90 per cent for communication skills (Nair *et al.* 1997). Although not yet confirmed by empirical evidence, in palliative care, students report great appreciation of bedside teaching particularly because this experience helps to reduce their fears of talking with dying patients. They are often surprised by the depth of clinical learning that can be achieved in terms of diagnostic history-taking, identifying physical signs and patient involvement in planning management.

Patients

Clinical staff are often protective of patients and concerned about their involvement in bedside teaching, particularly in the palliative care setting. Yet there is evidence that patients who participate in bedside teaching are generally positive about the experience (see Table 13.2). There are certain prerequisites, mainly those of common courtesy and thoughtfulness, including:

◆ requesting consent in advance

◆ respecting boundaries which are agreed with the patient beforehand and which may be further negotiated by the patient during the teaching

◆ avoiding too much use of technical language

◆ facilitating patient participation at their preferred level

◆ not staying too long, and

◆ thanking the patient afterwards.

Models of bedside teaching

There is no empirical data about which strategy is most effective for bedside teaching. The literature is littered with models for bedside teaching, of which only a few will be mentioned here. All these models incorporate:

◆ preparation before approaching the patient's side

◆ teaching at the bedside

◆ after-care for students and patients.

Cox (1993) described a two-cycle model of experience and explanation (see Figure 13.1). In the *experience cycle*, teachers start by ascertaining where students are coming from and what they already understand; students are briefed before approaching the patient. After the patient encounter, debriefing takes place away from the bedside. This is described as the *explanation cycle* in which students reflect on the experience and consider how this fits in with prior learning and turns it into working knowledge by thinking about what could have been done differently, in preparation for meeting the next patient.

Table 13.2 Literature evidence: patient participation in bedside teaching

Reference	Description	Patient response
Howe and Anderson (2003)	UK workshop of 49 participants: one-third each of patients, clinical staff and educationalists	Patients could be empowered by: • Receiving adequate information that can be understood, • Having opportunity to communicate, • Being asked for consent, • Having their feedback valued • Open approachable attitude from person in power, usually the teacher
Stacy and Spencer (1999)	UK semi-structured interviews with 20 patients involved in longitudinal patient study	Patients saw themselves as: • Experts in their medical conditions, • Exemplars of their condition, • Facilitators of the development of students' professional skills and attitudes • Having benefited through talking about their problems, learning more about themselves and satisfaction of helping and receiving gifts
Simons et al. (1989)	US study – monitored heart rate, blood pressure and plasma norepinephrine of 20 patients in critical care unit, measured at one-minute intervals during bedside case presentation and discussion between physician and patient.	Physiological measurements: • Small increase in blood pressure, • No change in heart rate and • No change in plasma norepinephrine Patients reported: • Pleased with bedside presentations, • Helped them understand their medical problems • Reassuring experience
Nair et al. (1997)	Australian cross-sectional survey of 160 general medical inpatients, 100 of whom had experienced bedside teaching every 2–3 days	• 77% enjoyed bedside teaching; • 83% said it had not made them anxious; • 84% would recommend to others; • 12% felt that bedside teaching could breach confidentiality
Lehmann et al. (1997)	US three-week randomized cross-over trial: discussion at patient bedside or in conference room – structured questionnaire administered blind to patients	Patients who had bedside case discussion: • Physicians spent more time with them, • More favourable perception of their inpatient care, • Suggested physicians should use less confusing medical terminology and allow more patient participation; Differences were not statistically significant
Linfors and Neelon (1980)	US survey of 50 patients about their response to bedside presentation of case histories	• 95% reported positive experience; • 66% understood their illness better as a result; • none considered disclosure to be improper or a breach of confidentiality Suggestions offered: • Attending doctor should introduce self, state purpose of bedside rounds and be sensitive to the need to translate technical terms, • Patients should receive advance notice • Should not be so long as to tire patient

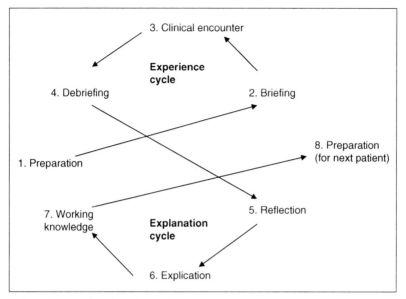

Fig. 13.1 Experience and explanation cycles
Reproduced from Cox K. Planning bedside teaching – 1. Overview. *MJA* (1993) **158**, 280–2.
©Copyright *The Medical Journal of Australia*, reproduced with permission.

Building on this and other models, Janicik and Fletcher (2003) developed a further teaching model (see Table 13.3), testing it with over a hundred clinical educators in workshop settings. Their model specifies three domains: attending to patient comfort, focused teaching and group dynamics, each of which has a specific goal and requires a set of skills or behaviours.

Other useful models for busy clinicians include the one-minute teacher (Furney *et al.* 2001) and SNAPPS (Wolpaw *et al.* 2003). In the former, the clinician asks students to outline their diagnosis or management plan, questions students for their rationale, teaches key learning points around that topic, provides feedback on what was done well and offers suggestions on what could be improved or corrected. SNAPPS is a mnemonic for student-centred learning: the student summarizes the case, narrows the differential diagnosis, analyzes the differential diagnosis, probes the teacher about areas not understood, plans the management and selects an issue for further learning.

Students can be given responsibility to video-record clinical encounters, with consent from patients. Feedback and discussion with a clinical teacher can take place subsequently, i.e. staged bedside teaching. In Oxford, student-led teaching sessions in which they take responsibility for organizing the session, getting consent from patients and teaching their peers, with a clinician present only as resource and back-up, have been popular with medical students.

Teaching palliative care at the bedside

The models described earlier have been developed within medical education and lend themselves well to clinical teaching on ward rounds and outpatients in the general

Table 13.3 Model of best bedside teaching practice (Janicik and Fletcher 2003)

Domains	Goal	Skills
Attending to patient comfort	To remain patient-centred and respectful	Ask ahead of time Introduce everyone to patients Brief overview from primary person caring for patient Explanations to patient throughout Avoid technical language Base teaching on data about that patient Genuine encouraging closure Return visit by a team member to clarify misunderstandings
Focused teaching	To conduct an effective teaching session in a focused manner that is relevant to an individual patient's and learner's needs	Microskills of teaching, modified for the bedside: Diagnose the patient Diagnose the learner – observe – question Targeted teaching: – role-modelling – assisting student with procedure or physical exam skill – teaching general concepts – actively involving patient as teacher – giving feedback
Group dynamics	To keep the entire group active during the session	Set goals and a time limit before entering the room Give all participants a role in the encounter Pay attention to everybody within the room Involve quieter members and control dominant members Patients should be encouraged to teach and ask questions Review the session and answer any questions

hospital setting. They may be easily modified for use in palliative care. In the following section, I shall draw attention to some issues which are specific to bedside teaching in palliative care.

Patients

Palliative care patients are often weak and frail. This creates two difficulties. First, they are easily exhausted by prolonged bedside teaching and cannot tolerate being moved around much. However, in Cox's model (see Figure 13.1), two-thirds of the teaching time, before and after the patient encounter, takes place away from the bedside. The time spent with the patient can be focused and brief. Palliative care is excellent for modelling whole patient care but it is not necessary to do it all within one encounter. Learning can be staged, hearing about different aspects through different patients or by learning from a single patient over a series of meetings. Second, the patient's frailty makes advanced planning difficult. Teachers need to be ready to involve other patients or to use alternative strategies. This can be a good learning opportunity for students to appreciate clinical unpredictability and to learn to cope with uncertainty.

Palliative care patients are vulnerable. Staff may be so protective of patients that they regard student learning to be an unacceptable imposition on patients' time. It is certainly important to respect patients' wishes not to be involved in teaching: however, to assume that decision for patients is unethical on two points. First, it does not respect patients' autonomy to make decisions for themselves. Second, if students do not have the opportunity to learn directly from palliative care patients, they will emerge from undergraduate or pre-qualifying education with only a theoretical understanding of palliative care. It is pointless decrying our colleagues' lack of understanding of palliative care while denying future professionals the opportunity to learn from patients. In palliative care, when patients' control of their lives is fast diminishing, it is particularly important for them to be allowed to make their own decisions about whether or not they wish to participate in teaching. It often provides a useful diversion from the monotony of the day. As yet there is no hard evidence available about patients' views on their involvement in teaching palliative care. However, the experience of palliative care educators in UK is that these patients are generally positive provided informed consent is obtained and patients' ability to withhold or withdraw consent is safeguarded.

In hospices, patients' relatives and friends spend prolonged periods at the bedside. Clearly, there are times when it is unfair to interrupt their time with the patient. However, the arrival of a student often provides a welcome distraction for patients and their visitors and a focal point for dialogue when they are reunited after the event. Family members or friends who have been closely involved as carers also provide a rich source of learning. Interprofessional workshops involving lay carers in palliative care were first developed at Southampton (Wee *et al.* 2001) and such carers are now also regularly involved at Oxford University. The skills that students acquire in communicating with carers and taking their views into account, as distinct to patients', are valuable transferable skills for learning and working in other environments, both before and after qualifying.

The subject of palliative care

The idea of talking with dying patients may be scary for students who often acknowledge fears of asking insensitive questions, upsetting the patient or not being able to respond to patients' questions. The reality is that patients rarely ask students about prognosis or expect answers in the way they do with professionals. Preparing students is crucial. A direct method to demystify clinical encounters with palliative care patients was introduced into the palliative medicine curriculum at the University of Southampton over two decades ago (Hillier 1995). A hospice inpatient would be invited, with informed consent, into the seminar room to converse with the clinical teacher, observed by students. As the conversation progressed, students gradually joined in and the clinical teacher quietly stepped back and assumed a background role, though remaining vigilant. The safety created by this process stimulated free-flowing and wide-ranging conversations that were often deeply revealing and rich in learning. The reactions of the students and patients were addressed separately after the interview.

Sometimes, the stories that patients told were positive, other times disturbing but they were always informative, authentic and valuable. Students reported feeling less apprehensive and more ready to converse with patients in the palliative care setting following that encounter. Patients who participated in such events reported feeling positive and some were exhilarated by the experience, even when they had been emotional. They also often reported being surprisingly impressed by the students. This model is now used in a number of medical schools in the UK.

Palliative care as a learning resource

There is a growing demand on clinical placements across all health and social work professions. While it is often daunting for patients in any setting to interact with a lot of students at any one time, it is well nigh impossible in palliative care. Keeping to the principle that only one-third of bedside teaching time needs to be spent at the bedside, it is possible to have a group of students, each interacting with one patient only, sharing the preparation and post-encounter learning time together. Students from different professional groups who happen to be in the hospice at the same time may benefit from learning together and through each other's experiences. When taking a group of students to a patient's bedside, teachers need to be mindful of making choices and maintaining focus. They may pre-allocate specific tasks to each student, e.g. taking history, examining a specific aspect of the patient's condition, asking about the home situation or observing and reporting non-verbal cues. In this way, all students can stay actively involved and share learning from the one clinical encounter without the patient being overwhelmed. Alternatively, teachers can use the opportunity to demonstrate specific skills which can then be further discussed away from the bedside.

Palliative care staff who are well-informed and involved in the planning process are less likely to be resistant to bedside teaching. They need to know about the learning goals for that group of students, what stage the students are at, what instructions students have been given and how long they would expect to spend with patients. Staff also need opportunity to feed back their experiences of these students and how patients responded. Providing a legitimate route for concerns to be expressed and positive views to be shared builds commitment. It is also invaluable to involve other professionals in bedside teaching and to develop them as clinical educators. Such involvement demonstrates interprofessional teamworking, explicitly values the different skills and perspectives that other professional groups bring and helps to embed a culture of learning and teaching within the palliative care service.

Teaching in different palliative care settings

Palliative care offers a wide range of opportunities for bedside teaching, whether in the hospice, home, nursing home, day centre or outpatients (see tips, Box 13.1). Much of what has been discussed so far applies to institutional settings.

Box 13.1 Tips for teaching palliative care at the bedside

Beforehand

- Request the patient's consent; check their level of understanding about disease and management
- Check agreement of any relative in attendance
- If the teaching is planned as part of ward routine, e.g. ward rounds, discuss plans with other members of the team
- If you do not wish to be interrupted, brief relevant colleagues beforehand, e.g. nurses, health care assistants, housekeeping staff and ward volunteers
- Draw a road map in your head of what you plan to achieve in terms of student learning at the bedside – make sure you are clear about your goals
- Check out students' understanding and orientate them to your plan for the teaching session.

At the bedside

- Introduce everybody present courteously and reconfirm the patient's agreement to participate
- Encourage the patient to participate actively in the teaching event – role-model this through your clear involvement of the patient.
- Keep the encounter focused and brief – translate any technical terms for all concerned
- Challenge gently; be sensitive and aware of the possibility of the student, patient or other staff feeling humiliated or embarrassed by the process.
- Avoid asking impossible questions or those that others might feel it was impossible for them to answer at the bedside
- Summarize (or ask the student to do so) the learning that has taken place
- Invite the patient to check out any concerns that may have been raised through that encounter, offer their advice to students and thank the patient.

Away from the bedside

- Elaborate on the teaching and offer an opportunity for further questions and clarification
- Invite student feedback on the session and spend a little time on your own reflecting on your own teaching in that session
- Return to check on the patient and offer an opportunity for further questions and feedback
- Feedback to other members of the team to keep them interested and involved.

Patients at home provide a different but creative challenge for bedside teaching. Students may accompany doctors, clinical nurse specialists, rehabilitation therapists or social workers to patients' homes. The teacher and student may be from the same professional background or not. The three stages of bedside teaching still apply: preparation, clinical encounter and after-care. However, the clinical encounter is both a normal clinical consultation as well as a learning encounter, so the expectations and needs of patients, carers and students all have to be met within a brief focused period. Unlike an institutional setting, the professional lacks the opportunity to slip back later, so the time has to be used efficiently. Students are often sent off to talk with carers to give the professional an opportunity to talk to the patient in private, or vice versa. It is important to be honest with students when they are being used in such diversionary tactics. Sometimes, they may miss out on the most valuable learning, which is taking place in the room from which they have just been sent! This cannot always be helped or anticipated. However, adequate preparation and opportunity for reflection and discussion afterwards enable students to learn from both encounters, the one in which they were directly involved as well as the one they missed.

Preparing teachers for bedside teaching in palliative care

Resistance to bedside teaching often rests on perceived external barriers: fear of patient discomfort, lack of privacy, concern about confidentiality as well as more practical issues of patients being hard to locate and the pressure of time (Janicik and Fletcher 2003). The clinical teacher's lack of confidence may be a further block, particularly in palliative care when teachers may be from non-medical backgrounds and fearful that their knowledge and credibility may be challenged by medical students or doctors in training.

Confidence and skills in bedside teaching need to be nurtured and consolidated, if effective and enjoyable teaching is to take place. One way to do this is through peer observation and feedback, in which another clinician attends the teaching session as an observer and provides feedback in a safe environment using a structured approach. This process, and other useful approaches for educator development, is described in Chapter 23 in this book. Through Beckman's (2004) peer review of inpatient teaching at the Mayo Clinic, a number of helpful and unhelpful teaching habits were brought to light, including: a large range of effective teaching strategies were used, the teacher's ability to expose their own ignorance improved with clinical experience, feedback was rarely given to students and questions were asked either too often, too infrequently or with an expectation that the student should guess what was in the teacher's mind. Peer review and feedback of bedside teaching in palliative care has not been formally reported but there is growing experience of using this approach within teaching development workshops.

Conclusion

Palliative care is an ideal setting in which to teach and demonstrate whole patient care through bedside teaching. There are specific issues which make bedside teaching more challenging in palliative care but, carefully thought through, the benefit outweighs the burden. It is a useful mode of teaching for all aspects of palliative care, including symptom assessment and management, psychosocial and spiritual support, communication skills, ethical decision-making and patient and carer involvement and education.

Bedside teaching is highly experiential. For the student, there is nothing more authentic than the patient as teacher. For the patients, this is often valued as an opportunity to get actively involved in teaching and to have their legitimacy as experts in their own experiences respected. For the clinical teacher, bedside teaching is deeply rewarding because it brings together the essence of clinical care: the application of knowledge, skills and clinical intuition to that unique situation in partnership with the person most deeply involved, the patient, and the exhilaration of passing on the craft of caring for patients and their families.

Chapter 14

Work-based learning

Margaret Colquhoun and Kathy Munro

Introduction

The organizations to which we belong are committed to work-based learning (WBL) and have experience in developing, implementing and evaluating WBL programmes for palliative care. This chapter will:

- explore the nature of WBL and its relevance to palliative care education and practice
- discuss the structures and processes that are required to support this form of learning
- explore some of the challenges involved in WBL
- outline the outcomes that may be achieved for patients and carers, for learners and their employers in a variety of palliative care settings.

The examples used to illustrate the issues arising from WBL are drawn from post-registration degree studies in palliative care nursing. We have reviewed material from WBL module evaluations and from focus groups of learners, graduates and managers involved in the degree programme. Where an individual's words are directly quoted, permission has been given. While examples presented are about WBL in a nursing degree context, plans to extend WBL to a postgraduate interdisciplinary programme in palliative care are discussed.

WBL is a relatively new approach to learning and although the evidence base is growing, there is an identified need for more research (Boud and Solomon 2001a). A selection of the available evidence, in the form of published accounts and research studies, is used to underpin the text.

What is work-based learning?

WBL has been described as having the potential 'to ensure fitness for practice, fitness for purpose and fitness for award' (Flanagan *et al.* 2000: 361). There are, however, many different definitions and interpretations of WBL (Boud *et al.* 2001; Clarke and Copeland 2003). These range from learning through work or 'on the job learning' to clinically based learning experiences, defined within an educational programme leading to a professional qualification and designed to ensure that competencies and standards are met.

Learning through work may be structured and guided by virtue of a palliative care organization's system of learning and learning resources such as education facilitators or practice educators. However, it may also be informal and unstructured and take the form of 'learning from others'. Such learning may not meet the needs of the individual or the organization. Indeed informal learning may be negative learning, where a person learns about custom and practice, the routine care and norms within a clinical area, without advancing palliative care through knowledge and evidence-based practice.

Within this chapter we will consider the approaches to WBL that lie at the other end of the continuum from informal learning through work. These focus on the learner at the hub of a process of WBL that involves employers, practitioners and education providers in a tripartite partnership. This type of curriculum is intended to maximize opportunities for learning and professional development in the workplace that can be recognized and accredited academically. It is experiential learning that requires the completion of a work-based learning event or task and also reflection and analysis on what has been learned from adopting the role of learner in the workplace. WBL enables learners to take a different learning trajectory depending on the organizational context in which they practise palliative care (community, hospice, hospital, oncology centre, nursing home). All of this is crucial to ensuring that practitioners are offered a learning experience that facilitates the development of the cognitive, affective and psychomotor skills and knowledge needed to care effectively for patients and their families at the end of life. WBL therefore addresses the concerns of some critics that education programmes do not meet the needs of learners or indeed match the requirements of employers within a rapidly changing health sector (Chalmers et al. 2001; Clarke and Copeland 2003).

The BSc in Nursing Studies – Palliative Care is a modular programme developed collaboratively between St Columba's Hospice and Queen Margaret University College, Edinburgh. The programme is designed to allow experienced practitioners working with patients and families in the palliative care phase of illness to acquire an academic award and a specialist practitioner qualification recordable with the United Kingdom Nursing and Midwifery Council (NMC). Within this degree programme, learners have experienced two different approaches to WBL.

First there is defined WBL, in which performance standards for the specialist practitioner qualification are set out in the *Unifying Modules: Palliative Nursing Care* as part of a validated curriculum (Colquhoun and Dougan 1997). The performance standards, which reflect NMC requirements for specialist practice (UKCC 1994), span the modular programme. They are designed to integrate theory from taught modules into the reality of palliative care practice and avoid the danger that 'learning may be seen as a series of unrelated chunks of content' (Sheldon and Smith 1996: 101). In achieving the performance standards, learners address the main areas of specialist palliative care such as pain and symptom control, communication, psychosocial and spiritual care and ethical issues at the end of life (Clinical Standards Board for Scotland 2002; Calman 2004; Sneddon 2004). They also demonstrate achievement of core skills recognized as important for specialist practice, such as decision-making, teamworking, leadership, teaching and research (Hoy 2004; Sneddon 2004). The lecturer and a clinical supervisor provide support. In this approach to WBL the performance standards determine what is to be learned and the learner determines how this will be achieved within their workplace. This approach will be referred to as 'defined WBL' for the purpose of the chapter.

Second, some learners on the palliative care degree programme have undertaken the *Developing Professional Practice* WBL module. In this double module the situation is, to an extent, reversed. The student is primarily responsible for setting out what is to be learned and how they intend to achieve that learning. The lecturer and a workplace mentor provide advice and support. In this scenario the focus is on achieving academic credit for learning derived from the job and directly beneficial to the workplace. Credit acquired in this way can be used towards the degree or, in other situations, the modules may be taken for continuing professional development (CPD). A useful working definition of this is 'learner-directed WBL'. For both approaches to WBL in this programme the learner completes a portfolio of evidence that demonstrates achievement of the performance standards or learning outcomes.

The following case study illustrates these two approaches to WBL and demonstrates how these came together in one learner's experience of the degree programme.

Case Study

For the learner-directed WBL, a charge nurse in oncology wanted to learn about setting up an exchange for staff nurses between a hospice and the oncology centre. She devised a learning action plan indicating her intention to learn how to gather and assess information on this topic, how to negotiate plans with stakeholders and how to design, manage and evaluate an exchange programme. The plan, negotiated with her employer and palliative care lecturer, was approved by the University College.

An extensive literature review on trust, networking, effective mentorship and creating a learning environment was undertaken. Contacts were made with managers; information sessions run in both institutions; human resource, legal and training issues were addressed and the exchange set up. Evaluation tools were formulated. Active involvement of all the team was encouraged throughout. The student submitted a portfolio of evidence including correspondence, minutes of meetings, contracts, documentation for exchange participants and mentors. The student was awarded 20 credits at degree level.

One performance standard in the defined WBL requires students to lead the team in developing clinical practice. The degree programme regulations permit students to develop their learner-directed WBL project further to complete a performance standard. The charge nurse therefore carried out a formal stakeholder evaluation of the exchange, thus meeting the criteria for this performance standard. The exchange programme was commended by NHS-Quality Improvement Scotland (NHS-QIS 2004).

Why use WBL for palliative care education?

WBL is particularly relevant to palliative care practice and education in terms of the interdisciplinary and patient-centred context of care and in relation to the process of palliative care.

The concept of learning through work and focusing on WBL fits well with the team approach to palliative care, because the main field of learning is the work context. It is acknowledged that there are other places of learning such as university and hospice classrooms, library, private study areas and learning resource centres. However it is only in the workplace that the learner will effectively learn how to do the job of caring for people as a member of an interdisciplinary team. Interdisciplinary education and working are clear goals of both the health service and higher education (Carlisle *et al.* 2005) and by providing opportunities in practice it is hoped that learning will occur through interaction with other professionals (Salmon and Jones 2001, Wakefield *et al.* 2003). This interdisciplinary context was acknowledged by one learner on completion of her defined WBL thus:

> Working with experienced practitioners in a multiprofessional setting has enabled me to learn more about the clinical aspects of palliative care but also about group dynamics.

Less well documented in the literature is the learning that may occur through interaction with the patient or carer (Turner *et al.* 2000). Callanan and Kelly (1992) write about the "extraordinary gifts" presented to carers by dying people – our 'finest teachers'(1992: vi). Many students echo this in the final evaluation of their defined WBL. One learner, having reflected in her WBL portfolio on the holistic care of a patient with complex needs, wrote:

> I nursed this patient soon after starting at the hospice and learned so much about the diversity of human nature.

It has been suggested that palliative care education should mirror the process of palliative care (Sheldon and Smith 1996; Sneddon 2004). Palliative care is likened to a journey where the dying person is faced with enormous risks, but also often a search for meaning and the potential for growth. At its best palliative care is about a partnership between an autonomous individual and the interdisciplinary team working to achieve the best quality of life. Education is also likened to a journey (albeit a very different journey from that of the patient) and there is no doubt that for the learner embarking on WBL there are risks, such as those associated with adopting the identity of a learner in their own workplace (Boud 2001b, Boud and Solomon 2003). Learners are required to be self-directing, to negotiate and manage their own learning and reflect on the experience in terms of personal and professional growth. It has been suggested that palliative care education providers need to work as 'co-educationalists, establishing collaborative and caring relationships and a dialogue' with learners (Sheldon and Smith 1996: 100) and this is perhaps particularly true in the context of supporting WBL.

What structures are required to support WBL?

Although it has been said that work is the curriculum (Boud 2001a), there is still a need for meticulous curriculum development. WBL requires a validated module descriptor with an overall aim, learning outcomes, teaching/learning activities and content. The number of hours of study and the amount of academic credit are determined within the descriptor. Once partnerships with employing organizations have been established, academic and workplace support systems must be built. Although WBL is described as learner-centred, these support systems are essential for facilitating learning, especially in the light of the 'complex, uncomfortable and ultimately emotional nature of experiential learning' (Dewar and Walker 1999: 1463). Steps also need to be taken to ensure that all parties are prepared for their roles (Dewar and Walker 1999; Flanagan *et al.* 2000; Boud 2001a; Boud and Solomon 2001b). Maintaining lines of communication throughout WBL is pivotal and this may be achieved through face to face meetings, telephone calls, emails and web-based technology. Clearly articulated assessment processes and robust systems to support assessment are also essential components (Biggs 2003; Stuart 2003; Webb *et al.* 2003).

What challenges arise in the process of WBL?

It is clear from the literature and from experience that challenges may arise at any part of the learning journey but most commonly in relation to orientation to WBL, negotiation of learning outcomes, the process of achieving the learning and in the evaluation of what has been learned. Some challenges are commonly encountered, but each is also unique to the individual learner. All challenges need to be addressed sensitively within the tripartite arrangement. Where a pattern of challenging issues is identified, however, aspects of WBL may require more general review.

Orientation to WBL

Ensuring at the outset that all parties understand WBL is crucial. WBL may be a wholly new experience for the learner and some may struggle with the increased responsibility, the identity issues of being a learner in their own workplace (Boud and Solomon 2001b, 2003) and indeed with understanding the WBL process itself. One learner on the palliative care degree, reflecting on defined WBL learning, wrote:

> As I stood at the start I felt I would never find a way through to the end, but each piece of work led me into another and kept me captive.

One of the ways in which the issue of preparing learners has been addressed in the programme is to invite students who have completed the defined WBL to meet with new students for an informal discussion and reflection on the experience of completing the portfolio. Workplace mentors and lecturers also need to recognize that this is a different learning experience. A workplace mentor, who may also be the learner's manager, may have to clarify particular issues of role (Boud and Middleton 2003). A study by Dewar and Walker (1999) indicates that lecturers have not always developed their own educational practice in the light of the new educational philosophy of WBL. The study suggests that lecturers also need to formally reflect on the experience as educators in order to facilitate others in that process. Boud and Solomon (2001b) suggest that a mentoring relationship between an experienced and a less experienced facilitator may be of value.

Negotiation of learning

While WBL is described as learner-directed, what is to be learnt needs to be negotiated between the learner, the employer and the educational institution as part of the tripartite agreement (Boyd *et al.* 2003; Clarke and Copeland 2003). Tensions can arise if the parties have different views regarding the nature of the learning for the individual and what has to be achieved for the organization (Boud and Solomon 2001b). A lecturer, for example, may feel that a learning plan is too ambitious for the credit rating, the academic level of study or the time scale. An employer may want to influence the learner to undertake a project that they do not want to do. The learner may not appreciate that learning makes additional demands of its own beyond the workplace function. Ownership of learning by the learner is an important issue (Chapman and Howkins 2003) and the desire to gain greater professional knowledge is a prime motivator (Smith and Topping 2001; Ryan 2003). Therefore any tensions between the learner and the employer have the potential to threaten WBL and lead to demotivation. They need to be openly acknowledged by all parties as an integral part of the learning process and sensitively worked through to a satisfactory conclusion.

Achieving the learning

While learners and employers may initially view WBL as a way of getting academic credit for an activity that they are already required to do for work, WBL is rarely viewed as reducing workload (Flanagan *et al.* 2000), and is recognized as involving hard work and being more time-consuming than expected (Swallow *et al.* 2001) possibly because it combines the integration of the higher education concept of critical being (Barnett 1997) in the form of critical reasoning, reflection and action in an unconventional way (Major 2002). Learners in the palliative care degree indicate in module evaluations and focus group discussions that workload and time management are major challenges. One student wrote:

> Completing the performance standards has been a steep learning curve for me. The majority of the standards have been completed in my final year which made it more challenging.

Therefore it is important to review workload and planning issues regularly with individual students and in the curriculum more generally. In the palliative care degree, as a result of focus group feedback, the performance standards were refined and workload reduced as part of a degree review process.

Evaluation of learning

Evaluation of learning is a further challenge for those involved in WBL because traditional methods of assessing knowledge may not inform us about the ability to develop as a professional and to learn and work. Context-based assessment, therefore, that is integral to WBL, and accredited by higher education, is advocated (Prince 2003; McDonough 2004; Poikela 2004). Portfolios – 'a collection of material brought together for a specific purpose' (Wilkinson *et al.* 2002: 919) – are commonly used in WBL programmes. A recently published major study emphasizes the evolutionary nature of portfolio use in higher education (Endacott *et al.* 2004). Portfolios can be viewed as having a number of advantages in relation to WBL particularly in terms of demonstrating the achievement of learning outcomes (Gallagher 2001; Williams 2003), linking theory with practice (McMullan *et al.* 2003; Rees and Sheard 2004) and recording of personal and professional growth over time (McMullan *et al.* 2003; Williams 2003). There are, however, issues about their reliability and validity as a form of assessment (McMullan *et al.* 2003; Webb *et al.* 2003). Where used in this way debate arises about whether portfolios should be assessed as pass/fail or if they can be graded. Further research is needed.

In relation to WBL portfolios we have taken the view, like Davies and Sharp (2000), that in a practice discipline, reflection on and analysis of learning for practice should contribute to the learner's overall grade. Following an extensive review of the literature and research we have developed explicit criteria for grading portfolios with colleagues.

Robust internal and external quality assurance systems, as recommended by Webb *et al.* (2003), are already in place.

What are the outcomes of WBL?

There is a general consensus in the literature that WBL has the potential to benefit patients and carers, learners, employers and educators (Boud and Solomon 2001b; Clarke and Copeland 2003). A learner in the Dewar and Walker study (1999) highlighted the difficulty of articulating experiential learning:

> Okay, I can look back at this and say well there's certain bits in the project that I did, the sort of hands on bits that I did, you know, they're very tangible, but it's the other bits and the more important bits as far as the work-based learning aspects are concerned, that are a lot less tangible for me at the moment.
>
> Dewar and Walker (1999: 1465)

In exploring the outcomes of WBL more generally there is also a need to try to encompass both the 'tangible' and the 'less tangible' achievements.

Box 14.1 sets out a small number of examples of WBL projects from the palliative care degree programme and these give some insight into the range of topics addressed. It also indicates some of the tangible benefits for patients and carers and indeed for employers and learners. It is these benefits that allow employers to see learning not as a 'self-indulgent activity', but one that actively contributes to the goals of the organization (Boud *et al.* 2001: 6). It is interesting that in the focus groups conducted as part of the review of the palliative care degree, managers expressed particular appreciation of the WBL components of the programme. It could be argued that some of these projects might have been

---

Box 14.1 Examples of WBL projects

A day hospice sister led her team in selecting and implementing a quality of life tool

A charge nurse in a breast unit developed a protocol for the drainage of seromas by senior nursing staff and undertook supervised practice to lead the initiative

A staff nurse explored with the clinical team the use of music as therapy in a specialist palliative care setting

A staff nurse introduced and evaluated team nursing in an oncology ward

A day hospice staff nurse developed, implemented and evaluated a patient education leaflet on constipation

A ward sister in a hepato-biliary unit led the interdisciplinary team in the development of an evidence-based approach to breaking bad news

A staff nurse working with people with HIV and AIDS involved her colleagues and patients in devising an information leaflet on living wills/advance directives

completed without enrolling on a WBL module, but one learner, in evaluating the defined WBL experience, noted that WBL was useful

> in that it has compelled me to examine my own practice and identify areas for development … Completing the course work has maintained my motivation to press forward with development initiatives that might otherwise have been set aside in the face of resistance to change.

Tangible benefits for education providers include using the links with employing organizations to remain in touch with practice in a wide range of settings and to establish research and curriculum development opportunities.

Less tangible benefits from WBL are more difficult to capture. Much of this is personal learning, unique to each individual and all of it is significant because it undoubtedly provides evidence of the development of personal and professional critical knowledge through WBL. Analysis of learner evaluations of the defined WBL within the palliative care degree programme over a five year period identified several key themes. The completion of the portfolio had been 'hard work' and 'challenging', but 'worth it', 'exciting' and 'rewarding'. This kind of WBL, the learners indicated, demanded the integration of theory and practice. Some learners highlighted added value professionally and personally through developments in practice or positive changes in relationships in the workplace. Clinical supervision and the opportunity for reflection on practice were emphasized as invaluable aspects of WBL. Many learners commented on completing the portfolio as a starting point for lifelong learning and others recorded learning of a more personal nature:

> I have also learned about myself which is important when dealing with patients and families who are under stress and strain in the cancer journey.
>
> The learning process has not been purely academic but has been an indirect opportunity to learn about myself as a nurse, a manager and a person.

Box 14.2 Starter's tips for WBL

All parties involved in WBL should:

- Recognize that WBL is a wholly different approach to learning
- Try to forge links with others who have experience of WBL
- Ensure that they are thoroughly prepared for WBL
- Commit themselves to the tripartite arrangement
- Remember the importance of ownership of learning by the learner
- Anticipate tensions as an integral part of the process of WBL
- Communicate and negotiate within the tripartite arrangement
- Value the tangible and less tangible outcomes of WBL

These comments highlight the intensity and complexity of the WBL experience. Some starters' tips are set out in Box 14.2.

The future for WBL

Work-based learning is an approach to learning which can be challenging organization-ally, intellectually and emotionally. It can also be enormously rewarding for all parties in terms of the tangible and less tangible benefits it offers. Work-based learning as described in this chapter, however, is relatively new and there is a need to explore further and to develop the evidence base for this approach to learning (Boud and Solomon 2001a). This is particularly true in relation to demonstrating the impact of WBL on patient outcomes (Prowse and Heath 2005).

In terms of the future in our own organizations, we have developed a postgraduate interdisciplinary programme of palliative care education. Market research indicates a great interest from a range of disciplines in completing a significant work-based project in place of a conventional research dissertation – an alternative approach which is gain-ing recognition within our own organizations and elsewhere (Flanagan *et al.* 2000). We look forward to the challenge of extending our experience of WBL for palliative care to an interdisciplinary initiative and in the context of advanced practice.

Acknowledgements

We wish to acknowledge the interest and support of our colleagues at St Columba's Hospice and the School of Health Sciences – Nursing at Queen Margaret University College, Edinburgh. We thank Fiona Taylor, Charge Nurse, Western General Hospital, Edinburgh for allowing us to use her project as a case study. We are also grateful to all our learners over the years, with special thanks to those whose projects and words have been used to illustrate the chapter.

Chapter 15

Reflective learning

Nic Hughes

Introduction

The belief that a process of reflection can turn experience into learning originates in the world of adult education and in the last two decades has also permeated health and social care education and practice, along with other academic and professional disciplines (Schön 1983; Gould and Taylor 1996; NCIHE 1997; Harrison *et al.* 2003). Nursing literature in particular is full of texts on reflection, most of which assume its benefits for learning without being able to demonstrate unequivocal effects (Newell 1994; Mackintosh 1998; Rich and Parker 1995). Palliative care educators, whether practitioners or lecturers or both, may be called on to help learners from a range of professions learn by reflecting on their experiences.

This chapter aims to:

♦ explore briefly the nature of reflection
♦ outline a range of different ways to enable reflection
♦ discuss reasons why learners may find reflection difficult
♦ summarize arguments for and against learning through reflection.

Background

Much of the literature on reflective learning in health care practice and in education assumes that reflection is inherently a good thing (Boud and Knights 1996) though there are a few dissenting and critical voices who point to lack of empirical evidence of its effectiveness or to lack of rigour in thinking through some of the potential moral implications (Newell 1994; Mackintosh 1998; Rich and Parker 1995).

There is a rich and diverse philosophical background underpinning ideas about reflective learning, stretching from the pragmatist philosophy of John Dewey through the humanistic psychology of Carl Rogers to the critical realism of Jürgen Habermas and to postmodern ideas about self and reflexivity. This means that reflective learning carries a strong cachet, a weight of philosophical tradition which gives it kudos and enables its popularity to persist in the absence of strong empirical evidence of its effectiveness.

Where reflection is introduced into formal programmes of study there seems to be little choice offered to learners about whether they wish to learn in this way and there is no reference at all in any of the literature reviewed in preparing this chapter to the influence of learning style or preference (Honey and Mumford 2000a) or of personality type (Myers 2000) on the willingness or ability to learn by reflection. Learners' resistance (documented by Jasper 1995; Patterson 1995) to reflective methods is presented as an obstacle to be overcome by the teacher (Johns 2002) rather than considered as a principled choice to learn by other means.

The context in which palliative care practitioners or educators may be engaged in helping students learn through reflection is, I suggest, strongly affected by the extent to which learners have been given a choice of whether to use reflective methods of learning or whether they have been required to do so. Jasper (1999) notes that none of the participants in her study would have chosen spontaneously to learn by reflection but, having been required to do so by the demands of a formal education programme, they came to value the process. Learners who make an active choice to learn in this way may be more motivated to make it work, though they may still need detailed guidance about the process. Learners for whom this approach conflicts with their learning style preferences or their dominant personality traits may need additional support in integrating reflective methods into their repertoire of learning strategies.

This chapter will draw on a selection of the wide-ranging body of literature about reflective learning to explore the nature of reflection and to analyse some methods of reflective learning.

What is reflection?

A simple dictionary definition of the word 'reflection' is *the action of the mind whereby it is conscious of its own operations.* Taylor (2000) suggests that reflection involves

> the throwing back of thoughts and memories in cognitive acts such as thinking, contemplation, meditation and any other form of attentive consideration, in order to make sense of them and to make contextually appropriate changes if they are required.
>
> Taylor (2000: 17)

Like many definitions of reflection in recent and current literature this has its roots in the work of the pragmatist philosopher John Dewey who defined reflective thought as the 'active, persistent and careful consideration of any belief or supposed form of knowledge in the light of grounds that support it and further conclusions to which it leads' (cited in Burnard 1995: 81).

This cognitive, rational approach has been complemented in recent years by definitions which honour the non-rational so that reflection is also seen as

> a way of contemplating self, an opportunity to bring the self together, a self that may be fragmented within the turmoil of everyday existence [or as] a state of mind, like a quiet eddy in a fast moving stream, a place to pause in order to consider the fast moving stream and the way self swims within it.
>
> (Johns 2002: 11)

Taylor emphasizes the importance of critical thinking and reasoning in making cognitive acts but also acknowledges the worth of 'intuitive grasps', 'creative expression' and 'inner knowing'. Reflection becomes more than just a thoughtful approach to learning or to professional practice, it becomes 'a way of being, a state of mind' (Rich and Parker 1995).

The cognitive and the affective are combined in the well-known work of Boud *et al.* (1985) who define reflection as 'a generic term for those intellectual and affective activities in which individuals engage to explore their experiences in order to lead to new understandings and appreciations' (1985: 19). Ekebergh *et al.* move still further in the direction of holism in articulating an approach to 'embodied knowing' through drama in which reflection is seen as 'a comprehensive act in the human mind where, by reflecting on thoughts feelings and actions, a meaningful picture is created in the learner's experience of the world' (2004: 624).

Attitudes and qualities necessary for effective reflection

All learning involves risk (Claxton 1984). For some writers this risk-taking element requires special consideration in relation to learning by reflection. This seems to be because of the part played by examining feelings when reviewing experience whereby possibly painful emotions are revived and re-experienced. If learners are not able to complete the learning cycle by imagining alternative perspectives and re-evaluating the experience, including its affective components, they may become stuck in the painful experience. Rich and Parker (1995) go so far as to claim that this process can be damaging to the mental health of the learner by threatening deep-seated coping mechanisms and they strongly recommend careful supervision or coaching to minimize this potential effect.

The ability to take personal, emotional risks in exploring experience is, therefore, seen as an important aspect of learning by reflection (Jasper 1999). Other qualities needed are authenticity, sincerity, integrity and commitment (Johns 2002). Such qualities are necessary but insufficient to produce effective learning by reflection. They must be allied with a consciously applied method.

Methods

Key features in the process of reflection include accurate description of experiences, articulation of thought and feeling, imagination of alternative perspectives and planning for future action. The most common way of activating this process is through reflective writing in the form of a diary or journal, or reports of learning through critical incident analysis. Written reflections may be supplemented, but are rarely entirely replaced, by non-verbal methods (drawing, collage) or bodily action (drama).

Reflective writing

Jasper (1999) argues convincingly that reflective writing is itself a form of learning, that the act of writing contributes substantially to what is learned by the process of reflection. In addition writing helps develop analytical and critical skills and to make new connections between ideas and experience. In these ways writing facilitates personal and professional growth. The skills of reflective writing, Jasper emphasizes, have to be learned.

Box 15.1 Helping learners to prepare for reflective writing

- ◆ What can learners expect to gain from reflective writing?
- ◆ What should you encourage learners to write about?
- ◆ How often should they write?
- ◆ What format should they use for writing?
- ◆ What should learners do with their writing?
- ◆ How are learners to gain the skills of writing reflectively?

Writing may be accompanied by discussion with a teacher, mentor or supervisor or with a peer group. Box 15.1 offers some questions to think about when preparing to help learners to write reflectively.

Diary/journal

Keeping a daily or weekly journal is recommended by most authors (Durgahee 1998; Heath 1998; Jasper 1999; Johns 2002; Landeen *et al.* 1995). Most agree, also, that some kind of structure is needed for writing. Many models have been given for structuring reflection itself, i.e. the thinking and feeling processes by which experience is reviewed (Boyd and Fales 1983: Boud *et al.* 1985; Gibbs 1988; Johns 2002) and these frameworks can be used as a format for written recordings. Mallik (1998) suggests strongly that students should be introduced to reflection gradually, taking into account different levels of cognitive development or ability and level of professional and clinical experience. Heath (1998) offers a useful exploration of different diary formats for the beginner, recommending a fluid, flexible style of writing in which the individual develops their own style unconstrained by others' expectations.

How does reflective writing contribute to learning?

Landeen *et al.* (1995) report a study evaluating the use of self-reflective journals in a group of psychiatric nursing students during a 13-week clinical placement. Students were required to submit journal entries every two weeks to a member of teaching staff who would make written comments on the journal. This is very different from the approach to writing reflective journals in the UK where the content of journals remains private.

Landeen *et al.* note that the process of keeping a journal was a learned skill in which it took students several weeks to learn how to reflect on their experience rather than simply to report events. Some students were unable to reflect in depth either because of limited knowledge and experience of the field of study or lack of journal writing experience. Others appeared to write what they thought was expected. Overall the process enabled student and teacher to track the student's growth and development and, for most, the experience was positive and developmental. Landeen *et al.* conclude that journals are a useful learning strategy within an overall curriculum that promotes self-reflection.

Box 15.2 Structure for a reflective journal

Describe in detail an event which occurred in the clinical day which you think is significant in understanding the care of a person receiving palliative care

Discuss how this event may have been perceived by others involved

Discuss your personal interpretation of the event, focusing on one or more of the four ways of knowing (personal, empirical, aesthetic, ethical) and including the assumptions which are revealed in this interpretation

Explore alternative ways of interpreting and responding to this event, including an evaluation of the feasibility and acceptance of each of these alternatives

Identify what learning has occurred in reflecting about this event

Identify the objective(s) of the course which are addressed in the journal entry
Patterson (1995). Adapted and reprinted with permission of Elsevier

Patterson (1995) shows how journal writing can be effective in promoting critical thinking, self-awareness and the creation of alternative perspectives. She gives a detailed account of problems and potential solutions: for example, in overcoming resistance, stimulating motivation, developing reflective skills, as well as how to structure and write journal entries. Here, too, the journal is a vehicle for dialogue between the student and teacher rather than a private record of the learner's experience.

A structure for a journal entry expected from undergraduate nursing students caring for chronically ill patients is reproduced in Box 15.2. Typical features include the requirement to give a detailed description of events before seeking interpretations and explanations. Learning can only occur when this sequence is completed in the correct order (Kolb 1984). Specific features in this structure include the assumption of prior knowledge of a particular theory of knowledge in nursing based on the work of Carper (1978). The last point makes clear that the context for this journal writing is a specific programme of formal learning. The student is expected to make links between their clinical experience, their reflective journal writing and the specific course objectives.

Reports of critical incidents

A well-established method of focusing journal entries is to concentrate on critical incident reporting (Minghella and Benson 1995; Parker *et al.* 1995; Rich and Parker 1995). This method is widely described as originating in aviation engineering during the 1950s as a method of analysing errors or problematic situations. It is now seen as having wide application to any potential learning event. 'Critical' in contemporary usage seems not to imply risk of harm or danger but to signify 'important for learning'.

Most writers agree that attention should be paid to a detailed descriptive account of what happened, to the feelings experienced, to a consideration of the viewpoints of

Box 15.3 Structure for supervised critical incident analysis

- ◆ Critical incidents are deconstructed by questioning to generate a wide range of perceptions of the incident and its influencing factors.
- ◆ Imagination is then brought to bear on the influencing factors identified so that a range of options for behaving differently can be explored.
- ◆ A process of action planning then takes place to increase the likelihood of behaviour change.

Williams and Walker (2003)

others involved, to thinking about how the experience or the student's own behaviour might be made different in future, and to planning for change. Williams and Walker (2003) describe an approach to facilitating reflection in groups based on critical incident analysis (see Box 15.3).

Key success factors here would include the skills of the group facilitator and group members in asking appropriate questions to uncover and summarize a range of perceptions and the skills of the facilitator in managing this step-wise process.

Rich and Parker (1995) emphasize also the importance of continuity of structure and time for such group work in order to enable the provision of psychological safety for both students and staff. In addition, explicit guidelines should be created to make clear how reports of poor clinical practice should be responded to. Teaching staff should receive in-depth training in the theory, practice and facilitation of reflective learning.

Action is central to all these methods of reflection through writing and dialogue. The process of reflection is itself an active process, and the end point is some form of action, at least an intention to behave differently in future based on the knowledge and insight that has been achieved. It is an iterative process in which planned actions arising from the process of reflection are implemented and then subjected once again to reflective scrutiny. Only in this way is the learning cycle completed. Otherwise reflective writing remains at the level of a documentary record of thoughts and feelings rather than becoming a dynamic learning tool.

Some potential challenges of reflective writing

A number of writers report that learners grow to value and enjoy reflective writing after an initial reluctance to do it (Shields 1995; Jasper 1999; Johns 2002). Important influencing factors include the clarity of explanation as to the purpose and method (Parker *et al.* 1995; Patterson 1995), the learners' perception of the trustworthiness of the teacher and the quality of feedback, where journal entries are to be disclosed (Patterson 1995) or the quality of supervision (Williams 2000) and facilitated discussion (Landeen *et al.* 1995). The learner's developmental level (intellectual and emotional maturity, professional and life experience) is also crucial to successful learning by reflection (Burrows 1995; Patterson 1995). Where any of these attributes is missing learners tend to produce superficial, non-evaluative descriptions of experience, more orientated to producing what they think teachers want to see than to genuine, independent self- inquiry directed at achieving new insights or new ways of behaving (Patterson 1995; Hargreaves 2004).

Learning effectively through reflective writing also depends on a culture of literacy. Johns (2002) points out the difficulties nurses sometimes have with reflective writing because of the oral culture of nursing which privileges speech over writing. Johns presents this as an obstacle to be overcome. It may be that spoken reflection should be honoured and that ways of reflecting which are less dependent on writing should be considered.

Other methods of reflection

Most approaches to reflective learning and teaching are based on logical, analytical ways of processing information and experience (Boud and Knights 1996) which privilege writing as a method of learning. Korthagen (1993) presents a broader gestalt (i.e. whole) approach to ways of interpreting data and making decisions which integrates the rational and the non-rational through use of metaphor or through the production or analysis of visual images.

A number of authors report success in using non-literary forms of reflection, including drawing (Cruickshank 1995), collage (Williams 2000) and drama (Ekebergh *et al.* 2004). These are non-literary forms of reflection, but they are not non-verbal, as all involve verbal analysis and interpretation. Cruickshank argues that drawing allows access both to unconscious and subconscious processes which can then be discussed to generate knowledge in the three domains of knowledge outlined in critical social theory – technical, rational, emancipatory – all of which, according to Cruickshank, are important for nurses. Drawing is a skill which should be seen as important as writing.

For many practitioners, though, the effectiveness of drawing in reflection is not determined by skill in drawing. In practice, most people can produce visual images which represent meaning symbolically and which can form the basis for verbal interpretation and analysis. If perceived lack of skill in drawing does form a barrier this can be overcome by creating a collage of images from a range of printed sources. These can be used in guided reflection with a mentor or supervisor (Williams 2000). Specialist knowledge in art therapy is not necessary for effective use of this technique, but skill in supervisory methods such as probing, clarifying and reflective questioning is required.

Dramatic techniques such as role play, improvisations, sculpting and forum theatre can be used to create 'embodied knowledge' (Ekebergh *et al.* 2004). Embodied knowledge is a way of describing knowledge which arises from the combination of the physical act of movement along with the imaginative creation or recreation of scenes which mirror peoples' real life experiences. In Ekebergh's study such physical and imaginative action was found to clarify feelings and to give more structure and consciousness to thinking (see Box 15.4).

Box 15.4 Forum theatre

Forum theatre is a powerful style of role play in which a group of learners shares a story from their experience and re-enacts the story, after rehearsal, in front of an audience of co-learners. The audience (ie the 'forum') is invited to intervene and to change the behaviour of key actors in the story. This method of reflection re-creates experience in a powerfully immediate way by adding bodily action to thinking and feeling. It is this combination of all three which makes reflection through drama a 'comprehensive act in the human mind' and 'creates a meaningful picture of the learner's world' (Ekebergh *et al.*2004). Ekebergh *et al.* emphasize the need for intensive training for teachers in the use of these techniques as well as the importance of continuing supervision from drama therapists.

Assessing learning by reflection

In much of the literature, from nursing in particular, reflection is embedded as a learning strategy within a formal curriculum. Students may be required to create a structured, written account of their learning by reflection in the form of a portfolio of learning (Jasper 1999), a clinical journal (Patterson 1995) or a sequence of critical incident reports (Minghella and Benson 1995). In addition students may be required to engage in written dialogue with their teachers (Patterson 1995) or discussion with their peers (Landeen *et al.* 1995; Minghella and Benson 1995). The 'dialogue journal' is a simple format in which the student writes to the teacher about their clinical experiences and the teacher responds, with questions, ideas, clarifications, affirmations. A relationship of mutual trust is necessary for this method to create genuine learning (Patterson 1995).

Teacher feedback through a dialogue journal is a type of formative assessment. It is indicative of the popularity, among educators, of reflection as a learning strategy that in many professional educational programmes, both pre and post-registration, reflective learning is also assessed summatively. This is often problematic. It is not easy to define criteria by which learning through reflection may be assessed. Students may feel more vulnerable to adverse judgement from the teachers for the style and content of their reflections than in traditional forms of assessment where expressions of personal feeling are omitted. Where reflective learning is closely linked to professional practice there are particular challenges in assessment. If reflective learning is not assessed, on the other hand, students may not value reflection as a learning strategy (Patterson 1995).

Hargreaves (2004) makes some very powerful points about the problems inherent in trying to assess reflective practice in the current 'inspectorial' system in higher education in the UK. Students, she argues, are forced into a position whereby to gain marks they have to present reflections which reveal 'acceptable' professional and personal attitudes rather than what they might really feel and think. Much of the literature on reflective learning assumes a more benign, collaborative approach than really exists, not only to the process of learning, but to the process of assessment. The problem arises because of 'dissonance between the act of reflection, and the objective of reflective practice within a given professional domain'. This dissonance is a moral one: reflection as a private act is morally neutral, or open, whereas reflective *practice* is 'bound within the ethical code of the profession' (Hargreaves 2004: 200).

Limitations of reflection as a learning strategy

Burnard (2005) casts serious doubt on reflection, on the grounds of poverty of memory and consequent fictionalizing of reflective accounts, lack of evidence that we learn effectively in this way, the potential de-skilling effect of paying too much attention to our experience, the strangeness of assessing someone's reflections, and the even greater strangeness of failing them and having them re-reflect and, finally, on the grounds that mindfulness, as taught and practised by Buddhists, is more suited to living in a world of change and uncertainty. 'They know, perhaps, that the past is gone' (Burnard 2005: 86).

There are some persuasive points here but the conclusion does not do justice to experience. It is too simple to say that the past is gone. It may be gone, but it leaves a legacy. It is the creative working with that legacy, interweaving feelings and perspectives to fashion new insights and behaviour, that is the potential strength of reflective learning.

Turning experience into learning by reflection is not simply a matter of recollecting an event and giving transient thought to the experience (Williams 2000). It is a complex process involving analytical ability and emotional maturity. Moreover it is a way of learning which is more suited to particular learning styles or preferences (Honey and Mumford 2000a) than to others. For some individuals reflection simply conflicts too greatly with their preferred learning style or stage of life development (Burrows 1995) to enable them to learn effectively in this way. This does not indicate an inherent limitation of learning by reflection but a mismatch between the individual and the learning strategy. As suggested in the introduction to this chapter, it is important to consider the extent to which a learner has made an active choice to learn by reflection, having evaluated their own learning style against the requirements of the method, before deciding how best to help facilitate their learning.

Conclusion

There is continuing debate about the effectiveness of reflection as a strategy for learning in professional practice. For many educators and writers it is self-evident that, as health and social care practice are rooted in interpersonal relations, self-awareness is a crucially important aspect of professional learning. Reflection is seen as the route to self-awareness. A range of methods (verbal and non-verbal) and strategies (private reflection, dialogue with others, group work) may be used to engage a learner in this process. It is a learning process which epitomizes the learning cycle defined by Kolb, involving integration of thinking, feeling and action. There is a risk of failure to learn, and potentially of emotional or cognitive hurt, if the cycle is not completed, but the reward can be depth of insight which fuels commitment to acting in new and more productive ways.

For a smaller number of writers the assumptions underpinning the valuation of reflection as a method of learning are untested and its efficacy unproven. Consequently the widespread inclusion of reflective learning in formal programmes of learning is seen as unwarranted. In particular, the challenges posed by assessing reflective learning seem to be unresolved.

Chapter 16

Small group and one-to-one teaching

John Costello

Introduction

The primary role of education relating to palliative care is focused on improving practice and hence changing behaviours through the use of appropriate teaching and learning strategies. Moreover, traditional teaching methods with a reliance on passive forms of learning are inappropriate for palliative care practitioners who need active participation in their learning in order to acquire the necessary communication skills to improve practice (Sneddon 2004).

This chapter describes and examines:

- the role of the teacher as a group facilitator
- small group and individual teaching strategies relevant to palliative care
- the role of the teacher conducting individual learning supervision.

Throughout the chapter my experiences as a palliative care educator, and those of colleagues involved in this area for many years, are used to highlight aspects of teaching relevant to small group work. Small group teaching and learning not only improves students' knowledge of palliative care, it can develop self-confidence and enable students to develop effective communication with patients, families and members of the palliative care team.

The role of the teacher as facilitator

Palliative care practitioners are often specialists working at an advanced level. Such individuals have multiple roles as mentor, counsellor, staff supporter and expert practitioner for patients (Brykczynska 2002). A facilitator is a process guide, an enabler who is instrumental in helping students maximize their learning opportunities (Heron 1989; Hunter *et al.* 1995). The facilitator's role is to develop group cohesion as soon as possible by encouraging students to share ideas about themselves, their experiences and feelings. A cohesive group is one in which ideas are shared and positive contributions are made, with the entire group making helpful comments (Gibbs 1988). Effective facilitators promote student disclosure by being positive when personal disclosures are made, by helping less able students to make a contribution and by reiterating that all group members are expected to share their views. Students who express more personal feelings should be supported by the facilitator, as this validates their disclosure and expression of feelings and should be used as a model when patients express their feelings. One of my students informed the group that she recently visited an elderly lady with a fungating breast wound. Despite needing to dress the wound, she could not bear to stay in the house for long without feeling sick. Through group discussion, the nurse could see that it was the smell and also her own fear of cancer that was making it hard to offer appropriate support. Expression of personal feelings are a sign that the group is working cohesively and may also illustrate areas of communication which cause anxiety such as talking about death and dying.

The amount and depth of disclosed information should increase as the group becomes more comfortable with sharing ideas together, progressing from stating facts to the expression of feelings (Kagan and Evans 1994). The facilitator's role is to encourage participants to express feelings without them becoming too personal and avoiding participants feeling guilty afterwards about having shared them with the group. The facilitator is less of a 'fount of knowledge', more of an initiator, often standing back from the group but rarely outside it. This can be challenging if the teacher is used to traditional teacher roles where learning was more of a passive activity. Facilitators have a number of responsibilities, often shared with the group, for fostering a positive climate for learning. These include demonstrating respect for individuals and an acknowledgement of individuality; enabling students to ascertain facts and associated feelings (how did you discuss terminal care with the patient and how did you feel about it?). This can be carried out through group discussion, as part of a more formal teacher-led session or through simulated interaction using role play scenarios.

Setting the scene

A small group may consist of three to five participants in a clinical setting or be as many as eight to twelve students in a classroom. Small group teaching provides a number of opportunities for students to discover their strengths and weaknesses in communication skills (Mearns 1997). It also provides opportunities for developing self-confidence, and has the potential for promoting group skills to enhance individual learning (Jarvis 1983; Bolton 1986). The establishment of trust and mutual respect is largely influenced by the facilitator's approach, attitude and level of skill and experience (Rogers 1987). Effective small group teaching requires planning and preparation. Session preparation includes a written plan outlining the organization of the teaching experience that allows for appropriate reflection on practice.

Ground rules

Establishing ground rules is an important part of developing group cohesion. Knowledge of such rules at the outset helps provide students with a sense of ownership of their learning. There are many ways of setting ground rules, some take the form of a short discussion, others form part of initial 'ice-breaking' sessions; if carried out during the initial session, rule setting helps to recognize individual values, provide positive feedback, and enable students to hear and share constructive criticism. Ground rules are not set for the facilitator's benefit, although they should not feel constrained from expressing their views about rules such as being punctual! The setting of ground rules is an interesting exercise and provides students with the chance to express views on previous negative as well as positive experiences.

Ice-breaking exercises

An important part of beginning a small group session is getting to know individual members and helping them to relax, which is also an important part of effective communication with patients (Maguire 1999). Learning aims such as providing palliative and supportive care for vulnerable patients cannot be achieved unless we have the co-operation of others. Maguire points out that time spent getting to know one another and listening to ideas through active participation helps to foster a climate for learning by stimulating mind and body. Facilitators need to be both familiar with different ice-breaker exercises and aware of possible difficulties. One student who seemed unhappy about doing an exercise that involved students changing seats every few minutes explained that she would like to 'play the game' but was prevented by a back problem! Ice-breaker activities are often fun, designed to enable students to learn more through participation (Knowles *et al.* 2005). Basic exercises designed to encourage participants to disclose their personal biography, such as where you work, and course expectations can promote attention and listening skills (Burnard 1990). Such exercises carried out in pairs can have important benefits when applied to palliative care practice where listening, attending and empathy building are important parts of the professional's repertoire (Fallowfield *et al.* 2001; Wilkinson (J.M.) *et al.* 2002). Patients with life-threatening illness need effective communicators able to make empathic responses during times of distress such as when bad news is broken (Morton 1996), or when patients have uncontrollable physical distress (Kohora *et al.* 2005). Booth *et al.* (1996) argue that health care practitioners need to respond in a positive empathic manner without having to use 'blocking behaviour'. There is a need for practitioners caring for patients with life-threatening illness to recognize that developing their listening behaviours is an important part of promoting effective palliative care. Communication skills can be enhanced through the facilitation of a range of group exercises designed to actively involve students in their learning (Booth *et al.* 1996; Maguire and Faulkner 1988; Wilkinson (S.M.) *et al.* 2002).

Disclosure exercises

At the beginning of a course, an interesting and common way of finding out about individual group members is to encourage participants to disclose information about themselves through listening and communicating exercises. A basic example is an introductions exercise designed to enable group members to introduce each other to the group with the facilitator requesting specific information about individuals such as their expectations of the teaching experience. Such exercises enable students to experiment and develop their interpersonal skills, providing opportunities to learn more about other group members and for facilitators to discover what students expect from the teaching. Exercises like these initiate the process of students working in pairs and providing feedback

Box 16.1 'Fear in a Hat'

The exercise involves participants writing their anxieties on a sheet of paper, folding it and placing it in a box (or hat). Group participants take a fear out of the hat offered round the group. Participants discuss their anonymous worries, fears and concerns (putting their own fear back if picked out). This exercise, like many others, is relatively quick to do and can be adapted to promote discussion on a range of subjects such as breaking bad news, talking about death or supporting specific groups such as children or older people. It is important to acknowledge fears, accepting the individuality and diversity of apprehensions as well as their importance in the learning experience. At the end of the session, the facilitator may reflect on the general range of ideas thoughts and concerns of the group through discussion identifying specific concerns as well as strengths of group members that can be utilized in future group work exercises.

Brandes and Phillips (1985)

to the group. The facilitator can invite discussion on recurring topics such as concerns about practice issues or assignment failure, to ascertain group concerns about topics raised. Often students raise the issue of failure in their studies as an anxiety. In a small group, discussion like this can help promote cohesion as well as raise self-confidence by recognizing that the concern is shared by others.

A classic text full of ways for working with small groups and using exercises to achieve group goals and promote effective communication is the *Gamesters' Handbook* (Brandes and Phillips 1985). I use a number of the exercises and have had tremendous success and fun from activities such as *Control Tower* and *Blind Find* that have fostered personal development and trust in the group. Many activities require modification, customising them to suit individual needs. *Fear in a Hat* (see Box 16.1) is a useful game for getting participants to share their anxieties or apprehensions about the course of study (often exams and essay failure feature prominently), as well as enabling people to share personal fears in a safe, non-threatening way.

Group work

An interesting and useful way of teaching small groups is to utilize experiential learning strategies (Gibbs 1988). Group work exercises maximize learning through active involvement of students in the learning process (Brookfield 1991; Habeshaw *et al.* 1992). Not all students enjoy experiential learning and those with different learning styles may have different preferences (Honey and Mumford 1986). Like many exercises, the group need to be informed of its aim and the expected outcomes. Learning by active involvement has long been an important principle of learning, although in isolation, experiences do not mean learning takes place. Without reflecting on the experience, students may fail to consider the potential to improve future practice and the implications for learning are lost. Reflection helps to give meaning to life-encounters enabling individuals to reflect on

> ## Box 16.2 Starters' tips
>
> Group exercises can be fun and very stimulating when the group is new or dealing with a complex and/or sad scenario. Games should not be used just to 'jazz up' the session and the aim should be made clear to the entire group. When choosing a warm-up exercise ensure you clearly state the aim, have contingency plans for dealing with sudden emotional moments. Discussion of sensitive issues such as death and dying may evoke memories thought lost and forgotten. Respond appropriately as a group and keep a facilitator's note of individual and group expressions.

and change future behaviour (Kolb 1984; Boud *et al.* 1985). Palliative care practitioners often encounter end of life situations as critical incidents, such as making 'do not resuscitate' orders or requests for euthanasia, that are both complex and emotionally sensitive. They also involve communicating about issues practitioners find worrying because of a lack of knowledge and experience (Tripp 1993).

Small group work should be closely related to relevant palliative care practice with students invited to relate theory with practice issues. A useful way of doing this is to ask students to discuss current patients they are dealing with or to use case studies of patients known to students, asking students to give an account of current care and concerns. It is important to remind students of the need for confidentiality when sharing such material. Students often highlight ethical issues such as withdrawal of treatment or organ donation as challenging areas. By listening to their colleagues' accounts group members can comment and respond positively and constructively to areas of difficulty. Small group teaching can take on many forms including seminars, problem-based learning and role play simulations (Chapter 17, p 162).

Student-led seminar groups

Seminar group teaching is a very useful way of enabling students to gain self-confidence and for students to share knowledge and pool their own ideas and experiences. Students organizing their own seminars avoids the potential problem of teacher-led tutorials where the teacher's contribution dominates and prevents students thinking for themselves. Seminars led by students who present their work to other students prevent them becoming passive in their learning and encourage group discussion as well as enabling students to learn from each other (Brookfield 1991). Students can present their work as posters or through verbal exposition using a range of teaching media. Time is provided to enable students to prepare and plan with facilitators acting as advisors, helping them gain access to material. The topics for presentation can be selected from a range, such as quality of life issues or medication. Each seminar group can have 20 minutes to present their material with the remainder of the group contributing by providing positive feedback and constructive criticism.

Problem-based learning

The move towards more holistic assessment of patients, with less reliance on studying distinct subjects, has prompted educators to consider the use of problem-based learning (PBL) as a way of enabling students to become more self-directed in their learning (Biley and Smith 1998). PBL is a method of learning focused on integration of knowledge from wider sources to create, analyse and develop appropriate ways of investigating through progressive enquiry (Andrew and Jones 1996). The facilitator guides students through the process or procedure, without necessarily having to have a presence in the classroom. PBL scenarios can be gleaned from students or from real life aspects of practice; for example, a patient who has been told his cancer has returned and requires more chemotherapy or where treatment is stopped because the patient's quality of life is adversely affected by treatment. Students need to have the full scenario and rationale clearly described. Facilitators need to have a positive belief that students can use their own knowledge and experience to contribute to the session.

Effective PBL includes participants respecting individual contributions, reinforcing group work principles and challenging students to work together to find ways to manage and resolve issues arising from the scenario. Effective facilitation, including an understanding of the group dynamics, can help to make PBL sessions a success. A PBL scenario used on the undergraduate programme in my school encourages students to think about what to do for a patient dying from a malignant brain tumour at home. Students often feel challenged by their lack of knowledge and experience of specific medical conditions, although the majority find explanations and arguments to justify a range of potential decisions for treatment and care. PBL experiences demand active participation by all students, which is a major challenge for the facilitator to ensure that the scenario is relevant and credible. PBL focused on palliative care in small groups is an ideal way of sharing ideas and raising awareness of the patient's perspective. It can also highlight communication difficulties experienced by members of the multidisciplinary team working to resolve patient problems.

Learning from patients

Patients and their experiences of health care have been utilized in education for many years. In particular, the use of patients (or people, such as actors, simulating patients) to help students develop a range of skills and develop communication, is an important part of education in palliative care. Simulated patients are now one of the largest groups from the general public involved in medical education in the UK and have been so for many years (Kilminster *et al.* 2005). Simulated patients are actors who undertake specific training to enable them to reproduce situations that real patients may find themselves in. Some simulated patients draw on their acting experience to simulate a specific situation for the group.

Real patients can also become involved in clinical practice and invited to share their experiences in a classroom situation (Costello and Horne 2005). The principles of involving patients in teaching are similar to those for conducting good group work.

Individual respect and a shared belief that patient experiences are a valid and important source of learning form the basis of this approach. Practically, patients work in small groups with one facilitator. They are briefed about their role, often being asked to behave as they would in a clinical setting and answer questions from the group as fully as possible. They are not expected to act or undertake tasks beyond their capabilities. The facilitator's role in situations such as this is to keep the situation credible, appropriate and relevant to the group:

◆ brief and debrief the patient fully

◆ give constructive feedback.

Utilising patients or simulated patients provides students with a situation where they can learn by having the chance to ask the patient directly as well as exploring with them their feelings about their experiences. In this way students can reflect on the discussion and consider similar experiences in their own practice. Utilizing patients in a classroom or clinical scenario is a powerful form of teaching and learning. It is a way of learning being developed by medical students (Kilminster *et al.* 2005) and has the potential for not only improving learning but also providing patients with a therapeutic and safe environment to describe their experiences and discuss feelings with those who stand to benefit from listening to their stories and reflecting on the meaning within their own clinical practice.

Students may also wish to describe a patient and family they are involved with and seek group advice and guidance on future interventions. The facilitator can encourage and initiate such discussions without adopting a 'telling approach', instead listening and encouraging individual and group responses and promoting discussion. Such experience can shape group dynamics and promote active listening. An alternative to utilizing patients in teaching is to focus group work on authentic case study situations that are problematic to the student. The case study can be used to highlight a range of issues that concern members of the group, from pain and symptom control to spiritual care and truth telling.

Box 16.3 Teacher's tips

I was asked to teach a group of students doing a short HIV course. I explained that my presentation involved a patient who was HIV positive. The students said they had done this before with another teacher who told them it was a real patient. Unfortunately the patient was an actor and the students were not told this until after the session. This made them feel upset because the teacher had deceived them. Any trust and cohesion in the group had been damaged by the lack of honesty. Facilitators should not deceive students as it fractures trust and cohesion between the students and the teacher. The value of using patients in teaching situations is to develop credibility and to keep the teaching and learning real.

Managing difficulties

Effective small group teaching is based on students having a clear understanding of its aims. It can be a satisfying experience for students and facilitator. To ensure success, clear boundaries and aims should be set at the beginning so that individuals know where they are going and why. Problems often arise in groups where rules are not clear or are misinterpreted. For example, a student with a strong desire to talk about their personal experiences with a patient who died can be supported in this as long as the group is prepared to tolerate and support the individual. However, one person dominating group time in this way can cause tension and have a negative impact on group morale by causing an imbalance in the time allotted by the group to the task in hand.

The facilitator's role in these situations is to keep the group focused on their aims and to avoid individuals being harmed, for example through negative criticism or through persistently making personal disclosures that are ignored by the rest of the group. In particular the facilitator should not openly criticize individuals, but instead 'scan' the group for signs of tension such as students who remain silent or withdraw from the group and those who are scapegoated by others. Facilitators should look out for signs of difficulty and confront individuals, or the group as a whole, constructively acknowledging their behaviour and asking them to respond to the criticism. Often it is possible to work through problems, such as persistent lateness, or group disruption, with the individual(s) concerned, to the benefit of the whole group. Appropriate supportive responses made to problems in the group can give a positive sign to the rest of the group that the facilitator is trying to secure their wellbeing. Sensitively made responses by the facilitator can enable and promote group cohesion and trust.

Individual teaching

One-to-one teaching and learning in palliative care may take place in two different contexts: first, the teacher as a supervisor in a more academic role, and second as a clinically based teacher in a practice context. I will briefly examine both roles starting with the academic role. This could include supervising dissertation students on degree courses and acting as personal tutor to those undertaking post-registration courses. In both cases there is likely to be existing written guidance produced by the institution on how to fulfill this role. The role of the facilitator in one-to-one learning is to be familiar with the rules governing the submission of a student's work and to facilitate them in producing the best work they can within their capabilities.

Similar 'rules of the road' apply within this context that operate when teaching small groups. This includes a need to set clear ground rules with students about deadlines, boundaries, quality of work and joint expectations. Try to assess the student's writing ability as soon as possible if you are supporting them in their academic studies. This provides a chance to see what they are capable of and how much to expect. It is useful to ask about what expectations students have; for example, what mark or degree classification they hope to achieve. It is useful to gain insight into what type of pass the student is expecting in order to gauge how much you can reasonably ask them to achieve. Stretching a student intellectually forms part of the supervisory process, although skill and sensitivity are required to know how far and how much the student is capable of producing. By jointly agreeing on deadlines and quality, the learning experience is shared and the learning contract becomes clear and unambiguous. The student and facilitator need to document progress and outcomes as they go along recording each meeting and identifying future goals. Above all, both parties need to have a clear focus based on a learning contract that stipulates the amount of time involved and what realistic deadlines can be set. This will avoid any potential difficulties that can arise due to a lack of understanding about who is supposed to do what.

Individual teaching in a clinical setting

One-to-one teaching in a clinical setting is a very fertile form of learning with a huge potential for enabling the student to learn from their experiences in a safe and structured way. Teaching in the clinical setting is, as Schober and Hinchliff (1995) point out, a partnership between the teacher and the student. The teacher is able to utilize a wide range of methods including demonstrating procedures and methods (such as cannulation), invasive procedures or methods of suctioning. The clinical environment is ideally suited to utilizing patients in teaching and for exploiting *teachable moments*. The latter can occur when the teacher sees a situation with the potential for teaching and learning to take place and *seizes the moment* to conduct some spontaneous teaching. Examples of this include demonstrating how a procedure such as wound dressing should be carried out, positioning a patient for physiotherapy or discussing a sensitive issue with a patient with the student observing. Often the teachable moment occurs after the encounter with the client when the student is thinking about what has just happened. In this situation, the teacher needs to be receptive to the student's perception and curious about what they thought they were learning.

When demonstrating practical procedures, the teacher needs to feel confident in their ability. There are a few rules of the road that apply to clinical teaching, summarized in Box 16.4.

Box 16.4 Rules of the road for individual clinical teaching

- Never ask a student to do what you are not confident in doing yourself.
- Avoid compromising the student or the patient by placing them in a difficult situation.
- Obtain consent from the patient and agreement with the student about involvement.
- Ensure that the teaching is consistent with the student's ability and is consistent with their learning objectives.
- Always provide oral feedback on the experience outside of the clinical context (not in front of the patient or others).
- Ensure that criticism is constructive.

There are also a variety of ways for teaching in the clinical setting which utilize the principles of learning previously discussed; for example, preparation, planning, organizing and feedback. If you are doing a mini-teaching session in the clinical area with a student always ensure that you are not likely to be interrupted by other staff, patients or sudden emergencies. A range of teaching opportunities can occur in clinical practice such as during handover periods or ward rounds, in outpatient clinics, or during a home visit.

Successful teaching on a one-to-one basis often depends on the personality of the teacher (Reece and Walker 1998). The teacher who makes it known that they are interested in the learner and their needs, and is approachable and receptive to student concerns, is more likely to be asked for help. Activity is a central part of learning by doing and the clinical setting is ideally suited to this form of learning. Students learn quickly in the absence of a group and often the learnt material is more focused. Such teaching is often referred to as coaching and involves the development of previously acquired knowledge and the promotion of more sophisticated skills. The teacher who may not feel confident in a classroom setting may excel in a clinical environment simply by showing interest in the student and facilitating them to learn by utilizing opportunities available. Asking a student to sit in when bad news is broken or when a Hickman line is removed demonstrates an interest in the student's learning needs and does much to stimulate their interest in wanting to learn about patients in a palliative care setting. One of the keys to successful individual teaching is to foster the student's desire to learn and to promote intellectual curiosity when the opportunity arises.

Conclusion

This chapter utilized my teaching and learning experiences with nurses, although I recognize that all of the methods described could apply equally to many interprofessional groups. The future for palliative care education clearly lies in developing multidisciplinary education and training focused on the effective provision of care for all patients with life threatening medical illness. This needs to be based on utilizing much of the sound research evidence available through a critical evaluation of its application to practice. To do this, practitioners need to have opportunities to learn and use critical thinking and awareness. Small group teaching and learning in palliative care takes place in many areas outside as well as inside the classroom. One of the keys to success is the facilitator having a clear idea of their role, a positive attitude and motivation to want to share their knowledge and expertise with others. This may include the use of didactic methods of teaching as well as students learning through being active participants in their own learning. Through the use of innovative research-based teaching and learning methods, health care practitioners can develop effective interpersonal skills that can be utilized in practice with patients, as well as with other members of the palliative care team.

Chapter 17

Experiential workshops

Marilyn Relf and Bob Heath

Introduction

The goal of teaching is much broader than creating understanding. Effective teaching needs to translate knowledge into behaviours that make a positive difference to the people we work with, namely our colleagues, patients and all those who care for them. Whereas didactic teaching helps learners to 'know about' by stimulating interest and thinking and by providing frameworks to structure knowledge, there is substantial evidence that these methods alone are not sufficient to change behaviour. Experiential teaching helps learners to 'be able to' by focusing on their values, attitudes and behaviours. Experiential methods are, therefore, an important part of the spectrum of teaching and learning (Kurtz *et al.* 2005).

Experiential learning is used widely to describe many types of non-traditional classroom teaching. This chapter focuses on experiential workshops. When planning and delivering experiential workshops consideration should be given to all four elements of Kolb's well known 'experiential learning cycle' (see Chapter 1, p 4). Such workshops may offer opportunities for reflection, exploration and experimentation. Whatever the focus, a good experiential workshop will provide an opportunity to translate new insights into the context of practice.

In this chapter we shall:

♦ explain the purposes of experiential workshops

♦ describe the skills involved in planning and leading experiential workshops

♦ provide detailed examples of three methods of experiential learning: role play, sculpting and exploring experience through creative connections.

Experiential workshops in palliative care education

In order to bring the holistic philosophy of palliative care into reality in practice health care workers need to have a wide range of knowledge and skills. As well as managing the multiple physical needs of patients, a high level of competence in the interpersonal domain is required combined with insight into personal emotional states and how these influence relationships (Sullivan *et al.* 2005). Experiential workshops offer powerful ways for professionals and volunteers to develop their capacity to work effectively with people facing death and bereavement.

Experiential workshops provide opportunities for:

◆ Reflection and support. There are often few opportunities to share thoughts and feelings about the sensitive situations that are frequently encountered in palliative care. Structured, interactive workshops can help participants to explore and share what it is like to work in close proximity to serious illness, loss and grief, to reflect on how they manage the intensity of the work and how it is affecting them. The very nature of such workshops may prove a more comfortable and creative setting than the traditional support group.

◆ Raising awareness of what influences our attitudes, assumptions and the way we respond to others. Our individual capacity to use interpersonal skills in sensitive situations is influenced by a combination of factors including our professional knowledge and experience, personal values and cultural and social norms as well as our personal experience. What we 'hear' people say and how we respond is filtered through these 'lenses' (Relf 2003). Similarly, patients and family members 'hear' us through their own filters. Blocks to communication frequently lie at the level of attitudes and emotional responses. Experiential workshops provide safe ways of exploring these issues. Workshops can also be used in relation to team working. Stress frequently arises from relationships with colleagues rather than from our work with patients (Vachon 1997). Experiential workshops can help people reflect on the reality of providing holistic care in multiprofessional teams and to develop more effective ways of working together.

◆ Experimentation. Workshops offer opportunities to try out different interventions and ways of being with others that participants may not have the confidence to use in real life. For example, it is impossible to develop communication skills by reading or observation alone; they have to be practised in the interpersonal domain (Fallowfield 2005). There is substantial evidence for the effectiveness of workshops involving simulations and role play in improving communication with patients (Gysels *et al.* 2004).

Teaching using experiential methods

Bridget Proctor, a pioneer of counsellor training in the UK, describes experiential learning as follows:

> We enter into an experience informed by our past and present knowledge [and] understanding ... We 'do' the experience our way, sometimes predictably, sometimes creatively, depending on our level of inner tension or freedom and outer support or stress. If the experience has been good enough ... we reflect on it according to our current mental constructs, or we invent or borrow a new construct to play with, and draw our own conclusions. If it has not been good enough ... we may avoid such situations in future.
>
> Proctor (1991: 64)

How do we ensure that our workshops provide 'good enough' experiences? According to Rogers (1961), all human beings have a natural desire to learn. He suggests that learning and personal development are more likely to take place when they are directly relevant to the needs and 'wants' of the learner and conducted in a supportive atmosphere where external threats are kept to a minimum. New attitudes or perspectives are much more easily assimilated and learning proceeds faster when there is little or no perceived threat. Rogers argues that self-initiated learning is the most lasting and pervasive. This means that teachers not only need to have the necessary knowledge to deliver the learning content of the workshop, they also need to be skilled, flexible facilitators willing to vary the content to meet learners' needs. We need to be sensitive to the diversity of our students, their personalities and their learning styles and be able to create experiences that in themselves facilitate learning effectively within the given time boundaries. We need to be able to:

- plan and structure the event
- create safety and manage individual and group responses
- teach in ways that are congruent with the values of palliative care.

Planning experiential workshops

Experiential methods can vary in the degree of structure provided. Many of the workshops we provide will be intentionally structured and the teacher will have a clear idea about what people will learn from the experience. However, workshops may also have a more open agenda with greater emphasis on the experience itself. In these workshops the learning outcomes will be less predictable. We provide examples of both types of workshop later in this chapter.

Questions that might be useful when planning a workshop are provided in Box 17.1 We recommend that experiential workshops should be facilitated by two (or more) teachers at least one of whom should have training and experience in group facilitation. Both should be committed to co-working and be able to acknowledge and work with any feelings engendered by the workshop. It is important that facilitators should have direct experience of the workshop, otherwise they may be unprepared for what may be generated by it. Co-facilitation means that workshop preparation and delivery can be shared and co-facilitators can debrief each other and provide mutual feedback after the workshop. Co-facilitators from different backgrounds can also provide positive role modelling of interprofessional working. Co-facilitation can be challenging, however, and a key factor for success is to negotiate roles and responsibilities in advance. Hogan (2002) outlines several models of co-facilitation including shared responsibility, dividing roles according to expertise, dividing roles according to focus (i.e. one focuses on the task and the other on how the group is responding) or by taking it in turns to facilitate or to 'sit out'. Having two facilitators available also means that, should a participant become distressed, one of the facilitators can attend to their needs while the workshop continues.

Attention to the physical environment is also important. Experiential workshops should be held in rooms where the layout can be altered easily to suit changing requirements. Learners invariably appreciate an environment that is light and well aired as these help us maintain our energy and a positive approach. However, if this is impossible small human touches such as fresh flowers or plants make a huge difference. Providing refreshments also helps to promote a sense of community and encourages further group interaction.

Box 17.1 Teacher's tips: planning an experiential workshop

- What are your aims and objectives? Are they realistic for the time available?

- What information will participants need about the workshop? Do they need to do any pre-event preparation?

- Will you work with a co-facilitator? How will you negotiate your individual roles and responsibilities?

- How will you introduce the event? How will you help participants introduce themselves? What 'housekeeping' do you need to build in? (e.g. giving information about how you will respond if there are 'wants' that you have not anticipated?

- How will you bring out participants' fears and concerns? How will you help them to agree what behaviour will help the group to work together to maximize learning?

- How will you help participants begin to engage with the workshop and share with each other?

- What will be the focus of the event – the main experience(s)?

- What do you need to prepare in order to help participants 'do' the experience? (e.g. case studies, role play cards, materials etc.)

- What do you need to be particularly aware of when facilitating this workshop? (e.g. complex sequence of instructions, times when participants might be more anxious)

- How will you help people reflect on the experience and digest what they have learnt?

- How will you help participants think about how they might apply their learning to their practice?

- What theory input or teaching handouts will be useful to help people link their learning to wider models and understanding?

- How will you close the group?

- What do you want to evaluate about the event and how will you do this?

Creating safety and security

The author of Chapter 16 (p 147) has described the importance of creating a positive and supportive climate for learning in groups by clarifying both expectations and concerns and by establishing agreements (ground rules) about group behaviour. If experiential workshops are part of a larger course, then group behaviour and cohesion may already be established but it is always important to take time to address what people want, to clarify what expectations are unrealistic and, perhaps, to be prepared to alter the programme in response to unanticipated wants. Agreeing what behaviour will help participants to work together is an important first step. It helps people to feel at ease and begins to create the trust that will help participants feel prepared to take the necessary risks. Such agreements might include respecting others, being prepared to take risks, taking responsibility for oneself etc. It is helpful to give people permission to not participate if they do not want to (as long as they agree not to obstruct others) and to remind participants that during palliative care workshops it is not unusual to remember times of personal loss. Should they become emotional, we will not think that they have not coped but that they are remembering an important time.

An important aspect of creating safety is agreeing what is meant by confidentiality. In workshops, this needs to be established not only in relation to work undertaken by the whole group but also to work undertaken in subgroups. Typically, participants agree that they can talk about what they have learnt but that they will not disclose any personal information about other participants. It is important that individuals have ownership of personal information and that others do not speak for them. For example, we recommend that facilitators do not use the popular introductory exercise in which participants are asked to talk with a partner for a few minutes and then to introduce that person to the rest of the group. People are often anxious at the beginning of an experiential workshop, may not listen attentively or may be nervous when speaking for the first time in the group. As a result misinformation may be given at a time when people feel reluctant to correct what is said about them and the all-important sense of trust within the group can be undermined from the beginning.

A good experiential workshop provides opportunities to practise new skills and to experiment with new ways of working. Providing constructive feedback is an important part of this process as it is only through feedback that we can gain insight into our 'blind' areas (Lufts and Ingham 1970). Agreeing guidelines for constructive feedback minimizes insensitivity and helps to ensure that feedback is specific and refers to behaviour that can be changed.

One way of creating security is to keep the workshop small. Many workshops have between six and fifteen participants which allows flexibility to work in a variety of ways without being too exposing. However, experiential methods can be used with larger numbers depending on the number of experienced facilitators available.

Each participant brings their own personal history, values and beliefs. Consequently, facilitators need a good understanding of group dynamics and the psychological mechanisms therein. Experiential workshops may evoke or trigger emotional responses which are often fundamental to the power of the work itself. Facilitators, therefore, need the skill and sensitivity to help learners manage and understand their own feelings in relation to death and dying. For example, a participant in a workshop on grief found memories surfacing of her experiences as a teenager in Northern Ireland. Two friends had been killed by a car bomb. She chose to sit out for the rest of the exercise and talked to the co-facilitator about her experiences while the group continued. She felt able to rejoin the group for the next part of the workshop. If something particularly painful emerges, either for the group or for an individual, attention should be given to the hurt feelings. If a participant becomes distressed, other participants may become anxious and feel uncomfortable. However, such experiences also present powerful learning opportunities and participants often develop a better understanding of both self and others. Facilitators, however, should be alert to any particularly vulnerable member of the group who may need time to discuss his or her feelings outside the session.

It is important to remember that experiential learning groups are not therapy groups. While important and often sensitive issues emerge and can be explored it is essential to maintain a focus on the learning outcomes. Facilitators may well become involved in helping participants to identify their personal needs and may suggest where they can find suitable support. This can be an important role and needs to be treated in a positive and sensitive manner. We referred earlier to some of the psychological processes that will be present in any experiential group. It is important to recognize that as facilitators we are not immune to these processes and will from time to time be very aware of our own difficult feelings. It is good to acknowledge these feelings and to be aware of where they fit into the overall group process. However, it is of equal importance to remain mindful that our role is one of facilitation and that we need to continually monitor our own responses. For instance, a difficult phase during a session may lead to feelings of self-doubt or a temptation to rescue others. How we respond to these feelings will have a direct impact on the group and its potential learning outcomes. We will, therefore, need to continually develop our skills as teachers.

Teaching in a way that is congruent with palliative care

Our attitude as teachers is crucial to creating a positive climate for learning; we are constantly modelling skills, behaviours and attitudes. Our behaviour needs to be authentic and we need to demonstrate a sense of congruence with our students that actively reinforces learning. Central to palliative care is respect for patient and family and a willingness to understand and accept. We need to embody and model these values and behaviours and remain consistent with the philosophy that informs much of our work. Our approach to how we teach, therefore, is equally as important as what we teach.

Experiential workshops often focus on the psychosocial and spiritual aspects of palliative care. The role of the facilitator here is not to attempt to uncover the right or wrong approach but rather to support participants in discovering their own way forward. Facilitators should not see themselves as experts but have a genuine attitude of curiosity and respect for each participant's experience. This approach can be described as one of 'joint enquiry' where teachers and learners work together and is often referred to as forming a 'working alliance'. Shafer, a gifted Canadian teacher and musician, suggests that learning 'should be an hour of a thousand discoveries. For this to happen the teacher and the student should first discover one another' (Shafer 1975: 2).

Examples of experiential workshops

In this section we provide three examples of experiential workshops, including reflective workshops focused on developing self awareness and practice based workshops to enhance and develop the individual's capacity 'to do'.

Role play

Frequently learners will ask teachers to demonstrate skills so that they can 'see' good practice. This can be useful but teachers should be aware that observation alone is rarely sufficient and that participants may compare themselves unfavourably to the teachers. Role play provides an opportunity to practice communication skills and to gain insight through feedback. It involves a participant, or actor, simulating the role of a patient or relative in order to give another participant the opportunity to hone their skills. Other participants take on the role of observer so that constructive feedback can be given. Practice can be undertaken in front of the whole group, in which case there will be a number of observers, or in smaller groups such as triads. Participants may value the opportunity to practise in smaller groups as this is less threatening. It is not our intention to give detailed information about how to run a role play as this can be found elsewhere (e.g. Jeffrey 2002: 61).

A frequent criticism of role play and other simulated exercises is that they are phoney or contrived and that in a real situation both 'the patient' and 'the helper' would behave differently. This can often reflect an anxiety about performing in front of others or being given judgemental feedback. Simulated situations *are* unreal, but few palliative organizations have the resources to provide real time education e.g. using two-way mirrors or bedside cameras. As a result role play is often our only method of providing opportunities to experiment with new ways of being. Some argue that using non-group members (actors or colleagues) helps the role play to feel more authentic (Fallowfield 2005). However, using participants has the advantage of giving greater insight into what it feels like to step into the shoes of a patient or relative. It helps to use examples, such as learning to drive a car, that remind people that learning new skills *always* feels awkward.

Role play provides the safety to make mistakes without worrying about causing harm. However, many learners still feel self-conscious when learning in this way and it is important for us to recognize this discomfort. We should make the time to reflect on this part of the learning process. In any skills practice participants will become more aware of their behaviour and consequently may feel less competent and deskilled. Similarly, practising new ways of responding or intervening can feel awkward and unnatural to begin with. When new skills are absorbed they feel natural but this can take time and some participants, for various reasons, may not yet be prepared to make the journey. Rather than viewing this as failure, Moore (1992) reminds us that:

> Sometimes we can shape experience into meaningfulness playfully and inventively. At other times, simply holding experience in memory and in reflection allows it to incubate and reveal some of its imagination.
>
> Moore (1992: 198)

Choosing the scenario

There are different ways of choosing the scenario for the patient or relative role depending on the needs of the session. Brief role descriptions may be provided and used as a starting point for the interaction, which will quickly develop its own momentum. These descriptions may be scripted in advance by the facilitators or they may be prepared during the workshop in order to provide individual group members the chance to practise specific situations that they themselves have identified. Participants may also be asked to draw on their own experience when in the role of the person being helped. This provides a useful opportunity to reflect on the client's experiences as well as practising skills.

Facilitating role play

The role of the facilitator is to set the role play up, contain anxiety, provide clear instructions for the procedure, ensure that people have come out of role and facilitate discussion and reflection. Learning using role play takes time and decisions will need to be made about whether everyone in the group will have the opportunity to play each role or whether the role play will be restricted. Facilitator participation in role play demonstrations should only be tackled if working with a co-facilitator who is not part of the role play as it is impossible to maintain group awareness while also playing a role.

Role play frequently engenders anxiety and it is important that facilitators avoid giving negative messages and clearly explain the opportunities that role play can provide when conducted carefully. It is particularly important to discuss the process of feedback so that participants understand what helps feedback to be constructive, balanced and 'heard'. As well as verbal feedback, audiotape or video recorders can be used so that the interaction can be replayed and critiqued. Audiotapes are less obtrusive, while video captures non-verbal communication.

Verbal feedback should always start with the person who is practising their skills describing what they thought they did well and then what they thought they did less well. The facilitator (or observer if triads are being used) may need to help the person identify their strengths as the tendency is always to go straight to weaker areas. The person being helped should then give their feedback about what was helpful and what might have been done differently, followed by the observer(s) giving feedback about the specific skills and behaviour they observed. Feedback is a crucial aspect of role play and should be allotted sufficient time. If breaking into small groups, it helps to have written instructions about the process. Prepared observer sheets help observers note specific skills or behaviours. When audio and videotapes are used, feedback is usually given after watching the replay. After the feedback the participants need to be 'de-roled' before moving onto the next round of practice. At the end of the practice, sufficient time needs to be allocated for group debriefing and discussion to draw out what has been learnt in all the roles (helper, helped and observer).

Sculpting

Sculpting is used to raise awareness and understanding of how relationships influence the way people think, feel and behave. Sculpting originated in family therapy where it has been used successfully to help family members understand and gain insight into each other's behaviour. The central technique is to create a tableau that depicts non-verbally the quality of the relationships between the people involved. This can provide a powerful insight into what the world looks like from the perspectives of the different roles depicted in the sculpt. It can give a sense of standing in another person's shoes. In palliative care education, sculpting may be used:

- to explore family relationships and dynamics such as power and conflict
- to explore the relationships between health care workers and patients and family members
- to develop team working, both within teams and across organizations

- to develop communication skills
- to explore clinical situations where an individual worker providing care feels stuck.

In all these situations, sculpting may be a prelude to other forms of experiential teaching. For example, new insights may be gained by sculpting and followed up by using role play to rehearse different ways of responding.

As with all experiential teaching, it is important that the facilitators have experienced sculpting themselves and it is important to create a feeling of group safety. Sculpting can be used with small to large groups of people depending on the type of situation. If the group is larger than the number of roles needed then some people can act as observers. As with all experiential exercises, it is best if two facilitators are involved with one taking the lead in conducting the sculpt.

Using sculpting to explore a family situation (1)

There are two methods of using sculpting to explore a family situation. In the first method, the situation is decided in advance by the facilitator and roles are allocated to participants during the workshop (see Jeffrey 2002:.63). In the second approach, the situation is generated by the participants. This method (Box 17.2) is more relevant to the learners' needs and may have a greater impact.

Using sculpting to explore a family situation (2)

So far we have explored how to use sculpting to increase understanding of what may be influencing behaviour within a family. Sculpting can also be used to explore the relationship between family members and professionals. In this case the assignment of roles includes the professionals in the scenario. The sculpt proceeds as before with the patient and family members being sculpted first and the professionals arranged in relationship to them and each other.

Using sculpting to explore a clinical relationship that has become stuck

Sculpting can provide a dynamic and immediate way of exploring a clinical situation and may be used in case review or group supervision. The worker sculpts the bodies of at least two people, herself and the person with whom she is working, with the aim of creating a representation of how the relationship feels. This can provide useful insights into transference and counter transference issues.

Using sculpting to explore team working

Sculpting can also be used to explore relationships within and across teams and organizations where individuals might, for example, represent the user, ward nurses, managers, nurse specialists, organisations such as a Cancer Network, NHS Trust, Strategic Health Authority, Board of Trustees, etc. This can be particularly useful to explore the pressures experienced at different levels.

Exploring personal experience through creative connections Saunders reminds us of the importance of attending closely to patients and knowing 'how to be silent, how to listen and how to just be there' (Saunders 2003: 7–8). Although this sounds simple, in practice our individual capacity to be close to others and truly attend to them often needs

Box 17.2 Teachers' tips: conducting a sculpt (45–60 mins)

1. Ask the participants to identify challenging family situations. Who wants to explore their situation in more depth?

2. Ask the 'volunteer' to draw a genogram and briefly describe the scenario. Check whether this has any personal resonance for others and keep this in mind during role allocation.

3. Ask the volunteer to choose others to represent the roles. Check that everyone is willing to participate and whether anyone has back problems.

4. Ask the volunteer to place the 'family members', sculpting their bodies into positions and postures that represent her perception of their relationships, paying attention to the space between the people, position of arms, facial expression etc.

5. Ask 'the family' to hold the tableau for a few minutes and notice their thoughts and feelings.

6. Ask for feedback in the order in which the bodies were sculpted.

7. Having heard the feedback, ask those involved to change position to one which feels 'right' *without speaking*. This is a dynamic process and may involve people changing position more than once as they are influenced by the moves the others make.

8. Ask 'the family' to hold the tableau again and to notice their thoughts and feelings.

9. Ask for feedback from the 'family'.

10. Ask the observers what they have seen happening.

11. Ask the volunteer to reflect on what has happened. What insights have they gained?

12. De-role the participants.

13. Facilitate general discussion about the issues raised.

to be developed. Experiential workshops are highly suited to helping people become more aware of the processes involved in this kind of relationship.

There are many ways in which we can use creative media to access our own experience and feelings. For example, we can use images (postcards are very useful), music, poetry or objects. This workshop is in two parts. The first part aims to develop our own capacity to listen and by doing so to become more aware of our environment and its impact on ourselves and others, including patients and carers. The second element involves the use of a medium, in this case music, to explore the dynamic relationship between listening and personal disclosure.

Part 1: Listening – what do we really hear? (40 mins)

The session begins with a simple breathing exercise. Breathing only through our noses we imagine a wheel in front of us, which we turn slowly towards us with the in-breath and away from us as we exhale. We connect our breath by making sure that the wheel never stops turning slowly, gently picking up our in breath just as our out breath is finishing. Any tension in the neck or face can often be relieved by placing the tongue between the teeth where it can rest comfortably. Repeat this two or three times, each time counting ten breaths.

At the end of this exercise invite the participants to close their eyes and simply listen to the sound of the room, concentrating on the different sounds that emerge, where they appear to be coming from and anything else that strikes them. After a few minutes invite them to cast their hearing outside the room and to listen to the sounds that seem the furthest away. Can they identify them? Where are they coming from? Finally invite them to slowly return the room and to concentrate once again on the sounds closest to them. Are they the same, has the sound of the room changed, did they bring back any of the sounds from outside the room?

Ask the participants to reflect on this experience. Common themes may begin to emerge such as:

- our hearing seemed to become far more acute as the exercise wore on.
- sounds that we previously had not noticed in the room became much louder, in some cases welcome and in others intrusive.
- listening to sounds in the distance often led us into visualizations. For example, the distant sound of a plane or train can trigger emotions around travel, escape, freedom or fond memories. Some participants may hear the distant roar of traffic, others may hear thunder.
- participants may begin to notice the sound of each others breathing, particularly when bringing their listening back into the room.

How can we relate this experience to practice? What soundscapes might patients encounter? They may hear voices both strange and familiar, whispers outside their room, the breathing of other patients; sounds from the outside world both resonant and symbolic. Listening and paying attention to detail in this way emphasizes not only how acute our listening skills can be but also how much we can overlook in our busy routines. By overlooking, we can miss vital information. The quality of our listening is directly related to the quality of our relationships.

Part 2: Disclosing (80 mins)

Ask each participant to bring a song or piece of music that is important to them to the session. They will each have about five minutes to talk about the piece and why it is important to them and to play an excerpt from it. The personal connection with the music enables us to access directly our own feelings, which may be richly diverse. What people choose to articulate will depend on their beliefs, personality and their relationship with the listeners (other group members). This will determine how they paraphrase and contain often-difficult emotions and how exposed they may feel.

When in the role of listener, participants will need to be aware of their own reactions, the influence of their own tastes and prejudices and their emotional response to the song. Do they already have a relationship with this piece and, if so, do they disclose it? How does this experience influence their relationship with the presenter of the piece?

Ask the participants to reflect on the experience. Common themes might be:

- the development of trust within the group
- surprise at the depth of disclosure
- how an external medium (the song) can enable powerful emotions to be shared and talked about safely
- balancing personal reactions to the music against attending to 'the discloser'
- the relationship between times of personal difficulty and resilience
- decision-making about how much to disclose.

This experience can be related to practice by making links with the extent to which we expect patients to disclose personal information and the importance of our responses. It also provides opportunities to teach about transference and countertransference by highlighting how personal reactions affect what we hear and how we react.

Looking after ourselves

Facilitating workshops can be demanding as this way of teaching is dynamic and influenced by how the group responds to the opportunities offered. As teachers we are constantly challenged to balance different needs and this can feel a bit like walking on a tightrope. Useful questions to check how well we are doing in maintaining this balance are summarized in Box 17.3.

We can help to look after ourselves by working with a co-facilitator who can give feedback and support and by ensuring that we have the time to both prepare and reflect on each workshop. Having regular supervision with an experienced practitioner can legitimize time for reflection and our own continued learning.

Box 17.3 How am I doing?

Can I keep a balance between:

- Structure and flexibility
- Awareness of individuals and awareness of the group
- Teaching content and group process (responses)
- Preparing people to take risks and raising anxiety
- Challenge and safety
- Being myself and sharing my experience while maintaining my role as teacher

---

Conclusion

Experiential workshops are valuable when teaching palliative care and offer rich experiences for developing self-awareness and teaching skills. Facilitators need to plan workshops carefully and to prepare for the unexpected! Workshops such as these will always have the potential to offer people powerful and meaningful learning experiences.

Chapter 18

Teaching large groups

Bee Wee

Introduction

Modern educators often oppose large group teaching, preferring small groups which facilitate interactive, experiential teaching and learning. Large groups can be daunting, both for teachers and students. However, resources are finite and large group teaching remains a reality with which most educators have to grapple sooner or later.

How big is a 'large group'? In this chapter, the term large group refers to class sizes of between 20 to 100 or more. This chapter does not deal with public speaking or conference presentations, for which many publications exist.

The aims of this chapter are to:

◆ explore the pros and cons of large group teaching

◆ confront fears and challenges in such teaching

◆ identify strategies for tackling this.

In palliative care, the most common situations for large group teaching that educators face are: teaching big groups of students in lecture theatre settings and delivering lectures or presentations to large conference audiences. The desire, on the part of the speaker, to convey information and understanding about the message to the audience is common to both situations; the strategies used to achieve this may be different. This chapter focuses on effective *teaching and learning* for large group settings.

Pros and cons

Educators and policy-makers tend to be polarized in the way they think about large group teaching. Proponents of large group teaching view its apparent cost-effectiveness as a significant advantage. It enables mass education to take place in an increasingly busy world. It saves busy lecturers having to repeat their session too many times. Lectures can be an efficient means of transferring core knowledge, explaining concepts, stimulating interest and directing student learning (Cantillon 2003). Some students enjoy the anonymity of the large group setting because they find small groups too intense and exposing.

Critics of large group teaching assert that it is no more economical than other methods and that the claim of being able to achieve greater coverage of the material is false. Lectures enable teachers to cover more ground but that does not necessarily mean that students achieve the same breadth or depth (Ramsden 1992). Students may be passive and dependent during lectures or become bored or somnolent.

Such debates often hinge around assumptions about what 'large group teaching' looks like. One stereotypical image is of a lone lecturer, standing at the front of the room, often behind a lectern, speaking didactically for their entire allotted time to a silent mass of individuals, some of whom are doodling, morose or even asleep. The lecturer grimly holds forth for fear that, once they stop speaking, the group will turn into an unruly mass and control would be lost. Of course, the problem here is lack of engagement and interaction with the learners, something which can happen, whatever the size of the group, unless effective teaching strategies are used. The focus of discussion should be on how to promote active learning in large group teaching, not on the number of students in the group. Therefore, it is worth confronting the fears and challenges posed by large group teaching.

Fears and challenges

The underlying concerns in teachers who are fearful of large group teaching seem to focus around exposure and loss of control. Teachers who do not regard themselves as natural performers envy those who appear to be self-confident and at ease with large audiences. They compare themselves unfavourably whereas it is preferable to focus on identifying and playing to their own strengths. This is more likely to build confidence in their own style. Teachers may also believe it is more difficult to acknowledge that they don't know the answer to a particular question in a large group than in a small one. They may deal with this by filling their entire allotted time, thereby denying the audience the opportunity to ask potentially awkward questions, nor any illuminating or stimulating ones.

Large group teaching brings a stronger probability that learners' prior knowledge, ability and interest will be varied. Palliative care teachers often encounter large groups of undergraduate students, at least a proportion of whom have been 'conscripted' and may feel resentful or even hostile. This creates apprehension in the palliative care teacher who may miss the point that those students have at least turned up and there is opportunity to capture their interest. As in any other group teaching, however small or large, the challenge of the dominating voices and withdrawn individuals have to be faced. The issue of equity and ensuring that minority views are heard and respected may be more challenging when teaching large groups.

The content of the teaching may pose a challenge. Teachers in some subjects suffer from the inherently dry nature of their subject. This is rarely true of palliative care, where the material is usually interesting, engaging and often moving. However, powerful emotions can be evoked and palliative care teachers need to make careful judgements about when and how to use such material to enhance learning. It is irresponsible and unhelpful to use sensitive material purely to evoke emotional responses amongst learners.

Finally, the teaching environment itself may pose other challenges. The size and shape of the room and seating arrangements both have big implications. Fixed seating hinders student movement. Mobile chairs are often set in theatre style in order to accommodate the required number of students in a room. Teachers and learners need to be able to see and hear each other with reasonable ease. Audiovisual aids may bring their own difficulties: technical hitches, lack of flexibility to divert away from prepared slides and opportunity and temptation for the teacher to hide behind the aids.

Table 18.1 Emotional impact of large group teaching (Hogan and Kwiatkowski 1998)

	Concerns
Students	Able to be 'invisible' or hide within large groups Able to remain passive and detached observers Feel isolated and alienated Difficulty finding a voice within these groups Difficulty getting engaged in non-aggressive dispute with others Increased anxiety may lead to diminished ability to pay attention to what is going on Subgroups and cliques may form – these may become disruptive or a focus for anger, resentment or fear for others
Teachers	Fear of exposure – brace themselves for attack, real or imagined; appear defensive High anxiety and stress levels Less satisfaction in teaching

Hogan and Kwiatkowski (1998) raise concern about the emotional impact of large group teaching and learning. Many strategies have been suggested to help teachers retain control, often through technical solutions such as audiovisual aids, or the use of small group work and student-centred approaches to promote student independence in learning. Hogan and Kwiatkowski argue that these strategies sidestep the main issue, i.e. that large groups inevitably have an emotional impact on lecturers and students (their concerns are set out in Table 18.1). They contend that if this is not acknowledged and grappled with, the problems are often exacerbated and that some teachers may adopt maladaptive practices, for example over-preparing for lectures or trying to be either over-friendly or too distant and remote with students. Their main concern was that these difficulties are often attributed by students and staff to individual failure and weakness, rather than being regarded and tackled as a group-related issue.

Managing large group teaching

Building teacher confidence

The prerequisite to building confidence as a teacher, particularly for large groups, is planning. This does not necessarily mean spending hours prior to the teaching session, which may help to boost some teachers' confidence but is not practical for most people and may be counterproductive. The essential ingredient is clear thinking time, however brief, devoted to both content and process. Many inexperienced teachers make the mistake of paying too much attention to the content, fearful of not appearing credible or knowledgeable to their students. Most palliative care practitioners underestimate the level of knowledge and understanding they have of their subject, particularly from practice, and further undermine their own confidence by being unwilling to admit when they do not know the answer to a question. One approach which this author has used in helping less confident palliative care teachers to build confidence is set out in Box 18.1.

Box 18.1 Building teacher confidence – one example

Context: One hour session on 'palliative care' for Senior House Officers (SHOs)

Group size: Potentially up to 40

Environment: Elongated seminar room; SHOs seated around large table; latecomers sitting behind those at the table; all eating lunch

Teachers: One palliative medicine consultant and one clinical nurse specialist (CNS); the latter is relatively inexperienced at teaching large groups of doctors

Process: Consultant chairs the session

    SHOs brainstorm topics they wished to cover – recorded on flipchart

    Voting to establish priority

    Consultant picks the first topic – teaches around it to warm up the group

    Consultant picks the second topic – refers to a recent clinical scenario relevant to this topic, in which the palliative care team was involved; invites the CNS to join in the discussion and gradually take over centre stage; consultant remains alert and chips in occasionally but leaves the CNS as the lead teacher

    Consultant picks up a third topic – invites the CNS to illustrate this with a real case study and continue taking the lead on this discussion.

By now the links between practice and teaching have become explicit and the two teachers and the SHOs settle into clinically grounded interactive teaching and learning. As chair, the consultant continues to take responsibility for timekeeping and ensuring that the relevant topics are covered but ensures the CNS (co-teacher) remains fully involved.

NB: In the above example, it happens to be the consultant who leads and chairs the session. This approach can be similarly used by any professional, with the more experienced teacher chairing and supporting the less experienced teacher, provided the latter has sufficient clinical experience to draw upon.

Teachers also develop their confidence and competence in teaching through other activities. Peer observation and feedback and some other approaches are described in Chapter 23 (p 257). Careful collection of student feedback can help the teacher to focus on areas of weakness. Although nerve-wracking and prone to technical difficulties, video recording of oneself teaching in large groups can provide the opportunity for critical review and suggest ideas for improvement, particularly if this is carried out in a safe environment with a trusted, but not overly reassuring, colleague.

Planning a large group teaching session

Teachers need to decide the key learning outcomes, i.e. what they hope students will have learnt by the end of that session. These should be simple, realistic and achievable within the time allotted to that session. These are important in any teaching event but even more so in large group teaching where it is more difficult for individual students to gain clarification about the aims of the session once it begins.

Once learning outcomes have been defined, teaching strategies need to be matched to these. Teachers may draw upon their understanding of different frameworks of teaching (see Chapter 1, p 2) to design learning activities which are appropriate for the subject and students with different learning styles and which are most likely to deliver the desired learning outcomes. Learning activities which incorporate dialogue and discussion are more likely to encourage a deeper level of learning than activities which encourage factual recall only.

Key points to keep in mind when planning lectures are set out in Box 18.2.

Managing large groups

Silencing noisy large groups can be difficult and will usually involve the teacher capturing the audience's attention by shouting, waving, holding up a hand or two, speaking loudly or standing quietly but prominently in the room and waiting until a sufficient number of people have noticed and quietened. Injecting energy and life into silent large groups can be equally difficult but is essential to promote active learning. One way to do this is by using 'buzz groups'. Learners are asked to undertake a task in pairs or threes, depending on the seating arrangements. They may be given time for brief individual reflection before 'buzzing', for example two to three minutes. It is surprising what people can think of in such a short time. After discussing or buzzing in pairs or trios, probably the most valuable part of the exercise, they join up with another pair or trio, usually in the row in front or behind, thus avoiding too much physical movement. This may be to share what they have already discussed or they may be given a further task which builds on their previous discussion. However this is done, it is vital that the tasks given to them are clear, meaningful and achievable within the allotted time. It may be valuable to write the instructions down explicitly on a flipchart. Generally buzz groups are brief and should last no more than 10 minutes at a time, but this exercise can be repeated later on.

Another advantage of using buzz groups is that individuals can share responsibility for the responses they offer to the rest of the class. This is less daunting than a lone voice, particularly if the view turns out to be a minority one. Each buzz group may have been asked to negotiate a rapporteur at the start to avoid the shuffling that can occur when responses are invited. If, on the other hand, the task requires a specific contribution from each individual in the buzz group, the teacher may include an element of timing. Each individual is then allotted a specific amount of time to speak without interruption, for example two to five minutes per person. The teacher needs to call time to ensure that each person, however dominant or quiet, gets an equal space to speak.

Holme (1992) describes a variation of this, bringing in the concept of the Socratic method. Classically, this is the method used by Socrates in which he develops his learners' understanding and challenges their assumptions by questioning and probing, getting them to come up with the answers themselves. Holmes describes how the teacher roams around the lecture theatre, throwing out questions to a group of students nearby.

Box 18.2 Planning and delivering lectures

Planning the lecture

- Be clear about aims, learning outcomes and essential points
- Be realistic about what can be achieved
- Be clear about the structure, shape and flow of session: how should it begin and end; what are the sections; are the links logical and explicit; include clear signposts of when moving from one section to another; how can you help students make links to previous learning and/or practice;

Deciding on teaching aids

- Do you need any?
- What aids are appropriate in terms of clear visibility for size of group and room?
- How flexible does each aid allow you to be?
- If using slides, keep them clear and simple

Delivering the lecture

- Introduce yourself clearly
- Give a clear introduction about title and aim of session
- Consider whether an ice-breaker is necessary or helpful
- Be mindful of your voice – don't gabble or mumble; don't drop your voice at the end of sentences; can those at the back hear?
- Questions from the audience – repeat the question for the benefit of those at the back
- Make eye contact around the room
- Incorporate opportunities for active learning – buzz groups; questions; individual tasks; keep in mind different aspects of the learning cycle (see Chapter 1, p 4); build in opportunity for debate and discussion
- Periodically remind students of structure of lecture and where you are at
- Slow down when explaining complicated concepts or showing complex graphs or text: allow learners time to absorb, understand and clarify
- Summarize key points or take home messages at the end; help students consider how they develop their learning further.

After the lecture

- Write down a few comments for yourself about what you might do differently next time – don't forget the things you did well and want to retain too
- Review student feedback and consider these in the light of your own reflections.

These students form an instantaneous buzz group in order to answer the question. The teacher moves on, developing the lecture by asking further questions of other groups of students. Occasionally the teacher elaborates teaching points further, in the form of a mini lecture, but the main thrust of the session is based on questioning in order to develop learning around the topic. Suchman *et al.* (2000), showed that 'small groups in large lectures can be an effective learning tool provided students are given well-designed activities with clearly defined, obtainable goals and clearly articulated guidelines' (2000: 121). It is this last that is vital but often missing in large group teaching.

Sometimes, experienced teachers may wish to give their audience a choice about the areas they wish the teaching to focus on. This can be an extremely effective way of motivating an audience and keeping the learning relevant for them, but equity of opinion is difficult to achieve in large groups so a majority view tends to prevail. Sometimes a dominant group of students may appear to be espousing the majority view, even if they are in fact a smaller number of individuals, and the teacher needs to be alert to this possibility. Voting is a simple and effective strategy for managing this. In smaller large groups, this can be achieved by giving each participant a set number of votes, expressed through marking on flipcharts, post-it notes or sticky dots. Participants may assign as many or all of their votes as they wish to one option if they feel sufficiently strongly. This has the added advantage of getting participants out of their seats if they have to move to the front of the room to place their votes. This is clearly impractical in even larger groups where participants need to remain seated and where a show of hands is most commonly used. Other methods that have been tried include coloured cards, as used in *Ready, Steady, Cook* (a cookery competition television programme in the UK and Ireland) or, rarely, electronic voting. For more major decisions, for example, deciding whether an important topic ought to be taught within the class or devolved to self-directed learning, participants can be asked to scribble their vote on a piece of torn-off paper and someone counts these.

Managing the content

Stories are a powerful medium for teaching, particularly in palliative care. They can be used to illustrate teaching, or to set a scene, and can provide the scaffolding for active learning. The story may be unfolded in stages, with the learners required to consider options and make decisions. This serves as punctuation points in the teaching session, with students buzzing or working individually on their responses. Groups of students may be given cases to work on, either within the teaching session itself or between sessions. Students may be given the task of bringing cases to the large group teaching session, swapping these with other groups or discussing them in plenary.

Patients and carers may be prepared to participate in large group teaching. Some palliative care practitioners argue that this is inappropriate when dealing with frail and vulnerable patients. However, many patients do enjoy contributing as lay teachers. Denying them the chance to accept or reject this opportunity is maternalistic and disrespectful. These events must be carefully managed and these lay teachers, as well as the learners, need to be adequately prepared and debriefed (see Chapter 13, p 119).

Teachers who cling tightly to a prepared lecture often do so because they are concerned that they will not be able to cover the required material if they allow any diversion. In doing so, they fail to make the most of learning that can come from the informal curriculum (see Chapter 1, p 2). The concern about covering specific topics is legitimate, particularly in palliative care where opportunities to teach undergraduates may be rare. However, there are other ways to help students cover material that gets excluded from the lecture because of diversion. Clear learning outcomes alert students to what the session had intended to cover, so that they can pursue any gaps themselves. Comprehensive annotated reading lists, supplementary handouts and additional material on the web are further resources. The teacher should devote a few minutes at the end of the lecture directing students to sources for further learning.

Throughout the session, teachers may wish to stop at certain points and ask students to write down key learning points for themselves. This is akin to the summarizing stage that we often use in communicating with patients. It provides an opportunity to take stock and check understanding, before moving on to a different section. Teachers may also take the opportunity to ask a few questions or run a mini quiz at those points. Web-based tools can be useful to support smaller group discussions beyond large lecture theatre-based teaching (Harden 2003).

The one-minute paper is a technique typically used at the end of the class. Each student is asked to write the most important thing they learnt and one question that remains unanswered. Students are literally given one or two minutes only to complete the exercise. The papers are collected and the teacher responds to the unanswered question individually or at the next class. Stead (2005) reports that students find this a useful learning technique. It is simple and flexible if sufficient time is allowed for it, but Stead cautions against using it excessively.

Further examples of strategies for large group teaching are shown in Table 18.2.

Environment

There is often little that a teacher can do about the environment. Most teachers, in palliative care or otherwise, can recount nightmare scenarios they have experienced of unsuitable teaching environments. What is important, however, is that the teacher examines the environment beforehand, if possible, and adapts it for the session accordingly. If this is not possible, an open sharing with the audience that 'we are in this together' can often enhance the relationship between the teacher and students, even in the worst circumstances. But teachers must never hide behind unsuitable environments as the excuse to abandon the effort of teaching or give up on helping the students to learn as effectively as possible.

Respect for the learners, which is an essential component of teaching, is almost always reciprocated. Another manifestation of respect for learners is good timekeeping. Starting on time rewards learners who have made the effort to turn up on time and sends out an important message to late comers for future teaching events. Finishing on time is equally essential. Not infrequently, teachers are confounded by previous speakers who run over time or by unavoidable problems such as the fire alarm going off. Teachers who can reduce or modify their plans and avoid exacting their pound of flesh are deeply appreciated.

Table 18.2 Examples of large group teaching strategies from literature

Activity (source)	Brief description
Integrated learning activity (Newble 2003)	Students view video of real patient then work in facilitated small groups within the lecture theatre. They work through problem definition, problem analysis and identify learning needs, which are then shared and collated for the whole class. Students leave with an agreed list of learning tasks to guide a period of self-directed learning. They have one facilitated small group tutorial and web-based guidance, then reconvene as a whole class to share learning and unanswered questions are tackled.
Active participation and learning in large groups (Nierenberg 1998)	Start learning exercise with clinical example or anecdote to demonstrate relevance of material. Frequently ask students whether they have ever seen examples of what is being described in their previous experience with patients, personal experience, etc. and whether they have heard similar material presented differently in other courses. Recruit students to help solve 'mystery cases' presented to them. Show examples of similar material from real life (e.g. patient descriptions or excerpts from favourite TV shows). Ask students to help summarize key points at the end of the session.
Cooperative groups (Ebert-May et al. 1997)	Students randomly assigned to permanent cooperative groups whose members were changed only if the group was not productive. Each group is given a question to probe students' prior knowledge and understanding (how, why, explain-type questions) – given 1 minute individual reflection and 3–5 minutes group discussion time. Mini-lecture, followed by further exploratory questions. Group quiz at the end of session.
Problem solving clinical seminars (Struyf et al. 2005)	Students are given a booklet with a series of clinical cases. Before the seminar, students study the case individually, discuss answers in groups of five and submit group report at start of seminar. One rapporteur per group speaks at seminar, followed by facilitated group discussion.
Collaborative learning groups (McKinney and Graham-Buxton 1993)	Brief written individual response to a projected question in lecture theatre. Students then move into groups of 3–5 to work out group response. Each individual response and written group response stapled together and submitted. Grade awarded to each student is the average of the individual and group score. This emphasizes the concept of interdependency and stops the 'free riders' who cannot participate unless they have an individual response to bring to the 'party'. Found that average grades improved with the introduction of collaborative learning groups.
Peer assessment (Learning and Teaching Support Network 2001)	Students are set problems to solve in their own time. At the start of class, they swap work with another student and the lecturer leads them through a model solution.

Those who have thought this through beforehand will be able to adapt their session quickly to ensure that the most important components are covered in this way. Students will remember a few key learning points whereas a plethora of information crammed into a reduced time will be lost.

Conclusion

Except for conferences, didactic large group teaching is out of place in modern education. Mere transmission of fact does nothing for deep learning and understanding. However, with interactive learning, large group teaching can be both effective and fun. It is practical and can be cost-effective, particularly in palliative care, where we need to reach large numbers of people with limited teaching resources and time. Like any other forms of teaching, careful planning and purposeful choices about both the content and process of the session are necessary. Interactive lecturing with the teacher talking 'with' rather than 'at' learners can be stimulating and rewarding for both teachers and learners.

Chapter 19

Distance learning

Stephen Jones and Ilora Finlay

Introduction

As Bosworth (1991) notes, the traditional image of distance (or open) learning is the correspondence course, where the student and the tutor/institution communicate intermittently by the use of paper and the postal service. Distance learning has evolved to mean various things to different people. There is now a myriad of distance learning programmes, offered and delivered across the globe, at all levels of complexity and utilizing the latest advances in technology. This chapter examines some of the issues that potential students should consider as they attempt to make sense of the opportunities available and select the right course.

Key considerations include:

- reasons for choosing distance learning
- understanding learning needs
- what to expect from a distance learning programme
- effectiveness of distance learning.

While intending to encourage students, we acknowledge some of the pitfalls that may be encountered, in order to help the student develop an advance strategy to cope with them. Practical tips are offered throughout the chapter, including 'phone box figures' that encourage the student to contact the distance learning provider and ask pertinent questions.

What can you expect from a distance learning programme?

You should expect:

- to be treated as an adult, capable of taking ownership for your own learning
- reflective learning – learning to effectively critique both your own and others' work
- ongoing assessment – both formative and summative
- feedback – support from the course tutors and guidance on how well you are doing (or not!)
- relevance – for work-related programmes, there should be a link to career and professional self-development.

Adult learning

Cantor (1992) noted that adults generally have different motivations for learning than children. Not surprisingly, the way in which adults are taught, a set of assumptions known as andragogy, differs considerably from the teaching of children, not least in that the responsibility for learning moves significantly from the tutor to the learner. Distance learning programmes acknowledge the following four concepts of adult learning identified by Knowles *et al.* (1998):

1. Adults need to be involved in the planning and evaluation of their learning. Distance learning places a great deal of control into students' hands, as they can (usually within limits) determine the pace and direction of their study

2. Experience, including the making of mistakes, is a key component of adult learning. A distance learning programme that is centred on students' everyday clinical practice allows closer interaction between the educational programme and their "real-life" experiences

3. Adults show most interest in studying those subjects that have immediate relevance to their roles. A distance learning programme that links each educational component to both the student's career aims and individual clinical practice will be the most attractive

4. Adult learning should be problem-centred. By using role-based scenarios which apply learning to the student's current clinical practice, a good distance learning course offers a learning experience that students can apply immediately to their own role.

From Von Prummer's (2000) work there also appear to be differences in learning styles between genders, with women exhibiting a preference for learning to be conducted, at least in part, within a social context. It flows from this that women students in particular may gain more from distance learning programmes that are supported by occasional residential study blocks, telephone conversations and local, informal support networks, each of which fosters direct contact between students, and between students and staff. This is also supported by Bosworth (1991) in his review of research in this area, which suggests a more general desire among co-learners to 'come together' at some point(s) in the programme.

Moore (1993) identified three key interactions in autonomous learning situations, such as distance learning, which are key to successful outcomes, namely between:

- learner and content
- learner and tutor
- learner and other learners.

Box 19.1 Learning styles

Each of us has our own preference for the way in which we learn. For those who wish to know more about their own preferences and how best to apply them, Honey and Mumford (1992) have developed a very helpful learning styles questionnaire.

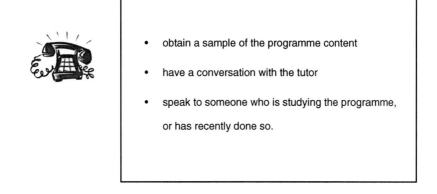

- obtain a sample of the programme content

- have a conversation with the tutor

- speak to someone who is studying the programme, or has recently done so.

Fig. 19.1 Before you join a programme.

The best professional development programmes offer students a reasonable measure of control over what they learn, how it is learned, and when and where their learning takes place. Garavan (1997) emphasizes the importance of the student's active participation in the learning process. Of, arguably, even greater importance, is the need to make all aspects of this learning reflective.

Reflective learning

While reflective learning is considered in more detail in Chapter 15 (p 137), it is worth emphasizing how important an aspect this is in an effective distance learning programme. Reflective activity can be undertaken at two distinct points: during an event, or after an event. Busy practitioners may wonder where the time can be created to engage effectively in reflective activity, but this should not be considered as a daunting activity. Reflection permits an effective critique on personal or group activity, focused on that activity in practice, permitting that practice to be developed in light of current understanding of the relevant issues and acknowledged best practice. Over time, the practitioner will adopt an approach that permits reflection on the issue both during and after the event, where the post-event reflection may be conducted as a group activity, possibly in an online community.

Assessment

Throughout a programme of study students expect feedback on their performance, both to highlight the strengths of their work and to identify areas for improvement. A good distance learning programme will include both formative and summative assessment at various times and stages. The distinction between these two categories of assessment may be expressed by the point in the programme at which the assessment occurs.

Formative assessment is typically conducted from the beginning of, and throughout, a programme. Hodgson (1993) describes this as 'the ongoing process of improving'. As its purpose is to improve the quality of student learning and enhance the student experience, it is not evaluative, i.e. formative assessment provides guidance rather than grades or marks, but it still provides an opportunity to learn. Students also play an important role in their formative assessment through self-evaluation. By providing contextual opportunities within the programme for professional development activities, the student gains maximum value from applying the learning to a real world situation, while receiving feedback that is both structured and helpful.

In comparison, *summative assessment* takes place at the end of the programme (or stage thereof) to ensure students have achieved the learning outcomes. It provides a measure of accountability for the quality of the programme. This assessment leads to grades or marks for the student.

Feedback opportunities

Distance learning can be a very isolating experience (Philpot 1997; Purcell-Robertson and Purcell 2000; Simpson 2000). In addition to the structural feedback offered by assessments, there should therefore be innumerable opportunities for the tutor and student to communicate and offer/receive support.

Good communication

Communication is the foundation stone in distance learning and it is imperative that the student is able to keep in regular contact with their tutor(s), the programme material and the administrative team. Today, email provides a prompt and relatively inexpensive method to keep in touch, which is a significant advantage in those parts of the world where local postal systems are unreliable. This is particularly important where course work has to be submitted by scheduled dates.

Supporting learners

The effectiveness of support from the distance learning team makes all the difference to the student experience. Bosworth (1991) draws a clear distinction between *supported self-study* and *self-supported study*, with the emphasis clearly on 'support'. Nevertheless, as Talbot (2003) points out, the emphasis is more on the 'learner *learning*', rather than the 'teacher *teaching*'. She also notes that support from both tutors and fellow students can be critical to success.

Unlike the students, the tutors are familiar with the programme and can empathize with the student's situation. The student should therefore maximize the benefit to be gained from the tutors' advice. A friendly tutor with a good knowledge of their subject may be important, but one who has been in the student's position themselves is invaluable. As Simpson (2000) notes, a support system can benefit students by:

- helping them clarify and contextualize their problem
- conceptualizing their problems, which offers new insights
- challenging their thinking.

While telephone support may seem a very attractive method, because of its convenience and immediacy, it can prove difficult and frustrating to make contact when both student and tutor are busy clinical practitioners. When such calls are international, there are additional problems with costs and time zone differences.

Race (1998) highlights the critical issue, for tutors, of giving effective feedback. Tutors need to embrace the enthusiasm that the students bring to their learning, but also recognize their anxiety. They need to recognize the cross-cultural sensitivities that can be offended by a lack of care and/or precision in their written feedback. If it's difficult to phrase in writing, why not pick up the phone and discuss it directly?

Career and self-development

Many practitioners see further learning as a key component of their career development. There has been a sea change in the nature of professional training and careers in the UK over the last decade. Consequently, as Hirsch and Jackson (1996) suggest, 'career' is being less thought of as a progression up an organizational ladder and more as a descriptor of an individual's professional experience over time. As Kanter (1989) and MacDermid *et al.* (2001) note, many professionals who think carefully about their careers have recognized that enhanced learning opportunities and reputation are, at least, as advantageous as formal promotion.

In a study conducted by Hirsch (2000), 71 per cent saw career management as their own responsibility. So how can distance learning help individuals to manage their career development? Because distance learning rarely requires the student to abandon their current role, it has the flexibility to be complementary to their work. It is doubly advantageous if it offers the capacity for that study to be based directly around the work itself, giving greater immediacy and relevance.

Distance learning is a good exemplar of self-development as the individual conceives, plans and controls much of their own learning. According to Hague (1978) the essence of self-development is that the individual takes the initiative in challenging and stretching themself, within real situations. As Preston and Biddle (1994) emphasize the notion of continuous learning within career paths and Frazee (1996) suggests that self-development is best attained through 'regular daily doses', distance learning would seem ideally placed to support such approaches.

Learning needs

What are the students' needs?

Many students will have a specific stimulus to learn. For example they may be:

- already working in the palliative care field and looking for a particular qualification for career development
- looking to change their career direction into palliative care and need to develop greater knowledge or particular skills

- just interested in the subject, for wider professional development or continuing professional education, but without necessarily gaining further qualifications
- looking for new stimulation which breaks their established routine at home or work and offers a new dimension to their life.

Through a clear understanding of their needs, it will be easier for students to assess how well individual distance learning programmes meet these.

Are clinicians' needs different?

Many clinicians will be on a programme of higher professional training, such as the Specialist Registrar programme in the UK, and should give thought to the relevance of the end point qualification to their career path. There are clear advantages to be gained from educational courses that recognize links to other professional training e.g. where activities count to both educational qualifications and the requirements of higher professional training.

To what extent does the provider recognize and credit previous study?

Most institutions now offer a variety of entry routes and the standardization of postgraduate qualifications has simplified these processes. There are two main routes:

1. *Accreditation of prior learning* (APL) enables a student with a qualification or part-qualification to enter another programme, in the same or a different educational institution, directly at a point in the study programme other than the initial entry point. For example, a postgraduate certificate in palliative care from one institution may allow the student to enter directly a postgraduate diploma programme at another.

2. *Accreditation of prior experiential learning* (APEL) permits the educational institution to recognize the student's prior experience in the palliative care field, without reference to specific educational attainment. For example, the student may be able to demonstrate that they have satisfactorily covered all the material relating to one module or one year of a study programme. This similarly may permit entry directly at a point in the study programme other than the initial entry point.

Is the qualification valued and/or professionally recognized?

It is worthwhile assessing the value that a particular qualification will offer a student, who should check with the appropriate professional body whether the qualification being considered is on their approved list.

Consult professional colleagues to see how many of them have either studied or considered studying for the qualification. Ask them for their opinions on the course and, importantly, how it has helped them develop their career paths.

Box 19.2 The value of the qualification

- What qualification(s) will the programme lead to?
- Is the qualification widely known and respected in the palliative care field?
- Who is the awarding body and what reputation does it have?
- Is the qualification well known and respected by palliative care colleagues and the wider profession?

What qualifications are offered?

Are there options to exit at various points in the programme with one of a range of qualifications? A good course will recognize one of the key realities of adult learning: students may change jobs, become pregnant, fall ill, or lose motivation. It can respond with various solutions that accommodate students' needs and preferences. This may include permitting formal study breaks, extended completion times or opportunities to graduate with an interim qualification.

Why study palliative care?

As Hillier and Wee highlight, 'many of the skills in palliative care are useful in every other health setting' (2001: 468). A good palliative care programme will be equally valuable whether palliative care forms the core or just an occasional component of the student's role. Kenny (2003) stresses the strong link between good clinical practice and education in cancer and palliative care, such that it is difficult to develop one without the other. But can the all-important artistry of palliative care be taught by distance learning?

Hillier and Wee (2001) suggest that professional artistry cannot be learned from books. While this may be true (and the reason a purely correspondence programme would be unsuitable for palliative care education), it is contended that a comprehensive distance learning programme with residential study periods and a strong audiovisual component, whether online or not, can permit effective teaching of both judgemental and communication skills, and interprofessional working.

Kaufman (2003) suggests that effective reflective learning is one aspect by which professionals may develop artistry in their practice. As noted above, if distance learning does promote reflective practice, it flows from this that such a programme is suitable to educate clinicians from all backgrounds in aspects of the artistry of palliative care.

Why study at a distance?

Some of the reasons why individuals follow distance learning pathways include:

- a desire not to take a break, or a difficulty in being released, from work
- to complement part-time work or family responsibilities

♦ a lack of suitable learning opportunities in their geographical region

♦ reduced costs, in comparison to other programmes.

What are the alternatives?

1. Attending a part-time programme at a local centre, within reasonable commuting distance:
   ♦ will there be a need to reduce working hours?
   ♦ would employers offer financial support?
   ♦ what are the financial and time implications of commuting?
   ♦ can students commit to a regular pattern of attendance?

2. Attending a full time programme at a centre within their home country or abroad:
   ♦ can students cope with the loss of income for 1–2 years?
   ♦ do they have sufficient funds to meet all the course fees and living expenses while being a full-time student?
   ♦ will their employer keep their job open for them at the end of the course?
   ♦ would a year's sabbatical adversely affect their career plans?

3. Deferring (or abandoning) plans for further study:
   ♦ will the situation be better or worse in one or two years time?
   ♦ could the lack of the qualification adversely affect their promotion prospects and/or career plans?

Does distance learning work?

Yes, where the student approaches distance learning with the right attitude and motivation. Some of the qualities desirable in the ideal distance learning student would include:

♦ good self-discipline and the self-confidence to work independently

♦ effective organization and time-management skills

♦ good IT skills, where e-learning is a component of the programme

♦ the ability to pace their learning and incorporate it effectively into other dimensions of their lives (work, family, health)

♦ creating an effective support network (colleagues, employer, family, tutors) that accommodates conflicting demands.

Distance learning programmes have certainly withstood the test of time. Bell and Tight (1993) note, for example, the strength of the distance examining system operated by the University of London since its inception in 1836. Rumble and Oliveira (1992) acknowledge that the success of distance learning programmes has led to a re-evaluation of their contribution as a legitimate and effective means of study. At the same time, there has been an increasing acceptance that the skills taught by distance education have effectively moved beyond cognitive (comprehension and understanding) skills, to include teaching of psychomotor (practical skills) and affective (values and emotions) concepts. This makes distance learning highly applicable to professional education.

Talbot (2003) suggests that a key corollary of distance learning is that students become better *learners*. In addition to the subject matter being learned, students gain valuable skills to enable them to become independent lifelong learners. As distance learning spans many cultures, Williams *et al.* (1999) point out that students and tutors also benefit from the cross-cultural understanding that flows from such programmes.

Salmon (2004) considers the key success factors to be time, motivation and the quality of support. Over time, a great deal has been learned, researched and delivered along the way to enable distance learning programmes to evolve to meet student needs. So, for many people, distance learning works. However, there are further relevant questions that the potential student should ask, and have answered to their satisfaction, before embarking on a programme of study. These are considered further in this chapter, but may best be encapsulated as 'it works, but is it for me?'

How is distance learning different from other forms of learning?

Distance learning and open learning

Confusingly, there has been a tendency to use terms interchangeably, with 'distance', 'open' and 'flexible' learning meaning different things to different people. As Bosworth (1991) points out, the important thing is that, irrespective of descriptors, the student clearly understands exactly what they are being offered. Fletcher (2001) contrasts distance learning, as a function of geography, with open learning as a function of time. The student has the freedom to determine how much time to devote and when to do so. Flexible learning, in his view, is an overarching term. Lewis and Spencer (1986) suggest that open learning describes a programme with a learner-centred approach which attempts to overcome traditional barriers of access to education, giving greater autonomy to the student.

As Von Prummer (2000) suggests, while the 'distance' aspect of distance learning is primarily thought to acknowledge geographical distinctiveness, there are traditional and established learning systems across the world that may be constrained by gender, national, cultural or institutional factors. Distance learning programmes therefore have the potential to transcend these boundaries.

Open learning does not require a geographical dimension, as Talbot (2003) suggests, whereas distance learning implies an element of remoteness. Bates (2005) emphasizes that openness is goal-directed to the removal of access barriers, and may be considered as an education policy, whereas distance education is a method of achieving this policy. However, distance learning programmes may not be open if barriers to access (e.g. compulsory attendance at a central location for some aspect of the programme, ready access to particular types of technology, or specified educational attainment prior to entry) exist. Distance learning and open learning cannot be considered synonymous.

What about e-learning?

This involves a particular delivery medium – electronic technology. The Internet, according to Bates (2005) has revolutionized distance learning programmes, but the technology makes it equally applicable to both traditional and distance learning. One of the advantages of e-learning, identified by Fletcher (2001) is 'the ease of asynchronous communication by email'. This type of communication method works well in distance learning programmes, where many students may be distributed across time zones. It overcomes the limited availability of office hours, provided there is an acceptable response time.

Bates (2005) suggests that commercial forces have been behind the growth in e-learning, rather than promotion of the philosophy of openness. The wider availability of home computers and faster Internet access has fuelled this growth. Williams *et al.* (1999) suggest growth has been encouraged by faster telecommunications networks and the improved reliability of home computer systems. Nevertheless, despite the popularity among doctors of the internet as a learning tool, Curran and Fleet (2005) found that most evaluation had been directed toward user satisfaction rather than changes to clinical practice. Despite innovative approaches and continued growth as a learning medium, no evidence was available to show any particular type of web-based learning changed actual practice.

Nevertheless, Cook and Dupras (2004) suggest e-learning has great potential, as the student sets the pace of the learning. This potential is reinforced in Hacker and Niederhauser's (2000) view as an opportunity to build upon existing online delivery systems. The self pacing element of e-learning is emphasized by Race (1996) and Clark (2002) as leading to higher retention of learning content.

Some challenges with e-learning

Students and tutors alike may be computer-phobic, but computers play as integral a part in clinical practice as any other aspect of life. Using a computer effectively has now become a life skill and an e-learning programme can help develop this. How? Use the resources available – play with the Internet, use it to research something. This is an important component of learning to learn.

Key areas where online sensitivity is needed by users, as Salmon (2004) highlights, include the expectations of formality and hierarchy in online activities: issues of openness, age, gender, forms of address and relative status have greater significance in some societies than others. Be aware of this.

Factors which determine when and where distance learning works best

Realistic student expectations

Potential students should conduct careful research before deciding to study by distance learning. For many, this will be a return to study after a considerable period outside an academic environment. Returning to an environment with deadlines, coursework submitted by a variety of means (e.g. writing essays, projects, audits and/or reports), and possibly formal examination, may prove to be quite a culture shock. In addition, many established

> ## Box 19.3 Practical considerations in distance learning
>
> - Does the programme acknowledge some of the cultural sensitivities that may apply to you and your clinical setting e.g. language, gender power balance?
> - Will the programme structure allow your daily routine to continue?
> - Do you have sufficient self-discipline to undertake distance learning?
> - Have you considered how you will ensure that you stay motivated in the depths of winter or when work pressures pile up?
> - Do you have the explicit support of colleagues and family for the duration of the programme?
> - Are you able to guarantee yourself some protected time for directed self-study?
> - Are there any unresolved emotional issues that would surface as a result of palliative care studies, e.g. the recent death of a family member or close friend?
> - Will you be able to cope with your tutor being at a considerable geographical distance?
> - If you are studying outside the UK, have you thought about the effect of different time zones upon communication?

practitioners may be unfamiliar (and uncomfortable!) with having their professional opinions, as expressed in their coursework, scrutinized and challenged. Some practical aspects are considered in Box 19.3.

Clear learning objectives

The programme should be explicit about what the student will have learned and may expect to be able to do upon successful completion. It should also have sufficient flexibility built into its delivery. Clarke (2001) notes the importance of giving the students some choice within the overall framework, to meet their specific needs. For example, if the student has a real life issue in advanced pain management, it would be frustrating and demotivating if this part of the programme was not accessible until the next term.

Good support mechanisms

Clarke (2001) suggests that the programme should make clear at the outset the range and extent of student support, whether this is:

- built into the material, e.g. frequently asked questions (FAQs), further reading and resources, etc.
- provided by the tutor(s), e.g. face-to-face, telephone conversations, emails or postal feedback
- provided by fellow students, e.g. informal local help groups, moderated online chat rooms, etc.

Box 19.4 Learn to study effectively

- Establish a study pattern or routine and keep to it;
- Take short breaks from study at regular intervals – especially if you're using a VDU/computer;
- Don't let study eat into your sleep time – you will not get the best out of study time if you're overtired;
- Limit your intake of caffeine and alcohol – neither makes for a clear head;
- Expect the unexpected, from the sublime to the ridiculous (e.g. the book you need urgently from the library is on loan, your phone line is damaged by workmen in the street, etc.) and allow for them in your study plan. If it can go wrong, it probably will – but not until you least need it to!

The components of an effective support system, proposed by Simpson (2000), cover both academic and non-academic aspects, and include both those built into the programme material itself and that provided by the programme team. This could include providing information, guidance on future direction, stimulating ideas to solve problems, or pragmatic advice on study techniques.

How much support should the student expect? While some programmes offer students unlimited access to tutors (by telephone, fax, or email), others may limit contact to the marking of assignments (only by post). Alternatively, online courses may have interactive features that largely replace tutor support.

Simpson (2000) points out that the support of partners, families and friends cannot be underestimated. This would include practical support, such as giving the student time and space, as well as emotional and moral support.

Effective assessment methods

As mentioned earlier, formative and summative assessment are essential academic support aspects of the programme, in addition to being assessment tools in their own right.

Does the programme include an exam at any point? If so, check when and where students are able to sit the exam. Some programmes hold examinations only in the country where the home institution is located, while others offer venues in various regions of the world.

- What is the balance between examination and continuous assessment in the programme?

Fig. 19.2 Assessment

> ### Box 19.5 Language proficiency
>
> Do you need to undertake any prior tuition to improve the standard of your written or spoken English before you begin to study the programme?

Check whether there are additional fees for sitting the examination. The majority of distance learning students are likely to travel considerable distances to sit the examination(s), so travel and accommodation costs can mount up very quickly. Have these been budgeted for?

Language skills

For the purpose of this chapter, the focus is on courses delivered in English, although courses in other languages may be available. Where the designated language for a programme of study is English, certain assumptions may be made:

- all study materials will be delivered and summative assessments will be exclusively in English, although some formative assessment may be available in other languages
- programme tutors will not provide extensive guidance on the correct use of English
- students should not expect a translation service to be available.

Students on postgraduate medical study programmes whose first language is other than English are normally expected to demonstrate an acceptable standard of academic English prior to entry to the programme. Successful completion of the International English Language Testing System (IELTS) qualification at Level 7.0, or equivalent, is typically acceptable. Potential students should contact individual educational establishments for details of their specific requirements.

Libraries and online resources

An important consideration in distance learning programmes is the range of resources available to students, either through traditional libraries or online. Even in distance learning programmes without considerable e-learning components, it is likely that students will often be able to access library catalogues and databases online only after appropriate password security has been established. This may then give students:

- references to acquire the book or journal through their local libraries
- some abstracts to help narrow their search for an appropriate article
- access to interlibrary loans, dependent upon location
- the possibility of obtaining a photocopy of part of a book or journal from the institution's own library, usually for a fee.

Effective technology

Developments in technology have permitted considerable progress to be made in the way educational opportunities are delivered, not least in the field of palliative care.

Kwa Kwa (2004) suggests that the World Wide Web ('the web') is the second most utilized element of the Internet, after email. It would there be sensible for innovative education providers to develop learning technologies that harness the power and potential of the web and email. In their survey of palliative care practitioners, Pereira *et al.* (2001) identified an increasing use of communication technologies across the globe, which suggests that practitioners are enabled for online educational programmes.

We live in an increasingly pressurized world and the new technologies allow students to access their studies from home or work, without worrying whether they have the correct books or materials with them in a particular location. Students have reduced concerns about fixed moments in time, such as library opening hours or set study events (e.g. a lecture on a part-time course), or being overtaken by work and life pressures, because they can access the learning resources wherever and whenever it best suits them. This meets the test for open learning, set earlier.

Rumble and Oliveira (1992) cite Nipper (1989) when acknowledging the generational aspects of distance learning development. From printed material (first generation) through broadcast and audiovisual media (second generation), distance learning has continually embraced the latest technologies to adopt computer-based, Internet-enabled technologies such as webcasting, instant messaging and teleconferencing (third generation). Williams *et al.* (1999) note that distance learning has evolved into the 'virtual classroom' where students learn from a variety of media including live broadcast, audio or video on demand and computer-based interactions that may be both synchronous (online tutorials) and asynchronous (email, etc.).

It has to be recognized that some tutors and students will be more familiar with, and attracted by, web-based technology than others. As Clarke (2001) suggests, ease of use must be a prime consideration in e-learning, giving the user the maximum degree of freedom to navigate the material to find what they are seeking.

- Is there an open-access web site that you can view?

- What specification of technology will you need to participate?

- Is your current software compatible/sufficient? What is the replacement/upgrade cost?

- Do you need a licence to operate any of the software or to access any resources?

Fig. 19.3 Learning resources

The reliability of the underpinning technology is critical to effective delivery of programmes which operate through e-media. As Bates (2005) points out, this is equally applicable to students' own computers and their Internet service providers, as it is to the platform delivering the learning programme. In many areas of the world, as Williams *et al.* (1999) point out, problems with the technical infrastructure remain. Programmes with a high e-learning component should offer the equivalent of a 'low graphics' version. If not, they may prove to be unattractive to students in developing countries.

A broad range of learning materials

A good programme will have developed a range of materials to engage the student in a process of active learning. These could include:

- structured written materials: course manuals, textbooks, etc.
- broadcast materials: audio or videotapes, or CDs
- online materials: web site, webcasts, online tutorials, etc.

Both technology and palliative care practice are rapidly evolving, so it is important to evaluate how relevant the programme materials are for your needs. Race (1996) highlights the importance of interactive materials for effective learning.

It is often helpful to learn more about the authors of the materials. Are they experts in their field? Their biographies should be available. Similarly, find out a little more about the programme's external examiners, as part of their role will be to evaluate the quality of the programme and its materials. Perhaps the most realistic assessment will be gained from former students, who may provide a wealth of insider knowledge.

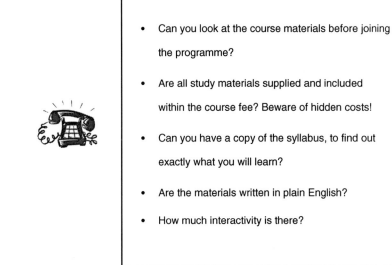

- Can you look at the course materials before joining the programme?

- Are all study materials supplied and included within the course fee? Beware of hidden costs!

- Can you have a copy of the syllabus, to find out exactly what you will learn?

- Are the materials written in plain English?

- How much interactivity is there?

Fig. 19.4 Course materials.

Box 19.6 Pitfalls to avoid

- *Insufficient life and career planning.* It is often easy to fall into the trap of beginning studies at the wrong point in your career path. Check what others have done.

- *Poor adjustment of learning style.* Distance learning places more responsibility on you, the learner. It will not be like studying at medical school again!

- *Too much, too soon.* Don't set overly ambitious time limits or progress points when you start the programme. Settle in, commence your studies, pace progress, and then review your ambitions.

- *Getting behind with studies.* The majority of learners fall behind at some point. If you feel this is happening to you, talk to your tutor straight away. It is usually easier to mutually agree a progress plan before the problem snowballs.

Tips for potential students

This section offers some ideas about what aspects potential students should consider as they compare and contrast study options.

Will distance learning suit them?

It is important for potential students to assess, as objectively as possible, their preparedness to commit to a programme of study. Some considerations might include:

- are they comfortable with studying for prolonged periods by themselves?
- what impact will it have on other aspects of their lives?
- are they prepared to critique existing practices and ways of thinking (including their own)?
- do they have sufficient confidence in their ability to cope with reviewing academic papers, statistics, etc.?
- are their IT skills good enough?
- what if they do not do as well on the programme as they expected?
- what are the financial considerations?

Residential blocks – travel and accommodation costs

Overseas students on distance learning programmes may find advantages of convenience and flexibility, when compared with the fixed structures and geographical upheaval that flow from a full-time programme based in the UK. Typically, traditional full-time, and often part-time, study requires the student to forego income and at the same time meet additional expenditure on accommodation and UK living costs.

While a distance learning programme may be, superficially, cheaper than travelling to the UK or elsewhere to study, there may be additional costs incurred if the programme has one or more compulsory residential study periods and/or examinations. Some academic institutions deliver these study periods and/or examinations in regional centres, which may significantly reduce the total cost to the student.

Are bursaries available for those from resource-poor countries?

Where students work in a resource-poor country, it is well worth checking with education institutions whether any bursaries are available to meet course fees and/or other associated expenses, such as travel and accommodation costs. Even if they meet only part of the costs, they are well worth having. Similarly, consider charities and other philanthropic institutions, which may have funds available for educational purposes.

Are fees payable in stages?

Check whether the provider will allow payment of fees in stages. This may be particularly important where students are self-funding or come from resource-poor countries. If the programme is a pathway programme (typically, Certificate/Diploma/Masters) students should be able to pay for each stage separately. Even within stages, some institutions permit fees to be paid over an extended period of time, e.g. by term or semester. If this option is available, check whether any deferred payment incurs an interest charge.

Will studying make a difference?

Back to work and making change happen! This is where the student puts learning into practice to improve the service provided to patients by themselves and their teams. Fear of the unknown is often considered as one of the main barriers to change. Recognizing this may be the first step to removing this barrier. There have been countless books published on the management of change, so this section is limited to reminding the student that their distance learning studies will provide them with:

- support for implementing a learning culture in the workplace
- useful information resources
- the skills to produce personal development plans
- credibility among their peers
- enthusiasm to drive the process forward.

Track record

It is worth asking the provider whether it is possible to talk to other students on the programme. This will provide real insight into the way that the programme is delivered. If possible, benefit may also be gained from talking to former students, who may be well placed to recommend the course. Much of this may not be available or not possible, but it is still worth asking.

- Check the experience and quality of tutors. Are they leaders in the field? Are they former students of the programme?

- How many students are on the course? How are groups allocated to tutors?

- What proportion of students from outside the UK? Which countries?

Fig. 19.5 Students and tutors

Currency of course content

Another dimension is currency. Given the fact that distance learning programmes may have been prepared months (or even years!) beforehand, a readily updatable online programme has an advantage here.

Other education providers

Often, similar programmes are offered by a number of providers. Make a real effort to compare them in terms of content, delivery and costs. If there are significant differences in cost, ask the provider to justify their costs. What added value does their programme offer, compared to the others?

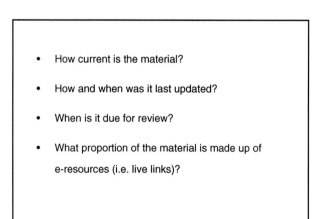

- How current is the material?

- How and when was it last updated?

- When is it due for review?

- What proportion of the material is made up of e-resources (i.e. live links)?

Fig. 19.6 Learning material

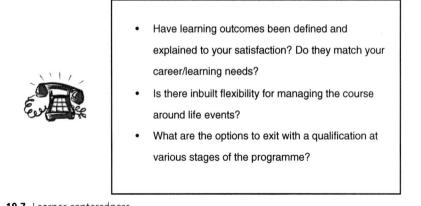

- Have learning outcomes been defined and explained to your satisfaction? Do they match your career/learning needs?
- Is there inbuilt flexibility for managing the course around life events?
- What are the options to exit with a qualification at various stages of the programme?

Fig. 19.7 Learner-centeredness

Single versus multiprofessional programmes

Good palliative care involves a team comprised of many professions. Should individuals from these professions learn separately? Are their needs so markedly different? Is palliative care best taught through a multidisciplinary environment? Hostad (2004) suggests that insufficient research has been undertaken to answer these questions. While these may be difficult questions to answer in a wider context, the individual student needs to make a personal preference at an early stage, if they are to select the most appropriate course.

Programme delivery, structure and organization

To ensure that the chosen educational provider meets their learning needs, students must make sure that they understand:

- the programme entry requirements
- how the work programme or timetable is scheduled across the year
- the balance between traditional and online delivery of course components
- what commitment the tutor has given to deal with enquiries at certain times, the turnaround times for marked work, etc.
- the policy for marking work (e.g. blind and double-marking) and feeding back results and markers' comments
- how the programme is balanced between continuous assessment and examination. If examined, in how many exam centres and in which countries?
- whether there are compulsory practical skills activities that can only be delivered in residential settings; and
- the range of library facilities available that will be available for distance learners.

Table 19.1 Decision-making

Resitting examinations or resubmitting coursework	It is unlikely that every student on a programme will pass each component at the first attempt. What is the provider's policy on resitting the examination or resubmitting coursework? Can you re-take the exam if you fail? Or are there any restrictions? Will the syllabus be the same at that time? If not, what are the implications?
Time limits	Are there built-in time limits? Do you have to complete components of the programme by certain dates after you have commenced the programme?
Leaving the course	You may decide the course is not right for you at this time. Is there any kind of 'cooling-off' period after you join? How easy will it be to withdraw from the course later on? If you do withdraw, can you get a refund of (any part) of the fees?
Feedback and complaints	How is student feedback captured? What is the student complaints procedure? Find out now – when you *need* to know, it's probably too late

What if things go wrong?

No one wants to think of failure, but an element of pragmatism is necessary in any adult learning environment.

Organizing to get maximum benefit from distance learning

Build a study zone

Similar to home workers, distance learners may find considerable benefit in creating a separate 'zone' at home that helps them distinguish study time from other aspects of their life and to maximize the potential from this study time. The following list gives some ideas that may be useful:

♦ space – a room or area to work in, preferably with natural light

♦ furniture – a desk and an adjustable chair plus some storage space

♦ an answerphone or answering service – to switch on for uninterrupted study periods

♦ technology – the minimum software, hardware and communication links that permit effective participation.

Having built a study zone, use it effectively. Try to establish regular study routines, such as set days and/or times of day when you study, to maximize the benefit. Find the list of key dates (submission deadlines etc.) for the programme and do some forward planning. Knowing what has to be done and by when, then pacing study to match this, will take away some of the stress of studying at a distance.

Make some space in life to study

There is some evidence that gender remains an important dimension in the organisation of study. Von Prummer (2000) found that, while studying placed additional demands upon women by partners and children, men tended to be relieved of childcare and similar responsibilities to undertake the same activities. It is therefore suggested that these potential pitfalls are acknowledged and that students' individual learning strategies take them into account.

Conclusion

This chapter has considered what students should expect from distance learning programmes in relation to their learning needs. From considering whether to study palliative care and, if so, by what means, the potential student should now appreciate that for many distance learning is an ideal study choice. Ultimately, the maximum benefit will obtained by the student from distance learning by:

♦ understanding the unique characteristics of distance learning programmes

♦ ensuring that their individual learning needs will be best met by this approach

♦ being organized and effectively fitting study requirements into the competing demands on their personal and professional time

♦ adopting the same rigour as with their earlier studying – while not being the easy option many suspect it to be, distance learning works well and delivers learners' expectations.

Chapter 20

Assessment

Bee Wee and Karen Forbes

Introduction

Palliative care practitioners may be involved in assessment in a variety of ways. First, as teachers, we use assessment to motivate, promote and test student learning in palliative care. Second, as part of a wider community of teachers, we contribute to assessments that are organized by others in the university and workplace. Third, we may be invited to sit on course organizing committees at which discussions about assessment happen. Therefore a good understanding of assessment enables the palliative care teacher to be more effective in every setting.

In this chapter we shall:

◆ set out the purposes and sources of assessment

◆ differentiate between formative assessment to aid learning and summative assessment which tests student achievement

◆ discuss the pros and cons of a range of assessment methods.

Purpose of assessment

The purpose of assessment is to examine students' behaviour in order to identify where they have achieved the learning outcomes and also when they fail to do so. Setting clear learning outcomes, which specify precisely what the student should have achieved by the end of this unit of learning, is a prerequisite of deciding how and what to examine. For example, it would be legitimate to test a student on how to set up a syringe driver if this had been clearly set out in the learning outcomes and there had been opportunities to learn how to do this. Student learning is often driven by assessment, so the choice of assessment methods will influence the quality of student learning. For example, setting questions which require students to memorize facts out of context will achieve precisely that, i.e. surface learning, whereas assessments which require students to work out how and when they would apply such facts will drive much deeper learning.

Assessments may be carried out in order to:

◆ aid student learning: providing motivation and feedback to students and staff about the quality of learning that has taken place

◆ test student achievement: checking whether student achievement has reached the desired level, comparing students against each other, providing assurance to others (e.g. the public) that student achievement has taken place and that they may proceed to certification or the next stage of training.

Clarity about the purpose of assessment is essential as this drives every decision about the choice and conduct of assessment strategies. Miller (1990) proposed a useful framework for assessing clinical competence. This is set out in Figure 20.1 with examples of assessment methods which may be used at each level. There is a trade-off between assessments that are easy to apply en masse but test at a lower level (e.g. multiple choice questions) and those that use more resources but test a more real situation (e.g. direct observation of a 'live' clinical encounter between a learner professional and a patient).

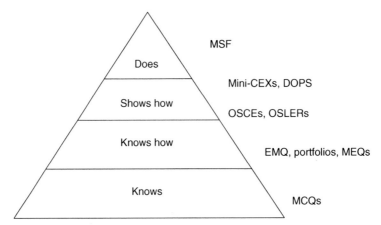

Fig. 20.1 Assessment of clinical competence (Miller 1990). These abbreviations are explained in detail on pages xvii and 339.

There is no perfect assessment method, nor one that is totally objective. Knowledge and skills are relatively easy to assess; attitudes and professionalism much less so. One way to ensure that all learning outcomes are widely sampled is to create a blueprint (Tombleson *et al.* 2000). This is simply a grid on which generic competencies, e.g. communication skills or theoretical understanding, are mapped against specific learning outcomes (see example in Table 20.1). This demonstrates wide sampling of student achievement using a variety of assessment strategies and quickly throws up essential gaps in the areas tested.

Source of assessment

The source of assessment is the person responsible for carrying it out. This is usually the tutor, but clinical practitioners may also be asked to assess students as clinical mentors or supervisors.

The students themselves and their peers may also be legitimate sources of assessment. It could be argued that when the task is intrinsically personal, e.g. reflective diaries, the student is best placed to know how well the evidence meets the assessment criteria. But there is a danger here: self-assessment may be influenced by a tendency to make judgements on what the student meant rather than what was actually demonstrated.

Table 20.1 An example of an assessment blueprint in palliative care

	Pain management	Constipation	Spinal cord compression	Depression
Theoretical knowledge	Writing prescription for analgesia (written exam)		Cause, signs and symptoms, and management of *SCC (written exam)	
History-taking	Taking history from patient with any chronic pain (video review)	Actor–patient presenting with history of overflow diarrhoea (OSCE)*		Actor–patient presenting with symptoms of depression (OSCE)
Physical examination			Examination to outrule SCC (OSCE or OSLER)*	
Communication skills	Actor–patient presenting with chest pain (OSCE)	Discussing patient's understanding and preferences for laxatives (OSCE)		Actor–patient presenting with symptoms of depression (OSCE)
Procedures	Setting up a syringe driver (OSCE)			

*SCC, spinal cord compression; OSCE, objective structured clinical examination; OSLER, objective structured long examination record.

Peer assessment can be both valid and reliable in assessing areas such as professional competence, which requires cognitive and interpersonal skills (Dannefer *et al.* 2005). It works most effectively when each piece of work is assessed by a number of students and where assessors are randomly chosen to reduce distortion by relationship factors.

Self- and peer-assessments may deepen the understanding and learning that occur when students have to actively seek evidence from their work to demonstrate learning achievements. It also helps students to become more independent learners and to develop lifelong learning skills through the habit of self-appraisal, fairness in appraising others' work and giving constructive feedback to others.

Formative assessment

When the prime intention of assessment is to help students learn and develop, it is called formative. The basis of formative assessment is feedback which is relevant and encourages discussion and self-assessment. Good feedback takes place in private and focuses on the actual behaviour or outcome of that behaviour, i.e. things that the student can change, not the intrinsic characteristics of the student. Constructive feedback requires the person giving feedback to be kind but honest. The beneficiary of such feedback should be solely the student, not the person giving feedback, other students, the reputation of the course or the public.

It is often worth asking the student to comment on how they performed first as this will demonstrate the level of that student's insight and open up a two-way dialogue. The more specific and accurate the feedback is, the easier it is for the student to see what needs to be different and to respond accordingly. If the feedback is unexpected, the student may need time to reflect upon it and return for a subsequent discussion. Before the end of the meeting, the student should identify some strategies for change. Formative assessments should be recurrent and built into the ethos of the educational programme.

Summative assessment

When the prime intention of assessment is to test student achievement, it is called summative. However, summative assessments should also incorporate feedback to aid learning wherever possible. Earlier on, we asserted that assessments cannot be totally objective because clinical assessments involve a level of judgement about the student's performance. Even written examinations with single correct answers require judgement at the question setting and standard setting stages. Clear marking criteria and a rigorous approach to assessment planning improve fairness and reduce bias.

Assessments must be fit for purpose, i.e. capable of assessing or testing what they are being used to assess. The quality of a test will depend upon its power to discriminate between students and its validity and reliability. Students may be measured in comparison with their peers (norm referencing) or against a predetermined standard (criterion referencing). In criterion-referenced assessments, students need to demonstrate achievement against preset criteria, which may be statements or hurdles, e.g. achieving 60 per cent pass mark. If all students achieved at least 60 per cent in that situation, they would all pass. Norm-referenced assessments allow comparison between weak and good achievers, e.g. students who come in the top ten in the class are awarded merits. It only discriminates between students within a cohort, not between cohorts or from year to year.

The validity of a test tells us whether it is measuring what it is designed to measure (see Box 20.1). The test should be appropriate for the learning outcomes to be assessed. For example, most multiple choice question (MCQ) exams test lower level cognitive function, whereas assignments, projects or portfolios are used to assess higher level cognitive function. Assessment of psychomotor skills should be through observation of skills at examinations, such as objective structured clinical examination stations (OSCEs) or objective structured long examination records (OSLERs), or in the workplace. Affective learning objectives are best assessed through self-assessment, by peers or during tutorial discussions.

The reliability of a test (see Box 20.2) is about how consistently it measures the relevant learning outcomes. It requires broad sampling of those learning outcomes, consistency within individual assessors (assessing different students on the same test) and consistency between assessors (assessing the same student or different students on different occasions). Reliability improves if marking schedules are clear and assessors are trained.

> ## Box 20.1 Validity
>
> To what extent is the assessment method measuring what it is designed to measure?
>
> A test with high content validity will be:
>
> ◆ Based on a sample of the objectives of the curriculum, and
>
> ◆ Ask questions relevant to those objectives
>
> A test with high *construct validity* will be appropriate to the course or objective being assessed.
>
> A test with high *consequential validity* will influence what and how students learn.

Methods of assessment

There are over fifty types of assessment used in higher education (Knight 2000). In the remainder of this chapter, we discuss the benefits and pitfalls of assessments commonly encountered in health care education and those which are particularly applicable to palliative care. These may be broadly divided into clinical, written, work-based and online.

Clinical assessment

The long case

A fundamental skill for most health professionals is their ability to meet a patient for the first time, learn about them and their problems, examine them where appropriate and negotiate a management plan. In medicine this process-history, examination, discussion of necessary investigations and management plan-was traditionally assessed during the 'long case' examination. Candidates were given up to an hour with a patient to complete a history and examination and then to present the case and discuss the diagnosis, management and possible investigations with two examiners.

The content validity of such an examination is high, in that it reproduces real clinical practice (see Box 20.1). However there are a number of problems. Construct validity is potentially poor. Because students see patients unobserved they can successfully obtain all the necessary information but do so in a brusque, arrogant or insensitive way which the examiners would never see. Students only report the examination findings they

> ## Box 20.2 Reliability
>
> How consistent is the outcome of the asssessment?
>
> A reliable test will consistently measure what it is supposed to measure.
>
> The reliability of a test will be influenced by the objectivity of the scoring.

are asked about, so poor examination technique can also be missed, while the student may be subjected to an oral examination about the condition, rather than the patient in question.

The reliability of the long case is also problematic. Fatigue would prevent a single patient seeing more than one or two students. Patients may feel unwell and different candidates and examiners may have different approaches so that no encounter is the same. Long case examinations also require extensive organization: ensuring patients are well enough to be seen, sometimes arranging for patients to come into hospital specifically for the examination, moving patients to a central area where the examination is being held and ensuring sufficient equipment, beds, linen, pillows and chairs are available for patient and student comfort. Difficulty with validity, reliability and practicality in long case examinations means that, although once common, they are rarely used now.

Objective structured long examination record (OSLER)

Long case examinations have largely been replaced by other formats where the student's performance is directly observed by examiners. Where examination of a complete clinical assessment is necessary the traditional long case has been replaced by the objective structured long examination record (Gleeson 1992), first reported in 1992.

In this examination the student is given up to an hour to take a history and examine a patient not known to them, observed by one or two examiners throughout. The student is then asked to summarize the history and examination findings and to discuss a differential diagnosis and initial management plan. As in the traditional long case, the content validity of such an examination is high. Reliability is improved by the use of a pre-agreed assessment schedule.

Objective structured clinical examination (OSCE)

First described in 1979 (Harden and Gleeson 1979), the objective structured clinical examination involves students moving around a series of five to ten minute stations, being observed undertaking a wide variety of clinical tasks. Where there are more than ten stations, rest stations may be included. Examples include tasks such as examining a patient's chest, interpreting a chest x-ray, explaining a clinical procedure and obtaining informed consent, performing cardiopulmonary resuscitation on a mannequin or setting up an intravenous infusion. In palliative care, OSCE stations could take the form of pain assessment, setting up a syringe driver or breaking bad news to an actor–patient.

Like the OSLER, reliability is improved by using mark sheets which include rating schedules, checklists and/or a requirement for a global impression score. Examiners may be trained by watching simulated and/or video recorded stations or consultations in order to standardize the level of achievement expected.

The validity of OSCEs is more challenging. Their construct validity is high, in that they test aspects of real clinical performance. However they are only a valid assessment of competence within the context of an OSCE. The OSCE is 'unchallenged in its position as the assessment instrument at (the "shows how") level of Miller's pyramid' (Davis 2003: 260). However, like the OSLER, it does not assess competence at the 'does' level of the pyramid (Figure 20.1). The driving test is a useful analogy. It checks that the driver has the basic and necessary skills at the time of the test but most people agree that they do not necessarily drive in that way in real life.

In medical education, OSLERs and OSCEs are often used in high-stake examinations for qualification. Most patients receiving palliative care are too unwell to be involved in hour-long OSLERs or to be seen repeatedly by a number of students for the OSCE. However, the OSCE format provides an ideal opportunity for all students to be examined in an aspect of palliative care, using actor–patients or simulated patients. Areas such as communication skills and dealing with difficult ethical issues can be assessed as well as palliative care knowledge or skills.

Viva voce

The viva voce or oral examination is another traditional form of assessment which has come under increasing criticism. Typically, the student is questioned by one or two examiners in an interview setting. Supporters of this form of assessment argue that it allows direct personal contact and enables problem-solving, reasoning and in-depth knowledge to be assessed directly. However some studies have shown a correlation between the scores and the candidate's personality (Thomas *et al.* 1992) and verbal style and dress (Rowland-Morin *et al.* 1991; Burchard *et al.* 1995). The reliability and validity of this assessment is so poor that its use is diminishing. Where this form of assessment is still favoured, it can be improved by structuring the viva on preset clinical scenarios, asking all candidates the same questions, using a number of vivas and a number of examiners, using preset criteria and training the examiners (Davis and Karunathilake 2005).

Written assessment

Written assessments are used both for formative and summative assessment. Most schools assessing health care professionals, particularly for licensing, have moved to written assessments which are increasingly structured because government and standard-setting bodies, e.g. Medical and Nursing Councils, require valid and reliable tests to demonstrate fitness to practice.

Essays

Essays are now used less often for summative assessment and licensing purposes because of problems with the objectivity of marking and their low validity and reliability as assessment tools. Essay marking is subjective, even with schedules, although marking rubrics do improve objectivity. Different examiners will award different marks for the same essay, indeed the same examiner may give the same essay different marks on different occasions. Students may be penalized for their style of writing and for grammar, rather than content. Essays tend to assess one area of the curriculum in depth, rather than covering a broad topic area. However, essays are useful in formative assessment. They encourage students to organize ideas, solve problems and develop arguments coherently. They also enhance writing skills which are necessary for recording in case notes, writing letters and creating papers. They also allow exploration of values, attitudes and opinions, which are otherwise difficult to assess. Their main disadvantage is a practical one. Essays are relatively simple and quick to set, but extremely labour intensive to mark.

Short notes or short answer questions

To replace the poor validity and reliability of essays, more structured questions can be used. Short answer questions which require students to respond to questions with single word answers, sentences, lists or brief paragraphs, can cover the syllabus rapidly and efficiently. Structured marking schedules also increase objectivity. Higher marks can be awarded for a completely correct answer, although a partially right answer can still gain credit. Whilst short answer questions make it clearer to students what is required of them, and are quick and easy to mark, they may lead to assessment of more superficial learning.

Multiple choice questions

Multiple choice question (MCQ) examinations are commonly used to assess students and postgraduate trainees of all disciplines because they provide good coverage of the syllabus and can assess knowledge, understanding and higher cognitive skills. Question banks can be formed and questions used over years. They are quick, easy and cheap to mark (usually using an optical reader), and have high reliability. But they have also been widely criticized. They can promote superficial learning and recollection or recognition of facts, out of context, rather than higher order thinking. Clear, unambiguous MCQs are difficult and time-consuming to create. They have become less prevalent over the last twenty years, however, they are coming back in vogue as pressure increases with the rise in student numbers and frequency of testing.

MCQs test factual recall so it is inevitable that, in palliative care, they will assess learning about more technical rather than holistic aspects of care. However, it is important to recognize that technical knowledge also matters in patient care. Questions on palliative care emergencies, the WHO analgesic ladder, opioid prescribing and management of common symptoms can be easily assessed with MCQs.

MCQs are made up of a stem question followed by a number of possible answer options or branches. For A-type questions, only one of five options will be true. This is also called the single-best answer question. For this to work well, the stem should give as much information as possible and be followed by five brief options. The incorrect answers (distractors) need to be plausible and there should be an even spread of the a, b, c, d and e answers being correct across the examination. The stem should be positive, for example: 'Which of the following are symptoms of spinal cord compression?' If negatives must be used, they should be highlighted, for example: 'Which of the following is *not* an opioid for moderate to severe pain?'

In B-type MCQs, more than one of the options may be true, so that the question becomes a series of true/false questions; the so-called 'multiple true/false' format. These are difficult to write because the incorrect answers (distractors) must be plausible. The correct answers must not be implied by the way the question is asked. The options in multiple true/false format MCQs need to be unequivocally true or false so that terms such as 'associated with', 'never', 'commonly', 'frequently', 'rarely', 'may' and 'can' should be avoided. The pattern and number of true and false answers must be random.

In order to avoid guessing, negative marking is often used, awarding one mark for a correct answer and deducting one mark for an incorrect one. This is an area of continuing controversy. Proponents of negative marking assert that this is a fair way of penalizing guesses and incorrect knowledge. However, others would argue that this is confounded by students' risk-taking behaviour, rather than testing true knowledge. Students who are less prepared to take risks, e.g. some female students, may be disadvantaged. Other students may gain marks through informed guessing and 'while some examiners may argue that they do not want to condone incomplete knowledge, performance under conditions of uncertainty and using a limited database to make crucial decisions is not something foreign to practicing clinicians' (Premadasa 1993: 240). Students probably perform best when they are encouraged to act on partial knowledge, but not to guess. If negatively marked MCQ examinations are to continue, students need to be carefully briefed about appropriate examination techniques.

Fowell has argued that many 'assessment methods and practices that might be considered to be less educationally desirable are still used by many schools, such as true/false multiple choice questions and negative marking of MCQs' (Fowell *et al.* 2000: 2). However, these practices continue.

Extended matching questions

Extended matching questions (EMQs) are a modification of the single-best answer MCQ described above. Here, the number of options may be extended up to twenty or thirty. The increased number of branches available in the EMQ format means, if used imaginatively, a single oncology or palliative care scenario could be used to assess learning about the symptoms and signs, management of an oncological emergency or symptom cluster as well as multiprofessional involvement and the patient's ongoing care needs.

Although EMQs are difficult to write, they allow a higher level assessment to take place. Unlike MCQs, students' knowledge is tested in context. They need to discriminate between the range of options to decide which is most applicable to the scenario they face in the question.

Modified essay questions

Modified essay questions (MEQs) allow students to give free text responses, but provide more structure than a traditional essay question. MEQs were first developed for the examination leading to membership of the Royal College of General Practitioners (Hodgkin and Knox 1975). An unfolding scenario is presented in the form of a booklet. After initial instructions, a clinical scenario is outlined with one or more questions posed which are relevant to the scenario. Candidates answer the questions by writing in the space below the information given. In the following section or on the next page, candidates are given further information, questions and space for their responses.

MEQs may explore different aspects of a clinical presentation or follow a patient through a series of episodes. Since MEQs require students to provide free text answers, the more holistic aspects of palliative care can also be explored.

The advantages of MEQs over other free text assessments are that the questions are clear, marking is made more reliable by using marking schedules, credit can be given for partially correct answers and higher skills such as problem-solving can be tested. Disadvantages of MEQs are that they are difficult and time-consuming to write, time-consuming to mark, and without tight marking schedules inter-rater reliability may be poor. Questions need to be carefully written so that information given in one section does not give the answer to the previous section or many invigilators are required to ensure candidates do not turn back and alter previous answers, something which is rarely practical.

Project work

Projects differ from assignments. The latter are often quicker to complete and are usually set by the teacher or assessor. Projects tend to be work over a period of time and the student develops the content and structure, within specified guidelines. Projects are therefore more focused on individual student learning.

Project work allows students to explore a topic in depth. The project may be developed and presented by an individual or group. Members of the latter could be asked to work on different aspects of a topic and present it as a group verbally or in writing, modelling and demonstrating teamwork. Projects can pose realistic situations for students and if chosen carefully can be motivating, enhance student ownership and promote independent, active learning. A large number of study skills, key professional skills and transferable skills can be assessed at various levels. Multiple areas of the curriculum can be covered.

Projects must be carefully managed. Students need clear learning outcomes and help with study skills and supervision, though this may be time-consuming. They must have access to library facilities and other resources. Some may need to have set boundaries, for example a weaker student might need encouragement to explore the topic in more depth whereas a highly motivated student might need help in drawing boundaries and not taking over group projects.

Project work can be theoretical, classroom based or work-based. It can discriminate well between students and has high validity. However, as every student's project will be different, objectivity of scoring will be low and reliability is only moderate.

In its 1993 publication *Tomorrow's Doctors* (General Medical Council 1993) the General Medical Council made recommendations about balancing the core curriculum with opportunities for student selected components in undergraduate medical education. Student options are common to other professional schools too. These options allow students to explore an area that interests them in some depth. Palliative care lends itself well to such projects.

Work-based assessment

Earlier in the chapter, we emphasized the importance of aligning assessments with learning outcomes and learning opportunities. Assessment of work-based learning is therefore required to test what students do in the clinical setting. Such assessments may be written, or direct observation of practice. Work-based projects allow assessment of the student's integration of classroom teaching into clinical practice. Case-based projects allow assessment of problem-solving skills and reflective practice.

Direct observation of practice within the workplace has been part of nurse assessment for some years, but is only now being formally introduced in medical practice. The Postgraduate Medical Education and Training Board (PMETB) has defined a satisfactory system of assessments as

> an integrated set of assessments which is in place for the entire postgraduate training programme, and which supports the curriculum. It may comprise of different methods, and be implemented either as national examinations, or as assessments in the workplace. The balance between these two approaches principally relates to the relationship between competence and performance. Competence (can do) is necessary but not sufficient for performance (does do), and as experience increases so performance-based assessment becomes more important.
>
> PMETB (2004)

The trio of assessments to be used for medical trainees are the mini-clinical examination record, direct observation of procedural skills and multisource feedback.

Mini-clinical evaluation exercise (mini-CEX)

The mini-CEX provides a structured way for a trainer to observe, score and give feedback to a trainee on a patient-related activity, e.g. an outpatient or ward consultation, note taking, prescribing or discussion about a clinical letter. Trainees are scored on a one to nine scale for medical interviewing skills, physical examination skills, consideration for patient/professionalism, clinical judgement, counselling and communication skills and organization/efficiency, except in areas which are not observed in that encounter. They also receive an overall clinical competence score.

The aim of the mini-CEX is primarily to assess and record the trainee's competence. There is also a formative component, in that trainers give feedback to help the trainee develop. The Royal College of Physician's pilot study indicated that a trainee's competence can be reliably assessed by eight assessors, each completing two mini-CEXs over the four to five year training period (Royal College of Physicians of London 2005). The construct validity of the mini-CEX is high because it assesses clinical practice in the workplace. Junior trainees should be encouraged to carry out mini-CEXs in patients who are ill, e.g. palliative care patients, in addition to fitter ones who might enable quicker mini-CEXs to be carried out.

Direct observation of procedural skills (DOPS)

Direct observation of procedural skills (DOPS) is similar to the mini-CEX but the trainee is directly observed carrying out all, or part of, a clinical procedure. A score is assigned and the trainee receives feedback from the supervisor. This is common practice in nurse education but has only recently been introduced formally as a method of assessment in medical training. The procedures specifically relevant to palliative medicine will be limited but there will be particular emphasis on discussing the benefits and burdens of the procedure in sick and frail patients. Prior agreement between the trainer and trainee about how the trainer should signal their intention to take over the clinical procedure during DOPS is helpful, to ensure smooth transfer of responsibility, if necessary, without undue distress for the patient.

Trainees are scored on a one to nine scale for a number of domains, including indications for procedure, obtaining informed consent, technical ability, professionalism and counselling and communication of results to patient/relatives, as well as an overall score.

Six assessors, each observing two DOPS, provide a reliable measure of trainee competence over the specialist registrar period of training (PMETB 2004).

Multi-source feedback (MSF)

Multi-source feedback involves obtaining feedback from a variety of sources, including patients, carers, clinicians from the same and other backgrounds and administrative and support staff. Medical trainees are required to ask up to 20 individuals to provide confidential, written feedback which is submitted directly to the trainer. They are scored on a one to nine scale on attitude to staff, attitude to patients, reliability and punctuality, honesty and integrity and team-player skills. They also receive a score for overall professional competence. The trainer collates the feedback, compares it to the trainee's self-assessment and provides feedback to the trainee, often as part of the annual appraisal. As a minimum, trainees are required to carry out an MSF at the end of the first year of training and again, as s/he approaches the final year.

Portfolios

Portfolios have long been used for appraisal and employment purposes in areas other than health care. Within medicine and other health professions portfolios are seen as having high face validity and are useful as formative assessment tools. They encourage reflective practice and self-directed and lifelong learning.

A portfolio is a collection of material brought together for a specific purpose (Challis 1999). There are various models, depending on the purpose of the portfolio. They may provide anything from an unstructured record of materials relevant to students' learning to those which require students to demonstrate achievement of learning outcomes through a variety of sources with an analytical reflection on the process. A portfolio is thus more than the sum of the individual parts. Students might include course work, assignments, learning cycles, assessments, written accounts of clinical interactions, videos and reflective writing to illustrate their achievement of learning outcomes.

Portfolios need to demonstrate (Rees and Walker 2000):

* validity – the evidence relates to the standards
* authenticity – the evidence is produced by and about the candidate
* currency – the evidence is current
* sufficiency – there is evidence sufficient to demonstrate competence.

Portfolios are used increasingly in the assessment of postgraduate students and trainees, for example for the award of certificates in education or medical education, diplomas in palliative medicine and for documenting achievement of learning outcomes in specialist registrars in palliative medicine. While portfolios are well established as formative assessment tools, the challenge is for the assessment process to be sufficiently rigorous if they are to be used reliably for summative assessment.

Learning contracts

These have been used in nursing and other professional education for some years. They are written agreements between the student, clinical supervisor and module leader indicating the focus for the assessment and how the student intends to set about achieving this focus. Students are encouraged to start their learning contracts at the beginning of a period of study. They are often used in conjunction with reflective dialogues and are intended to demonstrate student learning over the whole period.   •

Online assessments

The exponential growth in distance-learning and online learning means that assessment strategies have to be developed accordingly. Fortunately, computers lend themselves well to written assessments and some forms of simulated clinical assessments. The modified essay questions, with their unfolding scenarios, can be particularly rigorous when assessed online because the forward progression of responses can be forced. The key to designing effective online assessments is to recognize that the workload lies at the designing stage. Once assessments are properly set up, there are obvious advantages in the marking process.

Conclusions

It is widely acknowledged that assessment drives learning. While many health care professionals will want to learn about palliative care in order to improve patient care, the most powerful driver for all students and health care professionals to learn something about palliative care may be the anticipation that this would be assessed. Palliative care practitioners therefore have a duty to take any opportunity offered to be involved in assessment. Not all assessments need to be purely about palliative care, but if we can incorporate elements of palliative care into assessments, particularly summative ones, we will raise the importance of learning palliative care for our students and the profile of palliative care for our colleagues. This can be achieved if we offer to write questions, mark papers, find patients for examinations, coach actor–patients and, finally, act as examiners.

Chapter 21

Evaluation

Heather Campbell

Introduction

The term 'evaluation' may be applied to a diversity of situations and activities, ranging from a formal systematic evaluation of a planned intervention to the often unrecognized, informal subjective appraisal of everyday experience. It contributes to informing the individual, the organization and policy (Wilkes and Bligh 1999; Kenny 2003) and may have important consequences within the discipline of health if undertaken well or badly (Scriven 1991). In a health care and education system driven by a market philosophy, the move towards developing a quality assurance infrastructure has meant that evaluation is possibly the new randomized controlled trial (RCT). As a result there is a plethora of information around evaluation models, designs and methods, theoretical and anecdotal, but a less impressive portfolio of good evaluation reports in health care education (Bailey and Littlechild 2001; Roberts *et al.* 2001).

This chapter aims to:

- provide a practical guide to undertaking evaluation in health care education, with particular reference to palliative education when appropriate
- stimulate an interest in evaluation in health care education in order to fill the evidence gaps.

Background

Evaluation may be defined as 'the systematic collection of information about the activities, characteristics and outcomes of programs for use by specific people to reduce uncertainties, improve effectiveness and make decisions with regard to what those programmes are doing and effecting' (Patton 1986: 126). This definition is particularly useful because it provides guidance to a number of the acknowledged key characteristics of contemporary evaluation in whatever context:

- there is a general consensus that it is good for you in as much as it informs decision-making and the development of new initiatives (Rowntree 1985; Parfitt 1986; Chambers 1988)
- it is mainly concerned with establishing the worth, value or merit of something (Scriven 1996; Clarke and Dawson 1999; Roberts *et al.* 2001)

- it aims not to prove but to improve (Stufflebeam and Shinkfield 1985), differing from basic research by its focus, evaluation being more decision orientated and basic research more conclusion oriented (Cronbach and Suppes 1969).

However, evaluation can contribute to and apply theory in order to explain why things happen, rather than just describe what is happening (Pawson and Tilley 1997; Roberts *et al.* 2001) and therefore may prove *and* improve (Rogers and Badham 1994, cited in Roberts *et al.* 2001: 2).

In order to clarify this situation Scriven (2005) argues that evaluation is not always decision-oriented and that indeed every serious evaluation should lead to the conclusion about the merit or worth of something, and likewise that research is concerned with evaluation. These aims are met by applying a formal, systematic approach to the collection, analysis and dissemination of data (Crohnbach and Suppes 1969; Lincoln and Guba 1986; Clarke and Dawson 1999). Finally, evaluation should provide a service (Stufflebeam 1971) and one way of doing this is by being responsive to the information needs of stakeholders (Stake 1983 in Torrance 2003, Cowman 1996).

If all these criteria are part of the purpose of evaluation then it could be considered a powerful and influential means of bringing about change. For example, the National Audit Office (2001) recognizes evaluation as:

> important for determining the extent to which a policy has met or is meeting its objectives, and that those intended to benefit have done so. Evaluation can also help departments learn lessons and share good practice in policy design and implementation. For long term policies, evaluation can identify ways in which the policy can be improved or developed to increase its impact.

> National Audit Office (2001: 61)

The role of evaluation in policy development strengthens with a growing appreciation of the role of evidence-based practice and as Powell 1999 (in Sanderson 2003: 334) states: 'what counts is what works'. The emerging relationship between evaluation and evidence-based practice may contribute towards, and will be a consequence of, a political system where targets and achievement of results indicates quality, effectiveness, efficiency and value for money. This is evident where data aimed at evaluating the quality of education provision is collected for comparative purposes (Wilkes and Bligh 1999; Kwan 2001; Roberts *et al.* 2001) and to market universities (Bailey and Littlechild 2001).

So on the face of it evaluation appears to have moved away from its initial focus of improvement. Although this may appear an academic debate there is a growing sense that evaluation should: contribute to, and draw from, theory to inform not only what is happening but also how and why it is happening (Kapborg and Fischbein 2002; Sanderson 2003); explore causal relationships and contribute to the evidence base (Kapborg and Fischbein 2002; Sanderson 2003).

Evaluation in health care education

Educational evaluation contributes to programme development by appraising the quality of teaching and learning, contributing to improving the learning environment and establishing how effective the educational input has been (Wilkes and Bligh 1999). Tyler (1950 in Bailey and Littlechild 2001: 354) defines educational evaluation as:

> determining to what extent the educational objectives are actually being realised …. However since educational objectives are essentially changes in human beings…evaluation is the process for determining the degree to which these changes in behaviour are actually taking place.

The emphasis here is taking evaluation away from the educational setting into practice, from determining how much has been remembered to how it is applied.

Jordan (2000) highlights the growth of continuing professional education (CPE) within health care and this may not be disputed with a £2.5 billion education and training budget promised in the Working Together and Learning Together paper (Department of Health 2001). This is despite misgivings by the Department of Health (Department of Health 1998) about the relationship between performance and education. The need for evaluation, therefore, is apparent in health care education with authors agreeing that there are deficits in a range of areas. For example: appropriate insight into the process of learning and the effectiveness of teaching methods (Lloyd Williams and MacLeod 2004); approaches devoid of theory that do not enable educators to identify relevant outcomes for practice (Prideaux 2002); a dearth of evaluation reports and the necessary evidence that education changes knowledge, skills and practice either in the short or long term (Jordan et al. 1999; Bailey and Littlechild 2001); lack of evidence that education enables transferability (Mahara 1998); whether education is 'useful knowledge?' (Cox 1987 in Jordan 2000: 3) and, perhaps most importantly, little evidence that suggests that education in health care has an impact on practice (Jordan et al. 1999; Jordan 2000; Krujiver et al. 2000).

However, the evidence of the effectiveness of CPE is conflicting. For example, some studies (Waddell 1991; Sheperd 1995) have indicated an improvement in practice of over 60 per cent of participants participating in health care education. Likewise, immediate increases in knowledge and skills and confidence have been demonstrated (Bullock et al. 1999; Fineberg et al. 2004; Adriaansen 2005). However, this has not usually been sustained or evidence for demonstrating it has not been provided (Corner and Wilson-Barnett 1992).

Studies evaluating the impact of a communication skills programme suggested that there was little effect for both nurse or patient outcomes (Hulsman et al. 1999; Krujiver 2000) and Georgenson 1982 (in Bailey and Littlechild 2001; 352) suggests that only 10 per cent of learning through CPE gained from off the job courses results in changes in effectiveness at work. Hutchinson (1999) suggests that one reason for the lack of evidence in medical education is that there is reluctance on the part of the medical profession to address educational evaluation. Despite a potential lack of evidence the Royal College of General Practitioners opted for demonstration of competence through Accredited Professional Development (APD) performance rather than the traditional routes of medical education (Gray 1998).

If this is the reality of the situation Prideaux (2002) suggests that education providers are powerless to refute claims of irrelevance without appropriate and significant evidence-based outcomes providing a legitimate measure of achievement. However he contends that 'improved patient care' and similar outcomes may be too broadly expressed taking into account the number of variables that may influence it.

Evaluation in palliative care education

The issues that apply to measuring the effect in general CPE can be extrapolated to palliative care education, not only in relation to lack of practice measurements but also to contradictory evidence. For example, Fineberg *et al.* (2004) demonstrated that education around the centrality of a multiprofessional approach to palliative care demonstrated gains immediately post-course and some sustainability in understanding, compared to a comparator group which did not have the educational intervention. This was not the case in a study by Lloyd Williams and Macleod (2004), who demonstrated no difference in students having additional teaching. In neither study were practice behaviours measured and this was highlighted as a limitation in the studies. A small survey by Field and Wee (2002) exploring evaluation methods highlighted the use of feedback questionnaires in just under half of the medical schools targeted. The questionnaire issued at the end of the palliative education input suggested a favourable response and formative assessment suggested an intellectual benefit but nothing else.

Extending evaluation to stakeholders other than students is particularly difficult in palliative care because of a reluctance of health care professionals to ask for patient consent and also because of the deterioration in the health of participants. As a result the only useful data collected from patients might be around patient satisfaction. It is anecdotally acknowledged that collecting data from patients may give rise to the Hawthorn effect with patients not wishing to criticize their professional carer. This might be particularly pertinent to patients with life-threatening illness, and their informal carers, who are perceivably more vulnerable. A review of the literature on communications by Aspergren (1999) indicated that lay people tended to rate students' knowledge higher than students themselves. In contrast, Chant *et al.* (2002) highlighted the fact that while students perceive an improvement in skills, patients do not.

Approaches to evaluation

Although there is some disagreement in defining terms there are a number of evaluation approaches characterized by their specific intention of use. Traditionally evaluation has had two main purposes, formative and summative, and evaluation tools have been developed to that end. Harvey (1998: 2) provides a cooking analogy to hint at a key difference between the two: 'when a cook tastes the soup it is formative evaluation; when the dinner guests taste the soup, it is summative evaluation'.

Formative, process or implementation evaluation

This type of evaluation can be directed towards assessing the extent to which a programme is operating as intended. This is often called process or implementation evaluation. It assesses quality assurance and the data collected can contribute to immediate as well as long term change by informing stakeholders of what is working and what is not (Patton 1987). This type of evaluation is most commonly used to gather data on an ongoing basis on existing programmes and often presents as satisfaction data or measurement of perceived knowledge and skills attainment.

Summative evaluation

There is an element of dissent around the definitions subsumed under this heading and it may well be worth clarifying with stakeholders what their understanding of particular terms are before undertaking an evaluation. For example, summative evaluation is sometimes used interchangeably with 'impact evaluation' (Policy Hub 2003) or subsumed under the heading of impact evaluation (Bailey and Littlechild 2001).

Impact evaluation as described by Owen and Rogers (1999 in Daly and Carnwell 2001) has a retrospective emphasis which embraces all elements of evaluation in relation to implementation, outcome achievement and whether differences in programme implementation affect programme outcomes. The Policy Hub Magenta Book, however, sees impact evaluation as a form of outcome evaluation that compares the outcomes of a particular programme intervention to the outcomes from a comparator group (no intervention or another intervention). This usually involves evaluation research as it involves manipulating variables or using a comparator group.

Polit and Hungler (2001) concur and discern between outcome evaluation and impact evaluation, suggesting that impact evaluation is concerned with identifying the net effects of an intervention i.e. over and above what would have occurred in its absence. Comparison would be one approach to eliciting the effect. Outcome evaluation is concerned with examining whether a programme achieves its outcomes intended and unintended.

However, from the author's viewpoint, the debate around definitions of outcome and impact are a distraction. Impact evaluation will have to include measurement of outcomes, both explicit and implicit, and outcomes are the criterion against which an effect or impact is measured. The main aim of summative evaluation should, therefore, be essentially to determine whether the aims of the evaluation strategy have been achieved. Invariably this will mean ascertaining the overall effect of a programme (Bailey and Littlechild 2001) by evaluating the final results achieved (Scriven 1991).

A number of models have summarized the different levels of evaluation that can be measured (Dixon in Bailey and Littlechild 2001, Kirkpatrick 1967, cited in Hutchinson 1999: 3). These can be represented in an evaluation ladder. The analogy is intentional demonstrating not only complexity in achievement but also 'distance' in terms of time from input to output and being able to attribute outcome to the input.

The characteristics of evaluation at each rung of the ladder are described in Box 21.1.

A programme evaluation may include all or just some levels of evaluation. However, because the relationship between formative evaluation and summative evaluation is symbiotic, education programmes will require examples of both, at least in the early stages of a programme life cycle. For example, if formative evaluation is undertaken efficiently then it can be cautiously taken that the reliability and validity of the programme outcomes can be relatively assured because one can assume that the programme has been implemented as intended (OERL 2005). This, of course, may not be the case, as any educationalist knows. Lecturers may interpret expectations of the curriculum. One way of reducing this is to have prescriptive session outcomes to provide a framework within which the lecturer may work and provide a measure for achievement. This does not account for individual, group or institutional factors, however, which may well influence

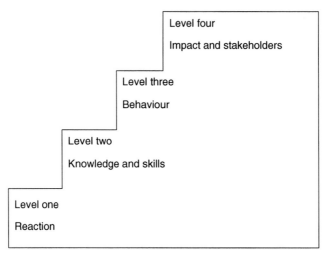

Fig. 21.1 An evaluation ladder

the successful achievement of programme outcomes. Likewise, evaluation of learning outcomes may highlight issues, barriers or facilitators to achievement linked to programme design, content or resources.

Another issue for summative evaluation is that of sustainability. One of the main concerns for evaluators and programme planners is the long-term effect of education in terms of retention of what has been learned and its impact on practice outwith the learning environment. Studies have demonstrated that some knowledge gained from educational programmes has been retained up to six weeks (Bullock *et al.* 1999), three months (Fineberg *et al.* 2004) or six months (Jordan *et al.* 1999). However, it is worth noting that attributing an effect to an educational programme is difficult as the variables that may

Box 21.1 Levels of evaluation

Level one: examines immediate effect of a programme often characterized as capturing immediate reactions for example 'happy sheets' (satisfaction). This would be seen as formative evaluation and is sometimes termed 'reactive evaluation'.

Level two: examines changes which may influence behaviour. This may include whether knowledge and skills have been gained and whether they have been sustained. This may have a formative and summative purpose.

Level three: examines whether there has been change in behaviours or performance in the individual. Usually summative evaluation.

Level four: examines the effect or results, intended or unintended, on stakeholders directly or indirectly. Usually seen as summative evaluation.

impact are numerous. These include having the right participants on the programme, the relevance of the programme to practice and inadequacies in the practice milieu (Chant *et al.* 2002; Ellis 2003).

Evaluation: research or audit?

Education programme evaluation probably aligns more closely to audit than to research although the process often utilizes existing research methods. The key differences between research and audit are that audit is often an ongoing process rather than one-off research; aims in the main to improve rather than prove and is specific and local to one particular institution or programme. The findings of many interventions, including education programmes, may only be applied internally or locally and will not have much meaning to other providers, stakeholders and may not contribute to theory (Parahoo 1997).

The main difference between evaluation and audit is the use of recognized standards or best practice as a benchmark in the audit cycle whereas evaluation uses aims and out-comes. However, audit findings may contribute to an evaluation. As a general rule, evalu-ation does not usually require ethical approval primarily because it is usually concerned with determining the effectiveness and value of existing, established programmes, interventions or policies (Polit and Hungler 2001). However, good practice should consider informed consent, confidentiality and the right to opt out (Eisner in Rosser *et al.* 2004).

There will be times when summative evaluation may be considered research or may include a research element to it. Parahoo (1997: 164) defines an evaluative study as a 'sys-tematic appraisal using research methods'. Although the aims may differ from other types of research, evaluation research utilizes the same research methods as any other research project (Robson 2002). As a result rigorous standards of reliability and validity should be assured in the methodologies used (Hutchinson 1999). Some evaluation projects involve contributing to an evidence base, generating or utilising theory, even if this is a secondary aim, and may involve methods which require controlling or manipulating variables. In these cases they would be considered evaluation research and would require appropriate ethical approval. A visit to the local audit department should help in the decision-making process.

Undertaking the evaluation

The most appropriate structure to an evaluation is to follow the evaluation cycle:

- planning the evaluation
- choosing the approach
- collecting the data
- analysing the data
- disseminating the results
- revisiting the purposes.

Planning the evaluation

When to plan?

One of the commonest mistakes made is to consider the evaluation as an after thought (Parahoo 1997). The issue with this is that costing may not be considered. For example, it is estimated that a comprehensive evaluation of an education programme may cost between five to ten per cent of the programme delivery costs. Also collection of the data may be mistimed (Harvey *et al.* 2000) and the method may not be appropriate to the evaluation aims. Ideally the evaluation strategy should be included at the programme planning stage.

Defining the purpose of the evaluation

Feinstein (2002) suggests that all evaluations have a cost but not a value and therefore each evaluation should be designed for a specific purpose (Hutchinson 1999). Determining the aims and objectives of the evaluation, or which questions require answering, will help focus on what level of evaluation is appropriate and who should be involved in the process (Hutchinson 1999). This applies to an evaluation for a study day or evaluation research into a new programme of study. Equally as important are the aims and outcomes of the education event. The outcomes will provide a measure against which to evaluate.

Who should be involved in planning the evaluation?

Cowman (1996) reminds us that there is a need to take into account the interests and concerns of stakeholders, recognizing that stakeholders may need different questions answered (Learning Technology Dissemination Initiative 1999). Traditionally the evaluation is designed by academic staff or education deliverers (Giles *et al.* 2004) even though it may include stakeholders as part of the data collection process. It may well be that evaluation is part of a wider quality strategy and the approach may be uniform across the institution. This in itself, although pragmatic, raises difficulties because a standardized tool used for all programmes may not be sensitive enough (Roberts *et al.* 2001). One way of overcoming this is adapting the tool with common core- and area-specific questions.

It is important to consider the benefits of including stakeholders in the evaluation design when the focus is to establish whether there has, for example, been any effect in practice as they may have clearer ideas of what they would want to find out. Giles *et al.* (2004) suggest including students in designing evaluation tools to highlight the areas of priority for them while providing them with an insight into evaluation processes.

Who will undertake the evaluation?

Bailey and Littlechild (2001) discuss the reasons for sharing the evaluation process between internal and external evaluators. Recognizing that evaluation of a long programme will probably involve all levels of evaluation, it may be that key stakeholders require an external evaluator. The advantages and disadvantages of this are presented in Table 21.1.

Table 21.1 How to commission an evaluation (Renewal.net)

Advantages for internal evaluator	Disadvantages for internal evaluator	Advantages for external evaluator	Disadvantages for external evaluator
Knows the project	Difficult to be objective	Easier to be objective	May not know the Organization/culture
Probably known to staff	May have difficulty breaking bad news, may experience role conflict	Fresh perspective	May not know the constraints which may affect the organization
May be seen as more credible in following up on recommendations	May avoid contentious issues	Free from organizational bias	May be seen as an adversary
Less expensive	Less experience	Should be experienced	May be expensive
Doesn't require negotiation time for contract	Not enough time to do it/too busy	Serve as an arbitrator	Needs time for contractual arrangements

However, in the evaluation undertaken by Bailey and Littlechild (2001), a collaborative approach was adopted with the writers being involved in the formative evaluation and external evaluators for the summative evaluation, while both groups of evaluators were involved in informing participants of the evaluation process and dissemination of the results to stakeholders. At evaluation levels three and four the method of evaluation will probably have strong research elements and it is worth approaching external evaluators (see Box 21.2).

Box 21.2 Suggested tips for commissioning an external evaluation

1. Be clear on the specification of the project including aims, objectives and or questions, timescales and resources. Prepare to offer a range within the financial budget. External evaluation has a cost but quality is not free (Kwan 2001).

2. Decide what can be done in-house.

3. Advertise for an independent evaluator or researcher or approach the local Higher Education provider who may offer this service from the research department.

4. Select and interview. It is worth looking at examples of their work before hiring their services to establish the rigour of their approach and the quality of their presentation.

(Renewal.net)

Choose the approach

Summative or formative?

The aims and objectives of the evaluation or the evaluation questions and the nature of the educational event should provide focus for identifying whether it is formative or summative evaluation, which level, who should be involved in the evaluation, the data and methods to collect it (see Table 21. 2).

Choose the level

The most appropriate way to evaluate courses is limited by resource and time costs (Bullock *et al.* 1999) but it is worth remembering that although evaluation is costly in the short term, ineffective education is likely to be even more expensive (Kenny 2003). Therefore, where at all possible, it is important to include all levels of evaluation at some stage of a programme life. Evaluation at one point in time does not give a complete picture and likewise focusing on one area will mean that others are neglected (Kapborg and Fischbein 2002).

Factors that influence the level of evaluation to be used are:

- the nature of the education event: established or pilot
- the experience of the evaluators
- the resources available
- the nature of the educational input.

The level of evaluation will vary depending on whether it is a short or long programme. Evaluation of a study day will differ considerably from evaluation of an established programme. For example, it is unlikely that evaluating impact on practice from a study day is feasible, although it is useful to ask questions that give insight into its usefulness or relevance to practice or role. With a longer programme, sustainability and

Table 21.2 How different levels of evaluation can be applied to different education programmes

Nature of programme	Level one evaluation (reaction)	Level two evaluation (knowledge, skills)	Level three evaluation (behaviour change)	Level four evaluation (effect on stakeholders)
Study day	x			
Short programme e.g. 2–5 days	x	x	?	?
Long programme e.g. a number of modules or action learning sets	x (for each component or module and at the end)	x	x	x
6 months–year:				
Formative	x	x	?	?
Summative	x (if an outcome)	x	x	x

impact on practice will probably be an issue to determine. Consider also whether the aim of the evaluation is to establish if a pilot programme should become part of an education portfolio or provide evidence for an exit strategy.

It can be seen that for some short programmes it may be appropriate to take the evaluation into practice or adopt a methodology which uses simulation e.g vignettes or objective structured clinical examinations (OSCE). Factors that may help towards decision-making are whether it is politically expedient to do so. For example, if an area of education is lacking in evaluation data, or a particular programme is seen as not being cost effective or strategically viable, the results may contribute to future planning or to the evidence base. The cost needs to be assessed against the benefit and this may be a personal or political decision.

Methods

The aims and outcomes of the evaluation strategy and/or evaluation questions will influence the methods used. There is no single best method (Harvey *et al.* 2000). It is recommended that a variety of methods are used (Bradley *et al.* 2005) and that 'best fit' determines the methods chosen (Clarke and Dawson 1999; Roberts *et al.* 2001). Historically there have been difficulties in combining methods from different paradigms (Bailey and Littlechild 2001) but a number of authors acknowledge the benefits of multi-method evaluation research including the complementary nature of the approaches and the opportunity to explore more than one dimension of the phenomena (Parahoo 1997; Mahara 1998; Polit and Hungler 2001; Bradley *et al.* 2005). Certain education interventions, a study day for example, will generate mostly quantitative data. Other more complex evaluations will involve methods which generate both quantitative and qualitative data.

It is generally accepted, though, that there are some methods which are not suited to educational evaluation. These include the RCT because of the numbers normally required (Hutchinson 1999), the method being too deterministic for the complexities of education (Ellis 2003) or not feasible or justifiable (Prideaux 2002).

Stakeholders

Gaining different perspectives is important to the evaluation process and a 360° evaluation tool is useful. The perspective of stakeholders who may have an interest in the findings of the evaluation may be sought: for example, managers who have fiscal responsibility for CPE, colleagues who may have to backfill while practitioners are off the job and, of course, clients. It is important to be clear when eliciting opinion from managers, colleagues and other stakeholders that the emphasis is on evaluating the impact of the programme and not assessing the participants' performance.

Collecting the data

Level one evaluation: scaled response sheets, questionnaires and the nominal group technique

'Questionnaire' is a generic word used for a variety of different tools, usually self-report, to collect opinion or data around a certain subject (Parahoo 1997). These are commonly used in formative evaluation. The most obvious way to collect opinions is through scaled responses. Parahoo (1997) reminds us that a rating scale is not the same as a questionnaire, a main difference being that a rating scale usually generates a number of statements around the same subject whereas a questionnaire has items which measure different things.

Scaled response sheets

A scaled response sheet, or Likert-type rating scale, is a pragmatic way of collecting level one evaluation data particularly if there are large numbers of participants or delegates e.g. a conference or study day. It can generate both quantitative and qualitative data with a focus on providing formative data. Munn and Drever (1993: 19) recommend that a questionnaire should be:

- attractive to look at
- brief
- easy to understand
- reasonably quick to complete.

Before the evaluation questions you may wish to collect biographical data e.g. profession. If it is a multiprofessional event, it is likely that you will already have this information on a delegate list. However, including it on the evaluation will enable you to see what was useful to each professional group.

Select a measure e.g. goodness, value, or satisfaction and provide intervals within the range. Avoid leading questions like 'would you agree?' (Robson 2002).

Example:

How would you rate the organization of the day?

Excellent ☐   Good ☐   Average ☐   Poor ☐   Very poor ☐

Or

How satisfied were you with the content of the day?

very satisfied ☐   satisfied ☐   neither satisfied nor dissatisfied ☐   dissatisfied ☐   very dissatisfied ☐

You may also wish to ask participants to rate:

- the organization of the event
- the venue and hospitality arrangements
- the content and its relevance to practice
- whether the content meets the delegates expectations
- the quality of the presentations.

Not all areas will be relevant. For example, gaining insight into a venue or hospitality arrangements may not be necessary if it is not going to be used again or you are aware of existing problems with it. However, venue proprietors may wish feedback, hence the importance of including key stakeholders in the development process. Where possible the questionnaire should be piloted beforehand. It is important to give delegates an opportunity to give feedback, therefore include a couple of open questions. Once again this will depend on the aims of the evaluation.

Table 21.3 Evaluation of longer programmes

5 = very satisfied 4 = satisfied	3 = neither satisfied nor dissatisfied	2 = dissatisfied	1 = very dissatisfied
			Rating
Experience of this programme			
Aims and objectives			
Design of the programme			
Amount of work required prior to the programme			
Academic demands of the programme			
Quality of teaching			
Variety of teaching methods and learning strategies used			
Quality of teaching material			
Quality of resources e.g. reading lists			
Links made between theory and practice			
Clinical content of the programme			
Clinical relevance of the programme			
Support provided by teaching staff			
Clarity of information provided by administrative staff			
Quality of teaching accommodation			
Opportunities to participate in learning activities			

For longer programmes you may wish to collect more information.

Table 21.3 provides some examples of information that can be collected. These can be rated using a satisfaction rating scale with the option of providing qualitative comments if desired.

A further section to the satisfaction component would be a satisfaction rating of the speakers. This can include all aspects of the teaching including content and resources used.

Key points for presenting questionnaires

Longer events may require a more detailed questionnaire which could provide the basis for an interview, focus group or 360° evaluation with a number of stakeholders. For short events or study days this should be one-sided if at all possible, bearing in mind that not every one will have as much enthusiasm for evaluation as you! Take into account any recent local or national policy. For example, the Special Education Needs and Disability Act (2001) provides guidance for preparing educational resources: use pastel-coloured paper or presentation background not white; avoid glossy paper; utilize Ariel font no less than size 12 (but not too big!); use black or blue ink; avoid underlining and italics (University of Plymouth 2005).

Box 21.3 The nominal group technique

Generate two or three questions around the programme. For example, what is the most important aspect of the programme to be changed?

1. Participants generate their own ideas around the questions posed.

2. Each participant in turn is given the opportunity to give an idea starting with their best one first. Further ideas can then be offered. Cluster similar items together.

3. Allow each person to allocate a number of votes; for example, six each. These may be allocated to just one item or across a number. This identifies high and low scores.

4. Repeat the exercise with the remaining questions.

5. In groups participants can discuss the high and low scores, giving possible reasons for scores, analyse problems and propose actions.

(Learning Teachnology Dissemination Initiative 1999)

A key consideration is to get as many evaluation forms back as possible. As with research a good response rate enables greater representation of the 'population' (Parahoo 1997; Polit and Hungler 2001). However, it is worth bearing in mind that if a long time is spent answering questionnaires it is more likely to be negative feedback. Surprisingly people find it easier to be negative than positive in this context!

The Gibson technique or nominal group technique

This approach can be used for a smaller group. It is suitable for the mid-point and end of a short programme and at the end of a long programme. However, it is not suitable for a large group as it takes time as well as participant preparation, organization and explanation. The advantage of this approach is that it provides feedback and problem-solving in the one process (see Box 21.3).

Level two evaluation: pre and post-course questionnaires

This level of evaluation attempts to measure whether educational outcomes have been achieved in relation to knowledge, skills and attitudes. It is important to demonstrate this as it could be argued that knowledge acquisition may be the *raison d'être* of education. Measurement using appropriate tools can really only be done once process data has been collected and used in programme development. Measuring this level of outcome may well inform this process if perceived positive changes in knowledge and skills have not been achieved.

This type of evaluation may be part of an evaluation strategy for either a short or a long programme. A baseline measure of the areas to be measured is advisable in order to evaluate any changes. A self-assessment of perceived knowledge and skills could be used, although the obvious weakness here is the notion of perceived or self-report and the pre- and post-design (Robson 2002).

Self report as the name suggests in this example is a subjective assessment of one's perceived knowledge and skills in a certain area. The difficulty here is determining accuracy. Polit and Hungler (2001) advise questioning whether the method is preferable over more objective measures; for example, an assessment of knowledge and skills in the appropriate area. Subjects using self-report may over- or underinflate their ratings for a variety of reasons. Ensuring anonymity may help to minimize this tendency.

Pre- and post-design using a single group is seen by Robson (2002) as being weak although commonly used. The main weakness is that in any intervening period between measures a number of variables may influence the outcome including maturation, history and vicarious learning. This may not be an issue if measures are taken over a number of days, but determining and isolating the effect of the intervention (programme) over a longer period of time will be more difficult.

Utilizing a specific level of learning outcome the participant would be asked to rate themselves using an attitudinal-like rating scale against the outcomes at the beginning of the programme and at the end of the taught component of the programme. The more detailed the learning outcomes the better. For example, session outcomes will provide more detail than module outcomes, which are likely to be broad. The disadvantage of this is that the evaluation form may be long and there may not be specific outcomes for each session, although it is a good idea to develop these even if they seem prescriptive.

Choose a measure, e.g. 'understanding', which may be used to evaluate the knowledge of the participants using a goodness value. Bear in mind that knowledge itself is not being measured – just the participant's perception.

Example:

Please use the five-point rating scale below to indicate your level of *understanding* in the following outcomes where:

1 = Very Good	2 = Good	3 = Neither good nor poor	4 = Poor	5 = Very Poor

Deciding which outcomes are knowledge-based will be determined by the descriptors used. For example, knowledge-based outcomes may use terms like 'describe', 'evaluate', 'discuss'. Those that are more skills-based will have descriptors like 'demonstrate', 'develop', 'perform' etc. A different measure should be used for skills-based outcomes, for example, confidence or competence.

Example:

Please use the five-point rating scale below to indicate your level of *confidence* in the following outcomes where:

1 = Very confident	2 = confident	3 = Neither confident nor unconfident	4 = unconfident	5 = Very unconfident

In order to compare between pre- and post-evaluation scores an identifier is necessary. As a general rule date of birth is adequate although it has been known for that to cause offence, especially if there is other data being collected e.g. gender or role which could be matched to the person. Analysis of the data should be able to demonstrate any changes in perceptions of knowledge and skills pre- and post-education intervention and may even provide some insight into particular lessons or sessions, although causal relations should be treated with caution.

This tool may be used as a measure of sustainability (delayed impact) following the end of the programme at a recommended time. Jordan (2000) suggests six months, but aforementioned difficulties about attributing causality to education interventions must be borne in mind.

Level three and four evaluation: interviews, observation, objective measures

It is recognized that outcome and impact evaluation is more difficult to measure and is most suited to long programme evaluation. Outcome evaluation is only as good as the outcomes to be measured and because of its focus may ignore contextual and unintended outcomes. Both types of evaluation will benefit from triangulation of data, methods and subjects, with a quasi-experimental design being more appropriate to these levels of evaluation than true experimental. Impact evaluation in particular will require research questions and should probably be considered as evaluation research. The benefits of using a comparator group for both levels of evaluation are seen by Jordan (2000) as important but complex, with practical difficulties.

Determining reliability and validity

Tanner (2001) suggests that for evidence to be credible it should be ensured that evaluation tools measure what they intend to measure. A number of tools including questionnaires, tests and vignettes should be piloted first prior to administration. Content validity or face validity can be estimated by using a panel of experts (Polit and Hungler 2001). For example, in the use of vignettes and response options it would be expected that experts would select the correct answer. A self-rating questionnaire around knowledge and skills would demonstrate face and content validity if appropriate outcomes were used. However, as previously mentioned, outcomes may be restrictive, prescriptive and may not be adequately sensitive or comprehensive (Prideaux 2002).

Reliability could be measured by administering rating scales around knowledge and skills to the same participants with a time lapse in between. This is called 'test–retest reliability'. However, knowledge may not be considered a stable attribute. As previously mentioned, determining causality between intervention and outcome may be influenced by a number of variables which may increase over time. Equivalence or inter-rater reliability can be used for observation methods.

Analysing data

The analysis of data will depend on the evaluation methods used. However in the author's experience some knowledge of statistical packages (e.g. SPSS) is useful, particularly for quantitative data analysis in pre- and post-designs. Guidance for this is best found in a research book or from a friendly statistician. It is also useful to note that it is time-consuming and boring if a large quantity of data is being analysed on a regular basis. It is worth debating when considering a rolling programme what level of evaluation will be used. For example, it may be useful to undertake level one and two evaluation over a period of time to determine reliability and validity of the programme and the measurement tool. If this is then used to inform changes to the programme then it may well suffice to continue with a short satisfaction questionnaire and periodically take snapshots using outcomes, e.g. annually. Level three and four evaluation is often restricted to a single occasion and is frequently associated with pilot programmes.

Dissemination and revisiting the purposes

There are a number of issues to consider when disseminating evaluation results. Who should receive the report? Is there a risk management strategy if the results are not as expected or are negative? Harvey *et al.* (2000) reminds the would-be evaluator that the very act of evaluating may affect findings. Bullock *et al.* (1999) and Feinstein (2002) argue that the collection of evaluation data is of little value unless something is done with it. It is generally recognized that evaluation activities generate knowledge that is significantly underused (Feinstein 2002).

Suggested format for an evaluation report

The majority of comprehensive evaluations produce a formal report, for which Morris (1987 cited in Harvey *et al.* 2000) suggests the following format:

- executive summary
- background to the evaluation
- description of the evaluation
- results of the evaluation
- discussion and interpretation of the results
- costs and benefits
- conclusions.

Summary

It can be seen that the type of evaluation undertaken depends on the purpose of the evaluation and the education event being evaluated. However, it is widely acknowledged that impact on practice both directly and indirectly is difficult to measure, this being pertinent to education in palliative care. Unfortunately, the notion of cause and effect is still notoriously difficult to measure in education research; whether establishing that increases in satisfaction or knowledge and skills is related to a particular teacher, teaching approach or content or whether determining that improved patient care or practice is a result of a particular education intervention. The latter remains elusive, particularly in palliative care. The domain of theoretical evaluation remains to date a relatively new area.

A range of methods and tools may be used, the important issue being that they are fit for purpose. It can be seen that traditional quantitative approaches are being combined with a more qualitative approach to take account of context. Likewise the importance of including stakeholders both in the development of the evaluation and data collection contributes to demonstrating the plausibility of success if they are pointing to the same conclusion. Evaluation can be an expensive and time-consuming process, so

> If the answer to the question 'why evaluate?' is that the results will lead to action to improve the teaching and learning within the course or institution, then all the effort will be worthwhile.
>
> Shaw in Harvey (ed) (1998: 6)

Part III

Building a Culture of Learning in Palliative Care

Chapter 22

Interprofessional education

Rod MacLeod and Tony Egan

Introduction

In this chapter we shall:

- introduce some theoretical underpinning for our view of interprofessional education in palliative care
- discuss the meaning of care in an interprofessional context
- suggest ways of developing a shared vision of care
- discuss ways in which we can learn about the delivery of interprofessional care.

Despite being a discipline which prides itself on the interprofessional nature of its functioning for the provision of care there have been remarkably few publications in the international literature about interprofessional education in palliative care. The problematic nature of palliative care education has been explored by James and MacLeod (1993) who drew distinctions between palliative medicine and palliative care, between care and cure, and identified some of the challenges of providing care interprofessionally. One major problem, which has significant implications for education, is that the goals of palliative care differ in kind and degree from those of curative care (Fox 1997). The ageing population and the emergence of chronic illness have required a reordering of the goals of care in the process of which the patient has resumed a central position in medical care (Kleinman 1988). What constitutes 'good palliative care' is still open to debate, but we would argue that it begins and ends with the patient in context.

Patient-centredness

We choose the term 'patient in context' in order to signify that the efforts of palliative care will extend beyond the individual patient and will take into account relatives and significant others. By defining the locus of care in this way we are directing attention to the patient's story rather than the medical history. Indeed an understanding of the stories of both the patient and the family will help us construct the meaning of patient well-being in each particular context. As a result 'well-being' may have physical, emotional, spiritual, intellectual and social connotations and good care will be responsive to all of them. This patient-centred approach is entirely consistent with the transformation of the clinical method proposed by Stewart *et al.* (1995, 2003). The model was originally developed in the context of family medicine as an attempt to integrate the biological, psychological and social components of illness. Both the patient-centred clinical method they describe and the learning and teaching methods they propose for developing it are well-suited to the provision of palliative care.

Clinical work

James and MacLeod (1993) also explored the problematic nature of interprofessional work and education, topics which have received a good deal of attention in the intervening years (Barr 1998; CAIPE 2002). However we will begin our consideration of interprofessional work (and education) with a very brief review of the social organization of medical work as described by Strauss and colleagues (1985). We begin with this study because it provides detailed descriptions of the work of different professionals in a clinical setting and sets out a provisional taxonomy of this work. Strauss *et al.* identify five distinct types of professional clinical work: machine, safety, comfort, sentimental and articulation (planning). These five types can be subdivided further and in myriad combinations they form lines of work which characterize everyday clinical practice. We believe all five types apply to palliative care and argue that the profile of clinical work varies from situation to situation.

Immediately of interest is the issue of which profession does which type of work. Even at a theoretical level there is no simple resolution to this question, although legally defined scopes of practice will give some indication. However at the level of clinical practice responsibility for different types of work is unlikely to be determined simply by professional identity (allegiance). For instance sentimental work might focus on helping the patient maintain composure under duress and on preserving the patient's identity when the body is objectified. This kind of work is carried out by all professional groups and might be accomplished by small acts, timely glances, shared sentiments and so forth. Interestingly, sentimental work in hospitals has usually been seen as the domain of the nurse. Of equal interest is the low accountability for sentimental work; generally, references to it do not figure large in clinical notes when compared to notes about other forms of clinical work (Strauss *et al.* 1985; Donnelly 2005).

Box 22.1 Ways of working

You can work:

Alone	Above	Before
With	Under	After
Alongside	For	Together
Around	Against	In spite of
Through		

Communities of practice

If we are to deliver quality palliative care, we must be able to perform all varieties of work in a timely, responsive fashion which will often require that the work is performed by a member of any one of a number of professions. At this point it will be useful to introduce some of the ideas of Etienne Wenger (1998). In some early field work with Jean Lave (Lave and Wenger 1991) models of apprenticeship were described as 'situated learning' and apprentices were seen as legitimate, peripheral participants in the delivery of services. Thus the novice's journey was one inward, from the periphery of activity, to increasingly legitimate participation at the centre of activity. Subsequently Wenger extended these ideas by locating activity in 'communities of practice' (1998); in so doing he provided a very useful conceptual structure for understanding group work in the delivery of clinical care. Briefly, communities of practice are purpose-built joint enterprises in which (in our case) professionals mutually engage in shared repertoires of behaviour which in total amount to palliative care.

Wenger offers us a social (as distinct from a cognitive) theory of learning in which socialization into the community of practice is a crucial part of the learning process. The shared repertoires of behaviour may reflect professional scopes of practice, but Wenger's emphasis is on what actually happens in contrast to what is prescribed at a professional or institutional level:

> One can design systems of accountability and policies for communities of practice to live by, but one cannot design the practices that will emerge in response to such institutional systems. One can design roles, but one cannot design the identities that will be constructed through these roles …One can design work processes but not work practices; one can design a curriculum but not learning.

> Wenger (1998: 229)

> Practice is where policies, procedures, authority relations, and other institutional structures become effective. Institutionalisation in itself cannot make anything happen. Communities of practice are the locus of 'real work'.

> Wenger (1998: 243)

From an educational point of view it is important that students of whatever profession have some understanding of the distinction between care and cure, of the meaning of

Box 22.2 Reflecting on your community of practice

How do you (collectively) construct the patient narrative?
How and what do you record?
How do you compose your vision of care? How do you validate it?
How do you determine the elements (physical, spiritual, social etc) of the care plan?
How do you communicate the above to newcomers or students?

well-being in a palliative context, of the derivation of this meaning from the patient's story and of the relationship between that sense of well-being and the types of work that professionals do. In addition it would be useful for them to have knowledge of each other's roles (as defined formally and informally), to recognize the importance of communication and be able to communicate effectively in a team setting, to value and participate in briefings, debriefings and supervision as part of professional practice. Regardless of how this knowledge base is built up, we believe its final form will be determined through interaction with communities of practice.

The meaning of care in an interprofessional context

If we are to provide interprofessional education in palliative care we also have to have a clear understanding of the notion of care, and this may be very different from discipline to discipline. The literature on care has come mainly from the nursing profession with remarkably little having been written about the concept of medical care. Palliative care must espouse all dimensions of care. Caring can be thought of as a behaviour or as a motivation. The behaviour is such that it implies 'looking after people and seeing to their needs'. In palliation 'needs' should be interpreted broadly and we suggest Maslow's hierarchy as a suitable starting point for reviewing needs (Maslow 1970).

As motivation, care refers to being fond of someone, feeling sympathy or empathy for that person and being concerned for their well-being. Humanistic models of caring such as those characterized by moral obligation or duty have been proposed (MacLeod 2000). Caring can also be seen as an art requiring the deepest knowledge of the person and incorporating effort, respect and responsibility before any sort of interprofessional education is undertaken. A shared understanding must be achieved. For many, a feminist model of caring would appear to be quite attractive. Some authors suggest that human caring is a phenomenon and an attitude that expresses our earliest memories of being cared for by our mother. There is however, still considerable debate about the nature of care – none less so than in the area of specialist nursing. In a specialty where the emphasis has been predominantly on caring for people with malignant disease there is a significant shift or broadening of outlook in what constitutes care. However, it is agreed that nurses are still heavily reliant on, and influenced by, medical diagnoses and regard them as essential to the delivery of care (Payne *et al.* 2000).

Rather than focusing on medical diagnosis and problems, it is proposed that those requiring specialist palliative care at least should have that care structured around the complexity and disruptiveness of patient problems (by listening to the voices of the patients). 'Until patients are able to discuss their experiences of illness in shared language, using symptoms and problems remains a starting point for initiating discussions with them' (Skilbeck and Payne 2005: 329). There are examples of where the patient voice can be clearly heard, but sadly they often tell of inadequacies and problems in the ordering of a caring approach (Armstrong-Coster 2005). Nonetheless, we would like to suggest that caring can be learned effectively and nurtured in the educational profession.

Interpersonal responsiveness

The ethics of caring assume that connection to others is central to what it means to be human (Branch 2000: 127): that 'relationships, rather than alienation give meaning to our existence'. Central to the effective provision of palliative care by an interprofessional team is that those people create a relationship with each other and assume not only a responsible attitude to their learning and care but also a receptivity to the needs of both their patients and other team members. The creation of an environment where value is placed on each individual irrespective of their profession or their experience is one way of ensuring that a caring and empathetic atmosphere is also created for patients. Perhaps unsurprisingly, Stewart *et al.* (2003) advocate a learner-centred approach in developing the knowledge, skills and attitudes that underpin a patient-centred method. Whatever view is adopted a clear understanding of the goals of care must be reached before progress can be made. In so many ways this approach mirrors the focus of patient-centred medicine that so far has failed to impinge adequately on much of medical practice and education, despite evidence of effectiveness (see, for example Howe 2001; Evans 2003).

Interprofessional education

Fifteen years ago (Carpenter 1990) there was evidence to support impressions that interprofessional education would be effective in overcoming barriers to education if it:

- explored similarities and differences in roles, skills, knowledge and ideology
- recognized the complementary skills and resources of different divisions
- brought together course members of equal status in equal numbers
- allowed communication in whole groups which are not too large
- had full institutional support to ensure participants' involvement.

A survey undertaken by the Institute of Community Studies for the Advancement of Interprofessional Education (CAIPE) in 1987 and 1988 identified specific course objectives for interprofessional learning which emphasized the ability to increase understanding of the roles/views of other professions, to promote team work/cooperation between professions, to increase knowledge of the course topic and to develop practical skills. More recently CAIPE has produced an extremely useful review of interprofessional education with the following definition for the health care professions: 'Occasions when two or more professionals learn with, from and about each other to improve collaboration and the quality of care' (CAIPE 2002).

Parsell and Bligh (1998) drew a distinction between interprofessional, multiprofessional and multidisciplinary. They defined interprofessional as learning activities which involved two professional groups. Multidisciplinary learning activities were defined as activities which involved members of differing branches of one profession and multiprofessional activities involved three or more professional groups. They suggested that interprofessional approaches to learning were essentially about the integration and synthesis of knowledge to solve problems or explore issues. In 1994 MacLeod and Nash reported the effects of workshops designed for primary health care teams or specialist units from hospitals in the area of palliative care and then in their evaluation looked not only at the structure and process but also outcomes of such learning. Nash and Hoy (1993) described an evaluation of residential workshops for general practitioner and district nurse teams in providing terminal care in the community. Both sets of workshops were evaluated by participants as being of value in developing their understanding of each other's approaches to care and enhancing teamwork in this area. Other authors (Carpenter and Hewstone 1996; Wee *et al.* 2001) have looked at interprofessional training programmes for undergraduates and postgraduates in this field.

Interprofessional education is potentially different from uniprofessional education because the values and learning objectives of the participating professions may not be aligned or correspond. Also there is likely to be a different balance in terms of content and process, with interprofessional education requiring a greater emphasis on process.

Overall in providing interprofessional care one might expect:

+ shared values, particularly with respect to patient (and family) outcomes
+ combined or integrated practices
+ discernible scopes of practice.

The first two could be the subjects of interprofessional learning, whereas the latter is more likely to be uniprofessional.

Professionalism

Part of the difficulty in writing a chapter on interprofessional education is that in order to begin we have to have a clear understanding of what we mean by a profession. George Bernard Shaw suggested that 'all professions are conspiracies against the laity' and identifying a common belief in what a profession is has proved problematic. Traditional definitions range from references to status and educational attainments through to 'noble callings' and claims such as the right of practitioners to autonomy.

Arnold (2002) has reviewed over thirty years of literature on professionalism in an attempt to outline the core values of what professionalism is. These values include altruism, accountability, excellence, duty and advocacy, service, honour, integrity, respect for others and ethical and moral standards. In a more succinct form professionalism has been defined as incorporating the primacy of the patient's interest above self interest (altruism), respect for patient autonomy and social justice. Part of the difficulty for a discipline like palliative care is that in order to preserve much of the professional nature of what it is that we do we must first separate out each of the elements of care. If professionalism entails commitment to a particular body of knowledge, attitudes and skill for its own sake then we must be able to identify what that is for each single discipline before we can go on to learn together in an interprofessional way and, finally, translate that into daily practice.

A profession is defined by a particular form of communication using specialized vocabulary, similar approaches to problem-solving, common interests and understanding of issues (Hall and Weaver 2001). Members of each profession have a theoretical basis through which they interpret and address issues which arise in their work. For professional practitioners – especially expert ones – it is often easy to forget that such work is complex and difficult and it can be hard to explain to others what each profession actually does. This is in part because the knowledge that practitioners draw on is broad, deep and multifaceted. In palliative care in particular there are technical elements to each profession but also ethical, moral, political, spiritual, social and economic elements as well. In many health care professions and perhaps particularly in palliative care, because of the nature of the human interaction in the caring process it is essential that each professional has an understanding of themselves, their personal values and their own insights. This might be achieved through a number of means but personal reflection and supervision are ways that many have found helpful.

For many professions, the context in which their work is carried out is clearly understood, but in palliative care the context may be constantly changing requiring a continual refocusing, a reanalysing and a renewing of intentions and actions. Subsequently it can be very difficult to explain exactly what it is that each professional does. Imagine trying to articulate just what a doctor does. In many ways the context of palliative care fits well into what Schön, in writing about theories of reflective practice, called 'the swampy zones of practice' where 'confusing problems which defy technical solutions' often lie (1997: 3).

In palliative care the team is used as a strategy to achieve a goal of improving the quality of life for people whose life expectancy is short. In their chapter on the interdisciplinary team Lickiss *et al.* (2005) have suggested some fundamental prerequisites for effective and efficient team work:

- consensus and clarity regarding goals/objectives/strategies
- recognition of specific personal contributions of each team member
- competence of each team member in his or her own discipline and understanding and respect for the competence and role of each other team member and procedures
- clear definition of tasks and responsibilities/accountability and means of communication within the teams
- competent leadership appropriate to the structure and function of the team and the task at hand
- procedures for evaluating the effectiveness and quality of team efforts
- bereavement care of staff as appropriate
- recognition of the contribution of patients in furthering professional understanding.

The goal of the team is to achieve the *patient's* outcomes (desires, wishes, goals etc.) and in order to achieve this we have to first know what they are. Part of the problem with teamworking is that each profession will have different goals of care depending on the various emphases of physical, psychological, social and spiritual approaches. Consequently these goals must cohere in a shared vision of care derived from the patient narrative and the team will require a forum in which to articulate this vision. Trying to describe the provision of care is also problematic, because initially professional practice depends on the process of socialization which each team member has undergone to gain membership of their profession, but subsequently it will depend on the communities of practice to which they belong.

James and MacLeod (1993) outlined the difficulty of sharing knowledge in the care setting. They suggested that the complexity of palliative care knowledge and its use as a basis for action presented a particular challenge for those faced with the task of explaining aspects of palliation to others. They pointed out that the 'frameworks for understanding' which are essential if the sharing of understanding is to take place may be challenging in this field partly because the framework is not yet developed. Most professional groups within health care teams employ a task-oriented or problem-solving approach to care, whereas in palliative care a more patient-centred approach demands the development of flexibility and supportive skills to foster such care. In order to do this, different disciplines have to understand fully and be able to articulate to others their espoused theories and bases for action and to develop in other caregivers a framework for the understanding of practice.

Educational methods

There are risks in removing interprofessional education from an interprofessional context and, in particular, from an interprofessional workplace. One risk is that decontextualized education becomes idealized, creating difficulties when it comes to putting into practice the knowledge, skills and attitudes learned. Another is that uniprofessional education can lead to isolation and insularity, creating rigid professional boundaries and power structures that militate against the shared care that characterizes communities of practice. Nonetheless there will be times when, at both the inter- and the uniprofessional level, it is valuable and productive to do educational work intraprofessionally. For example, while we advocate interprofessional reflection on practice as a means of exploring knowledge, skills and values and of evaluating the practice of care against a shared vision, we recognize that it is important to withdraw from the practice setting in order to review current practice, including its scope, from the point of view of an individual profession.

The affective quality of work (and learning) is higher in a palliative care context; there is more emotional work to do. In addition there may be more dimensions to care (physical, emotional, spiritual, relational) and more recipients (e.g. family). Consequently the emotions and values of both patients and professionals must be on the educational agenda. Case studies and role plays are good vehicles for the exploration of these issues away from the workplace. Briefings, debriefings and case reviews can serve a similar purpose in the practice setting. In clinical practice, professional boundaries are likely to be less rigid and the delivery of care more flexible.

Much education in palliative care will take place at work, indeed the shared understandings we are promoting could be seen as educational outcomes. However there may be compromises and other negotiations (e.g. boundaries) in achieving those understandings and they may require further educational work outside the care setting. Value can be added to work experiences through systematic processes of reflection using portfolios, logbooks, journals and/or thought-provoking episode reports to facilitate post-encounter

Box 22.3 Getting professionals together: starting tips

Use ice-breaking exercises and/or 'baggage drops'

Provide or develop clear aims and objectives

Explore similarities and differences in roles

Acknowledge differing skill sets, knowledge and expectations

Ensure courtesy and respect for each participant

Identify any hierarchical perceptions and minimize these (reduce territorial hostility between professions)

Identify common values and cultural beliefs

Ensure content has common interest to all

Reinforce the central position of the patient in learning and practice – use case-based and/or problem-based examples wherever possible

Identify ways to transfer learning into experiential practice

Develop meaningful assessments and evaluations

processing and analysis (Greenhalgh and Hurwitz 1999; Henderson *et al.* 2002; Wilson and Ayers 2004).

Formal interprofessional programmes require considerable attention to process: parking personal and professional baggage, exploring and defining roles to diminish stereotyping; debriefing to examine system and individual responses. Much of interprofessional learning for palliative care will inevitably take place within small group settings. Small group work benefits from the usual considerations of the learning environment and brings with it additional requirements such as introductions, credentialling, agenda or objective-setting, agreement on ground rules and a modus operandi and so forth (see Box 22.5). Whether learning in a theoretical way through cases or problems, or reviewing clinical situations, there are certain considerations that can improve effectiveness for this sort of learning (Oandasan and Reeves 2005). For interactive learning to be effective there is a need to maintain a group balance, ensuring that disciplines are not likely to dominate by being over-represented. The group size must be of an order that facilitates easy communication

Box 22.4 Avoiding pitfalls

Ensure organizational or institutional commitment

Ensure enough space and time to develop programs

Meet the needs of contrasting perspectives, terminology/language and levels of experience

Balance numbers of students

Ross and Southgate (2000)

Box 22.5 Tips for creating safety in a group

- Use an ice-breaking exercise at the start of each session
- Arrive on time, be attentive, avoid interrupting, use non-verbals to signal your wish to join in
- Agree to some form of confidentiality (regarding patient stories, personal experiences)
- Be courteous and respectful to others, especially if you disagree or don't understand
- Respect boundaries and limits
- Acknowledge your ground rules and refer to them as necessary
- Adapt your ground rules to suit changing circumstances – make this a group activity
- Be gentle and helpful, wary of blaming, judging etc.
- Follow the principles of giving feedback constructively
- Build up to self-disclosure, establish trust first
- Listen actively and use non-verbals to show support, empathy, confusion etc.
- Don't dominate the group
- Speak in the first person singular – 'I' rather than 'one' or 'we' – own what you say
- Address others in the second person – 'you' rather than 'her', 'him', 'they' – if you choose to encounter, do so directly
- *But* be aware of when you intend encountering, otherwise use 'I' and offer subjective opinions, interpretations
- Avoid presuming to tell others what they are thinking or feeling
- Take risks in saying what is going on for you and be open to others doing the same
- Use the group to check out your own feelings, responses
- Reflect on your own experience and motivation and note how they influence your questions and comments to others
- Try to avoid dumping and displacing your own distress on others
- Show respect if someone wishes to withhold
- Leave options open: 'We could let this go, but if you want to talk, now or later,...'
- Give permission: 'Not everybody finds this depressing, difficult etc...' or 'lots of people get embarrassed at... how about you?' or 'Doctors can't always recognize their patients' feelings'
- Use personal examples to help others open up: 'When *I* get...'
- Finish intense sessions with an acknowledgement of group process and what has been achieved
- Identify changes the group would like to see in process
- Recognize the possibility of unfinished business and provide for follow-up

amongst the group. Finally the group is most effective for learning where there is stability with little turnover and members can learn together for some time.

In outlining his views of a social theory of learning, Wenger (1998) argues that in order to learn effectively, together we must:

- discover shared meaning, a way of talking about our abilities and our experiences that can be shared
- practice a way of talking about our shared histories and social frameworks that mean we can understand each other
- negotiate identity, a way of talking about how learning changes who we are.

To this should perhaps be added that we must also have a willingness to learn and work together, develop trust and confidence in each other's abilities and show mutual respect of each other's abilities and contributions. How we establish these attitudes and behaviours in the workplace is crucial. Students joining communities of practice that are already functioning more or less effectively are marginal members, inexpert to some degree. It is important for their development as professionals that they are made to feel legitimate members of the group and enabled to participate in the group's activities. There is some risk for students in this process since they may unknowingly wander from one professional jurisdiction to another. Introductions, inductions and role definitions will all help at this point but, day to day, the practice of the community is likely to be the greatest determinant of emergent professional identity. In an effectively functioning community of practice the student is likely to witness negotiations, favours, deals and trades between professionals conducted in the best interests of the patient. These are transforming experiences in the taking on of professional identity and can be the subject of further reflective work. It is also important to recognize that the social dynamics of the community of practice potentially present students with a variety of role models, a function of which the members may or may not be aware.

In a systematic review of the development of an evidence base for interdisciplinary learning Cooper et al. (2001) identified a number of educational interventions from the literature which used interdisciplinary learning. The prominent methods of teaching used were small group teaching, case studies (real or simulated) and experiential learning, but traditional didactic methods were also used in maybe a third of the interventions. The summary of the main findings of this review showed the largest effects of interdisciplinary learning were on students' knowledge and attitudes, skills and beliefs and in particular on understanding of professional roles in team working. The smallest effects were for a transfer of learning into students' experiential practice and an effect on the students' learning environments. It was also interesting to note that educational and psychological theories were rarely used to guide the development of interventions and outcome measures. This review concluded by reinforcing previously held views that there were no clear-cut answers in terms of the effects of interprofessional learning upon professional practice. These observations are particularly relevant for palliative care.

Hall (2005) has pointed out that physicians traditionally learn independently in a highly competitive academic environment. Nurses learn early in their career to work as a team, collectively working out problems and efficiently exchanging information. She also suggests that the physician-patient relationship tends to be authoritarian whereas other professions such as social work and nursing have placed more value on patients' self-determination. This variance has led to tensions within interprofessional teams in palliative care where role-blurring exists. There is the possibility with interprofessional learning of identifying where one role ends and another begins, which is clearly an attractive option. Collaboration in the development of effective team work is fundamental and Norsen *et al.* (1995) have identified six collaborative skills which are crucial for such team work that should be addressed in any professional education programme:

1. co-operation – acknowledging and respecting others opinions and viewpoints

2. assertiveness – supporting one's own viewpoint with confidence

3. responsibility – accepting and sharing responsibilities and participating in group decision-making and planning

4. communication

5. autonomy

6. coordination – efficient organization of group tasks and assignments.

Alternatively, if we identify competencies for palliative care practice in an interprofessional way we can utilize a format like that proposed by Barr (1998) in which 'collaborative competencies' are outlined:

- describe one's roles and responsibilities clearly to other professions
- recognize and observe the constraints of one's role, responsibilities and competence, yet perceive the needs of a wider framework
- recognize and respect the roles, responsibilities and competencies of other professions in relation to one's own work with other professions to effect change and resolve conflict in the provision of care and treatment
- work with others to assess, plan, provide and review care for individual patients
- tolerate differences, misunderstandings and shortcomings of other professions
- facilitate interprofessional case conferences, team meetings etc.
- enter into interdependent relationships with other professions.

Palliative care is the product of a shared vision of care derived from the patient narrative and incorporating values and goals expressed in that narrative. The patient care plan is directed towards realizing those values and goals and includes actions and activities that we believe will be instrumental in achieving these. The unique course of events and experiences taken by the dying patient and the family combined with all the accompanying professional work (i.e. what the professional carers do) constitutes the trajectory of dying. This professional work can be viewed at three levels which will often mirror the hierarchy of professions (partly following legislated requirements). In daily practice there will be many tasks which, *in toto*, constitute care but the tasks will not be performed strictly according to profession. Further, they may consist of different types of work brought together in one task (or bundle of tasks). For example a carer might combine 'machine' work with 'comfort' and 'sentimental' work and this might be instantiated using hand–eye coordination, kinaesthetic feedback, body position, non-verbal communication, eye contact, pitch and tone of voice and so on. To be effective these bundles of tasks need to be organized and coordinated by somebody knowledgeable about the patient and in regular contact with affected parties. Finally, there needs to be someone who is responsible for overall planning, managing interventions and changes to the care plan and ensuring that clinical practice is aligned with the shared vision of care. Historically, a medical practitioner has taken the latter role, although we see no compelling reason for this, provided there are effective means of managing medications.

One of the taxing questions for educators in palliative care is how and when to introduce the concepts and realities of interprofessional education. While it is clear that there are discipline-specific areas of learning there is no doubt that in an area of health care that relies so heavily on interprofessional working there is great merit in introducing these concepts of learning at an early stage. Harden's (1998) notion of a spectrum of learning is being adopted in a number of areas and this spectrum is well-suited to learning in palliative care. In the development of an interprofessional educational exercise we must ask:

- what are the goals we are trying to achieve in having students learn together?
- based on these goals when should we introduce the learning to students?
- what strategy of learning should be used to accomplish these goals? (Oandasan and Reeves 2005).

Examples of interprofessional learning

A half-day interprofessional workshop in palliative care for undergraduates was developed by the team at Countess Mountbatten House in Southampton, England (Wee *et al.* 2001). They were facilitated by a palliative medicine consultant, a palliative nurse lecturer and a lecturer in psychosocial palliative care (a senior physiotherapist and occupational therapist joined the group for the final session). Initially students were asked to:

- describe their course briefly to others in the group and say what they were doing now
- explain how the course has prepared the student for what they are doing now
- explain how the course as a whole is preparing the student for what they are going to be.

Later in the session each group of students is joined by a family carer who acts as a resource for the group. The students are given specific tasks:

- hear the carer's story
- consider which different professionals are involved
- discuss how the care was coordinated
- identify the 'key' person who made it work
- discuss what would have made the care provided better for the patient, carer and other health professionals.

Their evaluation showed that students responded positively to 'real' situations and in particular valued learning from the carer. That aspect provided insight for the students into their own profession and into health care provision generally.

MacLeod and Nash developed a series of multiprofessional workshops in the early 1990s (for examples see MacLeod and Nash 1991, 1994) that utilized the similarities and differences between professional groups in their approaches to death and dying. They addressed areas such as communication and counselling skills (drawing on the approaches and experiences of each profession), ways of coping with death and dying and differing ways of caring for the family carer, friends and other helpers. They used didactic sessions for some of the more practical issues and experiential methods such as creative writing, role plays and sculpting for some of the more personal aspects of caring for people near the end of life. During these workshops participants were able to explore preconceived ideas about the nature of professional work in other disciplines and dispel some myths. Work with primary health care teams in particular was constructive in that despite working together on a regular basis participants often commented on their ability to see a new side of their colleagues. A shared understanding of values and approaches to care emerged from the majority of these workshops that participants felt would enhance their care for patients and families.

Carpenter and Hewstone (1996) report on a shared learning programme for final year social work and medical students who worked in pairs and small groups on shared tasks looking at topics including alcohol abuse, dealing with psychiatric emergencies, deliberate self-harm and community services for people with learning disabilities. Those participants reported increased understandings of the roles, attitudes and duties of other professions and how to work together.

Box 22.6 Examples of innovative practice in interprofessional education

- The training ward – medical, nursing, physiotherapy, occupational therapy, biomedical technician and social welfare students work together on practical issues of patient care at different wards and practices (Wahlström *et al.* 1997)
- Senior pre-qualification students in medicine, nursing, physiotherapy and occupational therapy work together caring for orthopaedic and rheumatology patients (Reeves *et al.* 2002)
- Educating health care students in professionalism (McNair 2005)
- Listening to and learning from the family carer's story: nursing, medicine, social work, physiotherapy and occupational therapy students (Turner *et al.* 2000)
- Shared learning for doctors and social workers: evaluation of a programme (Carpenter and Hewstone 1996)

An interprofessional ward placement for medical, nursing, occupational therapy and physiotherapy students, developed from the work in the training ward in Linköping (Wahlström *et al.* 1997), is reported from the UK (Reeves *et al.* 2002). Senior pre-qualification students learned and worked together to plan and deliver care for a group of orthopaedic and rheumatology patients. Students found it a valuable and relevant learning experience and the patients reported a high level of satisfaction with the care and attention they received from the student teams.

Conclusion

In this chapter we have argued that professional caregivers must be responsive to the range of needs of the dying patient and their family. In doing so they will perform a variety of work, some clearly determined by their scope of practice, but much determined by the unique needs of the patient at any given time. We have also argued that the patient's needs are to be discovered in the patient narrative and ideally lead to a shared vision of care. The patient and the shared vision of care are at the heart of every community of practice and we have suggested a theoretical underpinning of practice based on the patient-centred clinical method (Stewart *et al.* 2003) and on ideas about the nature of clinical work and how it is performed in communities of practice (Strauss *et al.* 1985; Wenger 1998). We argue that these intellectual tools will enable carers in diverse clinical settings to create a shared vision of care and a means of achieving that vision collaboratively. Finally, the same theoretical structures will help students make sense of their experiences and their emerging identities as health care professionals.

Chapter 23

Developing a community of teachers

Ruthmarijke Smeding, Bee Wee and
John Ellershaw

Introduction

Today, the perspective on the dying is shifting in many countries, moving from a passive cessation of curative treatment to a proactive integration of palliative care. With this movement comes the need to prepare professional and lay carers for their role in looking after dying people. In turn, those who take on the task of educating these carers require preparation and nurturing as teachers. The care of dying people, and their families, in the period leading up to the death and beyond, into bereavement, is much too important to be left to chance. The old maxim of 'see one, do one, teach one' is no longer good enough.

The focus of this chapter is on the development of individual teachers and a community of teachers within palliative care. The case for high-quality education and training in palliative care is made elsewhere in this book, along with the importance of interprofessional learning as a vehicle towards more collaborative teamworking. In this chapter, we shall:

- consider some of the relevant trends in the wider education world
- examine issues relating to the development of the individual teacher in palliative care
- propose organizational support for the development of a community of teachers within palliative care.

Trends in education

Shifts in educational theory

Teaching in palliative care has become a widespread activity now that palliative care is becoming a part of mainstream medicine in many countries across the world. Yet many teachers within palliative care are not given adequate time and opportunity to see the bigger picture or to acquire the necessary competence and confidence in teaching. By taking on teaching activities, these palliative care teachers join a third community beyond their own professional group and the domain of palliative care, namely the discipline of education. They need to develop their understanding and mastery of this domain, similar to that already achieved for their own professional background and the specialty of palliative care.

The research-driven advancement of education has been a long process of model-testing and systematic reflection on how to move students towards the desired direction in learning. The thinking about this process has changed dramatically over the last forty years. Until the late 1960s, students had been required to listen to knowledge offered, copy the skills demonstrated and somehow adopt the attitudes of their teachers. Paulo Freire, a Brazilian professor of learning theory called this the 'banking model' (Freire 1972), in which teachers seek to take out what they have put in. Creativity and independence were valued but constrained.

During the 1970s, educational theory and practice moved from an emphasis on knowledge acquisition to more process-oriented approaches. Learning became seen as the interaction between the individual learner and the material or content of what was being learned. Knowles set out his theory about the difference between learning processes in children and adults (Knowles 1970) whereas Kolb's experiential learning theory proposed a learning cycle, linking practical experiences to reflection, observation, theoretical thinking and further practical application (Kolb 1984). By the beginning of the twenty-first century, educational theory had focused further on the way individuals create the meaning of the materials they work with. It does not mean that education has become entirely learner-controlled, in terms of its outcomes. On the contrary, the emphasis on outcomes-based education means that careful goals have to be formulated. However, now, these goals tend to be jointly developed between teacher and learner, with the latter taking more and more control of this process as they move further along the learning trajectory. Once these goals have been agreed, learning methodologies appropriate to these goals may be identified, often by the teacher in negotiation with the learner.

The changes in educational thinking have been influenced by perspectives from other disciplines, including behaviourism, psychoanalysis (the role of the unconscious in learning processes), humanism (Maslow, Knowles, Rogers) and the belief in the value of experiences (Kolb, Mumford, Gardener). No doubt educational thinking will continue to be challenged, modified and enhanced through further unfolding of scientific enquiry.

What does all this mean for the teacher in palliative care? It is not necessary for such a teacher to agonize over which particular learning theory to adopt, to the exclusion of others. Understanding these theories offers the palliative care teacher some theoretical frameworks in which to reflect on their teaching approaches and to gain insights into the students' responses.

Where does training fit in?

Alongside shifts in educational thinking, a new set of designed learning experiences emerged from the business world. The need to pass on newly emerging technologies to the workforce quickly and efficiently was imperative. These learning exercises were aimed mainly at the 'doing' part of the learning cycle, to the detriment of reflection, observation and theoretical thinking. Steadman *et al.* (2006) offers a recent example of this in medical education and provides a comparison of the results of the two different approaches. While training may be a time-efficient way of inculcating certain behaviours where the end points are fixed and predictable, there are also inherent dangers in over-emphasizing training when it comes to health and social care.

In such a context training may have a quick but superficial effect, sacrificing the development of critical thinking and informed, emotional responsiveness, both equally necessary for interaction with other human beings, particularly those who are dying and vulnerable. Habituation, or for that matter underlying cognitive structures, cannot be replaced by one incident of training simply overruling previously existing ways of working (Nakashima 1997). Insight into the building of cognitive structures and how to achieve desired changes in existing behaviour and thinking are important aspects of the formation of educational theory. On the other hand, the assumption that knowledge will automatically translate into desired professional competencies needs revisiting.

Developments in professional education

Just as there has been a shift over the past decades in the position of the learner, from a passive absorber to a co-designer of their learning path, so there has been a shift in assumptions about the effect of learning. Previously, the aim was to help the student discover the truth, after which they would be charged as a keeper of the truth in their profession. Now, undergraduate and postgraduate learning is seen as part of a continuous, lifelong learning process (Toynton 2005). The role of education is thus to develop and support this dynamic process, through and beyond the gates of access to the professional world in which complexity and uncertainty abound.

Interprofessional teamworking is integral to palliative care. The contributing professions come from disciplinary backgrounds which are quite diverse in their philosophy and teaching methodologies. Some were historically university-based (medicine, psychology, sociology, theology) while others were more vocational-based (nursing, physiotherapy, occupational therapy, social work). These vary from country to country, although in some areas the distinction is becoming less relevant. For example, Europe will move, over time, to a 'BA-MA' system (like the American educational system, but with national variations) in which its polytechnic and university-based systems will eventually be restructured into new ways of defining academic degrees. One can see changes in the vocational realm moving towards theory development whereas academically designed educational pathways seem to be moving towards a stronger emphasis on practical approaches.

The challenge of palliative care education

Palliative care, like other specialties, has to address at least three different levels of education: undergraduate, postgraduate or post-qualifying and work-based.

When palliative care is taught at an undergraduate level within a curriculum, the cohort of students is unselected and the level of interest widely variable. Students at this level also have less clinical experience of dying patients but may already have personal experiences of illness, death or bereavement. Teachers of these unselected groups need to be aware of the range of responses that may arise, ranging from lack of interest to distressing emotional reactions. They need to have identified, and have available to them, a range of ways in which to support the students and learning processes appropriately. The teacher too may be affected by dying, death or bereavement in their own life and needs to be aware of the impact of this on the teaching process.

Postgraduate education poses different challenges to undergraduate education. In postgraduate education, health care professional students tend to be self-selected with an interest in learning and developing their skills in palliative care. This creates a different type of learner and a different learning environment.

The clinical setting offers opportunity for work-based experiential learning. One example is the Liverpool Care of the Dying Pathway (Ellershaw and Wilkinson 2003) or, indeed, any other integrated care pathways. These pathways provide educational content and have been found to be helpful frameworks in which to enhance education and training by bridging theory and practice.

Finally, a further challenge to education, beyond these three levels, is posed by the cohort of health care professionals who do not seek additional postgraduate education or qualifications in palliative care.

Developing the individual teacher

Developing a teaching workforce in palliative care requires a dual strategy. At a microlevel, it requires attention to the developmental needs of individual teachers; at a macrolevel, it requires organizational structures and processes, to initiate and enhance the development and professionalization of the community of educators. Some of the issues in palliative care teaching are generic to those in other areas of professional education, others are topic-specific.

The individual teacher

Where is the teacher coming from?

The starting point of the teacher, like any learner, has a strong influence on teaching practice. This starting point may relate to age, gender, ethnicity, early education culture, professional background and a whole host of other factors, much of which may be unknown, inaccessible or unacknowledged by the learner–teacher. This has particular relevance when teaching diverse groups. Even when the teacher shares a similar background to their students or learners, they may not share the same starting point, for example, in terms of values. The 'iceberg of professional practice' proposed by Fish and Coles (1998) highlights some of the hidden aspects of professional practice, such as assumptions, beliefs and values, which lie unseen and are often inaccessible but have a profound influence on the shape and nature of what is visible (see Figure 23.1). Teachers need to be willing to explore, expose and be appropriately challenged about some of those aspects of their professionalism, work that requires a deeper than surface approach. Such challenging must take place within a safe, constructive and respectful environment.

This is particularly relevant in teaching about palliative care. In addition to one's own life events, health and social work professionals who work in close proximity to intense emotions triggered by suffering, death and dying, often share values, assumptions and beliefs that are so deeply embedded that they seem to be difficult to access, e.g. for questioning, and not easily passed on to students and learners via quick teaching procedures.

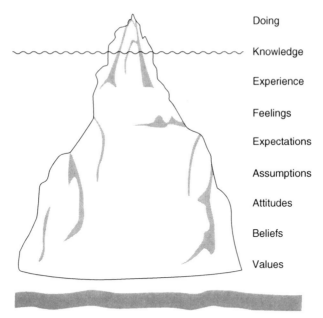

Doing

Knowledge

Experience

Feelings

Expectations

Assumptions

Attitudes

Beliefs

Values

Fig. 23.1 The iceberg of professional practice (Fish and Coles 1998). Reprinted from Fish D and Coles C (1998). *Developing professional judgement in health care: learning through the critical appreciation of practice*, p 306. Oxford: Butterworth-Heinemann, with permission from Elsevier

Harden *et al.* (1999) proposed a three-circle model to represent the learning outcomes appropriate for the development of a medical teacher: performance of the teaching tasks (e.g. how to teach on a ward round) as the inner circle, the approach to those tasks (e.g. having an understanding of the process of their teaching practice) as the middle circle and professionalism and self-development of those individuals as teachers (e.g. responding to critical comments) as the outer circle. Although this model was proposed within the medical context, it is relevant for all teachers in palliative care. We would suggest that the teacher's own understanding and critical awareness of where they are starting from, including the place of dying, death and bereavement in their lives, should permeate through all three circles because it underpins every aspect of this teacher's learning process.

Rights of the professional teacher

In the world of health and social care practice, it has become increasingly recognized that time and resources need to be devoted to continuing professional development so that practitioners stay fresh, up to date and deliver high quality care. Similarly, teachers require support to train as teachers and continue their own development as teachers. They have a right to expect that an organization which expects them to teach also provides them with the support to do so.

In a relatively young specialty such as palliative care, practitioners often find themselves in the position of having to (and wanting to) teach without adequate adjustments being made to their clinical responsibilities. The result is often feeling torn between their various duties. From the starting point of being a clinician, clinical work will almost always take precedence. While this is understandable, it can result in students and learners always taking secondary place and thus absorbing the implicit message that they, and their learning, are not important. In reality, most practitioners put themselves under tremendous pressure to fulfil both aspects of their job, with the danger that this becomes unsustainable. Organizations which value teaching have a responsibility to ensure that job descriptions and job plans adequately incorporate the teaching role of the practitioner.

Responsibilities of the professional teacher

In turn, the clinical teacher has certain responsibilities. First, they need to keep up to date with the subject of the teaching, just as they need to do so in order to practice safely as a clinician. In addition, the clinical teacher needs to keep up to date with teaching methodologies and wider issues in education. If they were to do the first (clinical update) without the second (teaching update), it would be akin to a clinician who knows everything about handling communication but insists nevertheless on teaching this in a completely didactic, i.e. frontal chalk and talk, manner.

Second, teaching cannot occur in a vacuum. Students and learners come with certain prior knowledge and understanding. If the teaching encounter is part of a course, students and learners come from one place before entering this encounter and subsequently move to another (learning) situation. Clinical teachers carry a responsibility for understanding where their teaching session sits within an overall curriculum, so that the learning process is made coherent for their students. Similarly, they need to consider where the students or learners are likely to be coming from, in terms of mindset, attitudes and emotion, so that they can help these students and learners make cogent links and prepare them for the next stage. In the study of palliative care, the subject matter may range from physical symptom control to spiritual issues or bereavement. The effective clinical teacher will use teaching methodologies which support students and learners in making the mental switch which the various aspects require. The clinical teacher who is oblivious to this will, at best, not get their message across and, at worst, cause confusion and dismay amongst his/her audience.

Third, selection of teaching methodologies requires care and understanding about its potential impact, both positive and negative. It is not enough for the clinical teacher to know 'how to' teach in a particular way. It is essential that they also understand the full impact that any one approach might have. They need to be able to use a variety of methods to suit different learning styles, as well as match appropriate methodologies to the content (Leung 2003). An obvious example would be the use of role play in teaching. This is an extremely effective way of teaching communication skills, empathy and practical application of knowledge. However, it is also a powerful tool to evoke strong emotions which might, if excessive, hinder learning or even harm learners. Another example would be a teacher who invites the audience to 'connect to your first loss in childhood' as an opening to a learning session on loss and grief. They may lose part or all of the audience for the rest of the session if these learners remain immersed in their emotions and unable to process further learning on the subject.

The fourth responsibility for the clinical teacher to which we wish to draw attention is that of the need to respect boundaries. The subject matter of palliative care, in particular teaching around death, dying and bereavement, has particular potential to trigger off personal emotions. The clinical teacher needs to be able to support the distressed learner but to remain in the relationship of teacher–learner, and to refrain from moving into a therapeutic relationship. This requires a high level of self-awareness, self-discipline and education skills on the part of the clinical teacher. The teacher who is also a practitioner at other times may find it easy to drift between the two but this is neither helpful for the learner, nor productive for learning. It is important to remember that it is not necessary to trigger deep emotional levels to achieve the required learning outcomes.

Methodologies for developing the individual teacher

In the section below, we set out a number of methods for developing teachers in palliative care. We do not claim superiority of any one method over others; indeed, many are complementary and the individual teacher may be exposed to one or more method depending on the opportunity that their situation offers.

A useful approach to thinking about teacher development is the framework proposed by Hesketh *et al.* (2001), building on Harden's three-circle model (1999). Although this was developed as a model for doctors who teach, it is also helpful for other health and social work professionals. The authors outline a set of 12 learning outcomes for the effective teacher, grouped around three themes (see Table 23.1):

- doing the right thing
- doing the thing right
- the right person doing it.

Teacher development through direct teaching experience

How does the individual draw on direct experiences of teaching to develop as an educator? We suggest that the clinical educator proceeds through a number of levels of sophistication in this process.

Table 23.1 Learning outcomes for the effective teacher (after Hesketh *et al.* 2001)

Themes	Learning outcomes
Doing the right thing (what the teacher is able to do)	Teach large and small groups Teach in a clinical setting Facilitate and manage learning Plan learning Develop and work with learning resources Assess trainees Evaluate courses and undertake research in education
Doing the thing right (how the teacher approaches the teaching)	With understanding of principles of education With appropriate attitudes, ethical understanding and legal awareness With appropriate decision-making skills and best evidence-based education
Right person doing it (the clinician as professional teacher)	The role of teacher or trainer within the health service and university Personal development with regard to teaching

First, there appears to be a *reactive phase*. At this stage, the teacher reacts and draws from a clinical encounter directly, seeking to translate this into an educational encounter. For example, a palliative care nurse takes a student with her on a home visit, acting for the first time as a teacher. When they leave the patient's home, the nurse (learner–teacher) goes over the experience with the student and helps them to identify the learning points from that situation. At this stage, the nurse may consider the task to be well done if the student expresses satisfaction from that learning encounter. If they do not, the nurse educator may be left with some doubt about the impact of that learning encounter.

After acquiring some basic teaching competencies, the next phase may emerge. This is the *responsive phase*, when the teacher begins to structure learning situations more clearly and develops the capacity to design in connection with the student as well as the teacher themself. This nurse–teacher has now taken a series of students on home visits. Perhaps they now feel confident enough to generate questions, which move the learning points from the straightforward to the more complex in an incrementally complex, organized way. They find it important to ask for feedback from the students or their organization may issue feedback forms for students to complete. The nurse educator reviews the feedback forms, reflects on the 'evaluation' of their teaching received and modifies practice on an informed basis, weighing up personal insights and educational knowledge with the feedback received (Ende 1983).

Taking this development onto a further stage, the nurse–teacher enters a *proactive phase*. They take a step back and consider their development as an educator in a more strategic way, carrying out action research in which they systematically evaluate, reflect and modify their practice as an educator, using various settings, learners and desired outcomes. The students, fellow learners from the beginning, now become co-researchers (not research subjects) in helping her to improve the teacher's practice. Such developments may occur at individual and/or organizational levels.

Teacher development through peer observation and structured feedback

Feedback is an essential and effective part of learning which is often underused (Beckman *et al.* 2003; Beckman 2004). In clinical practice, feedback about the effectiveness of care comes from comments by patients, relatives and colleagues and from the success, or otherwise, of care arrangements (e.g. satisfactory discharges). In teaching, feedback comes from many sources, including the student's or learner's reactions (as described in the above section), the quality of work produced by the students, the teacher's self-evaluation, reflection and comments from colleagues and senior managers and in the end, hopefully, from more satisfied service recipients (e.g. patients and their families).

Peer observation and structured feedback, if done professionally, is a constructive, useful and interesting method for enhancing the learning process for a teacher (Millard 2000). The teacher carries out a small piece of teaching (microteaching) in a safe, facilitated group setting. He/she receives observational feedback from his/her peers within a structured format. The teacher remains in the driving seat and determines the depth and extent of the discussion. In this approach, the prime beneficiary is the teacher (who carries out the microteaching) and their co-learners have to put that teacher's interests

Box 23.1 Building a community of teachers through microteaching

Within the palliative care service, first at Southampton, now at Oxford, microteaching has been established as a means of teacher development. Clinical and non-clinical staff in the hospice are invited to participate in this activity. Each microteaching set consists of up to six participants, facilitated by the second author of this chapter. Each set meets for three sessions. Learning styles and the microteaching process are explained and demonstrated at the first session. Each participant then undertakes microteaching at the second or third session. In each case, the participant who is taking on the teacher role prepares and delivers a ten-minute piece of teaching. One observer is assigned to document what they see and hear (observations only, they are not allowed to insert judgements or interpretations) and the rest of the participants are 'learners'. The feedback process is as follows:

1. Each person reflects in silence and makes brief notes.

2. The teacher comments first on how the microteaching session had gone – often, requiring encouragement from the facilitator to comment on what went well, as well as what did not.

3. Each 'learner' feeds back what they have learnt and what the teacher did that had supported that individual's learning. 'I' statements are mandatory; nobody is allowed to make sweeping statements or assume his/her views are shared by other 'learners'.

4. The observer gives a chronological feedback on what they had observed.

5. The teacher comments on the feedback received.

6. The facilitator closes the session and opens the discussion to wider issues raised by the teaching session.

   Within the organization, several microteaching sets were run concurrently or consecutively. Once every participant had had the opportunity to participate, a monthly microteaching event was set up, to which all those who had completed a microteaching set were invited. This gave them opportunity to explore and rehearse other teaching formats, and to continue receiving peer feedback within a safe, structured setting.

ahead of their own. This enables the teacher to explore different teaching methodologies and their impact safely. The way in which an organization has used this approach to build a community of teachers is described in Box 23.1.

Teacher development through group processes

Teachers who enjoy learning as part of a group may come together in learner sets. The group of teachers meets regularly and identifies a problem or issue about which they wish, or need, to gain a deeper understanding. The group then decides the tasks that are required to achieve this, divides up the work and sets off to find what they need. They later reconvene to share their learning. A well-recognized advantage of this method is that the group processes generate a depth of learning that is greater than simply adding together the knowledge that each has gleaned to contribute to the group. However, it does require discipline, coordination and leadership (albeit a rotating one) to ensure that the group continues to meet its objectives and to develop as a set of learner-teachers.

Strategies for development of a teaching workforce in palliative care

Development of mentorship

Although a learner–teacher can, and should, be able to seek information through reading books and published articles, a planned exchange with a senior colleague, in the form of a mentoring relationship, may come as welcome support in the beginning. The demonstration of mentoring in difficult situations may be an important learning experience for the less experienced palliative care teacher. Mentorship can empower less experienced teachers to refuse to undertake unsuitable teaching responsibilities. For example, a learner–teacher should not be asked to teach advanced communication skills, using role play, without adequate support or supervision.

As teachers become more experienced, peer mentorship may be used to achieve sustainability and build experience. International, national or regional schemes of mentorship in palliative care teaching can be established through email exchanges together with direct contact by telephone or face to face meetings.

Development of critical thinking

Organizations which aim to promote palliative care practice through education need to provide individual teachers with the encouragement, opportunity and resources to take a step back from their day to day teaching practice in order to critically appraise their provision of educational experiences on a regular basis. This may take place either with a peer or with a group of fellow teachers where feedback can provide a meaningful source of growth in competency and critical self awareness. Such interactive reflections are likely to yield higher and denser results than solo self-reflection or the use of feedback from students alone.

Training the teachers

The assumption that good clinicians necessarily make good teachers is a myth maintained by organizations to the detriment of the individual teacher and their learners. The assumption that clinicians are uninterested in learning how to become good teachers has been challenged by the eagerness with which many clinicians, including palliative care practitioners, have embraced educator programmes.

Educator programmes may be generic or subject-specific, uniprofessional or interprofessional. They vary in length, from one to two days, to week-long residential courses. An example of the latter is the Train the Teachers in Palliative Medicine course, developed in

1994 by the first author with other collaborators. The course has also been modified for interprofessional groups and addresses goal-setting, designing of educational processes, understanding of learning theories, assessment procedures and insights into various aspects of appropriate role play. These courses are not designed to produce fully trained professional teachers but do provide the basis for competent teaching which is specific to palliative care. So far, this course has reached a primarily European audience, but courses have also been held in South America and Australia and delivered in a variety of languages.

Those who wish to take a more academic or research-based approach may undertake certificate, diploma or masters level programmes in education (Allery *et al.* 2005). Others choose to develop specific aspects such as education leadership through courses run by other organizations such as the Association for the Study of Medical Education in UK (see Chapter 26, p 297).

Development of a community of teachers

In addition to developing individual teachers' ability to teach and enhancing their critical thinking skills, organizations might wish to focus some energy on developing a community of teachers. Wenger (1998) proposed a social theory of learning which consists of four components: practice (learning as doing), meaning (learning as experience), identity (learning as becoming) and community (learning as belonging). The discussion on the development of the teachers thus far has encompassed the first three of those components. Here we suggest that the fourth component, learning as belonging, may be nurtured by organizations through the creation of communities of palliative care teachers. One way to do this would be through organized activities, such as learning sets in which the topics of relevance to professional teachers are systematically addressed. Another way would be to develop microteaching sets in which teachers regularly come together to practice teaching, observed by their peers, learning together via structured feedback. A third way could be the creation of an education forum within the organization.

In our opinion, it is time for systematic reflection and a scholarly discourse. First on content, in order to define core and necessary knowledge for the various professions and secondly, on teaching methodologies proven to be successful in acquiring the necessary competencies for palliative care. This requires time, resources and commitment on the part of individuals, organizations and the wider palliative care community.

Chapter 24

Continuing professional development

Suzanne Henwood and Michelle McGannan

Introduction

In this chapter we shall:

- discuss continuing professional development (CPD) within the overall context of the palliative care workforce
- investigate perceptions and individual attitudes surrounding CPD and how CPD can be evaluated to show that it impacts on the patient
- examine ways of assessing CPD needs, both for the individual and for the organization
- discuss workforce development issues in relation to CPD with a specific emphasis on attempting to ensure the effective incorporation of CPD for all staff, in a complex working environment with multiple and competing priorities
- offer an analysis of selected CPD methods, including a range of practical hints to ensure that these activities are appropriate to the specific context within which the individual practises. The methods include examples of new or creative provision, which we believe can enhance the integration of learning within the palliative care workplace.

Setting the context for CPD in the twenty-first century

It is widely accepted that CPD in the context of health care uses the principles of adult learning, where learning is interactive and adults are involved in the whole learning process. CPD itself is not a new concept, and even before the term CPD was adopted there was an expectation that professionals would continue to learn beyond the point of qualification (Cervero 1988).

As CPD has been introduced across health care services a number of different definitions have been adopted. In addition different terminologies have also been used, often interchangeably, such as 'Continuing Professional Education' or 'Lifelong Learning'. It is generally accepted though that what is required is a deliberate, planned, all-inclusive and continuing process which is recorded and aims to develop the practitioner. In a nursing context, for example, the United Kingdom Central Council (UKCC 2001a) made it clear that CPD was 'more than simply keeping up to date' claiming that it 'requires an enquiring approach to the practice of nursing as well as to issues which impact on that practice'.

What is important then is to establish the concepts being advocated by any CPD policy, which individuals can identify with, rather than the title per se. One definition which was adopted by the engineering professions, and has been extended to encompass the necessity to ensure impact on practice, is shared here as a guide to how CPD can be, and should be, perceived:

> The continuous and systematic maintenance, improvement and broadening of knowledge and skills and the development of personal qualities necessary for the execution of professional and technical duties throughout the practitioners' working life which constantly works to improve the service provided.

Henwood et al. (1998: 6)

The only limitation to this term is the expectation that the process is about *professional* or *practice* development or *personal* development which *impacts on practice*, which may exclude some activities undertaken purely for personal gain.

The explicit expectation of professionals to undertake and record CPD has increased in recent years, with many professional groups adopting mandatory requirements for CPD and others writing clear guidelines in their codes of professional conduct. The main aim of CPD policies is reported to be public protection, although it is questionable whether any clear link has been empirically established between CPD activity and increased standards of practice – but that is the overriding belief, which pushes professions forward into ensuring adequate CPD activity. Caplan (1973) used an analogy of a hurricane to describe the impact of development activity – you cannot directly measure a rise in ocean level at the end of a hurricane, but you would not say there had been no effect.

In recent years the UK National Health Service (NHS) has also set out a clear expectation that professionals will ensure they remain up to date and the concept of clinical governance (Department of Health 1998) for the first time clearly established 'lifelong learning' as a *joint* responsibility between the employer and the practitioner. Agenda for Change (see the glossary) takes this one step further and links pay to the demonstration of appropriate skills and knowledge: CPD then is no longer optional. Core Dimensions 4 and 5 in the Knowledge and Skills Framework (see the glossary) looks specifically at service improvement and quality respectively and Dimension G1 and G2 looks at learning, development and innovation (Department of Health 2004a). Indeed, CPD systems will constantly need to evolve to take into account developments in post-registration requirements from professional and regulatory bodies (Department of Health 2001). However, it is outside the specific remit of this chapter to provide current regulatory body requirements for CPD activities. For up to date information pertaining to requirements, we would recommend visiting your regulatory or professional body's web site.

There are two significant issues from the definition of CPD given which are worth exploring – the development of personal qualities and continuous quality improvement.

The development of personal qualities

Unless the individual learner is entering into learning with the right attitude and is willing to invest in the process of CPD, it is unlikely that there will be a positive benefit. One of the most important things an individual can do to increase the effectiveness of CPD is to explore their own attitude towards learning and development in their work setting. In occupational therapy this has been termed 'The CPD Attitude' (College of Occupational Therapists 1996: 4) and is said to refer to 'a continuous improvement and self reliance in learning'.

In much work related to CPD the centrality of the individual is overlooked and the focus is placed on facilitation of CPD (issues related to funding and protected study time) or employer responsibility. Research in diagnostic radiography has shown that unless the individual is central to the process, the overall effect will be reduced (Henwood 2003), regardless of what policies or facilitation surrounds it. In nursing, Karp reported that 'Motivation is the causal factor, the mediator, and the consequence of learning' and 'that before learning can take place the learner must be motivated' and 'during learning motivation must be maintained' (1992: 171).

Some of the issues you might like to explore are set out in Box 24.1.

If you score lowly on motivation you will struggle to get the most out of any CPD activity, and you need to look inward to see what you can do to change things. If you are managing staff you need to look at motivation to learn and seek ways to facilitate increasing that motivation for your staff. If as a manager you do not value or enthuse about CPD, it is unlikely your staff will.

Continuous quality improvement

CPD can be any activity which impacts either on individual behaviour in practice or directly on practice. This does not have to be formal, attendance-based activities – although is often perceived to be that – (Eraut 1999), but it does have to link to the work environment. Without this link to professional activity, the activities undertaken are purely personal development, which may be individually valuable, but are not *professional* development. Clearly some activities will fall in both categories, but also it is clear some are for personal gain alone and can show no benefit to the practice setting.

A related issue is whether or not any activity is considered to be development. If almost by osmosis an individual experiences something new or is exposed to a learning opportunity,

---

Box 24.1 Attitude to CPD

On a scale of 1 to 10, how motivated are you to learn?

How much do you want to develop?

What barriers stand in your way and what are you prepared to do to break those barriers down?

What would increase your motivation and how can you get more of that?

What decreases your motivation and how can you reduce the impact of that?

Do you think CPD is worthwhile?

unless that is reflected on and used, it will not constitute effective learning. It is up to the individual to show how their ongoing learning impacts in practice and how *they* have made a difference. The Bristol Inquiry Report (2001) made it clear that just being able to do your job is no longer good enough: 'Clearly, health care professionals must be technically competent to do the task they profess to do, but technical competence is no longer sufficient' (Bristol Inquiry Report 2001: 325).

The report went on to suggest that the notion of competence should be broadened to include communication, knowledge of the organization of the NHS and how care is managed, teamwork, shared learning, audit, reflective practice and leadership. Possibly with this extended definition of competence some practitioners may even struggle to demonstrate existing competence, let alone extending their competence through CPD. So while the concept of CPD is no longer new, or even open to question, it is far from embedded – there is still much work to be done.

There are many issues to consider within CPD. The questionnaire set out in Box 24.2 might help you to identify some of the key aspects when considering any activity.

What is, however, missing from many of the discussions around CPD is how to ensure that any CPD undertaken is effective – indeed in much of the work written on CPD effectiveness is not considered, and there may be differences of opinion as to what actually would constitute effectiveness if it were measured. The American Association for Respiratory Therapy (1983) stated that the credibility of provision is based on impact on

Box 24.2 Is an activity worth doing?

Individual attitude

In what frame of mind are you undertaking this activity?

What do you expect to gain for yourself and for your practice?

Are you willing to invest time, energy, money into getting the most out of the activity?

What do you plan to do when the learning is over? How are you going to apply that learning in practice?

Quality

Have you explored what the activity entails?

Is there any accreditation (if a formal activity)?

Are learning outcomes clear?

Do you know anything about the provider/organizer?

What pre-activity information can you get hold of?

Has anyone else done the same or a similar activity – have you spoken to them about it?

How will you assess the quality of the activity?

Box 24.2 *(continued)* **Is an activity worth doing?**

Outcomes

What will you get out of this activity?

How will you know if you have achieved the learning outcomes?

Will you be able to share any of the learning with others?

How will you record what learning has taken place?

What obstacles might you encounter? How can they be overcome?

Relevance/context

How relevant is this learning to my role?

What will I be able to bring to my work place as a result?

How does this meet not only my needs, but my departments needs?

Who else should I speak to about this activity?

How is this going to move me on in my role and in my learning journey?

---

practice. If this is generally accepted then it is surprising that more attention has not been given to impact evaluation. Cervero (1985) and Henwood (2003) have both offered a reflective evaluation tool which looks at the various components which contribute towards making CPD effective, but beyond this there are few tools which look holistically at CPD effectiveness. At best, change in practice is measured following a skills-based course or knowledge increase is tested. Little or nothing is done to look at the wider and often 'softer' outcomes from CPD activity. Rarely within evaluation are the individual participant and their attitudes, the context of work or the work environment considered important, yet without considering these CPD cannot be fully evaluated.

Henwood's (2003) model (see Figure 24.1) gives one holistic reflective framework to explore effectiveness of CPD. Central to the framework is the 'individual' component, their attitude towards development, their motivation and previous experience of CPD. Surrounding the individual is 'facilitation', which looks at the broad aspects of support, enabling CPD to take place. Surrounding facilitation is the concept of 'external force' which includes mandates, for example. The three main elements are interlinked and interdependent, making the framework complex, but realistic. They also each have a relatively static element, which is unlikely to change in the short term and a more dynamic component, which moves them on to the next stage of the process.

If there is sufficient within the three components (and all three working together gives added value/impact) then the individual is likely to move on to 'participation' in CPD (using the broad definition of CPD outlined earlier). If the components of the individual and facilitation extend beyond participation it is likely that there will be some 'effectiveness' evident from that activity. The framework is dynamic and after each CPD activity the

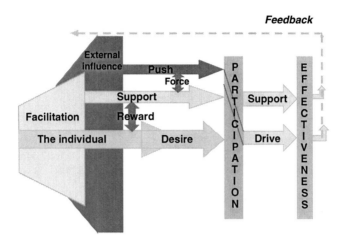

Fig. 24.1 Henwood's CPD process model

individual re-enters a new CPD phase, re-examining the individual components in the light of the latest activities. By subjectively measuring and quantifying the scope of each component the framework allows an individual to identify where improvements can be made.

While all components of CPD cannot be explored in one book chapter, hopefully the discussion above will have helped you to re-examine your involvement in CPD and what you can do to make it more effective. The remainder of the chapter will look at some of the creative ways of providing CPD. Many of these are or could be based in the workplace, which eliminates many of the problems associated with equality of access, geographic location of service and education providers. It also helps to break down some of the traditional barriers between professional groups and the inclusion of other key personnel within service provision. If CPD is to benefit the patient, it has to be accessible to all staff, regardless of grade, working patterns, professional (or not) background or any other variable and it has to be seen to be valuable. CPD is an exciting opportunity for us to make a difference, but it is up to us to make the most of that and choose to make the required changes.

Assessing individual and organizational CPD needs

To enable effective and appropriate CPD to be undertaken, it is essential that educational and training needs are assessed. Ideally this should incorporate both individual and organizational needs, thereby enabling an effective provision of CPD through appropriate planning.

Individual training needs analysis can be undertaken in several ways. Two examples are educational profiling and appraisal. Both of these exercises will culminate in the formation of a professional development plan relating to training and educational needs, and outlining strategies for undertaking these. This would appear especially important in the field of cancer and palliative care, as post-registration specialist training for cancer nurses is not yet mandatory in the UK, and nurses continue to have educational and training needs in oncology that are not addressed (Blunden *et al.* 2001). This is often similar for other professionals in this field.

A process of 'educational profiling' is particularly pertinent when assessing the educational needs of specialist palliative care practitioners. For example, the UK-based charity Macmillan Cancer Relief offers the opportunity for each Macmillan postholder to undergo educational profiling, facilitated by a Macmillan lecturer. This process allows in-depth exploration of the context of the current position, components of the specialist role and individual learning needs. It culminates in an action plan, specifying achievable CPD needs and identifying creative and practical ways of achieving these, within the context and confines of the working environment. Educational profiling is not exclusive to palliative care specialists; indeed it can certainly be most appropriate for other groups of staff, thereby affording opportunity for in-depth analysis of their needs.

As part of ascertaining learning needs, it is important to assess the individual's learning style. This will require the identification of appropriate learning style measures and promoting their use, as part of the assessment of need. A learning styles questionnaire, such as Honey and Mumford's (2000b) can categorize an individual's learning style and inform decisions about which form of education or development will be appropriate. Particular activities will be more appropriate for specific categories of learners: for example, maintenance of a reflective diary is likely to be more beneficial for a reflector than an activist (learning styles taken from Honey and Mumford 2000a). Where reflective records are required however, individuals, once having identified that potential area of weakness, will have to look at ways to acquire these skills, regardless of their learning styles.

In conjunction with the individual assessment, it is important to ensure that organizational needs are ascertained; indeed larger scale training needs analysis is intended to provide an in-depth organizational overview, enabling skills deficits to be identified and planned for. Larger scale organizational issues can be informed by collating data from individual needs analyses.

In addition to the use of an action, learning or professional development plan when planning a CPD activity, it is useful to refer back to Table 24.2 to ensure that the activity you are planning is worth doing, and will be relevant to your role. It is also important, as outlined earlier, that CPD opportunities are available to all staff within the palliative care setting, regardless of profession or level.

Workforce development issues in relation to CPD

When considering flexible workforce planning there is a need to consider the mandatory requirements from professional bodies in conjunction with local unit and statutory specifications. In planning provision, it is vital to ensure that CPD meets local service needs, as well as the personal and professional developmental needs of the individual (Pearson 2002). Employers should take the lead in designing and maintaining strategies for their workforce (Department of Health 2001), and this could be achieved through the development of effective CPD policies, thereby enabling equitable provision of access to appropriate CPD to enhance both the individual and the service. This could, for example, incorporate the provision of an in-house training guide, which would outline additional available opportunities for staff although potentially the consistency and quality of locally produced guidelines may not be effectively regulated and measured.

Support for CPD from employing organizations is crucial in allowing and supporting all staff of different levels and professions to undertake appropriate activities. In conjunction with this support there need to be robust systems to assure both quality and equality of opportunity (Pearson 2002). Although there is a large variety of activities available, participants often report that options may still be limited (MacGregor and Dewar 1997). This further emphasizes the importance of appropriate and flexible management support. Such support could incorporate raising awareness of, and valuing, wider CPD activities available, and encouraging appropriate diversity of opportunity and activity.

It is also important to be aware that specific workplace factors may affect the learning approach both positively and negatively. For example, a feeling of being overwhelmed at work is associated with a superficial and disorganized learning approach (Delva *et al.* 2002). These authors also state that, in contrast, physicians who believe they have choice, independence and support in their work will take a deep approach to learning, are also internally motivated and will use independent learning methods.

This demonstrates how the impact of workforce factors, in conjunction with learning styles, may affect the learning undertaken. In supporting staff it is important that managers are aware of, and act upon, the impact of both learning styles and workplace factors on CPD. By encouraging and empowering their team, especially in relation to developing an awareness of their own learning styles, managers can significantly improve the uptake and effectiveness of CPD for their staff. Additionally, it is essential that this interest and support is ongoing, with involvement and encouragement during the entire process.

Resource implications and constraints

Despite positive intentions by both unit management and higher level directorate management, there may still be potential resource implications and constraints precluding access to pertinent CPD activities. In many areas of palliative care provision, in both public and private sectors, there will be time pressures upon the service, which have the potential to negatively impact on CPD access and provision. It is therefore imperative to identify local barriers to CPD and work on ways to overcome them (Department of Health 2004b).

One way to address these issues can be through the use of an educational profile, as outlined earlier, where specific individual and service issues can be highlighted. A further potential solution could be ensuring the provision of protected time. This provision can be enhanced through the use of backfill or agency staff to ensure that the team has the opportunity to focus on their learning. Additionally, this can also be appropriate in allowing staff to apply to undertake sabbaticals for study.

The support of the line manager then is crucial, not only in helping to find space, time and resources, but also in motivating and encouraging staff and showing that they value the development they are undertaking. This can be as simple as taking an interest before, during and after the development, as well as encouraging the implementation of new skills and knowledge following any development opportunity. Just as the individual staff attitude has to be positive to ensure effective CPD (Henwood 2003), managers also have to have positive attitudes towards all aspects of CPD in order to support CPD activity in their departments.

With only limited funding being available it is essential that appropriate policies are put in place to ensure equitable and transparent access to CPD. This should incorporate all staff, especially as there have been past inequities in access between professional and non-professional groups. To ensure maximum gain from participation in CPD resources must be used efficiently (Brown *et al.* 2002). It is also important that there is creativity in attempting to access funds, if not available directly, especially in relation to accessing external funding bodies.

In conjunction with the use of employer funds for CPD, it is also vital to ensure that each workplace has clear, consistently implemented policies on self-funding and the use of staff's own time for CPD. In addition, it can be acknowledged that lifelong learning is one of the costs of being professional and that registered professionals should take responsibility for funding some of their own CPD (Department of Health 2004b). Current approaches in the UK to clinical governance identify this as a joint responsibility, thereby expecting both employer and individual to invest. However, this will need to be addressed on an individual basis.

After undertaking CPD activity, it is important that feedback is given to the manager and team on the CPD activity, specifically pertaining to potential impact on practice, and how it will contribute to the running and development of the unit. This would also be important for demonstrating the effective use of funds for, as Brown *et al.* (2002) acknowledge, resources for health care are scarce, and money spent on CPD could otherwise be used for direct patient care. The value of CPD activities may be gauged by completion of a routine evaluation document or questionnaire, which should include impact on practice and patients. Additionally, review of CPD activity could be incorporated into regular staff or development meetings, enabling other team members to benefit from shared learning, thus enhancing the investment in CPD.

Support and supervision: work-based activities

As discussed earlier in the chapter, it would appear essential that as part of CPD provision an emphasis is placed upon the value of learning in the workplace. Indeed, it could be argued that this element of education is crucial for effective learning to be undertaken in a palliative care context; especially in relation to Corlett's (2000) comment that there is strong evidence of a discrepancy between classroom theory and the learning which takes place in the clinical area. In addition, research findings have demonstrated the need to link both conceptual and procedural knowledge (McCormick 1999) for effective action and learning to take place. This form of CPD can also be perceived as resource effective, especially important from a workforce planning perspective, as it can be undertaken in the work setting (thereby reducing costs and time away from work setting) and should also have direct benefits on clinical practice (see Chapter 14, p 127).

In conjunction with CPD undertaken in your own place of work, there is also the possibility of structured educational visits to other workplaces. Exposure to clinical learning in other settings can be extremely valuable for furthering our own knowledge and skills. It can also be carried out in conjunction with structured documented reflection to enhance the learning and ensure new techniques and strategies can be applied to the current workplace. In addition to visiting other workplaces and developing links, expertise can be shared through the setting up of specialist networks and interest groups communicating via e-networking vehicles such as SMARTgroups (www.smartgroups.com). This provides opportunity for setting up and running a group, at no cost, for interested professionals to share, communicate and develop together within a password-protected discussion board. To ensure such learning is effective there is a need for a leader or champion to coordinate and promote such a group. More formal networking, for example through local cancer networks, may also be beneficial.

In addition to informal links between interested individuals for ongoing learning, links between practice and academic institutions are extremely important for ongoing development and enhancement of effective CPD. Indeed, if education and service institutions acknowledge a joint responsibility for clinical education, partnerships and collaborative structures can be set up to ensure a more comprehensive, rigorous and exploratory approach to practical education in relation to CPD (Edmond 2001). In conjunction with this, the role of a clinical teacher or practice-based educator/facilitator can be extremely valuable (Edmond 2001). Their role can include enhancing and facilitating the effective undertaking of experiential learning, whereby learning is centred around work practices, and reviewing and learning from these experiences. If undertaken in a structured way, and incorporating documentation of the process of reflection and subsequent learning, then this can be a recognized and valuable form of CPD. However, this requires a great deal of motivation and commitment from the practitioner undertaking it and financial investment by the unit to support such a role, but conversely can be an extremely valuable learning opportunity. To ensure that this learning is effective, it would be beneficial for the lecturer/facilitator to have a network whereby they can share, and thereby work towards enhancing and developing their own and colleagues' practice.

In addition, the practice-based educator/facilitator can take responsibility for the initiation of a research culture among staff in the clinical area (Field 2004), and provide support and motivation to encourage continuation of this activity. This is relevant in relation to journal clubs or research meetings, which can be especially valuable forms of CPD, and have been commonly utilized within palliative care settings. Through this format, knowledge can be gained both in relation to new developments in palliative care, and in enhancing critiquing and presenting skills. Interestingly, this more traditional format has also been widened, to a more formal clinically based learning opportunity, as described by Lockwood *et al.* (2004). Here, participants attend a regular two monthly meeting to review articles pertaining to a chosen topic. The evidence is critiqued and discussed with the aim of reaching a consensus, notes are taken and distributed to ensure a record of learning is also kept, with the conclusion focusing on updating clinical guidelines if appropriate. However, a high degree of motivation is required from all group members to ensure a journal club runs regularly, and an efficient and enthusiastic coordinator is especially important.

One further example of a potential CPD activity within the clinical area is the case conference, a traditional work-based learning format. However, through the use of tighter structure and specific knowledge gained through clinically focused discussion supported by relevant literature, this could become a more formal CPD opportunity. There is also an additional advantage of enhancing a multiprofessional learning environment and the sharing of expertise between the professions. This format could be strengthened through the introduction of a structured reflective element to further enhance the learning opportunity. It is certainly worth exploring the case conference format at a local level, and being creative with further enhancing and developing this forum. During such a process there is a need for active staff involvement to maintain ownership, ensure that it continues regularly and is still an effective learning opportunity.

Formal CPD opportunities

It would appear that the more traditional and often didactic format has been one of the mainstays of CPD. For example, the majority of nurses' experience of continuing education seems to be attendance at study days (Wood 1998). Indeed, research has found that for clinical nurse managers, their preferred method of receiving CPD is to attend study days (Gould *et al.* 2001). While there are potential benefits of formal study days for all professions, it is important to consider this as only one aspect of CPD provision, alongside many other and potentially more effective learning opportunities. In addition, the value of attending more formal learning will differ depending on the attitude of those attending and how the content is used and disseminated on the return to work.

When selecting study days or full courses, it is crucial to ensure that the content is going to be relevant in helping to achieve your own specific learning needs. This will depend on your own role specifications and individual learning needs. For example, in specialist and advanced palliative care roles, a Masters programme could be seen as a highly appropriate form of CPD, whereas an NVQ (see glossary, p 339) could be equally appropriate for a palliative care health care assistant. Again, selection of courses or study days should be undertaken in consultation with the individual educational profile or appraisal outcomes and plans, but it should be remembered that CPD is not undertaken purely by formal study days/courses. One advantage of the educational profiling process is that there is academic input, from the lecturer facilitating this process. This, therefore, should enable collaboration between practitioner, educationalist and manager in selection of appropriate programmes, relevant to both current position and future professional development. However, in relation to Agenda for Change (see the glossary, p 339) it is generally more important to ensure that all the current role requirements are met prior to moving into areas pertaining to future career development. It is also paramount to ensure equity of access for all groups of staff, and opportunities to attend relevant courses should be promoted. Additionally, it is important to ensure that feedback is provided.

Self-directed study

> Self-directed learning is described in adult learning theory, suggesting that adult learners can iden-
> tify their learning needs, find solutions to problems, base learning on experience and self-direct
> their education.
>
> Bravata *et al.* (2003: 7)

When considering promoting this form of CPD, it is important to be aware that there may
be a need to provide some degree of direction and support in assisting the development of
self-directed learning. Currently, many study guides are readily available, both in hard copy
and on the Internet, which could assist in this task, although no consensus exists regarding
the best method for providing self-directed skills training (Bravata *et al.* 2003). There may
well be a role here for clinical educators and managers in identifying individuals' gaps in
knowledge and skills in relation to self-directed study, and identifying, in conjunction with
the learner, a specific action plan for increasing these skills, thereby enhancing the benefits of
CPD activity.

Self-directed study may be commonly perceived as reading journals and paper copies
of distance learning materials. However, it is important that the reading is structured and
critical, and that learning can be demonstrated. This can be through documenting and
sharing new findings, in addition to preparing for presentations at journal clubs or other
meetings. To help focus reading, the use of specific clinical questions, formulated from current experience, can be beneficial in selection of appropriate reading (Bravata *et al.* 2003).

While journals are one element of this modality, it is important that other aspects are
additionally considered as part of CPD, often as part of a blended approach, comprising
several different methodologies. Indeed, more flexible modes of delivery such as distance
learning packages and off-site delivery (Blunden *et al.* 2001) can be important ways of
learning, but will require commitment, motivation and support. A study into physical
therapists' interest in web-based and computer assisted learning (CAL) found that there
was a large positive interest in CAL (Mathur *et al.* 2005). Additionally, new technologies
such as Blackberries, e-books, email updates and mobile phones can be added-value learning modalities in relation to CPD – but to enable maximum benefit from these technologies,
managerial support is especially important. This can comprise provision of protected time
to undertake such work and encouraging discussion of aspects of the study if appropriate.

In conjunction with these more traditional approaches, the use of medical narratives
and biographies can also be considered. Reading one of the published autobiographical
accounts of terminal illness critically and reflectively can offer a huge educational
resource from which to explore your professional response to death and dying (Read and
Spall 2005). To further learn in a more structured way from the experience of digesting
such an account, a critical reflection could be documented, and learning points summarized that could be taken forward and incorporated into practice. Additionally, learning
will also be undertaken from the day-to-day provision of care for patients, especially if
this is reflected upon in a structured and critical way.

Table 24.1 provides a summary of additional CPD activities (it is not an exhaustive list),
in addition to those discussed above. In conjunction with a brief summary, the suggested

Table 24.1 Summary of a selection of additional CPD activities

CPD activity	Overview of activity	Most appropriate learning style*	Relevant additional reading/suggested actions
Professional committee membership	Membership and active participation on specific committees as part of professional society membership. Opportunity for networking and increasing knowledge at higher levels.	◆ Theorist ◆ Pragmatist	Contact your own professional body to make enquiries regarding membership of specific committees.
Work-based project, i.e. audit	Through the undertaking of a specific work-based project, ongoing learning can be achieved through the experience of undertaking such a project, the methodology used and the ultimate outcomes.	◆ Theorist ◆ Activist	Higginson (1993)
Clinical supervision	This is defined as a framework whereby one professional guides the ongoing development of therapeutic competence in another by facilitating reflection (RCN Institute 2000). This is a facilitated process, focusing on specific practice issues, and either takes place individually or in groups.	◆ Reflector ◆ Pragmatist	Bond and Holland (1998)
E-resources	This self-directed activity comprises different elements, ranging from participation in an online course to accessing relevant web sites and communicating in discussion rooms to share and update knowledge. In addition, it includes the use of hand-held Blackberry, mobile phones and also accessing e-books and e-journals.	◆ Reflector ◆ Theorist	Use a search engine, such as Google, to locate details regarding specific online courses. Consider participating in relevant professional online discussion rooms. Investigate e-journal availability from you Trust, Professional body or University (if studying there)

* From Honey and Mumford (2000).

(Continued on following page)

Table 24.1 (continued) Summary of a selection of additional CPD activities

CPD activity	Overview of activity	Most appropriate learning style*	Relevant additional reading/suggested actions
Peers (networking)	This activity involves communication, through a variety of modes, with colleagues. The aim is to share and update on knowledge and skills. It can also be a forum to reflect upon and further discuss challenging clinical cases.	◆ Activist	Walsh (1997)
Conference attendance	Opportunity for both updating and gaining knowledge of new developments in your own specialist field, in addition to informal learning through sharing and critically discussing with peers.	◆ Theorist ◆ Reflector	Join specific mailing lists for conferences. Search Internet and professional journals for conference details.

appropriate learning style is included, and recommended references for further reading of each area.

Issues in future planning for delivery of CPD

Research

When considering future planning for effective CPD provision, it would seem important to ensure that these are informed by research findings and evaluation of prior CPD activity. However, Wood (1998) acknowledges the difficulty in identifying appropriate measurement tools of CPD. In addition, Grant and Stanton (1999) noted that although provision and funding for CPD activities had increased substantially since the late 1970s, the effectiveness of these activities in terms of producing changes in clinicians' behaviour and improved outcomes for patients was weak and inconclusive. In conjunction with measurement of change and patient outcomes, Brown *et al.* (2002) advocated that cost-effectiveness analysis must be applied to studies of educational effectiveness. This would appear particularly pertinent, especially when presenting accountability for utilization of charity funds, as is often the case in palliative care centres. It would seem that there is need for more research into the effectiveness of CPD, especially in the palliative care arena, to enable educational practice in this sphere to move forward appropriately.

Learner involvement in planning CPD

In addition to the importance of ongoing research into CPD effectiveness, it would appear, especially from perusal of the literature for this chapter, that there is a need to increase the role of learner involvement. In planning cancer care continuing professional education, it has been suggested that nurses representing groups of potential course applicants should be involved in the planning process (Gould *et al.* 2004). An increase in this type of participation would appear especially relevant in planning different types of CPD and more specifically in relation to planning curriculum content for more formal programmes and content.

Conclusion

CPD is an evolving area and, with a greater emphasis on its importance in palliative care, the next few years should prove an exciting time for ongoing development and expansion of CPD opportunities, informed by further research into its effectiveness. In conjunction with this, there is still a need for palliative care staff to maintain and further develop their individual benefit from CPD, in addition to working to increase the range of activities available, especially utilizing new methods of technology. It would also seem that there could be an increase of work-based learning, incorporating greater emphasis on inter-professional learning with equal opportunities for all staff to access CPD. To enable ongoing development opportunities should be made for increased collaboration between clinicians, educators and researchers in identifying and incorporating new modalities.

Chapter 25

Organizing education

Key concepts and processes

Barbara Gale

Introduction

Twenty years of experience in palliative care have taught me that each piece of work with a person and their family is unique. Similarly, each educational session has its own particular character. In this chapter I have tried to bring together ideas from my experiences in palliative care as a specialist nurse and systemic family therapist, as head of education in a hospice and as a keen consumer of education. Teaching and therapy both must pay attention to a number of key processes in order to create a safe space in which people can consider new ideas and concepts, learn about ideas that may challenge their beliefs and learn new ways of behaving. It is these key processes I will be focusing on in this chapter.

The ideas in this chapter have been greatly influenced by systemic and social constructionist models of thinking (Campbell 2000; Dallos and Draper 2000). Systemic thinking has challenged me to embrace connectedness and to explore how the contexts of past, present and future influence relationships and behaviour. A social constructionist perspective provides a better understanding of how knowledge has been constructed through individual, family and societal discourses.

In considering how to deliver palliative care education we can use the same principles of understanding, assessing, planning and reviewing that we use with patient and family care. Like patient care, education is a continuous and evolving process (see Figure 25.1) which needs to be underpinned by facilitated processes of communication, collaboration and cooperation.

Previous chapters have covered different aspects of palliative care education, and with so many educational resources readily available across the world there may be a temptation to transport models of palliative care education to your area. Although it might be simpler to offer a definitive instruction list on how to organize palliative care education, the key to success is to look closely at your particular context and needs and at the processes that influence your decision-making in the planning and delivery of palliative care education. This will ensure that what you use will really fit your requirements.

Understanding the path to successful organization does not need a specific map, but involves knowing the questions to ask and then understanding the answers. As education is about promoting a learning dialogue, I will suggest some questions for you to consider. When hearing the answers you will then need to reflect on the different perspectives that

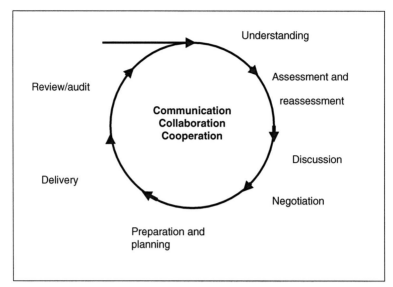

Fig. 25.1 Education: a continuous and evolving process

have influenced those answers and how your own perspectives have influenced what sense you make of them.

The processes I will be considering can be applied to any country and culture and for any student group and include understanding the:

- context within which palliative care sits locally and nationally
- needs of patients and their families requiring palliative care
- needs of your prospective students
- needs of those delivering the education.

In addition, it is important to know:

- the key relationships that need to be nurtured for your education to succeed
- the resources that will be needed, including who will deliver the education
- the preparation and planning process that will include the process of deciding the priorities and content and format of education that is to be delivered
- how to market, evaluate and assure quality of your programmes.

Understanding

Ideas from systemic family therapy help to clarify understanding of some important processes in designing and delivering education. This gives us a way to make sense of the relatedness of things around us (Campbell 2000), indicating that beliefs and behaviours are connected and that they all sit within the wider social and cultural contexts (Altschuler 1997; Dallos and Draper 2000). Recent developments in systemic family therapy have been influenced by social constructionist ideas which argue that meanings are created through the dynamic processes of conversations and that an individual's

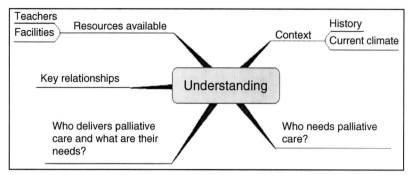

Fig. 25.2 Important areas for understanding in planning palliative care education

experience and identity are not static, but shift in relation to each social context (Dallos and Draper 2000). Similarly people's experiences and ideas about palliative care and their relation to it will vary, depending on the different contexts that influence them. Systemic thinking has particular resonance with the holistic principles of palliative care in the way that illness affects all parts of a family in relation to its history, wider community and social context. Figure 25.2 outlines important areas for understanding.

The context

To understand the context of palliative care in your area requires exploration of the past, present and future, taking local and national developments into account and anticipating the challenges palliative care might face. The wider context includes the different meanings that exist about illness, death and dying and how they have been constructed. When thinking about the language that is used, social construction reminds us that all the words we employ in our external and private conversation (either as patients or professionals) are 'soaked in the legacy of meanings of our cultural' and family contexts (Dallos and Draper 2000: 93). It is also important to understand how people's current practice has developed. Systemic thinking has taught me that while teaching is about helping people improve their practice and take on new ideas, it is important, first, to try and understand why and how people have come to use those methods. Box 25.1 suggests some questions to ask in exploring contexts of palliative care.

Foyle (2004) explored the impact of health and social care policy on cancer and palliative care education in the UK and describes how palliative care, which developed initially within voluntary organizations, is now being influenced by national government agendas and policies. In the UK it has been proposed that palliative care should be an integral part of mainstream care, but much of the responsibility for delivering hospice and specialist palliative care services, which includes education, still remains within the voluntary sector; for example, of the 220 hospices in the UK only 64 sit within the National Health Service (NHS) or statutory sector (www.hospiceinformation.info). Foyle commented that fragmentation and confusion can result from the involvement of many government departments in policy development, and encouraged those involved in education to be more proactive in their involvement.

Box 25.1 Exploring the context of palliative care

♦ If you described the *journey* that palliative care had had in your country and in your own local area – when and where would that journey have started?

♦ Who *started* it?

♦ What has *changed* along the way?

♦ What or who has *influenced* those changes?

♦ How is *palliative care defined* in your country?

♦ Has the *meaning* of palliative care changed and what has influenced those changes?

♦ How much do *national organizations* support the delivery of palliative care, or is it in the hands of volunteers or spiritual organizations?

♦ Who now *leads* the development of palliative care?

Most cultures and countries are bound and dominated by various systems – religious, political, health, educational and social systems. In the way illness and death affects the family system, it will in turn also affect surrounding systems. It is noticeable that the boundary between the family and health care system can become more permeable as the family allows professionals to become closer (Walsh and McGoldrick 1991; Altschuler 1997). It is therefore important to understand how illness and death are currently managed by the other systems, as this will affect the experience of palliative patients. Box 25.2 suggests some

Box 25.2 Exploring the influence of societal systems on palliative care and education

♦ What are the major influences on how healthcare is managed in your country are they *government/political agendas* and/or *societal or religious* beliefs?

♦ How do your *dominant systems* manage births and *deaths*?

♦ Who takes the *main role in caring*?

♦ If women take the main role – *how are women viewed by your society*?

♦ What are *the societal beliefs about death* and caring for those who are dying?

♦ What *model of health professionals' education* is used, is it unidisciplinary and/or multidisciplinary?

♦ What are *the main influences* on health professionals' education – professional model/gender/culture/power/religion?

♦ *How much* palliative care education already occurs in health professionals' training? Who *influences* the delivery of palliative care education?

questions to ask when exploring the influence of societal systems on palliative care and education.

Understanding the role of gender in society will play a major part in how your education is structured. Belenky *et al.* (1986) described the impact of learning on women in American society and found that in societies where education is predominantly designed and led by men, women have struggled to find their voice in education. Therefore courses that build on the knowledge of women will have the most powerful impact in helping those women 'translate their ideas from the darkness of private experience into a shared public language' (Belenky *et al.* 1986: 203).

Patients and families

While the principles of palliative care are clear, it is important to understand the specific needs of patients and families in your area and consider how you will maintain a connection to their needs in the planning and delivery of your education. Questions to ask when thinking about this are suggested in Box 25.3.

While we may feel we have a grasp of the key areas of need, it is always worth revisiting patients' and families' needs on a regular basis, as their needs will change as health care develops. To do this, you need to maintain connections with clinicians and hear the clinical problems that they and others are struggling with.

Who needs palliative care education?

The list of individuals and groups potentially needing palliative care education is extensive, as can be seen in Figure 25.3. How will you decide who to target and, for professionals, at what stage in their career?

Box 25.3 Patient and family needs for education

- Is there a particular *patient group* that has the greatest palliative care need?
- What would the patients and their families think their *greatest need* was, *spiritual* care or *pain* control or *practical* help, all of them or something else?
- If asked about their care, what would *patients and families want to improve*?
- What is your *community's understanding* of palliative care?
- How would your education *address patients' issues and understanding*?
- *Where* are people being cared for – at home or in hospital or somewhere else?
- *Who* does most of the care – *professionals or families*?
- How is *illness and death viewed* by your local community?
- How are families *supported*?
- Where is the *main focus of palliative care*, during the illness, around dying or before, or both?

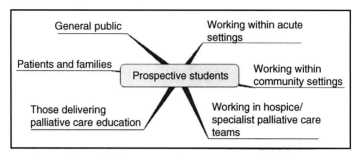

Fig. 25.3 Prospective students of palliative care education

Palliative care education for patients, families and the public

There is a danger that limiting education to the professionals involved with the person within the confines of the illness replicates the way that death has, in some places, been taken over by the medical world. What about the patients and families themselves? Education may also be needed by people facing illness, their families and local communities. If you find that the majority of care is delivered by families, friends and communities, perhaps that is where some of your education should be focused.

While public education was high on the agenda of Dame Cicely Saunders the founder of the hospice movement (Hostad *et al.* 2004), it now seems to have lost its way. Hostad *et al.* suggest that the lack of this public education may have led to inequitable access to palliative care across the UK. It is worth examining what the public perception in your country is about palliative care. How does the public receive information about palliative care? It may be through television or film dramas, which are not always accurate, but are certainly influential. Some may be through advertisements for charities describing the work of the practitioners it supports. There are disadvantages to this as it may increase public expectations of those practitioners, whose resources might be limited. For example in the UK, the successful national advertising by Macmillan Cancer Relief about Macmillan Nurses has meant that many people with cancer think that everyone should meet a Macmillan Nurse. In 2004 Macmillan increased its support to 3590 nurses yet, with over a million people in the UK with a cancer diagnosis (Macmillan Cancer Relief 2005), demand clearly outstrips resources. Therefore public education must be clear without raising unrealistic expectations.

Good public education has a part to play in health promotion, helping families to make choices about how and where they would like to be cared for: many people would often like to be cared for at home, but are concerned about placing the burden on their families. Information about services is part of the help that families need, but helping them learn practical skills and coping strategies may also be useful. Some hospices run courses for patients and families, giving them access to information and an opportunity to discuss how they are managing their illness with people in a similar situation. These courses are possibly best run by clinicians and educators, using the skills of both. There are many programmes helping families prepare for a birth – I wonder how many families would like a course or group to help to prepare for and manage a death?

Palliative care education for health and social care professionals

One of the difficulties in trying to assess the needs of those health and social care professionals working with palliative patients is that, because the concepts may be new to them, they may not know what to ask for. Conversely they may ask for anything and everything, which can also be overwhelming to a small education department. Therefore you might begin by targeting education at those who deliver care to the patients that have the greatest needs.

As palliative care increasingly becomes part of pre-registration training, some professional groups and institutions will be more advanced in applying this than others. Your degree of involvement may depend on your resources and your relationship with the institutions. For hospice and palliative care organizations, offering well-organized and supportive student placements can result in a variety of benefits: giving students insight into palliative care; stimulating hospice staff and enhancing their own teaching skills; improving future recruitment into hospice posts.

While the majority of education will focus on improving the skills of generalist practitioners, the needs of those who wish to specialize in palliative care must also be addressed. How do you move from being a novice in palliative care to an expert or advanced practitioner? Having reached a place where you feel you are working at a more advanced level, how do you maintain that level of practice? Providing high-quality modules that focus on the skills and the knowledge needed to become an expert practitioner may not be enough.

One way might be to provide a training placement within an organization where the practitioner can improve their confidence in their practice, working with experienced staff and having opportunities to reflect on their practice. However, many who have enjoyed placements within a hospice or palliative care setting have then struggled to maintain their expertise when returning to their own place of work. Therefore the ideal would be to follow up a placement with supported learning in one's own area, with someone like a practice facilitator. Advanced practice is not so much about getting it right all the time, but being able to continually reflect, learn and adapt. Maintaining advanced practice is especially difficult if one works in isolation. Regular clinical supervision is vital, but maintaining connections with other practitioners by meeting or keeping in touch through Internet chatrooms or discussion groups will also help.

Relationships

You may be reading this from different positions, perhaps as a teacher of palliative care either within

- an educational establishment or
- a hospice/palliative care service or
- a general hospital or community service.

Examining relationships both within your own organization and with external organizations will give an added dimension to your understanding and increase your effectiveness.

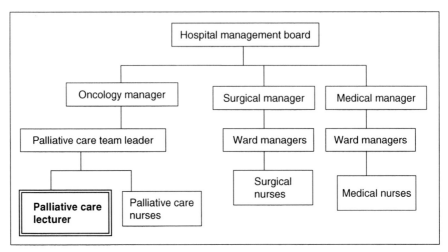

Fig. 25.4 An organization genogram

Examining internal relationships

Palliative care practitioners often ask families to draw a family tree or genogram (McGoldrick *et al.*1999), asking questions about key people in the family and at what level decisions are made. It is possible to do the same for an organization. To explain how this looks, I have used the same principles to draw a simple organizational map of a palliative care lecturer working within a general hospital setting (see Figure 25.4).

You can see from this example that the palliative care lecturer is a long way from where decisions might be made, and they might have to rely on the skills of the people hierarchically above them to make sure palliative care education is part of the decision-making processes. To add more information to the genogram you could also map good and poor lines of communication, and where decision-making about education sits in the organization. To better understand the current context it is also worth being aware of the pressures an organization is under. For example if this hospital is suffering from a large number of complaints about the quality of care, particularly around death, to provide support and teaching for staff to improve care around time of death may be particularly pertinent and receive support from senior management. Although the map helps identify the hierarchy in the organization and the lines of responsibility, it does not show the position that individuals or teams have within an organization. For example some individuals may be hierarchically low in the organization, but may exert significant influence or power on those around them.

If you drew your organizational map where would you fit and what advantages, disadvantages or opportunities would it highlight? You could also widen the map to include local and national groups that influence the hospital's structure. Having done that it would then help to ask some of the questions in Box 25.4 to understand where palliative care education fits within the culture of your own organization.

Box 25.4 Education in the organizational culture

- Is education and *palliative care education embedded* in your organization's culture and mission statement? How would you recognize the effect of this on your organization?

- What are the *key influences* on the culture of your organization – ethnicity, religion, gender (do you have a mainly male or female workforce, full or part time) what difference does this make in how you organize your teaching?

- How is *education funded* and supported within your organization, what *implications* does this have on the way you plan education?

- How are organizational and educational *objectives* decided?

- How are *staff and patients* involved in deciding objectives?

- What *relationship* does your organization have with other organizations and other education providers?

- If you asked other organizations to rate your *credibility* or *effectiveness* as an education provider, what would their answer be?

Examining external relationships

Having analysed your own organization in this way it is important to ask similar questions about external organizations. One way is to visually map the people and organizations you work with. Create a map which puts your closest partners nearest to you and the others further away, then examine what helps and what hinders relationships. To give an example of this I have mapped the relationships I had when I was running a hospice-based education department as a lecturer practitioner (see Figure 25.5).

Reflecting on this map now, I know the greatest need for palliative care education was within the community, often within nursing or residential homes, and that one of the key recognized providers of palliative care education was within Higher Education (HE) and yet they are both furthest away from me. Therefore if one of my objectives had been to increase education in the community and collaborate with HE, I would have had to plan on how to improve working relationships with those groups. Although the nearness of patients and families was something I was keen to maintain, as it was my regular contact with clinical work that grounded my teaching and enhanced my credibility as a teacher, it may have taken too much of my energy and hindered other relationships.

The doctors working in the community played a vital part in delivering care at home, yet they were difficult to engage with. This might have been because:

- the sessions were not academically accredited for doctors

- our sessions were often multiprofessional and facilitated by nurses or counsellors; our experience was that the doctors tended to be drawn towards sessions run by doctors for doctors

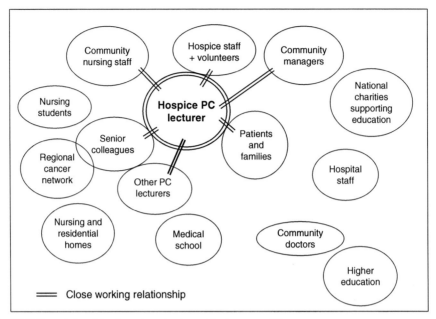

Fig. 25.5 Key relationships for a hospice-based lecturer-practitioner

- it was difficult for doctors to attend at the times that suited other professionals
- community doctors were facing other issues that had a higher priority than palliative care.

These difficulties started to resolve with the appointment of a doctor who was based at the hospice, whose role was to liaise with the community doctors and who was successfully setting up educational sessions in their practices. Having drawn your map you need to consider what needs to change, what is missing? Are there potential partners that you have not included, voluntary organizations or other education providers? Some of the questions I now ask of myself include: did HE really understand my role and perspective as a palliative care lecturer? How well did I understand what and how they were providing education? Did we have a trusting relationship or could misunderstanding affect our relationship? A sense of competition can result among education providers if one does not take care to make sure that different courses complement rather than compete with each other. Factors that might affect working relationships include trust, understanding of roles, time to discuss professional boundaries and effective ways of communicating.

A discussion that may help you in exploring the relationship between palliative care and HE could include understanding the perspectives held by clinicians in palliative care and the tutors in HE. Clinicians may believe that the palliative care educator needs clinical knowledge and experience, while tutors believe that they have the key skills in supporting and encouraging adult learning. These different perspectives can often cause conflict; therefore collaborative teaching could be the way forward, with clinicians teaching alongside tutors and/or offering courses or placements in palliative care specifically for those tutors working in HE in order to improve their understanding.

Having examined internal and external relationships it is worth considering your connections to wider relationships. These might include:

- other palliative care lecturers locally, nationally and internationally
- other palliative care providers
- national and local, statutory and voluntary organizations delivering health and education.

Better working relationships with other providers might then address the disparity in the different types and levels of palliative care education that is provided. Larkin (2005) gives an example of a European working group that agreed a set of criteria of levels of education against which palliative care nurse education could be judged. While this could start to help to provide some conformity, it needed to be expanded to other professional groups and if it were adopted in other countries, care would need to be taken that it took account of the local contexts.

As I outlined earlier, palliative care in the UK has grown up in the voluntary sector, so a question to consider is how educational processes and relationships might be affected by the role that charitable organizations play. If you are charitably funded, are there formal or implicit guidelines that influence how you provide or charge for education? In the UK most of the hospices are independent of the NHS, yet the majority of their education is aimed at staff within the NHS or other statutory bodies. Would hospices based within the NHS have any advantages? NHS hospices would hopefully be part of the NHS communication systems and have ready access to the training needs identified by NHS managers and their staff. They could develop education plans that would fit the workforce's educational needs and availability. Independent hospices, on the other hand, may have to work harder to gain access to information about needs and resources and therefore might run the risk of developing courses that do not fit the workforce needs or availability. Both need to develop good working relationships and the ability to have constructive discussions and negotiations with the organizations to whom they will be marketing educational programmes.

Resources

To complete your understanding you need to be clear about what resources you have available. Before considering what sort of education you would like to deliver, first explore what education is already happening and how successful it is. If your resources are limited, then it may be best in the short term to link with other providers and use your resources to enhance what is already being provided.

In considering where to deliver education you need to consider your prospective students. It may mean a lot to staff for education to be brought to their doorstep, particularly if travelling is difficult. Alternatively, being away from their environment may also play a part. Then, most importantly, what resources do you have to do this work? Do you have the personal resources and skills needed, or do you need further training or increased administrative support?

As teachers we need to improve the way we share resources. While this book will play its part in making the expertise of others more available, there are many resources that could be shared – ideas for programmes, modules, experiential work, worksheets etc. In the UK palliative care lecturers are considering starting an association for palliative care lecturers and hope to develop a web site to include access to such shared resources.

Finally, while I could discuss physical resources such as rooms, use of equipment, PowerPoint etc., I would encourage you to concentrate on the skills of those who will be teaching on your programmes. A teacher may have spent hours on a highly technical PowerPoint presentation, but if they lack the skill or experience in making their subject relate to their audience's needs and lack the skill to manage the audience, it will all be in vain. I have spent two hours packed into a tiny room with 20 other people listening to an inspiring teacher talk about their experiences about death in other cultures. In this situation the cramped environment did not matter.

Clinicians as teachers

One of the most important tasks you will have is identifying people who would like to be involved in teaching. Although I am using the term 'teacher', I am attracted to Belenky *et al.*'s (1986) idea of the teacher as a midwife, as adult students do not wish to be seen as empty receptacles, but as people who already hold some knowledge. The skill of the 'teacher midwife' is to support the student in acknowledging their own knowledge and then to help them give birth to their own ideas and develop them further. This way of teaching fits well with Gergen's (1999) view that constructionist teaching needs to be collaborative and develops it further, in that dialogue within the classroom should extend into the community and be relevant to society.

This is particularly important when bringing palliative care ideas into classrooms, where some of the ideas may not fit readily alongside that society's ideas about communication or death. The teacher will need all their skills in helping students interweave aspects of palliative care with their own dominant traditions. An example of this is given by Krause (1989) as she explored the Punjabi model of the 'sinking heart', an illness in which physical sensations in the chest are felt to be caused by heat, worry and/or social failure. Krause found that this experience did not easily translate into English ideas of depression or stress as it ignored the emphasis Punjabis place on the physical symptoms as well as the cultural and emotional aspects of the condition. Therefore the treatment offered by Western doctors was often refused, as it might be seen to aggravate rather than alleviate the symptoms.

Palliative care has aspects of both art and science to it. Students new to palliative care will value learning about what the experience of working in palliative care is like.

If they are able to, some of the best teachers are clinicians who feel able to share their experiences with students. Skills and abilities to look for in educators include:

- able to create a safe environment for people to learn in
- a good facilitator, encouraging people to speak in groups and able to pay attention to the processes that happen in groups
- confidence in using a variety of formats – from flipcharts to PowerPoint, from lecture to experiential
- passionate about their topic
- ability to work with and from different perspectives
- time to prepare
- skills in helping students explore the processes. Adult learning often needs to be able to give students an opportunity to explore their own beliefs and ideas and then take on new ones
- to focus on process rather than content, I mean by this encouraging students to think about the processes that happen during illness and why patients, families and professionals might behave the way they do
- good sense of humour
- able at times to work with increased levels of discomfort.

The list above looks daunting so teachers must be adequately resourced, with appropriate training and professional development. Jeffrey (2002) and Draper *et al.* (1990) give practical ideas and suggestions for teachers. Although Draper *et al.* is focused on family therapy, their First Aid Tips for stuck teachers (Draper *et al.* 1990: 175–83) offer some helpful suggestions.

Palliative care teachers also need to agree their own guidelines and structures with associated academic accreditation in the way that palliative care specialist professional development has occurred in some countries. Without this, palliative care teachers will not be keeping in line with clinicians' professional development or with their counterparts in HE, which could affect their credibility.

Patients and families as teachers

An important component of good palliative care is helping students learn to really listen to patients so as to not impose their assumptions of what is wrong and what the solution is. The best people to help with this are patients and their families themselves. In palliative care we may worry about exposing people at a vulnerable time in their lives, but if patients and families are given good support before, during and afterwards and the session is well facilitated, it can be a great success. While having a patient speak on their own with some students can allow for the students to hear a person's story in depth, bringing a group of patients together can be equally rewarding. Listening to a family member can help students understand the impact of illness on the family and the wider community.

Over the last few years I have been involved with taking a group of 25 five medical students to meet a group of eight to ten patients who were attending a day therapy centre in a hospice. Giving students the opportunity to meet palliative patients early in their clinical training can have tremendous benefits in increasing their insight into patients' or carers' perspectives (Wee *et al.* 2001). The patients definitely drew support from each other and they talked about the variety of feelings and ideas they all had in relation to the care and treatment they had received. During a lull in the discussion one patient turned to another and asked 'When did you know you were terminal then?'. The following conversation gave the students the permission to ask questions about how bad news was broken and what could have helped.

Preparation and planning

The time that has been taken in understanding the context you will be teaching in and the needs of your students will help you in the more detailed planning of your education programmes. Jeffrey (2002) gives a good practical guide on what you will need to consider when planning an educational session, detailing what needs to be covered from planning meetings to an administrative checklist for the session itself. Therefore this section focuses more on the factors that will affect those detailed plans.

Priorities

How do you decide where to start, having identified the areas of palliative care education you want to concentrate on, in the way that will best suit your audience and within the resources that you have available? I firmly believe that, in line with principles of palliative care, education should focus on quality rather than quantity. It is far better to run a few high-quality sessions where both students and teachers feel they have achieved what they wanted to do, rather than stretch yourself and others too much. If you need to rely on local clinicians for delivery, you might want to concentrate on their particular skills and passions or areas of interest. But I acknowledge in reality that there will be other factors that may influence your decision-making, although some of them may feel constraining or not quite in line with your vision, they still need to be considered (see Box 25.5).

Format and structure

A wide range of teaching methods is appropriate to learning about palliative care, as indicated by the chapters in Part Two of this book. Lectures or didactic teaching have a place in introducing new ideas to students. Facilitated discussion or experiential exercises can then allow students to discuss these ideas in relation to their own practice or culture. In imparting new ideas a skilled teacher will know that it is not enough for the students to be able to look at a new subject as if looking through the teacher's eyes, added to this the teacher needs to be able to look at the subject as if looking at it through the students' eyes (Belenky *et al.* 1986).

Educational programmes may be structured as short sessions, half or full days, longer courses or a mixture of all these. Decisions about structure will be influenced, among other things, by what you have learned about prospective learners' needs and wants.

Box 25.5 Factors influencing priority setting

- Who do you *involve* in the decision-making process?
- Are there *external influences* for funding, resourcing, or support that will affect your decision?
- Are there *topical areas* which may not be your priority but would increase your audience and potential for funding?
- If you could *separate your ideas* into must do, should do and want to do, which would have priority?
- How is the *success* of your department *measured* – quantitatively, qualitatively or both?
- If you have a major funder, are they interested in *quantity or quality*?

Teamwork is a vital part of palliative care involving professionals from many disciplines, many of whom will also be working alongside volunteers. Therefore, where possible, the learning in the classroom should encourage different disciplines to discuss and work together (see Chapter 22, p 235).

Teaching multiprofessional groups has both challenges and benefits (Koffman 2001; Wee *et al.* 2001). Different professional groups will be used to their own styles of teaching and learning, but the main advantage of teaching different professionals together is that it gives them the opportunity to discuss topics and challenge the ideas proposed. If well facilitated it can help students learn how to deal with disagreements and understand different perspectives (Gergen 1999).

If gender is an important factor in your society, it may be worth thinking about how you might manage either mixed education or education where one gender is in the minority. In those scenarios teaching a session with a member of the opposite sex may help those in the minority, particularly if discussing emotional topics. Gilligan (1993) reminds us about societal and family ideas that will influence how girls and boys develop and show emotions. Frosh *et al.* (2001) found, in researching understandings of boys in contemporary society, that boys were able to give a rich account of themselves and their relationships. While this research may not be directly translatable into adult education, childhood learning and influences will still play a part.

Accreditation

Accreditation poses another dilemma and will vary from one country to another. Accreditation in the broadest sense is an academic credit that can be used by a student to contribute to a HE qualification. But accreditation should be more than just a piece of paper, it should show prospective students and organizations that the course and its teachers and the learning outcomes have all been assessed, indicating that the whole

Box 25.6 Accreditation

- What would be the *advantages and disadvantages* of accreditation?
- What *percentage* of your education could or should be accredited?
- *Which organization* would you accredit with and how good is their reputation?
- What *percentage* of your prospective students would benefit?
- How *important* are these students in the delivery of care to palliative patients?
- What part does accreditation play in *your reputation* with local/national organizations?
- If you don't have the resources to manage the accreditation process, is there anyone you could hand it over to? Could you *collaborate* with another organization to do this?
- Are there any *risks* in going down the accreditation route or not going down it?
- If you don't accredit your courses, how will students be able to *evidence their learning* if they need to? Could you use *competencies and portfolios* as an alternative?

package of learning has been approved and meets agreed standards. There is the option of some courses having dual outcomes, whereby those needing the points can register to receive accreditation and other students can have confirmation of attendance and that they have achieved the learning outcomes. For those not going down the accreditation route it is worth thinking about how you might demonstrate the quality of your own courses and teachers, to ensure that standards of learning and teaching are met. Some questions you might ask in thinking about whether to seek accreditation of your education programmes are in Box 25.6.

Marketing

Having decided on the format and content you need to market the sessions and attract your audience. One does not want to do hours of preparation for an expected class of twenty to find that only eight turn up. Would you have run the session if you knew only eight would come? As I have become more experienced I have enjoyed the challenge of having to change the format of the session to allow for the change in numbers, but some teachers with less experience may find it daunting, as there is considerable difference in teaching a subject to a small group of eight compared to a large group of twenty.

Part of your marketing strategy will include deciding whether or not to charge a fee for attendance. This may depend on the type of session and the audience you are aiming to attract. A charge may make the course unavailable to a group of staff who particularly need the education. Conversely some people and organizations might place less value on a session that was offered for free. All areas will have a preferred way of circulating information, and keeping a database of those who like to receive information, but what may

---

Box 25.7 The cost of education

Should you make a charge for the session?

Should you make a charge if people do not turn up without letting you know – who pays – them or their manager?

Does filling in an application form and signing a contract help or would it put some people off? Should it include their manager's signature?

Do you have minimum numbers?

---

be more important is how you make sure the students manage to get there on the day. Charging may be a factor that may help or hinder the process of attendance. Some of the options you might consider are listed in Box 25.7.

Evaluation

Finally, how do you evaluate your education? Evaluation may be needed in different forms and for different reasons. It may be required by organizations you are working with, it could measure the effectiveness of the education and it could provide evidence for financial funding and support. It also is needed by teachers to improve or adapt the teaching and learning system. While there are many models of evaluation in HE, little is written about evaluating palliative care education (Taylor 2004).

Taylor (2004) outlines the potential areas that need evaluating from the different stakeholder perspectives of student, teacher, health and educational organizations and patient. A variety of methods is needed. Evaluations can include asking participants to complete a form either on the day or afterwards. In addition you might contact participants some weeks later to assess whether there has been any effect on practice. Auditing the attendance at your educational sessions will also give you an idea of at least their popularity and whether you are reaching your target audience. You may also seek or receive feedback from patients and the managers of staff to see if practice and patients' experiences are improving. The process of evaluation is discussed in detail in Chapter 21 (p 215)

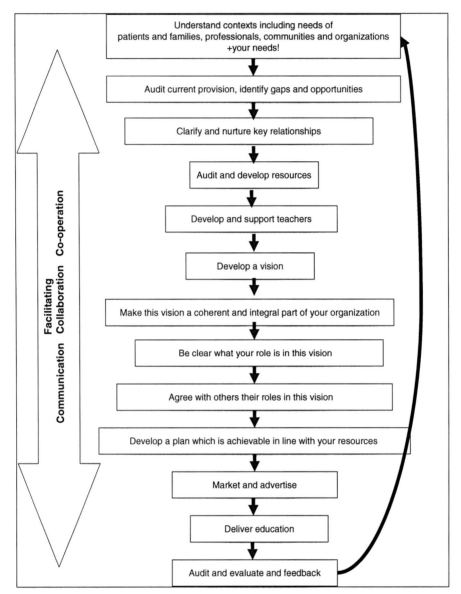

Fig. 25.6 Organizing palliative care education: key processes

Conclusion: developing your own palliative care education

As I have highlighted, there are many issues to be considered when planning and delivering high quality palliative care education. As the lead for education, one of your key tasks will be to facilitate these processes, using your skills to allow the different voices involved to be heard. In conclusion, and to bring some of these strands together, I have produced a flow chart (see Figure 25.6) that captures the key processes discussed in this chapter.

Chapter 26

Educational leadership

Bee Wee

Introduction

The strategic development and successful implementation of palliative care education requires effective leadership and management. This chapter focuses on leadership and aims to address the following:

- what makes a good leader
- the tasks and styles of leadership
- building a culture of learning in palliative care.

Publications on leadership abound. In this chapter, I shall not provide a comprehensive guide to leadership, nor an in-depth critique of the leadership literature. I shall draw together our current understanding of what leadership means, selected publications on leadership development where this is relevant to leadership in palliative care education and my own experience in this area. Most of this chapter is about educational leadership but first, there needs to be a brief discussion about the distinction between leaders and managers.

Difference between leaders and managers

Leadership and management are synergistic, not the same. Schein (1992) suggests that the significant difference between these two groups is that while leaders create and change cultures, managers seek ways to work within prevailing cultures. In essence, leadership is about coping with, or instigating, change to enable organizations to survive effectively within the wider world; management is about dealing with complexity within the organization and in its interface with the wider world (Kotter 2001). The characteristic activities of leaders and managers are contrasted in Table 26.1.

A quick glance at the headlines in Table 26.1 might suggest that leadership activities are more exciting and fun, charging from the front, whereas those of the managers are mundane and tedious, flogging from behind. However, in any effective organization, whether in health care, education or business, leadership and management are equally essential and must complement each other. In health care and education, however, a single individual often has to juggle both leadership and management responsibilities. Sometimes, they can excel in both: more often, they are much stronger in one than in the other. The key is for these individuals to recognize where their strengths lie and then either develop the other aspect in themselves or find somebody else to do it. It is essential that leaders

Table 26.1 Leadership and management activities (adapted from Kotter 2001)

Leader	Manager
Sets direction for change	**Plans steps and budgets**
Produces clear vision and strategic direction	Sets targets and goals, works out what resources are required and produces detailed plans
Aligns vision and people	**Creates organizational structures**
Communicates vision and strategic direction and secures commitment from everybody	Communicates plans, works out systems and structures to ensure that goals can be achieved efficiently
Motivates and inspires	**Monitors and problem-solves**
Keeps all staff moving in the desired direction, energizing and supporting them to achieve the organization's vision	Ensures that plans are achieved by monitoring results, problem-solving and keeping control on the process

and managers appreciate each other's role and their reliance on one another, otherwise frustration and jealousies can lead to dysfunctional organizations.

> Leading and managing are distinct but both are important. Organisations which are over managed but under led eventually lose any sense of spirit or purpose. Poorly managed organisations with strong charismatic leaders may soar temporarily only to crash shortly thereafter. The challenge of modern organisations requires the objective perspective of the manager as well as the flashes of vision and commitment wise leadership provides.
>
> Bolman and Deal (1991: xiii–xiv)

To be successful, education programmes need leaders to set the direction of the department or programme, ensure that everybody is behind that direction and then motivate and inspire the team to deliver high quality education and training. On the other hand, managers are required to set detailed plans, budget carefully, coordinate the whole process and ensure that everything works to plan. Both leaders and managers are particularly important in palliative care education where the teachers are often busy clinicians or managers, whose teaching activities are extra to their 'day job'. Equally, students may be busy clinicians who are trying to learn while juggling their daily responsibilities. Without clear direction and motivation (provided by leaders), balanced against planning, coordination and attention to detail (provided by managers), teachers and students would soon be disheartened, flounder and lose interest.

In this book, a whole chapter is devoted to organizational and managerial aspects of delivering an education programme in palliative care (see Chapter 25, p 279). This chapter focuses specifically on leadership.

What makes a good leader?

The assumption that leaders are born, not made, has been vigorously contested in the literature. In many ways, leadership is not unlike communication. Some individuals are born communicators but all can improve their skills with training, reflection and feedback, provided they are motivated to do so. Some are natural leaders and require little additional training. Others need much more help with development of skills, confidence and self-awareness.

The most effective leaders appear to have a high degree of emotional intelligence in common (Goleman 2004). This consists of five components:

1. self-awareness: a deep understanding of own strengths, weaknesses, emotions, values, needs and drive; honesty with self and others; ability to balance being critical and forgiving of self; often has self-deprecating sense of humour; ability to remain aware of own responses to others and situations

2. self-regulation: experiences bad moods and emotional impulses like everybody else, but able to control, and even channel, these constructively; reflective, thoughtful and measured

3. social skill: manages relationships effectively and in a friendly manner; has knack for finding common ground and building rapport with others

4. empathy: ability to sense, understand and consider others' viewpoints and feelings in the process of making thoughtful decisions; treats others fairly, not merely by doling out tea and sympathy

5. motivation: deep desire to achieve beyond expectations, for the sake of the achievement itself; passionate, creative and energetic about the work; takes pride in a job well done; able to retain a sense of optimism even when things are not going well.

The first two components are related to self-management; the third and fourth are about relationships with others. The final component is more controversial. Unlike the first four, which are generally positive and constructive, the final one could be destructive if motivation is followed through at the expense of others. Hence it needs to be balanced by the other components.

Cognitive abilities, often measured as intelligence quotient (IQ), and technical skills are also important but they appear to be only 'threshold capabilities', i.e. the starting point. When Goleman calculated the ratio of technical skills, IQ and emotional intelligence as indicators of performance, he found emotional intelligence to be twice as important as the others for jobs at all levels. He asserts that without emotional intelligence, all the training in the world would not make a great leader. Fortunately, his work also shows that emotional intelligence can be developed. Natural leaders have a high degree of emotional intelligence but others can develop this with self-motivation, through practice and being given constructive feedback. It may also improve with age and maturity.

Alimo-Metcalfe and Alban-Metcalfe (2000) surveyed over 2000 NHS staff in the UK to identify a profile of important leadership qualities. The top leadership qualities chosen by staff included genuine concern for others, inspirational communication, empowerment of others, transparency, accessibility and decisiveness. Based on extensive questionnaires and interviews, her findings led to the development of a leadership framework for the NHS, coupled with a multisource questionnaire which enables a variety of individuals interacting with the leader to feed back their views and comments.

Kouzes and Posner (2002) surveyed over 75 000 people, mainly in the US but also in other parts of the world, to identify the values, personal traits or characteristics which people look for in leaders. Being honest, forward-looking, competent and inspirational were the top four characteristics identified. Credibility and trust were also regarded as fundamental to leadership, i.e. did the leaders do what they said they would do and could they be trusted.

Trust and trustworthiness have been the subject of much discussion over the past decade. In 1995, at the request of the UK Prime Minister, the Nolan Committee was set up to examine the standards in public life (Nolan 1995). The Committee produced a set of seven principles to which all those in public office in the UK are expected to conform: selflessness, integrity, objectivity, accountability, openness, honesty and leadership. Many other bodies in the UK, including scientific advisory bodies and the National Council for Voluntary Organisations, now include these principles in their person specification for members and trustees. When delivering the BBC Reith Lectures in 2002, O'Neill (2002) contended that 'we cannot have guarantees that everyone will keep trust. Elaborate measures to ensure that people keep agreements and do not betray trust must, in the end, be backed by trust', but also stressed that this trust must be made with good judgement, based on active inquiry, not blind faith. O'Neill went on to assert that there are no rights without counterpart obligations or duties. Leaders are obliged to build trusting and trustworthy cultures, by encouraging active, even challenging, questioning. In turn they should expect all members of their team to balance their own freedom and rights with obligations and duties.

The concept of leadership can be daunting to those who do not think of themselves as natural leaders. Many individuals in palliative care are appointed to positions of leadership without prior training or, often, much warning or induction. Some have been fortunate to have worked with positive role models along the way, whom they try to emulate. Others have had negative experiences and try to behave differently. Importantly, the behaviours they choose to adopt or reject may not be congruent with their own personalities. There is no single perfect leadership profile. Each leader's personality, strengths and weaknesses are unique. Similarly, the way they adapt their leadership styles to the context in which they lead is crucial.

Everyone has leadership potential. For those who are less experienced in this field, it is helpful to think about leadership development at two levels. The first is to pay attention to the development and maturing of their emotional intelligence; this has already been discussed above. The second is to consider how they should set about accomplishing the tasks of leadership.

Tasks of leadership

According to Kouzes and Posner, effective leaders 'model the way, inspire a shared vision, challenge the process, enable others to act and encourage the heart' (2002: 13). Pendleton (2006) built on this and his own work, largely though not exclusively in the UK, and defined the tasks of leadership as follows:

- to inspire
- to focus

- to enable
- to reinforce
- to learn.

Pendleton asserts that the first task of leadership is to inspire confidence, trust and commitment. To do so, leaders need to be able to hold and communicate a vision which is credible and motivating, i.e. one that sets a direction of travel and destination that generates enthusiasm and commitment. The second task is to focus the team's efforts, by setting clear objectives, priorities and schedules. This prevents energy being too dissipated and the team becoming exhausted and losing confidence in themselves and their leader. Having inspired and set a clear focus, leaders need to enable others by ensuring that they have the mandate, skills and resources to act. This requires courage and faith in others but does not imply that blind faith and unlimited resources are required. The fourth task of leadership is to reinforce by appreciating and rewarding achievements appropriately. At the same time, the task of reinforcing includes the need to tackle those who have not achieved what is required, initially by helping and developing them, then challenging continuing failure and, finally, removing them. This is particularly difficult in hospice organizations where being supportive and 'nice' are so fundamental to the culture. However, avoidance of this less pleasant aspect of leadership is unfair to those who have strived to achieve what is required and undermines their trust in the leader and the process of leadership. The final task of leadership is to learn. Leaders and members of their teams need to reflect and learn from experiences and feedback from themselves and others. This prevents complacency and keeps raising the standard for the whole organization.

The leadership tasks set out as above are helpful because there is no prerequisite for a particular style of leadership or personality. Those styles will inevitably influence how the leadership tasks are tackled but it is easier to learn behaviours than change personality. This is similar to communication, where the goals of effective communication remain the same while the way in which communication occurs will be influenced by the personalities and styles of all those who are party to it. At this stage, it is probably helpful to pay a little attention to the concept of leadership styles.

We all have assumptions which underpin daily living. Most of the time, these assumptions lie quietly unchallenged but they have a profound influence on the way we view and interact with others. Self-awareness about these assumptions and a willingness to examine and challenge them increases one's effectiveness as a leader, just as it does one's effectiveness as a palliative care practitioner. Rooke and Torbet (2005) describe seven leadership styles (see Table 26.2) which are based on the premise that leaders' 'internal action logic' (assumptions) determine how they interpret their surroundings and respond when their safety or power is challenged. Rooke and Torbet suggest that leaders may be able to transform their leadership capabilities if they understand what kind of leaders they are, recognize their own assumptions and are prepared to undertake personal development.

In an area as complex as leadership and personal development, it is dangerous to rely too much on categorization. There is a temptation, when faced with lists such as in

Table 26.2 Leadership styles (adapted from Rooke and Torbet, 2005)

Leadership styles	Internal action logic (assumptions)
Opportunist	Wins in any way possible; assumes that others are competitors who are also out for themselves
Diplomat	Controls own behaviour, rather than gaining control of external events or other people; avoids overt conflict; rarely rocks the boat
Expert	Controls by perfecting own knowledge; continuously pursues improvement, efficiency and perfection; 'my way is the only way'
Individualist	Recognizes that assumptions are self-constructed; ignores rules which are regarded as irrelevant; high achiever but a wild card
Achiever	Open to feedback and recognizes that complexities and conflicts of everyday life are due to differences in perceptions and ways of relating; aware of need to be sensitive to relationships and achieves change through teams
Strategist	Regards organizational and social change as a developmental process; effective at handling conflicts, personal relationships and relations within and beyond organization
Alchemist	Ability to renew or reinvent self and organization in fundamental ways; extremely aware individuals; able to capture significant moments in the organization

Table 26.2, to seek to define one's own leadership style (or worse, somebody else's) within a particular box. Rooke and Torbet's (2005) work simply presents one way of considering styles of leadership. Others argue that leadership styles should be conceptualized as being situational or task-specific: directive, coaching, supporting or delegating (Blanchard *et al.* 1987). Later in this chapter (p 304), there is a reference to Bush (2003) whose models of educational management have implications for how leadership styles might influence, and be influenced, by organizational cultures.

Leadership may need to take a different style at times of conflict. Although clear direction and communication continue to be required, Patten (1998) suggests that at times of turbulence, leaders who constantly consult their teams and conduct surveys and focus groups to find out their wishes are unlikely to achieve or convey a sense of direction. Effective leaders need to exhibit courage and steady resolve at such times.

Building a culture of learning in palliative care

Developing values, vision and strategy

Leadership begins by defining a purpose and inspiring a common vision. Pendleton and King (2002) show that companies which are successful in the long term have predetermined and strongly held values. These values are real and credible. They act as guiding principles to help the companies take tough but crucial decisions. Values – what the organization stands for – are inextricable from vision, i.e. where the organization is

Box 26.1 Values underpinning palliative care education in one department

We value:

- making a difference to the care of patients and families
- having pride in what we do and the way we do things
- having integrity in what we do and the way we do things
- relationships within the team that are based on trust, an ability to be open with one another, a valuing of all contributions and a sense of corporate responsibility
- getting the best out of everybody within the team by having clear structures, good communication and effective teamworking, and by providing opportunities for personal and professional development.
- providing opportunities for others to get the best out of themselves, each other and their experiences, through education, training and research
- the belief that a group of learners coming together, actively learning from and with each other, creates more constructive energy than the sum of individual energy in the group
- the importance of the collaborative spirit – aspiring to build and maintain mutually beneficial relationships with other individuals and organizations, locally, nationally and internationally.

Wee *et al.* (2004)

going. The values are fixed and are core to the organization. But the vision has to move in response to the changing environment. Pendleton and King point out that at times of great change or stress, people and institutions often revisit their core values to remind themselves of what they stand for. Palliative care (like much of health care) and palliative care education (like much of higher and continuing education) are going through times of great change, so it is more necessary than ever to make sure that values are explicitly stated and owned by the whole team and organization. Box 26.1 provides, as an example, the set of values which we have developed in my own department. The process of developing these together and of asking ourselves the questions 'what really matters to us' and 'what motivates us in our work' enabled members of the team to share their assumptions and feelings, and to define a set of shared values.

Once the values of an education (or any other) department have been made explicit, it is possible to consider setting out a vision. This is about the future, so it requires some imagination and boldness. It needs to be compelling and describe what the department and its work would look like when the goal is achieved, so that the whole team knows what it is reaching for. Questions like 'How can the department meet the needs of those whom it sets out to serve?' i.e. learners, patients and carers, and 'How easily can the vision be translated into a realistic strategy?' are important. Although it is impossible to predict the future fully, effective leaders in palliative care education must work closely with their teams, to look beyond the 'tomorrow' and outside palliative care. A series of 'what if' questions can be helpful to provoke discussion, debate and lateral thinking. It is only after a vision has been defined that a clear strategy with goals and target dates can be set out. Once that has been achieved, the department has both focus and direction.

Recognizing and valuing the strengths and weaknesses of individual members of the team may be intuitive for some leaders. Shackleton, the famous Antarctic explorer, was a much respected leader who brought his crew safely back home after their ship, *Endurance*, became crushed in the ice of the Weddell Sea in Antarctica. He made sure that each man had challenging and meaningful work. He matched personality types with work responsibilities and gave his men constant positive or constructive feedback (Morrell and Capparell 2001). For those of us who do not have Shackleton's instinctive genius for leadership, there are now many tools available to help the process of identifying individual strengths and weaknesses, our own as well as our team's, notably Belbin (2004) and the Myers-Briggs Type Inventory (Myers 2000). The former helps individuals to look at the roles they play within teams, whereas the latter helps to identify preferred behavioural styles. Used wisely and not prescriptively, these tools can help leaders to harness natural talents effectively, appreciate individual strengths and understand the way in which they react and respond to different members of the team.

Like other leaders in palliative care, those in palliative care education have rarely had the opportunity for formal leadership training. Sadler (1997) suggests that leadership training programmes which focus on management rather than leadership skills do not develop real leadership potential. This is not surprising, given the distinction between leadership and management activities. Houghton (2005) provides a useful framework to assist leaders in developing their own leadership skills. The framework enables leaders to examine their environment, personal behaviour, skills and abilities, beliefs about themselves and their values, role in the context of the situation in which they lead and personal motivation. This framework can also be used to help whole teams explore their thinking as a group. Another useful strategy is feedback analysis, in which the leader writes down what they think will happen every time a key decision is made; then nine to 12 months later, the leader compares their expectations with the actual results (Drucker 2005). Mentoring, coaching and learning sets can also be extremely helpful in leadership development.

Organizational culture

Bush (2003) outlines a set of organizational models which provides a useful framework for considering the culture, assumptions and ways different organizations work:

- formal – these organizations function as hierarchical systems, with the leader's authority legitimized by their formal position
- collegial – decision-making in these organizations occurs through discussion leading to consensus

- political – policy and decisions in these organizations emerge through negotiation and bargaining
- subjective – there is a shared assumption that the organization is created by the people within them
- ambiguity – turbulence and unpredictability are dominant features of these organizations
- cultural – beliefs, values and ideology lie at the heart of these organizations.

Incoming leaders need to be able to recognize the prevailing organizational culture before they can function effectively in it or endeavour to change that culture. Their leadership style will, in turn, influence the organizational culture. This style may need to be modified to be effective in different situations. Leaders and managers with congruent styles or who are able to identify and appreciate the difference in each other's styles, and discuss this openly and honestly, are more likely to head up healthy organizations.

No organization begins with a blank page. Even when setting up a department from scratch, each individual, including the leader, arrives with a set of assumptions and expectations. Despite their importance, these are rarely discussed or made explicit. It is therefore hardly surprising that leaders may encounter early resistance when they try to bring in change. This can then be interpreted as the resistor's lack of commitment to the goals of the team and, if isolated, may result in that individual becoming a scapegoat for that team. On the other hand, a leader who underestimates the level of resistance to change in the team will usually fail in that attempt because they will not have done sufficient preparatory work to motivate the team to change.

Motivating change

There are two issues to be confronted here. First, some resistance to change almost always occurs. This resistance is not always bad. For example, it can prevent an ill-considered change from occurring. At other times, it prevents or delays positive things happening. Rogers (1995) suggests that there is an S-shaped diffusion curve in response to most innovations (see Figure 26.1). There are always a few innovators: individuals who proactively seek information about new ideas. Then there are some early adopters: people who may be influenced and enthused simply by having the idea mentioned to them. The diffusion curve (or idea) takes off once about 10–25 per cent of the group have adopted the change, usually through activation of interpersonal networks. At this point, the early majority, who require persuasion, then the late majority, who require proof, begin to come on board. Finally, there are some laggards, those at the top of the curve in Figure 26.1, who may never come on board. It is likely to be futile to spend further time and energy trying to persuade this group. However, it is important to remember that the laggard's resistance is to the innovation in question, not necessarily to the function of the whole organization. It is particularly important to ensure that these individuals are not made scapegoats, particularly by the enthusiasts. Staying alert to laggards enables the leader to involve them helpfully when the time is right.

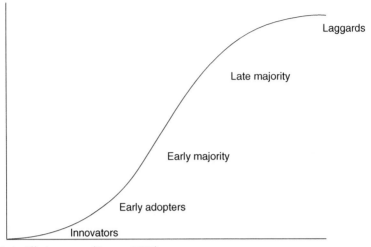

Fig. 26.1 A diffusion curve (Rogers 1995)

The second issue to be confronted in motivating change is that of the basic underlying assumptions held within organizations. Schein (1992) suggests that organizational cultures consist of three layers: artefacts, espoused values and basic underlying assumptions (see Box 26.2). Artefacts form the top layer. They are the visible phenomena of organizations, for example the lay out and decor of buildings and the way meetings are structured and chaired. Newcomers will be able to see this easily, but it is much harder for them to work out the basic underlying assumptions from the artefacts. Espoused values define the way the group works together and are reinforced by early success. These then gradually become transformed into basic underlying assumptions which are non-discussable, neither confronted nor debated, and are extremely difficult to change. Nobody speaks about them and they are often inaccessible or inexplicable to newcomers.

Bowe *et al.* (2003a) outline a process to help individuals uncover their own 'big assumptions' in a step by step approach, and to reframe gripes or complaints into well-considered strategies. These steps, using an example from palliative care education, are set out in Table 26.3.

First, individuals identify major personal dissatisfactions that they believe could improve their professional well-being. This is translated into the underlying values or commitments that these represent. Next, they identify behaviours which get in the way of what they wish to achieve. They consider how these behaviours might simultaneously express another less conscious, conflicting commitment that they also hold. They consider what would happen if they were to do something different. This uncovers the underlying big assumption which, if true, is blocking their ability to deal constructively with the major personal dissatisfaction they identified in the first place. Finally, this allows behavioural strategies to be developed to deal with the original dissatisfaction. Bowe *et al.* argue that unless these big assumptions, which feed individuals' personal

Box 26.2 Illustration of Schein's layers of organizational culture (1992)

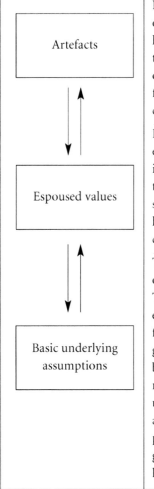

Artefacts

Espoused values

Basic underlying assumptions

Newly arrived staff nurse at a hospice is delighted to be offered exciting opportunities to attend courses, particularly 'chalk and talk' courses aimed at improving her factual knowledge about palliative care. But she is also keen on experiential learning, for example in-depth learning from critical incidents. However her managers appear curiously disinterested.

In this hospice, factual knowledge about palliative care, especially drug treatment, is valued. This is because, when it first opened, the hospice established its reputation as the regional 'centre of excellence' because of its staff's superior factual knowledge. Since then, managers have held on to the belief that factual knowledge about drugs contributes most to their reputation.

This belief has become so deeply engrained in the culture of the organization that it cannot easily be questioned. The new staff nurse finds that her efforts to learn experientially are tolerated but regarded as superfluous. She finds it hard to understand why, and even has difficulty getting her colleagues to discuss it. Eventually she leaves because she is frustrated by her own inability to memorise facts and by the lack of opportunity to deepen her understanding and improve practice through reflection and discussion. If her managers and colleagues had been prepared to listen, the whole organisation might have gained insight into the limitations of valuing factual knowledge alone.

defences, are challenged, professional development will be hindered. Challenging these assumptions can feel threatening and individuals may benefit from working with a mentor or experienced colleague. Ultimately, this may lead to some tough decisions and the realization that it is rarely possible to achieve everything in one's professional life to one's satisfaction. This process can also be used to explore whole institutional or organizational dissatisfactions. It can be a powerful way to avoid the simplistic solution of employing more and more people instead of tackling the root causes and conflicting commitments within organizations. However, this can feel even more threatening, so those involved should have had a chance to try out the process at an individual level first (Bowe *et al.* 2003b).

Table 26.3 Illustration: questioning your big assumptions (Bowe *et al.*, 2003a)

	Questions	Example
Gripe	What you need more or less of to make your professional life happier: '*I need..........*'	More protected time to teach junior doctors
Primary commitment	What personal commitment your statement reflects: '*I am committed to...*'	◆ Junior doctors' development and learning about palliative care ◆ Their satisfaction from this placement ◆ Good evaluations from them about the learning and support they received in this post
Contradictory behaviour	What you are currently doing or not doing, that prevents your commitment from being realized	Prioritizing patient care and attending management meetings
Competing commitments	What do you fear would happen if you did or didn't carry out the behaviour identified under 'contradictory behaviour': '*I am also committed to....*'	◆ Personally delivering good patient care and being attentive to my patients ◆ Influencing management decisions through my presence at management meetings
Big assumptions	What assumptions are embedded in your competing commitment: '*I assume that....*'	◆ Delegating patient care to others represents lack of attentiveness on my part and I would be failing in my duty ◆ If I don't attend management meetings, key decisions will be made without my input
Testing the big assumption	Delegating patient care to others represent a lack of attentiveness on my part and I would be failing in my duty: ◆ identify the last time I went on holidays ◆ what did I do to ensure that the continuity of care was preserved in my absence? ◆ to whom did I delegate responsibility? ◆ how did my patients respond to my absence – and my return? If I don't attend management meetings, decisions will be made without my input: ◆ identify a specific decision that is about to made ◆ consider how I can provide input without attending that meeting ◆ decide if my presence at the meeting is really important – are there other ways of influencing the decision?	

NB Sometimes, you will decide that the competing commitment is in fact more important than your primary one. This strategy helps you to clarify your thinking.

Conclusion

Leadership is a social process in which different people engage at different levels at different times. Foster (1989), as cited by Martin and Rogers (2004: 158), describes this as not residing 'in an individual, but in the relationships between individuals, oriented toward social vision and change, not simply, or only, organizational goals'. This may sound somewhat idealistic, but it is helpful and empowering to move away from the concept that leaders are born to the concept that there is leadership potential in everybody, to a greater or lesser degree. It might also seem more egalitarian to move from having one leader to that of *all* being leaders. However, in the complex world in which many clinical teachers and learners exist, the fashionable drive towards group leadership in all situations often leads to chaos and confusion, with continuous cycles of consultation, discussion and posturing – so called 'wading in mud'.

Effective and efficient leadership in palliative care education cannot be achieved as a group activity. This may be a bold statement, but it is not the same as stating that group processes have no role in leadership. Leadership is not the same as dictatorship. It requires credibility and earned authority. Here, I propose a different way of looking at leadership in palliative care education (also applicable to leadership in other arenas of palliative care), one which is compatible with our ethos of whole patient care and teamworking, but which does not over-encourage egalitarianism resulting in helpless floundering. Earlier in this chapter, I described two levels to think about leadership development:

1. development of emotional intelligence within individuals

2. accomplishment of leadership tasks.

The first requires motivation and commitment on the part of the individual, as well as support and investment by the organization. In a healthy organization, every individual at every level of the organization should be encouraged to develop their emotional intelligence, in preparation for situations in which they may take up a particular leadership role. People who provide effective leadership in important jobs have often had a chance, before they get into those jobs, to grow beyond the narrow base of their more junior roles, so offering these opportunities form an important part of the strategy for growing leaders within the organization.

The second, accomplishing leadership tasks, requires one person to lead and others to follow and share in achieving the whole task. Group processes, including communication, consultation and dialogue, are therefore essential to the achievement of leadership tasks. In a well-developed team, more than one individual would be capable of taking the lead for any single project or programme. The choice of who becomes the leader in each situation may depend on other factors, e.g. interest, enthusiasm, time, workload, credibility, responsibility and accountability. Constant rotation of leadership is not always appropriate. The size and scope of what is being led inevitably influences decisions about leadership. Large organizations require a clear leader at the helm, just as large ships require a single captain, to set the direction, ensure that the tasks of leadership are achieved and, ultimately, to be accountable for the whole enterprise. This is as true of education as it is of any other field.

Building the leadership capability of an organization requires:

- investment in individual leadership development

- an assumption that everyone has leadership potential and should have the opportunity to develop these skills

- a culture of open dialogue and discussion and a willingness to expose and challenge underlying assumptions

- preparedness for the leadership role to be assumed by the person most appropriate for whatever task, project or organization that needs to be led, and
- the moral courage to withstand political correctness about leading as a group activity.

The difference between a well-led team and a poorly led one is so marked that it is surely worth investing in building leadership capabilities. The cause of palliative care and palliative care education cannot be effectively championed unless strong, courageous leadership is at the helm.

References

Accreditation and The Liaison Committee on Medical Education (2001). *Standards for Accreditation of Medical Education Program Leading to the MD Degree*.

Adler J, Auret K, Brogan R *et al.* (2004). *Developing a curriculum for the training of specialists in palliative medicine*. Second National Palliative Care Education Conference, Adelaide, Australia.

Ahmed MEK (2002). What is happening to bedside clinical teaching? *Medical Education* **36**(12), 1185–8.

Albanese M (2000). Problem-based learning: why curricula are likely to show little effect on knowledge and clinical skills. *Medical Education* **34**, 729–38.

Alimo-Metcalfe B and Alban-Metcalfe R (2000). Heaven can wait. *Health Services Journal* **12**, 26–9.

Allard P, Maunsell E, Labbe J and Dorval M (2001). Educational interventions to improve cancer pain control: a systematic review. *Journal of Palliative Medicine* **4**(2), 191–203.

Allery L, Brigley S, MacDonald J and Pugsley L (2005). *Degrees of difference. An investigation of Masters and Doctorate programmes in medical education*. Edinburgh, Association for the Study of Medical Education.

Allshouse KD (1993). Treating patients as individuals. In M Gerteis, S Edgman-Levitan and J Daley, eds *Through the patient's eyes: understanding and promoting patient-centred care*, p. 21. San Francisco, Jossey-Bass Publishers.

Altschuler J (1997). *Working with chronic illness*. London, Macmillan.

Al-Wakeel Y and Handa A (2006). Foundation and beyond: is the future any clearer? *BMJ Careers* **7 Jan**, 3–5.

American Academy of Hospice and Palliative Medicine (2005). *Personal communication*.

American Association for Respiratory Therapy (AART) (1983). Competency-based continuing education. Aartimes – American Association for Respiratory *Therapy* **7 Jan**(1), 52–3.

American Society of Clinical Oncology (1998). Cancer care during the last phase of life. *Journal of Clinical Oncology* **16**(5), 1986–96.

Andrew M and Jones P (1996). Problem based learning in an undergraduate nursing programme – a case study. *Journal of Advanced Nursing* **23**, 357–65.

APM (Association for Palliative Medicine of Great Britain and Ireland) (1992). *Palliative medicine curriculum APM*. Southampton, Association for Palliative Medicine of Great Britain and Ireland.

APM (Association for Palliative Medicine of Great Britain and Ireland) (2006). *Association for Palliative Medicine workforce review* Southampton, Association for Palliative Medicine of Great Britain and Ireland.

Aries P (1974). *Western attitudes toward death from the middle ages to the present*, p. 76. Baltimore, The Johns Hopkins University Press.

Armstrong-Coster A (2005). *Living and dying with cancer*. Cambridge, Cambridge University Press.

Arnold L (2002). Assessing professional behaviour: yesterday, today and tomorrow. *Academic Medicine* **77**(6), 502–15.

Ashby M (2005). Broadening the concept of supervision in medicine and nursing according to the 'integrative model' of Hawkins and Shohet. *Grief Matters* **Autumn**, 5–8.

Ashby M, Brooksbank M, Dunne P *et al.* (1997). *Australasian Undergraduate Medical Palliative Care Curriculum*. Melbourne, Australia, Australian and New Zealand Society of Palliative Medicine.

Aspergren K (1999). BEME Guide no 2: Teaching and learning communication skills in medicine – a review with quality grading of articles. *Medical Teacher* **21**(6), 563–70.

Bailey D and Littlechild R (2001). Devising the evaluation strategy for a mental health programme. *Evaluation* **7**(3), 351–68.

Barnett R (1997). *Higher education: a critical business.* Buckingham: SRHE and OU Press.

Barr H (1998). Competent to collaborate: towards a competency-based model for interprofessional education. *Journal of Interprofessional Care* **12**, 181–7.

Bates AW (2005). *Technology, e-learning, and distance education,* 2nd edn. London, Routledge.

Beard J, Strachan A, Davies H *et al.* (2005). Developing an education and assessment framework for the Foundation Programme. *Medical Education* **39**(8), 841–51.

Becker R (2004). Education in Cancer and Palliative Care: an international perspective. In L Foyle and J Hosted, eds *Delivering Cancer and Palliative Care Education,* pp. 189–202. Oxford, Radcliffe Medical Press.

Beckman T (2004). Lessons learned from a peer review of bedside teaching. *Academic Medicine* **79**(4), 343–6.

Beckman T, Lee MC, Rohren CH and Pankratz WS (2003). Evaluating an instrument for the peer review of inpatient teaching. *Medical Teacher* **25**(2), 131–5.

Belbin RM (2004). *Management teams: why they succeed or fail,* 2nd edn. Oxford, Elsevier Butterworth-Heinemann.

Belenky MF, Clinchy BM, Goldberger MR and Tarule JM (1986). *Women's ways of knowing.* New York, Basic Books.

Bell R and Tight M (1993). *Open Universities: a British tradition?* Buckingham, Open University Press.

Bertolino M, Wenk R, Aresca L, Bagnes C, Rigel M, Vicente H. (1996). *Awareness of cancer diagnosis in patients at the first consultation with a palliative care team in Argentina.* Fifth Congress of European Association of Palliative Care, poster 133: Session 57. London, UK.

Biggs J (2003). *Teaching for quality learning at university: what the student does,* 2nd edn. Buckingham, University Press.

Biley FC and Smith KL (1998). Exploring the potential of problem based learning in nurse education. *Nurse Education Today* **18**, 353–61.

Billings JA (2000). Palliative medicine fellowship programs in the United States: Year 2000 survey. *Journal of Palliative Medicine* **3**, 391–6.

Billings JA and Block S (1997). Palliative care in undergraduate medical education. Status report and future directions. *JAMA* **278,** 733–8.

Billings JA, Block SD, Finn JW *et al.* (2002). Initial voluntary program standards for fellowship training in palliative medicine. *Journal of Palliative Medicine* **5**(1), 23–33.

Bines H and Watson D (1992). *Developing professional education.* Buckingham, Open University Press.

Bishop M, Heaton J, Jaskar D. Collaborative end-of-life curriculum for fourth year medical students. Presented as module W-11 A collaborative end-of-life care curriculum at the 11th annual assembly of the American Academy of Hospice and Palliative Medicine, June 23–26, 1999. Snowbird, UT.

Blanchard K, Zigarmi P and Zigarmi D (1987). *Leadership and the one minute manager.* London, Fontana Paperbacks.

Bliss M (1999). *William Osler: a life in medicine.* Canada, University of Toronto Press.

Block SD and Sullivan AM (1998). Attitudes about end-of-life care: a national cross-sectional study. *Journal of Palliative Medicine* **1,** 347–55.

Blunden G, Langton H and Hek G (2001). Professional education for the cancer nurse in England and Wales: a review of the evidence base. *European Journal of Cancer Care.* **10,** 179–82.

Bolman L and Deal T (1991). Reframing organizations: Artistry, choice and leadership. San Francisco, Jossey-Bass.

Bolton R (1986). *People skills.* New York, Touchstone edition, Simon and Schuster.

Booth K, Maguire P, Butterworth T and Hillier VT (1996). Perceived professional support and the use of blocking behaviours by hospice nurses. *Journal of Advanced Nursing* **24**, 622–7.

Bosworth DP (1991). *Open Learning*. London, Cassell.

Boud D (2001a). Creating a work-based curriculum. In Boud D and Solomon N, eds *Work-based learning: a new higher education?* pp. 45–58. Buckingham, Open University Press.

Boud D (2001b). Knowledge at work: issues of learning. In Boud D and Solomon N, eds *Work-based learning: a new higher education?* pp. 33–43. Buckingham, Open University Press.

Boud D and Knights S (1996). Course design for reflective practice. In Gould N and Taylor I, eds *Reflective learning for social work*, pp. 26–34. Aldershot, Ashgate.

Boud D and Middleton H (2003). Learning from others at work: communities of practice and informal learning. *Journal of Workplace Learning* 15(5), 194–202.

Boud D and Solomon N (2001a). Future developments for work-based learning: reconfiguring higher education. In Boud D and Solomon N, eds *Work-based learning: a new higher education?* Buckingham, Open University Press.

Boud D and Solomon N (2001b). Repositioning universities and work. In Boud D and Solomon N, eds *Work-based learning: a new higher education?* pp. 18–33. Buckingham, Open University Press.

Boud D and Solomon N (2003). 'I don't think I am a learner': acts of naming learners at work. *Journal of Workplace Learning* 15(7/8), 326–31.

Boud D, Keogh R and Walker D (eds) (1985). *Reflection: turning experience into learning*. London, Kogan Page.

Boud D, Solomon N and Symes C (2001). New practices for new times. In Boud D Solomon N, eds *Work-based learning: a new higher education?* pp. 3–17. Buckingham, Open University Press.

Bowe CM, Lahey LL, Armstrong E and Kegan R (2003a). Questioning the big assumptions. Part I: addressing personal contradictions that impede professional development. *Medical Education* 37, 715–22.

Bowe CM, Lahey L, Kegan R and Armstrong E (2003b). Questioning the 'big assumptions'. Part II: recognising organisational contradictions that impede institutional change. *Medical Education* 37, 723–33.

Boyd E, Knox H and Struthers J (2003). Work-based learning, theory and practice: a case study of Scottish SMEs. *Industry and Higher Education* 17(3), 163–78.

Boyd EM and Fales AW (1983). Reflective learning: key to learning from experience. *Journal of Humanistic Psychology* 23, 99–117.

Bradley P, Oterholt C, Nordheim L and Bjorndale A (2005). Medical students' and tutors' experiences of directed and self-directed learning programmes in evidence-based medicine. *Evaluation Review* **April**, 149–77.

Branch WT (2000). The ethics of caring and medical education. *Academic Medicine* 75(2), 127–32.

Brandes D and Phillips H (1985). *Gamesters' handbook*. London, Hutchinson.

Bravata DMT, Huot SJ, Abernathy S, Skeff KM and Bravata DMC (2003). The development and implementation of a curriculum to improve clinicians' self-directed learning skills: a pilot project. *BMC Medical Education* 3, 7.

Bray J and Cooper J (2004). The contribution of occupational therapy to palliative medicine. In D Doyle, G Hanks, N Cherney and K Calman, eds *The Oxford Textbook of Palliative Medicine*, 3rd edn, pp. 1035–40. Oxford, Oxford University Press.

Brookfield SD (1991). *Understanding and facilitating adult learning: a comprehensive analysis of principles and effective practices*. San Francisco, Jossey-Bass.

Brooksbank M (2005). *Personal communication*.

Brown CA, Belfield CR and Field SJ (2002). Cost effectiveness of continuing professional development in health care: a critical review of the evidence. *BMJ* 324, 652–6.

Brykczynska G (2002). The critical essence of advanced practice. In Clarke D, Flanagan J and Kendrick K, eds *Advancing nursing practice in cancer and palliative care*. London, Palgrave.

Bullock A, Belfield C, Butterfield S, Ribbins P and Frame J (1999). Continuing education courses in dentistry: assessing impact on practice. *Medical Education* 33, 484–8.

Burchard KW, Rowland-Morin PA, Coe NPW and Garb JL (1995). A surgery oral examination: interrater agreement and the influence of rater characteristics. *Academic Medicine* **70**, 1044–6.

Burge FL and Latimer EJ (1989). Palliative care in medical education at McMaster University. *J Palliat Care* **5**, 16–20.

Burnard P (1990). *Learning human skills.* Oxford, Butterworth-Heinemann.

Burnard P (1995). *Learning human skills: an experiential and reflective guide for nurses,* 3rd edn. Oxford, Butterworth-Heinemann.

Burnard P (2005). Reflections on reflection. *Nurse Education Today* **25**, 85–6.

Burrows DE (1995). The nurse teacher's role in the promotion of reflective practice. *Nurse Education Today* **15**, 346–50.

Bush T (2003). *Theories of educational leadership and management,* 3rd edn. London, Sage Publications.

CAIPE (UK Centre for the Advancement of Interprofessional Education) (2002). *Definition of Interprofessional Education.* http://www.caipe.org.uk/index.php?&page=define&nav=1. Accessed 4 Nov 2006.

Cairns W and Yates P (2003). Education and training in palliative care. *Medical Journal of Australia* **179**(Suppl. 6), S26–8.

Callahan D (2000). Justice, biomedical progress and palliative care. *Prog Palliat Care* **8**(1), 3–4.

Callanan M and Kelly P (1992). *Final gifts.* London, Hodder & Stoughton.

Calman K (2004). Education and training in palliative medicine. In Doyle D, Hanks G, Cherny N and Calman K, eds *Oxford Textbook of Palliative Medicine,* 3rd edn, pp. 1155–58. Oxford, Oxford University Press.

Calman K and Hine D (1995). *A policy framework for commissioning cancer services.* A report by the expert advisory group on cancer to the Chief Medical Officers of England and Wales. London, UK, Department of Health.

Calman KC (2000). *A study of story telling humour and learning in medicine,* p. 10. London, Nuffield Trust.

Campbell D (2000). *The socially constructed organisation.* London, Karnac.

Canning D and Yates P (2005). *New understanding of contemporary nursing practice: developing a competency framework for specialist palliative care.* New Horizons, 8th Australian Palliative Care Conference, Sydney, Australia.

Cantillon P (2003). Teaching large groups. *BMJ* **326**, 437–40.

Cantor JA (1992). *Delivering Instruction to Adult Learners.* Toronto, Wall & Emerson.

Caplan R (1973). Measuring the effectiveness of continuing medical education. *Journal of Medical Education* **48**(12), 1150–2.

Carlisle C, Donovan T and Mercer D (2005). *Interprofessional education: an agenda for healthcare professionals.* Salisbury, Quay Books.

Carpenter J (1990). *Research in interprofessional education: criteria for evaluation.* Report to CAIPE 1st National Conference, London, UK.

Carpenter J and Hewstone M (1996). Shared learning for doctors and social workers: evaluation of a programme. *British Journal of Social Work* **26**, 239–57.

Carper BA (1978). Fundamental patterns of knowing in nursing. *Advances in Nursing Science* **1**, 13–23.

Centeno C, Clark D, Rocafort J and Flores Perez LA (2004). EAPC task force on the development of palliative care in Europe. *European Journal of Palliative Care* **11**(6), 257–9.

Cervero R (1988). *Effective continuing education for professionals.* San Francisco, Jossey Bass.

Cervero RM (1985). Continuing professional education and behavioural change: a model for research and evaluation. *The Journal of Continuing Education in Nursing* **16**(3), 85–8.

Challis M (1999). AMEE Medical Education Guide No 11 (revised): Portfolio-based learning and assessment in medical education. *Medical Teacher* **21**, 370–86.

Chalmers H, Swallow VM and Miller J (2001). Accredited work-based learning: an approach for collaboration between higher education and practice. *Nurse Education Today* **21**(8), 597–606.

Chambers M (1988). Curriculum evaluation: an approach towards appraising a post-basic psychiatric course. *Journal of Advanced Nursing* **13**(3), 330–40.

Chant S, Jenkinson T, Randle J and Russell G (2002). Communication skills: some problems in nursing education and practice. *Journal of Clinical Nursing* **11**(1), 12–21.

Chapman L and Howkins E (2003). Work-based learning: making a difference in practice. *Nursing Standard* **17**(34), 39–42.

Chartered Society of Physiotherapy (2001). *Specialisms and specialists: guidance for developing the clinical specialist role*. London, Chartered Society of Physiotherapy.

Chartered Society of Physiotherapy (2002a). *Curriculum framework for qualifying programmes in physiotherapy*. London, Chartered Society of Physiotherapy.

Chartered Society of Physiotherapy (2002b). *Validation procedures*. London, Chartered Society of Physiotherapy.

Chittazhathu R and Moideen S (2005). Training community volunteers and professionals in the psychosocial aspects of palliative care. *Indian Journal of Palliative Care* **11**, 53–4.

Clark D (2002). Psychological myths in e-learning. *Medical Teacher* **24**(6), 598–604.

Clark D and Wright M (2003). *Transitions in end of life care: hospice and related developments in Eastern Europe and Central Asia*. Buckingham, Open University Press.

Clarke A (2001). *Assessing the quality of open and distance learning materials*. Leicester, National Institute of Adult Continuing Education (England and Wales).

Clarke A and Dawson R (1999). *Evaluation research: an introduction to principles, methods and practice*. London, Sage.

Clarke DJ and Copeland L (2003). Developing nursing practice through work-based learning. *Nurse Education in Practice* **3**(4), 236–44.

Claxton G (1984). *Live and learn: an introduction to the psychology of growth and change in everyday life*. Milton Keynes, Open University Press.

Clinical Standards Board for Scotland (CSBS) (2002). *Standards for specialist palliative care*. Edinburgh, CSBS.

Coles C (1996). Undergraduate education and palliative care. *Palliative Medicine* **10**(2), 93–8.

Colleau S (2002). Palliative care in Latin America and the Caribbean. *Cancer Pain Release, World Health Organisation Wisconsin* **15**(1).

College of Occupational Therapists (1996). *Professional Development Programme: Portfolio*. London, College of Occupational Therapists.

College of Occupational Therapists (2003). *COT/BAOT briefings. Occupational therapy clinical specialist*. London, College of Occupational Therapists.

College of Occupational Therapists (2004). *Occupational therapy intervention in cancer: guidance for professionals, managers and decision-makers*. London, College of Occupational Therapists.

Collins J (2005). *Personal communication*.

Colliver JA (2000). Effectiveness of problem-based learning curricula: research and theory. *Academic Medicine* **75**(3), 259–66.

Colquhoun M and Dougan H (1997). Performance standards: ensuring that the specialist nurse in palliative care is special. *Palliative Medicine* **11**, 381–7.

Committee on Care at the End of Life (1997). *Approaching death: improving care at the end of life*. Division of Health Care Services, Institute of Medicine, National Academies Press, Washington D.C.

Committee on Care at the End of Life (1997). Grauel RR, Eger R, Finley RC, Hawtin C *et al*. Educational Program in Palliative and Hospice Care at the University of Maryland School of Medicine. *J Cancer Educ* **11**, 144–7.

Cook DA and Dupras DM (2004). A practical guide to developing effective web-based learning. *Journal of General Internal Medicine* **19**(6), 698–707.

Cooper H, Carlisle C, Gibbs T and Watkins C (2001). Developing an evidence base for interdisciplinary learning: a systematic review. *Journal of Advanced Nursing* **35**(2), 228–37.

Corlett J (2000). The perceptions of nurse teachers, student nurses and preceptors of the theory-practice gap in nurse education. *Nurse Education Today* **20**(3), 499–505.

Corner J and Wilson–Barnett J (1992). The newly registered nurse and the cancer patient; an educational evaluation. *International Journal of Nursing Studies* **29**(2), 177–90.

Corner J, Clark D and Normand C (2002). Evaluation of the work of the clinical nurse specialist in palliative care. *Palliative Medicine* **16**, 275–7.

Corner J, Halliday D, Haviland J *et al.* (2003). Exploring nursing outcomes for patients with advanced cancer following intervention by Macmillan Specialist Palliative Care Nurses. *Journal of Advanced Nursing* **41**(6), 561–74.

Costello J and Horne M (2005). Patients as teachers: utilising patients in classroom teaching. In Warne T and McAndrew S, eds *Using patient experience in nurse education* pp. 86–103. London, Palgrave.

Cowley S, Bilss J, Mathew A and Mc Vey G (2002). Effective interagency and interprofessional working: facilitators and barriers. *International Journal of Palliative Nursing* **8**, 30–9.

Cowman S (1996). Student evaluation: a performance indicator of quality in nurse education. *Journal of Advanced Nursing* **24**(3), 625–32.

Cox K (1987). Knowledge which cannot be used is useless. *Medical Teacher* **9**, 145–154.

Cox K (1993). Planning bedside teaching – 1. Overview. *The Medical Journal of Australia* **158**, 280–2.

Cronbach LJ and Suppes P (eds) (1969). *Research for tomorrow's schools: disciplined enquiry for education.* New York, Macmillan.

Cruickshank D (1995). The 'art' of reflection: using drawing to uncover knowledge development in student nurses. *Nurse Education Today* **16**(2), 127–30.

Cullen CM and Vera MM (2001). International perspectives. South America: Argentina. In Ferrell B and Coyle N, eds *Oxford Textbook of Palliative Nursing,* pp. 797–801. New York: Oxford University Press.

Curran VR and Fleet L (2005). A review of evaluation outcomes of web-based continuing medical education. *Medical Education* **39**, 561–7.

Currie J, DeAngelis R, de Boer H, Huisman J and Lacotte C (2003). *Globalizing practices and university responses.* Westport, CT, Praeger.

D'Urbano E and Salguiero S (2003). Aspectos sociales de la enfermedad terminal e intervencion del trabajador social; la experiencia de un centro de dia. In *Avances en Cuidados Paliativos,* GAFOS **3**, 62–70.

Dallos R and Draper R (2000). *An introduction to family therapy.* Maidenhead, Open University.

Daly W and Carnwell R (2001). The case for a multi method approach. *Nurse Researcher* **8**(3), 30–44.

Dannefer EF, Henson LC and Bierer SB *et al.* (2005). Peer assessment of professional competence. *Medical Education* **39**, 713–22.

Davies C and Sharp P (2000). The assessment and evaluation of reflection. In Burns S and Bulman C, eds *Reflective practice in nursing,* 2nd edn. Oxford, Blackwell Science.

Davis MH (2003) OSCE: the Dundee experience. *Medical Teacher* **25**, 255–61.

Davis MH and Karunathilake I (2005). The place of oral examination in today's assessment systems. *Medical Teacher* **27**(4), 294–7.

De Simone G (2002). It takes two to tango. *Hospice Information Bulletin* **1**, 4–5.

De Simone G (2003) Palliative care in Argentina: perspectives from a country in crisis. *Journal of Pain and Palliative Care Pharmacotherapy,* **17**(3–4), 23–43.

De Simone G, Roca E, Solves A *et al.* (1990). *Psychosocial aspects of terminally ill cancer patients: an Argentine study*. Tenth Annual Meeting ASCO, Washington, USA. Selected abstract 1171, abstract book: poster presentation.

De Vlieger M, Gorchs N, Larkin PJ and Porchet F (2004). *A guide to the development of palliative nurse education in Europe*. Report of the European Association of Palliative Care Task Force, Milan, European Association of Palliative Care.

Delva MD, Kirby JR, Knapper CK and Birtwhistle RV (2002). Postal survey of approaches to learning among Ontario physicians: implications for continuing medical education. *BMJ* **325**, 1218.

Department for Education and Skills and Department of Health (2003). *The StLaR HR plan project: phase 1 consultation report*. London, Department for Education and Skills and Department of Health.

Department of Health (1998). *A review of continuing professional development in practice: a report by the Chief Medical Officer*. London, HMSO.

Department of Health (1999). *Making a difference: the new NHS*. London, Department of Health.

Department of Health (2001). *Working together – learning together. A framework for lifelong learning from the NHS*. London, Department of Health.

Department of Health (2002). *Requirements for social work training*. London, Department of Health.

Department of Health (2003a). *The NHS Knowledge and Skills Framework (NHS KSF) and development review guidance: working draft*. London, UK: Department of Health.

Department of Health (2003b). *Medical, health care and associated professions. The General Medical Practice and Specialist Medical Education, Training and Qualifications Order 2003 consultation document*. Available at www.dh.gov.uk/assetRoot/04/07/11/24/04071124.pdf. Accessed 30 Mar 2006.

Department of Health (2004a). *The NHS Knowledge and Skills Framework (NHS KSF) and the development review process: Appendix 2 The NHS KSF dimensions, levels and indicators*. London, Department of Health.

Department of Health (2004b). *Learning for delivery: Making connections between post qualification learning/ continuing professional development and service planning and contact*. London, Department of Health.

Department of Health (2004c). *Manual for Cancer Standards*. Available at http://www.dh.gov.uk/PublicationsAndStatistics/Publications/PublicationsPolicyAndGuidance/PublicationsPolicyAndGuidanceArticle/fs/en?CONTENT_ID=4090081&chk=hq28gu. Accessed 1 April 2006.

Dewar BJ and Walker E (1999). Experiential learning: issues for supervision. *Journal of Advanced Nursing* **30**(6), 1459–67.

Dharmasena HP and Forbes K (2001). Palliative care for patients with non-malignant disease: will hospital physicians refer? *Palliative Medicine* **15**, 413–18.

Dingle K and Yates P (2005). *Developing the allied health professional workforce in palliative care: a survey to assess learning needs*. New Horizons, 8th Australian Palliative Care Conference, Sydney, Australia.

Dixon J (1978). Evaluation criteria in studies of continuing education in the health professions: a critical review and a suggested strategy. *Eval Health Prof* **1**(2), 47–65.

Dixon NM (1996). New routes to evaluation. *Training and Development Journal* **50**(5), 82–85.

Donnelly WJ (2005). Patient-centred medical care requires a patient-centred medical record. *Academic Medicine* **80**(1), 33–8.

Dowell L (2002). Multiprofessional palliative care in a general hospital: education and training needs. *International Journal of Palliative Nursing* **8**(6), 294–303.

Dowling S and Broomfield D (2002). Ireland, the UK and Europe: a review of undergraduate medical education in palliative care. *Irish Medical Journal* **95**(7), 215–16.

Downing J (2005). Moving with education and training. *African Palliative Care Association. Journal of Palliative Care* **1**(2), 23.

Doyle L, McClure J and Fisher S (2004). The contribution of physiotherapy to palliative medicine. In D Doyle, G Hanks, N Cherney and K Calman, eds *The Oxford Textbook of Palliative Medicine*, 3rd edn, pp. 1050–6. Oxford, Oxford University Press.

Draper R, Gower M and Huffington C (1990). *Teaching family therapy*. London, Karnac.

Drucker PF (2005). Managing oneself. *Harvard Business Review* **Jan**, 100–9.

Dunn S and Yates P (2000). The role of Australian Chairs in Clinical Nursing. *Journal of Advanced Nursing* **31**(1), 165–71.

Durgahee T (1998). Facilitating reflection: from a sage on stage to a guide on the side. *Nurse Education Today* **18**(2), 158–64.

EAPC (European Association for Palliative Care) (2004). Taskforce on education for physicians: EAPC news and update. *European Journal of Palliative Care* **11**(1), 39–40.

EAPC (European Association for Palliative Care) (2005). http://www.eapcnet.org. Accessed 27 Oct 2006.

Ebert-May D, Brewster C and Allred S (1997). Innovation in large lectures: teaching for active learning. *BioScience* **47**(9), 601–7.

Edmond CE (2001). A new paradigm for practice education. *Nurse Education Today* **21**, 251–9.

Edmonds PM, Burman R and Sinnott C (2004). The goldfish bowl. *European Journal of Palliative Care* **11**(2), 69–71.

Eisenchlas J and De Simone G (2002). *The oncology/palliative care inter-phase – an audit regarding expectations and communication about palliative chemotherapy*. Diploma in Palliative Medicine, University of Wales, Cardiff (unpublished data).

Eisner E (1991). *The Enlightened Eye: Qualitative Inquiry and the Enhancement of Educational Practice*. Macmillan, New York.

Ekebergh M, Lepp. M and Dahlberg K (2004). Reflective learning with drama in nursing education – a Swedish attempt to overcome the theory–praxis gap. *Nurse Education Today* **24**(8), 622–8.

Ellershaw JE and Wilkinson S (2003). *Care of the dying: a pathway to excellence*. Oxford, Oxford University Press.

Ellis L (2003). Illuminative case study design: a new approach to the evaluation of continuing professional evaluation. *Nurse Researcher* **10**(3), 48–59.

ELNEC (End of Life Nursing Education Consortium) (2000). City of Hope National Medical Centre (Betty Ferrell PhD, FAAN, Principal Investigator) and American Association of Colleges of Nursing (Geraldine Bednash PhD, FAAN, Co-Investigator). Available at http://www.aacn.nche.edu/elnec. Accessed 11 December 2005.

Eluf-Neto J and Nascimento CM (2001). Cervical cancer in Latin America. *Seminars in Oncology* **28**(2), 188–97.

Emanuel LL, von Gunten CF and Ferris FD (1999). *The Education for Physicians on End-of-life Care (EPEC) Curriculum*. © The EPEC Project, The Robert Wood Johnson Foundation. Availabe at http://www.epec.net. Accessed 11 Dec 2005.

Endacott R, Gray MA, Jasper MA *et al.* (2004). Using portfolios in the assessment of learning and competence. *Nurse Education Today* **3**, 1–8.

Ende J (1983). Feedback in Clinical Medical Education. *JAMA* **250**(6), 777–81.

End-of-life Care (2000). *Journal of the American Association of Medicine:* themed issue **284.**

Eraut M (1999). *Learning in the workplace. Professional Development Network seminar*. London, Institute of Education.

Evans RG (2003). Patient-centred medicine: reason, emotion and human spirit? Some philosophical reflections on being with patients. *Journal of Medical Ethics: Medical Humanities* **29**, 8–15.

Fallowfield L (2005). Learning how to communicate in cancer settings. *Support Care Cancer* **13**, 349–50.

Fallowfield L, Saul J and Gilligan B (2001). Teaching senior nurses how to teach communication skills in oncology. *Cancer Nursing* **24**, 185–91.

Feinstein ON (2002). Use of evaluations and the evaluation of their use. *Evaluation* **8**(4), 433–9.

Ferris F, Balfour H, Bowen K *et al*. (2002). A model to guide patient and family care. Based on nationally accepted principles and norms of practice. *Journal of Pain and Symptom Management* **24**(2), 106–23.

Ferris FD, von Gunten CF and Emanuel LL (2001). Knowledge: insufficient for change. *Journal of Palliative Medicine* **4**(2), 145–7.

Field D (1984). Formal instruction in United Kingdom medical schools about death and dying. *Medical Education* **198**, 429–34.

Field D (2000). *What do we mean by psychosocial?* National Council Briefing Paper No. 4. London, National Council for Hospice and Specialist Palliative Care.

Field D and Wee B (2002). Preparation for palliative care: teaching about death, dying and bereavement in UK medical schools 2000–2001. *Medical Education* **36,** 561–67.

Field DE (2004). Moving from novice to expert – the value of learning in clinical practice: a literature review. *Nurse Education Today* **24**, 560–5.

Fineberg I, Wenger N and Forrow L (2004). Interdisciplinary education: evaluation of a palliative care training intervention for pre-professionals. *Academic Medicine* **79**(8), 769–76.

Finlay I (2005). *Personal communication*.

Fish D and Coles C (1998). *Developing professional judgement in health care: learning through the critical appreciation of practice*. Oxford, Butterworth-Heinemann.

Fitzpatrick JJ (1998). Building community: developing skills for inter-professional health professions education and relationship-centred care. *Journal of Nurse-Midwifery* **43**, 61–5.

Flanagan J, Baldwin S and Clarke D (2000). Work-based learning as a means of developing and assessing nursing competence. *Journal of Clinical Nursing* **9**(3), 360–8.

Fletcher M (2001). *Distributed open and distance learning. How does e-learning fit?* London, Learning and Skills Development Agency.

Foley KM and Gelband H (2001). *Improving palliative care for cancer*. Washington DC , National Cancer Policy Board, National Research Council, National Academies Press.

Fowell SL, Maudsley G, Maguire P, Leinster SH and Bligh J (2000). Student assessment in undergraduate medical education in the United Kingdom. *Medical Education* **34**(Suppl. 1) 1–49.

Fox E (1997). Predominance of the curative model of medical care. *JAMA* **278**(9), 761–3.

Fox S (2002). *Integrated community-based home care (ICHC) in South Africa*. Cadre: The Centre for AIDS Development, Research and Evaluation.

Foyle L (2004). The impact of health and social policy on cancer and palliative care education. In Foyle L and Hostad J, eds *Delivering cancer and palliative care education*, pp. 1–20. Oxford, Radcliffe.

Francis A (1993). *Facing the future: the internationalisation of post-secondary institutions in British Colombia, Canada*. Vancouver, British Colombia Centre for International Education.

Fraser HC, Kutner JS and Pfeifer MP (2001). Senior medical students' perceptions of the adequacy of education on end of life issues. *Journal of Palliative Medicine* **4**, 337–43.

Frazee V (1996). Develop your career 5 minutes at a time. *Personnel Journal* **75**(12), 28.

Freire P (1972). *Pedagogy of the oppressed*. London, Penguin.

Frosh S, Phoenix A and Pattman R (2002). *Young masculinities*. Basingstoke, Palgrave.

Furney SL, Orsini AL, Orsetti KE *et al*. (2001). Teaching the one minute preceptor. A randomised controlled trial. *J Gen Intern Med* **16**, 620–4.

Gallagher P (2001). An evaluation of a standards-based portfolio. *Nurse Education Today* **21**, 409–16.

Galucci M, Borsani M, Causarano R *et al*. (2001). *Advanced teaching methods in palliative care education adopted by the Italian School of Medicine and Care (SIMPA)*. Seventh Congress of the European Association for Palliative Care, Palermo, Sicily, Italy.

Garanganga E (2003). *Personal communication*.

Garavan TN (1997). Training, development, education and learning: different or the same? *Journal of European Industrial Training* **21**(2), 39–50.

Garrigue N, Fisman N, Junin M and De Simone G (2001). *Measure of clinical impact of education in palliative care: Pallium Latinoamerica distance learning advanced course.* Proceedings of the Annual Meeting of Argentinean Association of Palliative Care, Buenos Aires.

Georgenson DL (1982). The problem of transfer calls for partnership. *Training and Development Journal* **36** (10), 75–78.

General Medical Council (1993). *Tomorrow's doctors: recommendations on undergraduate medical education.* London, General Medical Council.

General Medical Council (2002). *Tomorrow's doctors,* 2nd edn. London, General Medical Council.

General Social Care Council (2005). *Post qualifying framework for social work education and training.* London, General Social Care Council.

Gergen KJ (1999). *An invitation to social construction.* London, Sage.

Gibbs G (1988). *Learning by doing: a guide to teaching and learning methods.* London, Further Education Unit (FEU).

Gibson B, Fancott C and Nixon S (2005). *Are you providing patient-centred care?* Toronto, College of Physiotherapists of Ontario.

Giles A, Martin S, Bryce D and Hendry G (2004). Students as partners in evaluation: student and teacher perspectives. *Assessment and Evaluation in Higher Education* **29**(6), 681–5.

Gilligan C (1993). *In a different voice.* Cambridge, Massachusetts, Harvard University Press.

Gleeson F (1992). Defects in postgraduate clinical skills as revealed by the objective structured long examination record (OSLER). *Irish Medical Journal* **85**, 11–14.

Goleman D (2004). What makes a leader? *Harvard Business Review* **Jan**, 1–11.

Goswami DC (2005). *Personal communication.* CEO, Indian Association of Palliative Care.

Gould D, Kelly D, Goldstone L and Maidwell A (2001). The changing training needs of clinical nurse managers: exploring issues for continuing professional development. *Journal of Advanced Nursing* **34**(1), 7–17.

Gould D, Kelly D, White I and Glen (2004). The impact of commissioning processes on the delivery of continuing professional education for cancer and palliative care. *Nurse Education Today* **24**, 443–51.

Gould N and Taylor I (eds) (1996). *Reflective learning for social work.* Aldershot, Ashgate.

Graham F and Clark D (2005). Addressing the basics of palliative care. *International Journal of Palliative Nursing* **11**, 36–9.

Gramsci A (1996). The intellectuals. In Q Hoare and GN Smith, eds *Selections from prison notebooks,* p. 10. Chennai, Orient Longman.

Grant J and Stanton F (1999). *The effectiveness of continuing professional development: a report for the Chief Medical Officer's review of continuing professional development in practice. Association for the Study of Medical Education, Edinburgh.* Cited in: Morrison J (2003). Research issues in CPD. Lancet **362**, 410.

Gray DP (1998). Continuing medical education. *Lancet* **351**, 1742.

Greenhalgh T and Hurwitz B (1999). Why study narrative? *BMJ* **318**, 48–50.

Gupta H (2004). How basic is palliative care? *International Journal of Palliative Nursing* **10**(12), 600–1.

Gwyther L (2002). Partnerships in palliative care training. Available at http://hab.hrsa.gov/publications/palliative/partnerships_in_training.htm. Accessed 2 Nov 2006.

Gwyther L (2005). *Integrating palliative medicine into medical curricula.* Family Practice Conference, Mtata.

Gysels M, Richardson A and Higginson IJ (2004). Communication training for health professionals who care for patients with cancer: a systematic review of training methods. *Support Care Cancer* **13**, 356–66.

Habeshaw S, Habeshaw T and Gibbs G (1992). *53 Interesting things to do in your seminars and tutorials.* Avon, UK, Technical and Educational Services Ltd.

Hacker DJ and Niederhauser DS (2000). Promoting deep and durable learning in the online classroom' In Weiss RE, Knowlton DS initial and Speck BW (eds) *Principles of effective teaching in the online classroom* pp. 53–64. Hoboken, NJ, Jossey-Bass.

Hafferty FW (1998). Beyond curriculum reform: confronting medicine's hidden curriculum. *Academic Medicine* **73**(4), 403–7.

Hague H (1978). Tools for helping self-development – Part 1. *Journal of European Industrial Training* **2**(3), 13–5.

Hall D, Jones R and Raffo C (1996). *Advanced business,* p. 125. Ormskirk, Causeway Press Limited.

Hall M (2004). The role and training needs of HOPE members. Unpublished Master's dissertation. University of Sheffield.

Hall P (2005). Interprofessional teamwork: professional cultures as barriers. *Journal of Interprofessional Care* **1**(Suppl. 1) 188–96.

Hall P and Weaver L (2001). Interdisciplinary education and teamwork: a long and winding road. *Medical Education* **35**, 867–75.

Harden JK (2003). Faculty and student experiences with web-based discussion groups in a large lecture setting. *Nurse Educator* **28**(1), 26–30.

Harden RM (1998). AMEE Guide No. 12. Multiprofessional education: Part 1 – Effective multiprofessional education: a three dimensional perspective. *Medical Teacher* **20**, 402–8.

Harden RM and Gleeson FA (1979). Assessment of medical competence using an objective structured clinical examination. *Medical Education* **13**, 41–54.

Harden RM, Crosby JR and Davis MH (1999). AMEE guide No. 14: outcome-based education: Part 1 – An introduction to outcome-based education. *Medical Teacher* **21**(6), 546–52.

Hargreaves J (2004). So how do you feel about that? Assessing reflective practice. *Nurse Education Today* **24**(3), 196–201.

Harrison M, Roberts C and Short C (2003). Reflecting on reflective learning: the case of geography, earth and environmental sciences. *Journal of Geography in Higher Education* **27**(2), 133–52 .

Harvey J (1998) (ed.). *The LTDI evaluation cookbook.* Edinburgh, The Learning Technology Dissemination Initiative.

Harvey J, Higginson C and Gunn C (2000). *On line tutoring e-book.* Available at http://www.scotit. ac.uk/onlinebook/otist504.htm.

Hawkins C (2005). *Personal communication.*

Health Workforce Advisory Committee (2005). *Fit for purpose and for practice: a review of the medical workforce in New Zealand.* Available at http://www.hwac.govt.nz.

Heath H (1998). Keeping a reflective practice diary: a practical guide. *Nurse Education Today* **18**(7), 592–8.

Henderson E, Berlin A, Freeman G and Fuller J (2002). Twelve tips for promoting significant event analysis to enhance reflection in undergraduate medical students. *Medical Teacher* **24**(2), 121–4.

Henwood S, Edie J, Flinton D and Simpson R (1998). Continuing professional development – a re-examination of the facts. *Radiography* **4**(1), 5–8.

Henwood SM (2003). Continuing professional development in diagnostic radiography: a grounded theory study. PhD Thesis, South Bank University, London.

Heron J (1989). *The facilitators' handbook.* London, Kogan Page.

Hesketh EA, Bagnall G, Buckley EG *et al.* (2001). A framework for developing excellence as a clinical educator. *Medical Education* **35**, 555–64.

Hill C Stratton, Fields WS, Thorpe DM (1989). A call to action to improve relief of cancer pain. In Hill CS and Fields WS, eds *Advances in pain research and therapy,* pp. 353–61. New York, Raven Press.

Hillier R (1995). *Personal communication.*

Hillier R and Wee B (2001). From cradle to grave: palliative medicine education in the UK. *Journal of the Royal Society of Medicine* **94,** 468–71.

Hinohara S (1993). Sir William Osler's philosophy on death. *Annals of Internal Medicine* **118,** 638–42.

Hirsch W (2000). Spinal accord. *People Management* **6**(11), 40.

Hirsch W and Jackson C (1996). *Strategies for career development: promise, practice and pretence.* Brighton, Institute of Employment Studies.

Hodgkin K and Knox JDE (1975). *Problem-centred learning.* London, Churchill Livingstone.

Hodgson B (1993). *Key terms and issues in open and distance learning.* London, Kogan Page.

Hogan C (2002). *Understanding facilitation.* London, Kogan Page.

Hogan D and Kwiatkowski R (1998). Emotional aspects of large group teaching. *Human Relations* **51**(11), 1403–17.

Holme TA (1992). Using the Socratic method in large lecture courses: increasing student interest and involvement by forming instantaneous groups. *Journal of Chemical Education* **69**(12), 974–7.

Honey P and Mumford A (1986). *The manual of learning styles.* Maidenhead, Peter Honey Publications.

Honey P and Mumford A (1992). *The manual of learning styles,* 3rd edn. Maidenhead, Peter Honey.

Honey P and Mumford A (2000a). *The learning styles helper's guide.* Maidenhead, Peter Honey Publications.

Honey P and Mumford A (2000b). *The learning styles questionnaire.* Maidenhead, Peter Honey Publications.

Hospice and palliative care services – UK summary 2005. Available at http://www.hospiceinformation.info/uploads/documents/hospice_&_palliative_care_facts_&_figures_2005.pdf. Accessed 27 Oct 2006.

Hospice New Zealand (2000). *Guidelines for nurses in palliative care.* Wellington, Hospice New Zealand.

Hostad J (2004). An overview of hospice education. In Foyle L and Hostad J (eds) (2004). *Delivering cancer and palliative care education,* pp. 205–224. Oxford, Radcliffe Medical Press.

Hostad J, MacManus D and Foyle L (2004). Public information and education in palliative care. In Foyle L and Hostad J eds *Delivering cancer and palliative care education,* pp. 37–52. Oxford, Radcliffe Medical Press.

Houghton A (2005). Personal support 6: for leaders and medical managers. *BMJ Careers* **23 July,** 37–8.

House of Lords Select Committee on Medical Ethics (1994). *Report of the House of Lords Select Committee on Medical Ethics: Volume 1.* London, HMSO.

Howe A (2001). Patient-centred medicine through student-centred teaching: a student perspective on the key impacts of community-based learning in undergraduate medical education. *Medical Education* **37**(7), 666.

Howe A and Anderson J (2003). Involving patients in medical education. *BMJ* **327,** 326–8.

Howe D (1998). Relationship-based thinking and practice in social work. *Journal of Social Work Practice* **12,** 45–56.

Hoy AM (2004). Training specialists in palliative medicine. In Doyle D, Hanks G, Cherny N and Calman K, eds *Oxford Textbook of Palliative Medicine,* 3rd edn, pp. 1166–1175. Oxford, Oxford University Press.

Hulsman RL, Ros WJ, Winnubst JA and Bensing (1999). Teaching clinically experienced clinicians communication skills: a review of evaluation studies. *Medical Education* **33**(9), 655–68.

Hunter D, Bailey A and Taylor B (1995). *The art of facilitation: how to create group synergy.* Tucson, AZ: Fisher Books.

Hussainy S, Beattie J, Nation R *et al.* (2005). *Development of an online educational programme in palliative cancer care for community pharmacists: using the nominal group technique (NGT) to assist in determining content material.* New Horizons, 8th Australian Palliative Care Conference, Sydney, Australia.

Hussainy SY, Beattie J, Nation RL *et al.* (2006). Palliative care for patients with cancer: what are the educational needs of community pharmacists? *Supportive Care in Cancer* **14**(2), 177–84.

Hutchinson L (1999). Evaluating and researching the effectiveness of educational interventions. *BMJ* **318**, 1267–9.

Illeris K (2004). *The three dimensions of learning*, 2nd edn. Frederiksberg, Roskilde University Press and Leicester, Niace Publications.

James C and MacLeod RD (1993). The problematic nature of palliative care education. *Journal of Palliative Care* **9**(4), 5–10.

Janicik RW and Fletcher KE (2003). Teaching at the bedside: a new model. *Medical Teacher* **25**(2), 127–30.

Jarvis P (1983). *Professional education*. London, Croom Helm.

Jasper M (1995). The portfolio workbook as a strategy for student-centred learning. *Nurse Education Today* **15**, 446–51.

Jasper M (1999). Nurses' perceptions of the value of written reflection. *Nurse Education Today* **19**(6), 452–63.

Jeffrey D (ed.) (2002) *Teaching palliative care: a practical guide*. Abingdon, Radcliffe Medical Press.

Johns C (2002). *Guided reflection: advancing practice*. Oxford, Blackwell Science.

Jolliffe J and Bury T (2002). *The effectiveness of physiotherapy in the palliative care of older people*. London, Chartered Society of Physiotherapy.

Jordan S (2000). Educational input and patient outcomes: exploring the gap. *Journal of Advanced Nursing* **31**(2), 461–71.

Jordan S, Coleman M and Hughes D (1999). Assessing educational effectiveness: the impact of a specialist course on the delivery of care. *Journal of Advanced Nursing* **30**(4), 796–807.

Junin M (2001). International perspectives. South America: Brazil, Chile, Paraguay, Peru and Uruguay. In B Ferrell and N Coyle, eds *Oxford Textbook of Palliative Nursing*, pp. 797–801. New York, Oxford University Press.

Kagan C and Evans J (1994). *Professional interpersonal skills for nurses: research and application*. London, Stanley Thorns Publishers.

Kanter RM (1989). *When giants learned to dance*. New York, Simon and Schuster.

Kapborg I and Fischbein S (2002). Using a model to evaluate nursing education and professional practice. *Nursing and Health Sciences* **4**, 25–31.

Karp NV (1992). Physical therapy continuing education part ii: motivating factors. *The Journal of Continuing Education in the Health Professions* **12**, 171–9.

Kaufman DM (2003). ABC of learning and teaching in medicine: Applying educational theory in practice. *BMJ* **326**, 213–6.

Kennedy I (2001). Chapter 25: Competent Healthcare Professionals, pp 321–50. In *Bristol Royal Infirmary Enquiry–Learning from Bristol*. The Report of the Public Inquiry into children's heart surgery at the Bristol Royal Infirmary 1984–1995. Presented to Parliament by the Secretary of State for Health. HMSO Stationery Office.

Kenny L (2003). An evaluation-based model for palliative care education: making a difference to practice. *International Journal of Palliative Nursing* **9**(5),189–94.

Keogh K, Jeffrey D and Flanagan S (1999). The Palliative care Education Group for Gloucestershire (PEGG): an integrated model of multidisciplinary education in palliative care. *European Journal of Cancer Care* **8**, 44–7.

Kickbush IS (2001). Health literacy: addressing the health and education device. *Health Promotion International* **16**, 289–97.

Kilminster S, Morris P, Simpson E, Thistlewaite J and Ewart B (2005). Using patient experiences in medical education: first steps in Inter-professional training? In Warne T and McAndrew S, eds *Using patient experience in nurse education*, pp. 104–124. London, Palgrave.

Kirkpatrick DI (1967) in Craig R, Bittel I (eds.) *Training and Development Handbook.* New York, McGraw-Hill.

Kleinman A (1988). *The illness narratives.* New York, Basic Books.

Knight PT (2000). The value of a programme-wide approach to assessment. *Assessment and Evaluation in Higher Education* **25**(3), 237–51.

Knowles M (1984). *The adult learner: a neglected species,* 3rd edn. Houston, Gulf Publishing.

Knowles MS (1970). *The modern practice of adult education. Andragogy vs. pedagogy.* New York, Association Press.

Knowles MS, Elwood EF and Swanson RA (eds) (2005). *The adult learner: the classic in adult education and human resource development.* California, Elsevier.

Knowles MS, Elwood FH and Swanson RA (1998). *The adult learner.* Houston, Gulf Publishing.

Koffman J (2001). Multiprofessional palliative care education: past challenges,future issues. *Journal of Palliative Care* **17**(2), 86–92.

Kohora H, Ueoka H, Takeyama H, Kurakami T and Morita T (2005). Sedation for terminally ill patients with cancer with uncontrollable physical distress. *Journal of Palliative Medicine* **8**(1), 20–5.

Kolb DA (1984). *Experiential learning – experience as a source of learning and development.* New Jersey, Prentice Hall.

Korthagen FAJ (1993). Two modes of reflection. *Teaching and Teacher Education* **9**(3), 317–26. Cited in Boud D and Knights S. Course Design for Reflective Practice in Goulds N and Taylor I (eds) (1996) Reflective learning for Social work, Ashgate, Aldershot.

Kotter JP (2001). What leaders really do. *Harvard Business Review* **Dec**, 3–12.

Kouzes JM and Posner BZ (2002). *The leadership challenge,* 3rd edn. San Francisco, Jossey-Bass.

Krause I (1989). Sinking heart: a Punjabi communication of distress. *Social Science and Medicine* **29**(4), 564–75.

Kruijver IPM, Kerkstra A, Francke AL, Bensing JM and Van de Wiel HBM (2000) Evaluation of communication training programs in nursing care: a review of the literature. *Patient Education and Counselling* **39**(1), 129–45.

Kubler-Ross E (1969). *On death and dying: what the dying have to teach doctors, nurses, clergy and their own families.* New York, MacMillan Publishing.

Kumar S (2004). Learning from low income countries: what are the lessons? Palliative care can be delivered through neighbourhood networks. *BMJ* **329,** 1184.

Kurtz S, Silverman J and Draper J (2005). *Teaching and learning communication skills in medicine.* Oxford, Radcliffe Publishing.

Kwa Kwa J (2004). Clinical governance in 'face to face' and 'online space' palliative care education. In Foyle L and Hostad J, eds *Delivering cancer and palliative care education,* pp. 21–35. Oxford, Radcliffe Medical Press.

Kwan Kam-Por (2001). *Evaluating an evaluation: a case study of the costs and effectiveness of a student feedback system in one university,* pp. 171–85. Available at http://cem.dur.ac.uk. Accessed 15 Aug 2005.

Landeen J, Byrne C and Brown B (1995). Exploring the lived experiences of psychiatric nursing students through self-reflective journals. *Journal of Advanced Nursing* **21**(5), 878–85.

Larkin P (2005). Developing a nurse education network across Europe. *International Journal of Palliative Nursing* **11**(8), pp. 420–2.

Lave J and Wenger E (1991). *Situated learning – legitimate peripheral participation.* Cambridge, Cambridge University Press.

Law M, Baptiste S and Mills J (1995). Client-centred practice: what does it mean and does it make a difference? *Canadian Journal of Occupational Therapy* **62**, 250–7.

Learning and Teaching Support Network (2001). *Assessment: a guide for lecturers.* York, LTSN Generic Centre.

Learning Technology Dissemination Initiative (LTDI) (1999). *Evaluation cookbook. Selecting a methodology.* Available at http://www.icbl.hw.ac.uk/ltdi/cookbook/preparation/selecting.html. 1–4 Accessed 10 Aug 2005.

Lee L (2002). Interprofessional working in hospice day care and the patients' experience of the service. International Journal of Palliative Nursing **8**, 389–400.

Lee V and Zeldin D (1982). *Planning in the curriculum,* pp. 118–50. Sevenoaks, The Open University.

Lehmann LS, Brancati FL, Chen MC, Roter D and Dobs AS (1997). The effect of bedside case presentations on patients' perceptions of their medical care. *New England Journal of Medicine* **336**(16), 1150–5.

Leung W (2003). Gaining experience in different teaching methods. *BMJ Careers* **25 January,** S27–8.

Levorato A, Stiefel F, Mazzocato C and Bruera E (2001). Communication with terminal cancer patients in palliative care: are there differences between nurses and physicians? *Supportive Care in Cancer* **9**, 420–7.

Lewis R and Spencer D (1986). *What is open learning? An introduction to the series.* London, Council for Educational Technology.

Lickiss J (1996). Australia: status of cancer pain and palliative care. *Journal of Pain and Symptom Management* **12**(2), 99–101.

Lickiss JN, Turner KS and Pollock ML (2004). The interdisciplinary team. In Doyle D, Hanks G, Cherny N and Calman K, eds *Oxford Textbook of Palliative Medicine,* 3rd edn pp. 42–6. Oxford, Oxford University Press.

Lincoln YS and Guba EG (1986). *Naturalistic enquiry.* Newbury Park, CA, Sage.

Linfors EW and Neelon FA (1980). The case for bedside rounds. *New England Journal of Medicine* **303**(21), 1230–3.

Lloyd-Jones G, Ellershaw J, Wilkinson S and Bligh JG (1998). The use of multidisciplinary consensus groups in the planning of an integrated problem-based curriculum. *Medical Education* **32**, 278–82.

Lloyd-Williams M (2005). *Personal communication.*

Lloyd-Williams M and Dogra N (2003). Caring for dying patients – what are the attitudes of medical students? *Support Care Cancer* **11**, 696–9.

Lloyd-Williams M and MacLeod RD (2004). A systematic review of teaching and learning in palliative care within the medical undergraduate curriculum. *Medical Teacher* **26**(8), 683–90.

Lockwood DNJ, Armstrong M and Grant AD (2004). Integrating evidence-based medicine into routine clinical practice: seven year's experience at the Hospital for Tropical Diseases, London. *BMJ* **329**, 1020–3.

Lorber J (1975). Good patients and problem patients: conformity and deviance in a general hospital. *Journal of Health and Social Behaviour* **16**, 213–25.

Lufts J and Ingham H (1970). *Group processes; an introduction into group dynamics.* Palo Alto, CA, National Press Books.

MacDermid SM, Lee MD, Buck M and Williams ML (2001). Alternative work arrangements among professionals and managers: rethinking career development and success. *Journal of Management Development* **20**(4), 305–17.

MacDougall G, Mathew A, Broadhurst V and Chamberlain S (2001). An evaluation of an interprofessional palliative care education programme. *International Journal of Palliative Nursing* **7**, 24–9.

MacGregor J and Dewar K (1997). Opening up the options: making the inflexible into a flexible framework. *Nurse Education Today* **17**, 502–7.

Mackintosh C (1998). Reflection: a flawed strategy for the nursing profession. *Nurse Education Today* **18**(7), 553–7.

MacLeod R (2000). Learning to care: a medical perspective. *Palliative Medicine* **14**, 209–16.

MacLeod R (2001). A national strategy for palliative care in New Zealand. *Journal of Palliative Medicine* **4**, 70–4.

MacLeod R and Robertson G (1999). Teaching about living and dying. *Education for Health* **12**(2), 185–92.

MacLeod R, Parkin C, Pullon S *et al.* (2003). Early clinical exposure to people who are dying: learning to care at the end of life. *Medical Education* **37**(1), 51–8.

MacLeod RD and Nash A (1991). Palliative care education in Malta. *Illness, Crises and Loss* **1**(3), 34–8.

MacLeod RD and Nash A (1994). Multidisciplinary palliative care education. *Journal of Interprofessional Care* **8**(3), 283–8.

Macmillan Cancer Relief (2005). Available at http://www.macmillan.org.uk/aboutmacmillan/. Accessed 28 August 2005.

Macmillan Cancer Relief (2006). *How to become a Macmillan nurse.* Available at http://www.macmillan.org.uk/healthprofessionals/dispage.asp?id=640. Accessed 22 March 2006.

Maddocks I (2003). Palliative care education in the developing countries. In Rajagopal MR, Mazza D and Lipman AG, eds *Pain and palliative care in the developing world and marginalised populations: a global challenge*, pp. 211–21. New York, The Harworth Medical Press.

Maguire P (1999). Improving communication with cancer patients. *European Journal of Cancer* **35**(14), 2058–65.

Maguire P and Faulkner A (1988). How to improve the counselling skills of doctors and nurses involved in cancer care. *BMJ* **297**, 847–9.

Mahara SM (1998). A perspective on clinical evaluation in nursing education. *Journal of Advanced Nursing* **28**(6), 1339–46.

Major D (2002). A more holistic form of higher education: the real potential of work-based learning. *Widening Participation and Lifelong Learning* **4**(3), 26–34.

Mallik M (1998). The role of nurse educators in the development of reflective practitioners. *Nurse Education Today* **18**, 52–63.

Marston J (2003). *The status of palliative care training in South Africa.* South Africa: Hospice Palliative Care Association Desk Review.

Martin V and Rogers A (2004). *Leading interprofessional teams in health and social care*, pp. 151–7. Abingdon, Routledge.

Maslow A (1970). *Motivation and personality.* New York, Harper and Row.

Mason S and Ellershaw J (2004). Assessing undergraduate palliative care education: validity and reliability of two scales examining perceived efficacy and outcome expectancies in palliative care. *Medical Education* **38**(10), 1103–10.

Mathur S, Stanton S and Reid WD (2005). Canadian physical therapists' interest in web-based and computer-assisted continuing education. *Physical Therap* **85**, 226–37.

Mcclure P, Shann S, Jeffers K and Mackenzie A (2005). *Case studies in occupational therapy. An overview of the nature of the preparation of practice educators in five health care disciplines.* Available at http://www.practicebasedlearning.org. Accessed on 13 August 2005.

McCormick R (1999). Practical knowledge: a view from the snooker table. In McCormick R and Paechter C, eds *Learning and knowledge.* Paul Chapman Ltd, London. Cited in: Field DE (2004). Moving from novice to expert – the value of learning in clinical practice: a literature review. *Nurse Education Today* **24**, 560–5.

McDonough R (2004). Accrediting work-based learning in primary care for an academic qualification. *Work Based Learning in Primary Care* **2**(3), 214–19.

McGoldrick M, Gerson R and Shellenberger S (1999). *Genograms, assessment and intervention.* New York, Norton.

McKinney K and Graham-Buxton M (1993). The use of collaborative learning groups in the large class: is it possible? *Teaching Sociology* **21**(4), 403–8.

McMullan M, Endacott R, Gray MA *et al.* (2003). Portfolios and assessment of competence: a review of the literature. *Journal of Advanced Nursing* **41**(3), 283–94.

McNair RP (2005). The case for educating health care students in professionalism as the core content of interprofessional education. *Medical Education* **39**, 456–64.

Mearns D (1997). *Person-centred counselling training*. London, Sage.

Millard L (2000). Teaching the teachers: ways of improving teaching and identifying areas for development. *Ann Rhem Dis* **59**, 760–4.

Miller GE (1990). The assessment of clinical skills/competence/performance. *Acad Med* **65**(Suppl. 9): 63–7.

Minghella E and Benson A (1995). Developing reflective practice in mental health nursing through critical incident analysis. *Journal of Advanced Nursing* **21**(2), 205–13.

Mkwananzi S (2005). Focus on training in palliative care at Island Hospice, Zimbabwe. *African Palliative Care Association. Journal of Palliative Care* **1**(2), 29.

Modernising Medical Careers UK Strategy Group (2004). *Modernising medical careers: the next steps: the future shape of foundation, specialist and general practice training programmes*. Available at www.dh.gov.uk/assetRoot/04/07/95/32/04079532.pdf. Accessed 30 March 2006.

Monroe B (2004) Social work in palliative medicine. In D Doyle, G Hanks, N Cherney and K Calman, eds *The Oxford Textbook of Palliative Medicine*, 3rd edn, pp. 1007–17. Oxford, Oxford University Press.

Moore M (1993). Three types of interaction. In Harry K, John M and Keegan D, eds *Distance Education: new perspectives*. Routledge, London. Cited in Jarvis P, Holford J and Griffin C (1998). *The theory and practice of learning*. Kogan Page, London.

Moore T (1992). *Care of the soul*. London, Piatkus.

Mor V, Greer DS and Kastenbaum R (1988). The hospice experiment: an alternative in terminal care. In Mor V, Greer D and Kastenbaum R, eds *The hospice experiment*, p. 6. Baltimore, Johns Hopkins University Press.

Morrell M and Capparell S (2001). *Shackleton's way: leadership lessons from the great Antarctic explorer*. London, Nicholas Brealey Publishing.

Morris LL, Fitz-Gibbon CT and Freeman ME (1987). *How to communicate evaluation findings*. Newbury CA, Sage.

Morton R (1996). Breaking bad news to patients with cancer. *Professional Nurse* **11**, 669–71.

Mpanga Sebuyira L, Mwangi-Powell F, Pereira J, Spence C (2003). The Cape Town Palliative Care Declaration: home-grown solutions for sub-Saharan Africa. *Journal of Palliative Medicine* **6**(3), 341–3.

Munn P and Drever E (1993). *Using questionnaires in small scale research. A teachers guide*. Edinburgh, SCRE.

Murray C and Lopez A (1996). *A global burden of disease*. Oxford, Oxford University Press.

Myers IB (2000). *Introduction to type: a guide to understanding your results on Myers-Briggs Type Indicator*, 6th edn. Oxford, OPP Ltd.

Nair BR, Coughlan JL and Hensley MJ (1997). Student and patient perspectives on bedside teaching. *Medical Education* **31**(5), 341–6.

Nair BR, Coughlan JL and Hensley MJ (1998). Impediments to bedside teaching. *Medical Education* **32**(2), 159–62.

Nakashima N (1997). The role of counter evidence in rule revision: the effects of instructing metaknowledge concerning non adhocness of theory. *Japanese Journal of Educational Psychology* **45**(3), 263–73 (only abstract in English).

Nash A and Hoy A (1993). Terminal care in the community – an evaluation of residential workshops for general practitioner/district nurse teams. *Palliative Medicine* **7**, 5–17.

National Audit Office (2001). *Modern policy making: ensuring policies deliver value for money*. London, National Audit Office.

National Hospice Organisation (1997). *Hospice standards. Approaching death: improving care at the end of life*. Arlington, Virginia, Committee on Care at the End of Life, Division of Health Care Services, Institute of Medicine, National Academy of Sciences.

National Palliative Care Strategy (2005). Available at www.health.gov.au.

NCHSPCS (National Council for Hospice and Specialist Palliative Care Services) (1996). *Education in palliative care: Occasional Paper 9*. Northampton: Land and Unwin Limited.

NCIHE (1997). *Higher education in the learning society. Report of the National Committee of Inquiry into Higher Education*, 2 vols. (Dearing Report) HMSO: London.

Newble D (2003). Large group integrated learning activities. Available at www.medev.ac.uk/resources/best_practice/display_single_item?BestPracIndex=240. Accessed 27 Oct 2006.

Newell R (1994). Reflection: art, science or pseudo-science? *Nurse Education Today* **14**, 79–81.

Newell-Jones K (2003). *Global perspectives in adult learning*. London, Development Education Association.

Newell-Jones K (2005). *International perspectives on learning and curriculum design*. Conference proceedings of International Society for the Scholarship of Teaching and Learning (ISSOTL), Vancouver.

NHS Workforce Review Team (2005). *National Specialist Palliative Care Workforce Survey. Personal communication*.

NHS–QIS (2004). *Specialist Palliative Care: St Columba's Hospice*. NHS–Quality Improvement Scotland, Edinburgh.

NICE (2004). *Guidance on cancer services. Improving supportive and palliative care for adults with cancer*. London, National Institute for Clinical Excellence.

Nierenberg DW (1998). The challenge of "teaching" large groups of learners: strategies to increase active participation and learning. *International Journal of Psychiatry in Medicine* **28**(1), 115–22.

Nipper S (1989). Third generation distance learning and computer conferencing. In Mason R and Kaye A, eds *Mindweave: communication, computers and distance education*. Pergamon Press, Oxford. Cited in Rumble G and Oliveira J (eds) (1992). Vocational education at a distance: international perspectives. Kogan Page, London.

NNPC (2004). *Palliative care – a handbook for community volunteers*. Calicut, Institute of Palliative Medicine.

Nolan Principles for Public Life (1995). Available at http://www.archive.official-documents.co.uk/document/parlment/nolan/nolan.htm. Accessed 27 March 2006.

Norsen L, Opladen J and Quinn J (1995). Practice model: collaborative practice. *Critical Nursing Care Clinics North America* **7**, 43–52.

Numpeli M (2003). *Personal communication*. Program Executive, NNPC.

Nursing and Midwifery Council (2002). *Requirements for pre-registration nursing programmes*. Available at http://www.nmc-uk.org/aArticleSearch.aspx?SearchText=post%20registration%20nursing. Accessed 1 April 2006.

Nursing and Midwifery Council (2005). *Consultation on a framework for the standard for post-registration nursing*. Available at http://www.nmc-k.org/aArticleSearch.aspx?SearchText=post%20registration%20nursing. Accessed 1 April 2006.

Nutbeam D (2000). Health literacy as a public health goal: a challenge for contemporary health education and communication strategies into the 21st century. *Health Promotion International* **15**, 259–67.

O'Neill JF, Selwyn PA, Schietinger H (2003). US Department of Health and Human Services, Health Resources and Services Administration, HIV/AIDS Bureau.

O'Neill O (2002). *BBC Reith lecture series*. Available at http://www.bbc.co.uk/radio4/reith2002/lectures.shtml. Accessed 27 March 2006.

O'Neill WM, O'Connor P and Latimer EJ (1992). Hospital palliative care services: three models in three countries. *Journal of Pain and Symptom Management* **7**, 406–13.

Oandasan I and Reeves S (2005). Key elements for interprofessional education. Part 1: the learner, the educator and the learning context. *Journal of Interprofessional Care* **Suppl. 1**, 21–38.

OERL (2005). *Professional development modules; methodological approach and sampling: strategy: step 2*, p. 1. Available at http://oerl.sri.com/module/mod4/m4_p2b.html. Accessed 9 August 2005.

Oliviere D (2001). The social worker in palliative care – the 'eccentric' role. *Progress in Palliative Care* **9**, 237–41.

Owen JM and Rodgers PJ (1999). *Program evaluation: forms and approaches.* London, Sage.

Paes P and Wee B (2006). *Consensus syllabus for undergraduate palliative medicine in Great Britain and Ireland.* Southampton, Association for Palliative Medicine of Great Britain and Ireland.

PAHO (Pan American Health Organisation) (1998). *La Salud en las Americas.* Ed. Oficina Sanitaria Panamericana, Publicación cientifica vol II: pp. 24–48. Washington, Pan American Health Organisation.

PAHO (Pan American Health Organisation) (2002). *Executive summaries: Health in the Americas.* Scientific Publication 587, pp. 4–14. Washington, Pan American Health Organisation.

Paleri A and Numpeli M (2005). The evolution of palliative care programmes in North Kerala. *Indian Journal of Palliative Care* **11**, 15–18.

Paleri AK (2004). *Personal communication.* CEO, Pain and Palliative Care Society.

Palmer A, Burns S and Bulman C (1994). *Reflective practice in nursing*, pp. 10–15. Oxford, Blackwell Science Limited.

Parahoo AK (1997). *Nursing research. Principles, process AND Issues.* Basingstoke, Hampshire, Palgrave Macmillan.

Parfitt B (1986). Steps in evaluating a programme of nurse education. *Nurse Education Today* **6**, 166–71.

Parker DL, Webb J and D'Souza B (1995). The value of critical incident analysis as an educational tool and its relationship to experiential learning. *Nurse Education Today* **15**(2), 111–16.

Parker J (2005). Social work education for palliative care – changes and challenges. In J Parker, ed. *Aspects of social work and palliative care,* pp. 1–19. London, Quay Books.

Parsell G and Bligh J (1998). Interprofessional learning. *Postgraduate Medical Journal* **74**, 89–95.

Patten C (1998). *East and West: China, power and the future of Asia.* New York, Times Books.

Patterson BL (1995). Developing and maintaining reflection in clinical journals. *Nurse Education Today* **15**, 211–20.

Patton M (1987). *How to use qualitative methods in evaluation.* Newbury Park, CA, Sage.

Patton MQ (1986). *Utilization – focused evaluation,* 2nd edn. Newbury Park, CA, Sage.

Pawson R and Tilley N (1997). *Realistic evaluation.* London, Sage.

Payne S, Hardey M and Coleman P (2000). Interactions between nurses during handovers in elderly care. *Journal of Advanced Nursing* **32**, 277–85.

Pearson M (2002). *Developing a shared framework for all health professionals learning beyond registration.* Official communication from the DoH office of Prof Pearson, Deputy Director of Human Resources. UK, Department of Health.

Pendleton D (2006). Edgecumbe Consulting Group. *Personal communication.*

Pendleton D and King J (2002). Values and leadership. *BMJ* **325,** 1352–5.

Pereira AL (2003). Pedagogical approaches and educational practices in health sciences. *Cad Saúde Pública, Rio de Janeiro* **19**(5), 41–5.

Pereira J, Bruera E and Quan H (2001). Palliative care on the net: an online survey of health care professionals. *J Palliative Care* **17,** 41–5.

Philpot M (1997) Educational courses in Britain. *Distance Learning.* **18**(6) Cited in: Talbot CJ (2003). *Studying at a distance: a guide for students.* Maidenhead, Open University Press.

Poikela E (2004). Developing criteria for knowing and learning at work: towards context-based assessment. *Journal of Workplace Learning* **16**(5–6), 267–74.

Policy Hub (2003). *Magenta Book,* Chapter 1. Available at http://www.policyhub.gov.uk/ evaluating_policy/magenta_book/chapter1.asp. Accessed 7 August 2005.

Policzer JS (1999). *Approach to teaching palliative medicine to medical students.* Presented as module W-11 A collaborative end-of-life care curriculum at the 11th annual assembly of the American Academy of Hospice and Palliative Medicine, June 23–26, 1999. Snowbird, UT.

Polit DF and Hungler BP (2001). *Nursing research: principles and methods*, 6th edn. Philadelphia, Lippincott.

Porchet F, Schaerer G, Larkin P and Leruth S (2005). Intercultural experiences of training in the Maghreb. *European Journal of Palliative Care* **12**(1), 35–7.

Postgraduate Medical Education and Training Board (2004). *Principles for an assessment system for postgraduate medical training*. London, Postgraduate Medical Education and Training Board.

Powell M (ed.) (1999). *New Labour, new welfare state?: the 'third way' in British social policy*. Bristol, Policy Press.

Premadasa IG (1993). A reappraisal of the use of multiple choice questions. *Medical Teacher* **15**, 237–42.

Preston AP and Biddle G (1994). 'To be or not to be?': making a professional career choice. *International Journal of Career Management* **6**(1), 28–32.

Prideaux D (2002) Researching the outcomes of educational interventions: a matter of design. *BMJ* **324**, 126–7.

Prince C (2003). Corporate education and learning: the accreditation agenda. *Journal of Workplace Learning* **14**, 179–85.

Pringle HM (2005). Learning how to care. *The Royal College of Anaesthetists Bulletin* **34,** 1719–21.

Proctor B (1991). On being a trainer. In Dryden W and Thorne B, eds *Training and supervision for counselling in action*, pp. 49–73. London, Sage.

Prowse MA and Heath V (2005). Working collaboratively in health care contexts; the influence of bioscientific knowledge on patient outcomes. *Nurse Education Today* **25**(2), 132–9.

Purcell-Robertson RM and Purcell FP (2000). Interactive distance learning. In Lau L (2000). *Distance learning technologies: issues, trends and opportunities*, pp. 16–21. London, Idea Group Publishing.

Quality Assurance Agency for Higher Education (2000). *Subject benchmark statement. Health care programmes: social policy and administration and social work*. Gloucester, Quality Assurance Agency for Higher Education.

Quality Assurance Agency for Higher Education (2001a). *Subject benchmark statements. Health care programmes: occupational therapy*. Gloucester, Quality Assurance Agency for Higher Education.

Quality Assurance Agency for Higher Education (2001b). *Subject benchmark statements. Health care programmes: physiotherapy*. Gloucester, Quality Assurance Agency for Higher Education.

Race P (1996). *How to win as an open learner: a student's guide to tackling an open learning course*. Coventry, National Council for Educational Technology.

Race P (1998). *500 tips for open and flexible learning*. London, Kogan Page.

Race P (2005). *Making learning happen*. London, Sage Publications.

Rajagopal MR and Kumar S (1999). A model for delivery of palliative care in India – the Calicut experiment. *Journal of Palliative Care* **15**, 44–9.

Ramani S, Orlander JD, Strunin L and Barber TW (2003). Whither bedside teaching? A focus-group study of clinical teachers. *Academic Medicine* **78**(4), 384–90.

Ramsden P (1992). *Learning to teach in higher education*. London, Routledge.

Read S and Spall B (2005) Reflecting on patient and carer biographies in palliative care education. *Nurse Education in Practice* **5**(3), 136–43.

Reece I and Walker S (1998). *Teaching, training and learning: a practical guide*. London, Business Education Publishers.

Rees CE and Sheard CE (2004). The reliability of assessment criteria for undergraduate medical students' communication skills portfolios: the Nottingham experience. *Medical Education* **38**, 138–44.

Rees R and Walker S (2000). Planning and design for teaching and learning. In *Teaching, training and learning: a practical guide*, pp. 235–350. Sunderland, Business Education Publishers Limited.

Reeves S, Freeth D, McCorie P and Perry D (2002). 'It teaches you what to expect in future...': interprofessional learning on a training ward for medical, nursing, occupational therapy and physiotherapy students. *Medical Education* **36**, 337–44.

Relf M (2003). Bereavement care. In Oliviere D and Monroe B (eds). *A voice for the voiceless: patient participation in palliative care*. Oxford, Oxford University Press.

Renewal.net. *How to commission an evaluation?* Available at www.renewal.net./documents/RNET/toolkit/howcommissionevaluation.doc. Accessed 27 Oct 2006.

Rhodes L (1997). Links between education and practice. *Information Exchange* **Dec**, 14.

Rich A and Parker DL (1995). Reflection and critical incident analysis: ethical and moral implications of their use within nursing and midwifery education. *Journal of Advanced Nursing* **22**, 1050–7.

Roberts P, Priest H and Bromage C (2001). Selecting and utilising data sources to evaluate health care education. *Nurse Researcher* **8**(3),15–29.

Robertson G (1997). Palliative nursing in New Zealand. *International Journal of Palliative Nursing* **3**(5), 244.

Robertson G (2005). *Personal communication*.

Robinson D (2000). The contribution of physiotherapy to palliative care. *European Journal of Palliative Care* **7**, 95–8.

Robson C (2002). *Real world research,* 2nd edn. Oxford, Blackwell Publishing.

Rogers A (1996). *Teaching adults,* 2nd edn. Buckingham, Open University Press.

Rogers C (1961). *On becoming a person*. London, Constable.

Rogers CR (1987). Client-centred ? Person-centred? *Person-Centred Review* **2**(1), 11–4.

Rogers EM (1995). *Diffusion of innovation,* 4th edn, pp. 1–37. New York, The Free Press.

Rogers G and Badham L (1994). Evaluation in the management cycle. In Bennet N, Glatter R and Levacic R (eds). *Improving Educational Management through Research and Consultancy*. London, Paul Chapman.

Rooke D and Torbert WR (2005). Seven transformations of leadership. *Harvard Business Review* **April**, 67–76.

Ross DD, O'Mara A, Pickens N, Keay T *et al.* (1997) Hospice and palliative care education in medical school: a module on the role of the physician in end-of-life care. *Journal of Cancer Educ* **12**, 152–6.

Ross F and Southgate L (2000). Learning together in medical and nursing training: aspirations and activity. *Medical Education* **34**, 739–43.

Ross, DD, Keay T, Timmel D *et al.* (1999). Required training in hospice and palliative care at the University of Maryland School of Medicine. *J Cancer Educ* **14**, 132–6.

Rosser M, Rice AM, Campbell H and Jack C (2004). Evaluation of a mentorship programme for specialist practitioners. *Nurse Educ Today* **24**(8), 596–604.

Rowland-Morin PA, Burchard KW, Garb JL and Coe NP (1991) Influence of effective communication by surgery students on their oral examination scores. *Academic Medicine* **66**, 169–71.

Rowntree D (1985). *Developing courses for students*. London, Harper Row.

Royal Australasian College of Physicians Chapter of Palliative Medicine (2005). **Curriculum for the Training and Continuing Professional Development of Specialists in Palliative Medicine.** Available at http://www.racp.edu.au/public/pallmed.

Royal College of Nursing (2004). *A framework for nurses working in specialist palliative care: competencies project*. London, Royal College of Nursing.

Royal College of Nursing (RCN) Institute (2000). *Realising clinical effectiveness and clinical governance through clinical supervision*. Oxford, Radcliffe Medical Press.

Royal College of Physicians of London (2005). *On-the-job assessment for SpRs: delegate pack*. London, Royal College of Physicians.

Rumble G and Oliveira J (eds.) (1992). *Vocational education at a distance: international perspectives*. London, Kogan Page.

Ryan J (2003). Continuous professional development along the continuum of lifelong learning. *Nurse Education Today* **23**, 498–508.

Sadler P (1997). *Leadership: styles – role models – qualities – behaviours.* London, Kogan Page.

Salmon D and Jones M (2001). Shaping the interprofessional agenda: a study examining qualified nurses' perceptions of learning with others. *Nurse Education Today* **21**, 18–25.

Salmon G (2004). *E-moderating: the key to teaching and learning online,* 2nd edn. London, Routledge Falmer.

Saunders C. History of Hospice Care. In: Oxford Textbook of Palliative Medicine, 2nd edition, Oxford University Press, New York, 1998.

Sanderson I (2003). Is it what works that matters? Evaluation and evidence-based policy making. *Research Papers in Education* **18**(4), 331–45.

Saunders C (1998). History of hospice care. In D Doyle, G Hanks and N Cherney, eds *Oxford Textbook of Palliative Medicine,* 2nd edn, pp. xvii–xx. New York, Oxford University Press.

Saunders C (2003). *Watch with me: inspiration for a life in hospice care.* Sheffield, Mortal Press.

Schein EH (1992). *Organisational culture and leadership.* San Francisco, Jossey-Bass.

Schober JE and Hinchliff SM (eds) (1995). *Towards advanced nursing practice.* London, Arnold.

Schön D (1997). *Educating the reflective practitioner.* San Francisco, Jossey-Bass.

Schön DE (1983). *The reflective practitioner.* London, Temple Smith.

Schon DA (1987). *Educating the reflective practitioner.* London, Jossey-Bass.

Scopinaro M and Casak S (2002). Paediatric oncology in Argentina: medical and ethical issues. *The Lancet Oncology* **3**, 111–6.

Scriven M (1991). *Evaluation thesaurus,* 4th edn. Newbury Park, CA, Sage.

Scriven M (1996). The theory behind practical evaluation. *Evaluation* **2**(4), 393–404.

Scriven M (2005). *The most important part of evaluation.* Available at http://evaluation.wmich. edu/scripts/wa.exe/A2=ind0504&L=eval-wmu&F=&S=7P=. Accessed 6 August 2005.

Sewpaul V and Jones D (2005). Global standards for the education and training of the social work profession. *International Journal of Social Welfare* **14**, 218–30.

Seymour J, Clark D, Hughes P *et al.* (2002). Clinical nurse specialists in pallative care. Part 3: issues for the Macmillan Nurse role. *Palliative Medicine* **16**, 386–94.

Shafer RM (1975). *The rhinoceros in the classroom.* New York, Universal Edition (Canada) Ltd.

Shaw R (1998). Why evaluate? In Harvey J (ed.) *The LTDI Evaluation Cookbook* p 6. Edinburgh, Learning Technology Dissemination Initiative.

Sheldon F and Smith P (1996). The life so short, the craft so hard to learn: a model for post-basic education in palliative care. *Palliative Medicine* **10**, 99–104.

Sheperd J (1995). Findings of a training needs analysis for qualified nursing practitioners. *Journal of Advanced Nursing* **22**, 66–71.

Shields E (1995). Reflection and learning in student nurses. *Nurse Education Today* **15**(6), 452–8.

Simons RJ, Baily RG, Zelis R and Zwillich CW (1989). The physiologic and psychological effects of the bedside presentation. *New England Journal of Medicine* **321**(18), 1273–5.

Simpson O (2000). *Supporting students in open and distance learning.* London, Kogan Page.

Singleton JK and Green-Hernandez C (1998). Interdisciplinary education and practice: has its time come? *Journal of Nurse-Midwifery* **43**, 3–7.

Skilbeck J, Corner J, Bath P *et al* (2002). Clinical nurse specialists in palliative care. Part 1: a description of the Macmillan Nurse caseload. *Palliative Medicine* **16**, 285–96.

Skilbeck JK and Payne S (2005). End of life care: a discursive analysis of specialist palliative care nursing. *Journal of Advanced Nursing* **52**(4), 325–34.

Sloan PA, Donnelly MB, Schwartz RW, Sloan DA (1996). *Cancer pain assessment and management* **67**, 475–81.

Smeding R and Oderkerk R (1997). *Training for teachers in palliative medicine,* pp. 1–9. Netherlands: Stichting Pallium 2.

Smith J and Topping A (2001). Unpacking the 'value added' impact of continuing professional education: a multi-method case study approach. *Nurse Education Today* **21**(5), 341–9.

Smith T, Loprinzi C and von Gunten CF (2001). *ASCO curriculum: optimizing cancer care – the importance of symptom management*. Virginia, US American Society for Clinical Oncology.

Sneddon M (2004). Specialist professional education in palliative care. How did we get here and where are we going? In S Payne, J Seymour and C Ingleton, eds *Palliative care nurses, principles and evidence for practice*, pp. 636–54. Buckinghamshire, England, Open University Press.

Societal Working Needs Group (1996). CanMEDS 2000 Project. *Annals of the Royal College of Physician and Surgeon of Canada* **29**, 206–16.

Sonobe HM, Hayashida M, Costa Mendes IA, Fontao Zago MM (2001). The Arch method in the preoperative education of laryngotomized patients. *Revista Brasileira de Cancerologia* **47**, 425–33.

Special Educational Needs and Disability Act (2001). London, HMSO Stationery Office. Available at http://www.opsi.gov.uk/acts/acts2001/20010010.htm. Accessed 28 June 2006.

Spencer JA and Jordan RK (1999). Learner centred approaches in medical education. *BMJ* **318**, 1280–3.

Spring B (2005). *Personal communication.*

Stacy R and Spencer J (1999). Patients as teachers: a qualitative study of patients' views on their role in a community-based undergraduate project. *Medical Education* **33**(9), 688–94.

Stake R (1983). Program evaluation, particularly responsive evaluation. In Madaus GF, Scriven MS and Stufflebeam DL (eds.) *Evaluation models: viewpoints on educational and human services evaluation.* Boston, Mass., Kluwer-Nijhoff, pp 287–310.

Starr P (1982). *The social transformation of American medicine*, pp. 342–3. New York, Basic Books.

Stead DR (2005). A review of the one-minute paper. *Active Learning in Higher Education* **6**(2), 118–31.

Steadman RH, Coates WC, Huang YM *et al.* (2006). Simulation-based training is superior to problem-based learning for the acquisition of critical assessment and management skills. *Crit Care Med* **34**(1), 252–3.

Steen PD, Miller, T, Palmer L *et al.* (1999). An introductory hospice experience for third-year medical students. *J Cancer Educ* **14**, 140–3.

Sterling S (2001). *Sustainable education: revisioning learning and and change.* Totnes, Green Books.

Stewart A and Catanzaro R (2005). Can physician assistants be effective in the UK? *Clinical Medicine* **5**(4), 344–8.

Stewart M, Belle Brown J, Weston WW, McWhinney IR, McWilliam CL and Freeman TR (1995). *Patient-centered medicine: transforming the clinical method.* Thousand Oaks, CA, Sage Publications.

Stewart M, Belle Brown J, Weston WW, McWhinney IR, McWilliam CL and Freeman TR (2003) *Patient-centered medicine: transforming the clinical method*, 2nd edn. Oxford, Radcliffe Medical Press.

Stjernsward J, Kumar S and Thottathil Z (2003). *Consensus Report from the Workshop on Palliative Care and Hospice Services.* Kuwait Palliative Care Initiative. Submitted to the Government of Kuwait.

Stjernsward J (2004). In LA Reynolds and EM Tansey, eds *Innovation in pain management*, p. 45. London, Wellcome Trust Centre for History of Medicine at UCL.

Stjernsward J and Clark D (2004). Palliative medicine – a global perspective. In D Doyle, G Hanks, N Cherny and K Calman, eds *Oxford Textbook of Palliative Medicine*, 3rd edn, pp. 1209. Oxford, Oxford University Press.

Strauss A, Fagerhaugh S, Suczek B and Wiener C (1985). *Social organization of medical work.* Chicago, Chicago University Press.

Struyf E, Beullens J, Van Damme B, Janssen P and Jaspaert H (2005). A new methodology for teaching clinical reasoning skills: problem-solving clinical seminars. *Medical Teaching* **27**(4), 364–8.

Stuart C (2003). *Assessment, supervision and support in clinical practice: a guide for nurses, midwives and other health professionals.* Edinburgh, Churchill Livingstone.

Stufflebeam G (1971). *Educational evaluation and decision making.* Itasca, IL, Peacock.

Stufflebeam G and Shinkfield AJ (1985). *Systematic evaluation: a self instructional guide to theory and practice.* Nijhof, Dordrecht, Kluwer.

Suchman E, Smith R, Ahermae S, McDowell K and Timpsom W (2000). The use of small groups in a large lecture microbiology course. *Journal of Industrial Microbiology and Biotechnology* **25,** 121–6.

Sullivan AM, Lakoma MD and Billings A (2005). Teaching and learning end-of-life care: evaluation of a faculty development program in palliative care. *Academic Medicine* **80,** 657–68.

Sulmasy DP, Dwyer M and Marx E (1995). Knowledge, confidence and attitudes regarding medical ethics: how do faculty and housestaff compare? *Acad Med* **70,** 1038–40.

SUPPORT (Study to Understand Prognoses and Preferences for Outcomes and Risks of Treatment) Principal Investigators (1995). A controlled trial to improve care for seriously ill hospitalized patients. *JAMA* 274, 1591–8.

Swallow VM, Chalmers H, Miller J, Piercy C and Sen B (2001). Accredited work-based learning for new nursing roles: nurses, experiences of two pilot schemes. *Journal of Clinical Nursing* **10,** 820–1.

Talbot CJ (2003). *Studying at a distance: a guide for students.* Maidenhead, Open University Press.

Tanner C (2001). Measurement and evaluation in nursing education. *Journal of Nurse Education* **40**(1), 3–4.

Taylor BJ (2000). *Reflective practice: a guide for nurses and midwives.* Maidenhead, Open University Press.

Taylor P (1993). *The texts of Paulo Freire,* pp. 25–52. Buckingham, Philadelphia, Open University Press.

Taylor V (2004). Palliative care education: establishing the evidence base. In Foyle L and Hostad J, eds *Delivering cancer and palliative care education,* pp. 147–160. Oxford, Radcliffe Medical Press.

Tebbitt P (1999). *Commissioning through partnership,* pp. 23–4. London, National Countil for Hospice and Specialist Palliative Care.

Ten Have H and Janssens R (2001). *Palliative care in Europe concepts and policies.* Oxford, IOS Press.

The Medical School Objectives Writing Group (1999). Learning objectives for medical student education: guidelines for medical schools: Report I of the Medical School Objective Project. *Academic Medicine* **74**, 13–8.

The SUPPORT Principal Investigators (1995). A controlled trial to improve care for seriously ill hospitalized patients. *JAMA* **274,** 1591–8.

Thomas CS, Mellsop G and Callender K (1992). The oral examination: a study of academic and non-academic factors. *Medical Education* **27**, 433–9.

Thompson AR, Savage MH, Travis T (1999). *Palliative care education—the first year's experience with a mandatory third-year medical student rotation at the University of Arkansas for Medical Sciences.* Presented as module W-11 A collaborative end-of-life care curriculum at the 11th annual assembly of the American Academy of Hospice and Palliative Medicine, June 23–26, 1999. Snowbird, UT.

Tieman J (2005). CareSearch: finding and evaluating Australia's missing palliative care literature. *Biomed Central Palliative Care* **4**(4). www.biomedcentral.com/content/pdf/1472-684x-4-4.pdf/.

Tombleson P, Fox RA and Dacre JA (2000). Defining the content for the objective structure clinical examination component of the Professional and Linguistic Assessments Board examination: development of a blueprint. *Medical Education* **34**, 566–72.

Tookman AJ, Hopkins K and Scharpen-von-Heussen K (2004). Rehabilitation in palliative medicine. In D Doyle, G Hanks, N Cherney and K Calman, eds *The Oxford Textbook of Palliative Medicine,* 3rd edn, pp. 1021–32. Oxford, Oxford University Press.

Torrance H (2003). When is an evaluation not an evaluation? When it's sponsored by the QCA? A response to Lindsay and Lewis. *British Educational Research Journal* **29**(2),169–73.

Toynton R (2005). Degrees of disciplinarity in equipping mature students in higher education for engagement and success in lifelong learning. *Active Learning in Higher Education* **6**(2), 106–17.

Tripp. D (1993). *Critical incidents in teaching*. London, Routledge.

Tulsky JA Chesney MA and Lo B (1996). See one, do one, teach one? House staff experience discussing do-not-resuscitate orders. *Archives of Internal Medicine* **156**, 1285–9.

Tulsky JA, Chesney MA and Lo B (1995). How do medical residents discuss resuscitation with patients? *Journal of General Internal Medicine* **10**(8), 436–42.

Tulsky JA, Fischer GS, Rose MR and Arnold RM (1998). Opening the black box: how do physicians communicate about advance directives? *Annals of Internal Medicine* **129**(6), 441–9.

Turner K and Lickiss J (1997). Postgraduate training in palliative medicine: the experience of the Sydney Institute of Palliative Medicine. *Palliative Medicine* **11**(5), 389–94.

Turner P, Sheldon F, Coles C *et al.* (2000). Listening to and learning from the family carer's story: an innovative approach in interprofessional education. *Journal of Interprofessional Care,* **14**(4), 387–95.

Tyler RW (1950). *Basic principles of curriculum and instruction.* Cited in Guba EG and Lincoln YS (eds.) *Effective evaluation: improving the usefulness of evaluation results through responsiveness and naturalistic approaches.* San Francisco, Jossey Bass.

UKCC (United Kingdom Central Council for Nursing, Midwifery and Health Visiting) (1994). *The council's standards for education and practice following registration.* Registrar's letter 20/94. London, UKCC.

UKCC (United Kingdom Central Council for Nursing, Midwifery and Health Visiting) (2001a). *Supporting nurses, midwives and health visitors through lifelong learning.* London, UKCC.

United Kingdom Central Council for Nursing, Midwifery, and Health Visiting (2001b). *The PREP handbook.* London, UKCC.

University of Plymouth. Available at http://www.plymouth.ac.uk/assets/swa/5preparing%20documents.pdf. Accessed 12 August 2005.

Vachon M (1997). Recent research into staff stress in palliative care. *European Journal of Palliative Care* **4**, 99–103.

Von Gunten CF (2002). Secondary and tertiary palliative care in US hospitals. *JAMA* **287**, 875–81.

Von Gunten CF, Ferris FD, Marquis D *et al.* (1999). The EPEC Project: education for physicians on end-of-life care. *Journal of Cancer Education* **14** (Suppl.), 14.

Von Gunten CF, Ferris FD, Robinson K, *et al.* (2001). The Education for Physicians on End-of-life Care (EPEC) Project. *Journal of Cancer Education* **16**(3, Suppl.), 14.

Von Gunten CF, Sloan P, Portenoy R and Schonwetter R (2000). Physician board certification in hospice and palliative medicine. *Journal of Palliative Medicine* **3**, 441–7.

Von Prummer C (2000). Women and distance education: challenges and opportunities. London, Routledge.

Vygotsky LS (1978). *Mind in society,* pp. 28, 78–80, 86. London, Harvard University Press.

Waddell D (1991). The effects of continuing education on nursing practice: a meta-analysis. *Journal of Continuing Education in Nursing* **22**, 113–8.

Wahlström O, Sandén I and Hammar M (1997). Multiprofessional education in the medical curriculum. *Medical Education* **31**, 425–9.

Wakefield A, Furber C, Boggis C, Sutton A and Cooke S (2003). Promoting interdisciplinarity through educational initiative: a qualitative evaluation. *Nurse Education in Practice* **3**(4), 195–203.

Wald FS, Foster Z and Wald JH (1980). The hospice movement as a health care reform. *Nursing Outlook* **28**, 173–8.

Walsh F and McGoldrick M (1991). Loss and the family: a systemic perspective. In Walsh F and McGoldrick M Living beyond loss: death in the family, pp. 1–29. New York, Norton.

Webb C, Endacott R, Gray MA *et al.* (2003). Evaluating portfolio systems: what are the appropriate criteria? *Nurse Education Today* **23**, 600–9.

Wee B, Hillier R, Coles C, Mountford B, Sheldon F and Turner P (2001). Palliative care: a suitable setting for undergraduate interprofessional education. *Palliative Medicine* **15**, 487–92.

Wee B (2005). *Personal communication.*

Wee B, Relf M, Foot C, Allen K, Roberts M and Roy Y (2004). *Personal communication.*

Weissman DE (1995). Palliative medicine education at the Medical College of Wisconsin. *Wis Med J* **94**, 505–8.

Weissman DE and Block SD (2002). ACGME requirements for end-of-life training in selected residency and fellowship programs: a status report. *Academic Medicine* **77**(4), 299–304.

Weissman DE and Dahl JL (1995). Update on the cancer pain role model education program. *Journal of Pain and Symptom Management* **10**(4), 292–7.

Weissman DE, Mullan P, Ambuel B, von Gunten CF, Hallenbeck J and Warm E (2001). End of life graduate education curriculum project. Project abstracts/progress reports – years 2. *Journal of Palliative Medicine* **4**, 525–47.

Weissman DE, Mullan PB, Ambuel B and von Gunten CF (2002). End-of-life curriculum reform: outcomes and impact in a follow-up study of internal medicine residency programs. *Journal of Palliative Medicine* **5,** 497–506.

Wenger E (1998). *Communities of practice: learning, meaning and identity,* pp. 3–15. Cambridge, Cambridge University Press.

Wilkes M and Bligh J (1999). Evaluating educational interventions. *BMJ* **318**, 1269–72.

Wilkinson SM, Gambles M and Roberts A (2002). The essence of cancer care: the impact of training on nurses' ability to communicate. *Journal of Advanced Nursing* **40**(6), 731–8.

Wilkinson TJ, Challis M, Hobma SO *et al.* (2002). The use of portfolios for assessment of the competence and performance of doctors in practice. *Medical Education* **36**, 918–24.

Williams B (2000). Collage work as a medium for guided reflection in the clinical supervision relationship. *Nurse Education Today* **20**(4), 273–8.

Williams B and Walker L (2003). Facilitating perception and imagination in generating change through reflective practice groups. *Nurse Education Today* **23**, 131–7.

Williams M (2003). Assessment of portfolios in professional education. *Nursing Standard* **18**(8), 33–7.

Williams ML, Paprock K and Covington B (1999). *Distance learning: the essential guide.* Thousand Oaks, CA, Sage.

Wilson HJ and Ayers KM (2004). Using significant event analysis in dental and medical education. *Journal of Dental Education* **68**(4), 446–53.

Wilson IB, Green ML, Goldman L, Tsevat J, Cook EF and Phillips RS (1997). Is experience a good teacher? How interns and attending physicians understand patients' choices for end-of-lie care. *Medical Decision Making* **17,** 217–27.

Wolpaw TM, Wolpaw DR and Papp. KK (2003). SNAPPS: a learner centred approach for outpatient education. *Academic Medicine* **78,** 893–98.

Wood I (1998). The effects of continuing professional education on the clinical practice of nurses: a review of the literature. *International Journal of Nursing Studies* **35**, 125–31.

Woof R (2005). *Personal communication.*

Worcester A (1935). *The care of the aged, the dying and the dead.* Springfield, IL, Charles C. Thomas.

World Health Organisation (1990). *Cancer pain relief and palliative care.* WHO Technical Report series 804. Geneva, World Health Organisation.

World Health Organisation (2002). *WHO definition of palliative care.* Available at www.who.int/cancer/palliative/definition/en/. Accessed 12 Mar 2006.

Wykurz G and Kelly D (2002). Developing the role of patients as teachers: literature review. *BMJ* **325**, 818–21.

Yates P, Nash R, Parker D *et al.* (2004). *Scoping undergraduate palliative care education in the health profession. Implications for the future.* Third Annual Research Conference, Centre for Palliative Care Research and Education, Brisbane, Australia.

Further Reading

Amery J and Lapwood S (2004). A study into the educational needs of children's hospice doctors: a descriptive quantitative and qualitative survey. *Palliative Medicine* **18**, 727–33. (Chapter 3)

Atkins J (1998). Tribalism, loss and grief: issues for multiprofessional education. *Journal of Interprofessional Care* **12**(3), 303–7. (Chapter 22)

Blewitt J and Cullungford C (eds) (2004). *The sustainability curriculum: the challenge for higher education*. London, Earthscan. (Chapter 12)

Bonwell CC. Active learning workshops. http://www.active-learning-site. com/bib1.htm#large%20class. Accessed 27 Oct 2006. (Chapter 18)

Boursicot K and Roberts T (2005). How to set up an OSCE. *The Clinical Teacher.* **2** (1), 16–20. (Chapter 20)

Bruera E (2001). Palliative care in Latin America. *Journal of Pain and Symptom Management* **8**(6), 365–8. (Chapter 11)

Buber M (1958). *I and thou.* New York, Scribrer.

Case SM and Swanson DB (2001). *Constructing written test questions for the basic and clinical sciences,* 3rd edn. Philadelphia, USA: National Board of Medical Examiners. www.nmbe.org/PDF/2001iwgin-dex.pdf (Chapter 20)

Chapman DM and Calhoun JG (2006). Validation of learning style measures: implications for medical education practice. *Medical Education* **40**(6), 576–83. (Chapter 3)

Corttrell S (2001). *Teaching study skills and supporting learning.* Basingstoke and New York, Palgrave Macmillan. (Chapter 1)

Downing SM (2003).Validity: on the meaningful interpretation of assessment data. *Medical Education* **37**, 830–837. (Chapter 20)

Farrow R (2003). Creating teaching materials. *BMJ* 2003; 326: 921–923. (Chapter 18)

Fletcher SH and Barrett A (2004). Developing effective beginning teachers through mentor-based induction. *Mentoring and Tutoring* **12**(3), 321–33. (Chapter 23)

Forsyth P (1995). *Making successful presentations.* London, Sheldon Press (Chapter 18)

Freire P (1995). *Pedagogy of hope. Reliving pedagogy of the oppressed*, pp. 7–22. New York, Continuum. (Chapter 11)

Gibbs G and Habeshaw T (1989). *Preparing to teach. An introduction to effective teaching in higher education.* Bristol, Technical and Educational Services Ltd. (Chapter 18)

Gupta H (2004). How basic is palliative care? *International Journal of Palliative Care* **10**(12), 600–1. (Chapter 12)

Henderson P, Ferguson-Smith AC and Johnson MH (2005). Developing essential professional skills: a framework for teaching and learning about feedback. *BMC Medical Education* **5**(11), 1–6. (Chapters 1 and 23)

Higgs J and Edwards H (2002). Challenges facing health professional education in the challenging context of university education. *British Journal of Occupational Therapy* **65**(7), 315–20. (Chapter 12)

LaCombe MA (1997). On bedside teaching. *Annals of Internal Medicine* **126**(3), 217–20. (Chapter 13)

McGregor J, Cooper JL, Smith KA and Robinson P (2000). *Editors' notes – strategies for energising large classes. New Directions for teaching and learning,* no. 81, Spring. Jossey-Bass Publications. (Chapter 18)

McKimm J, Jollie C and Cantillon P (2003). Web based learning. *BMJ* **326**, 870–3. (Chapter 19)

Maguerez C and Bordenave JD (1985). Alguns fatores pedagógicos, capacitação pedagógica para instrutor, supervisor da área de Saúde. *Bulletin do Ministério da Saúde*, pp 19–26, Brasilia. (Chapter 11)

Neher JO, Gordon KC, Meyer B and Stevens N (1992). A five-step "microskills" model of clinical teaching. *Journal of the American Board of Family Practice* **5**, 419–24. (Chapter 13)

Norcini JJ (2003). Setting standards on educational tests. *Medical Education*. **37**, 464–69. (Chapter 20)

Norcini JJ (2005) The Mini Clinical Evaluation Exercise (mini-CEX). *The Clinical Teacher*. **2** (1), 25–30. (Chapter 20)

Oxman AD, Thompson MA, Davis DA and Haynes RB (1995). No magic bullets: a systematic review of 102 trials of interventions to improve professional practice. *Can Med Assoc J* **153**(10), 1423–31. (Chapter 24)

Parsell G, Spalding R and Bligh J (1998). Shared goals, shared learning: evaluation of a multiprofessional course for undergraduate students. **32**, 304–11. (Chapter 22)

Pavlov, IP (1927). *Conditioned reflexes*. London, Routledge and Kegan Paul. (Chapter 1)

Race P, Brown S and Smith B (2005). *500 Tips on assessment*. London, Routledge-Falmer. (Chapter 20)

Rawlinson F and Finlay I (2002). Assessing education in palliative medicine: development of a tool based on the Association for Palliative Medicine core curriculum. *Palliative Medicine* **16**, 51–5. (Chapter 21)

Schuwirth L. Assessing medical competence: finding the right answers. *Clinical Teacher*. **1**, 14–18. (Chapter 20)

Steinert Y and Snell LS (1999). Interactive lecturing: strategies for increasing participation in large group presentations. *Medical Teacher* **21**(1), 37–42. (Chapter 18)

United Kingdom Central Council for Nursing, Midwifery, and Health Visiting (2002). *Report of the higher level of practice pilot and project: executive summary*. London: UKCC. (Chapter 4)

Verney RE (1960). *The Student Life. The Philosophy of Sir William Osler*, pp. 70. Edinburgh and London: E. & S. Livingstone Ltd. (Chapter 13)

Walsh K (2005) Advice on writing multiple choice questions (MCQs). *BMJ Careers*. Jan, 25–27. (Chapter 20)

Glossary

Accreditation of Prior Learning (APL) enables a student with a qualification or part-qualification to enter another programme of study, in the same or a different educational institution, at a point in the programme other than the initial entry point.

Accreditation of Prior Experiential Learning (APEL) a process whereby an educational institution recognizes a learner's prior experience in professional practice, and gives academic credit for it, without reference to specific previous educational attainment.

Agenda for Change new pay and reform package designed to ensure that all non-medical clinical and support staff of the National Health Service in UK are paid on the basis of equal pay for work of equal value, linked to skills and competencies identified by the Department of Health. See also **Knowledge and Skills Framework**.

andragogy a set of assumptions about the way adults learn and the most appropriate ways of helping them learn (teaching them). One key feature of andragogy is that the responsibility for learning moves significantly from the tutor to the learner.

basic underlying assumptions deeply held ways of thinking about the way the world works which influences the way an individual perceives and responds to others and different situations; may be so embedded that the individual is unaware of these assumptions.

bedside teaching clinical teaching which takes place at the patient's side, usually integrated within or alongside the normal process of care.

case-based learning learning from experiences of individual situations, usually clinical. Learners may be required to record and/or discuss the anonymized details of the case and their own reflections about what happened, how they felt, how they might have handled things differently, etc.

collaborative working a way of working together with others which requires tolerance, generosity and cooperation, readiness to listen to others' viewpoints, willingness to explain and negotiate, and an underlying belief that the whole is greater than the sum of the parts.

communities of practice a conceptual structure for understanding group work in the delivery of clinical care.

Credit Accumulation and Transfer (CAT) a system in higher education in some countries whereby academic credit gained for courses taken in one institution may be added to credits achieved in a different institution, cumulatively creating sufficient credits, or points, for the award of a degree or diploma.

criterion referencing a method of assessing student work where achievement is measured against preset criteria. Contrast with **norm referencing** where students are measured against a cohort of peers assessed at the same time.

critical incident analysis a form of reflective learning in which an experience is examined through detailed descriptive reporting, along with review of accompanying feelings, a consideration of the viewpoints of others involved, imagining how the experience or the learner's own behaviour might be made different in the future, and planning for change.

critical thinking critical response to ideas and thoughts; scrutinizes and dips below the surface of what is heard or read; not accepting dogma or statements at face value but thinking deeply about these.

direct observation of procedures (DOPs) assessment method in which trainee is directly observed carrying out all, or part of, a clinical procedure. A score is assigned and the trainee receives feedback from the supervisor.

emotional intelligence capacity for self-awareness, self-regulation, social skill, empathy and motivation which contributes to success in creating and sustaining effective working relationships. A high degree of emotional intelligence is particularly important for successful leadership behaviour.

experiential learning a philosophy of learning which acknowledges the importance of experience as a source of learning. Also refers to a range of methods designed to maximize learning gained in this way.

formal curriculum declared statement of what will be taught in a teaching session, course or programme of study. Contrast with **informal curriculum,** which is the learning that comes from unscripted interactions between teachers and learners, and **hidden curriculum,** which is the culture in which learning occurs.

formative assessment any assessment where the primary intention is to help students learn and develop. The basis of formative assessment is feedback which is relevant and encourages discussion and self-assessment.

forum theatre a powerful style of role play in which a group of learners shares a story from their experience and re-enacts the story, after rehearsal, in front of an audience of co-learners.

genogram diagrammatic representation, using agreed symbols, of family and social network connections created to gain understanding of a patient in the context of their significant relationships.

Hawthorn effect the possibility that the mere fact of being observed (in a research project) can influence the behaviour of those observed. Translated to evaluation the effect is that recipients of a service or intervention may be less likely to report negatively if the evaluator is known to them.

hidden curriculum the culture in which learning occurs, incorporating the values, beliefs and assumptions held by the teacher and organization. Contrast with **formal curriculum** which is the declared statement of what will be taught in a teaching session, course or programme of study and **informal curriculum,** which is the learning that comes from unscripted interactions between teachers and learners.

ice-breaking activities, often in the form of short games requiring active participation of learners, designed to introduce group members to each other and prepare them for active learning in small groups.

informal curriculum learning which comes from unscripted interactions which take place between teachers and learners, and between learners themselves. Contrast with **formal curriculum** which is the declared statement of what will be taught in a teaching session, course or programme of study and **hidden curriculum** which is the culture in which learning occurs.

interprofessional learning occasions when two or more professions learn together with the object of cultivating collaborative practice. Compare **multidisciplinary** learning, which involves different branches of the same profession, and **multiprofessional learning,** which involves two or more professions learning together but not necessarily interacting during the process of learning.

Knowledge and Skills Framework a set of skills and competencies set out by the UK Department of Health as guidelines for appointment, payscale and progression of non-medical health professionals. See also **Agenda for Change**.

learning styles the idea that individuals have preferences for the way they learn; these are ways which are likely to be most effective for these individuals; non-preferred ways of learning will cost that individual more energy and effort.

lifelong learning the idea that professional learning extends beyond the point of registration to include continuing learning, incorporating both work-based learning and further education programmes or courses.

mini-CEX provides a structured way for a trainer to observe, score and give feedback to a trainee on a patient related activity, e.g. an outpatient or ward consultation, note taking, prescribing or discussion about a clinical letter.

multisource feedback (MSF) obtaining feedback from a variety of sources, including patients, carers, clinicians from the same and other backgrounds and administrative and support staff.

National Institute of Clinical Excellence (NICE) an institution set up by UK government to scrutinize the evidence base and make recommendations about treatments that should be funded on the National Health Service.

National Vocational Qualification (NVQ), England and Wales designed to assess skills and knowledge gained through learning at work or on work-placement/simulation.

norm referencing a method of grading assessed work in which students are compared with their peers. Allows comparison between weak and good achievers. Contrast **criterion referencing** in which student performance is measured against preset criteria.

pedagogy the art or science of teaching. Contrast **traditional pedagogy,** which is based on teachers being transmitters of knowledge and students being recipients, with **conditioning-based pedagogy,** which focuses on the behavioural outcome of an educational process like training and **empowerment pedagogy** which regards students as key agents who identify real problems and develop creative solutions.

practical wisdom the combination of good judgement and action, knowing what is required in a particular moral situation and being willing to act on this knowledge.

Post-Registration Education and Practice (PREP) requirement for nurses in UK to undertake minimum continuing professional study and to keep evidence of doing so.

portfolio a collection of material which provides evidence of work-based learning, often structured to show that defined learning outcomes have been achieved.

problem based learning (PBL) a method of learning focused on integration of knowledge from a wide range of sources to create, analyse and develop appropriate ways of investigating through progressive enquiry.

Quality Assurance Agency (QAA) statutory body responsible for carrying out quality monitoring of higher education programmes in UK.

reflective learning an approach to learning which situates the self in a central position in the process of knowledge production.

reflective practice an approach to practice in which learning occurs through thinking through a practical experience in relation to theory and previous learning.

role play a method of experiential learning in which learners imagine themselves into the role of another person and act out a real-life situation relevant to the intended learning. Other learners take on the role of observers who give constructive feedback. Skilful facilitation, careful preparation and debriefing are required.

sculpting a method of experiential learning used to raise awareness and understanding of how relationships influence the way people think, feel and behave. The central technique is to create a tableau that depicts non-verbally the quality of the relationships between the people involved. This can provide a powerful insight into what the world looks like from the perspectives of the different roles depicted in the sculpt.

simulated patients actors who undertake specific training to enable them to reproduce situations in which real patients may find themselves.

summative assessment assessment whose primary function is to test student achievement. Summative assessments should also incorporate feedback to aid learning wherever possible.

viva voce an oral examination in which, typically, the student is questioned by one or two examiners in an interview setting.

work-based learning experiential learning and professional development in the workplace that can be recognized and accredited academically.

Useful web sites

Cross reference to chapter	Name	Website address
2	Occupational Therapy in HIV/AIDS, Oncology, Palliative Care and Education (HOPE)	www.cot.org.uk/specialist/hope/intro/intro.php
2	Association of Chartered Physiotherapists in Oncology and Palliative Care (ACPOPC)	www.acpopc.org.uk/acpopc/home.asp
2	Association of Palliative Care Social Workers (APCSW)	www.helpthehospices.org.uk/NPA/socialworkers/
3	Royal College of Physicians, London	www.rcplondon.ac.uk
3	Postgraduate Medical Education and Training Board	www.pmetb.org.uk
3	Moderning Medical Careers	www.mmc.nhs.uk
3	Joint Committee on Higher Medical Training	www.jchmt.org.uk
3	General Medical Council–Tomorrow's Doctors document	www.gmc-uk.org/education/undergraduate/tomorrows_doctors.asp
5	African Palliative Care Association	www.apca.co.ug
5	Hospice Palliative Care Association of South Africa	www.hospicepalliativecaresa.co.za
5	Hospice Africa Uganda	www.hospiceafrica.org
6	Asia-Pacific Hospice Network	www.aphn.org
7	New Zealand Hospice	www.hospice.org.nz
10	Educating Future Physicians in Palliative and End-of-Life Care Project	www.efppec.ca

Continued

Cross reference to chapter	Name	Website address
10	Joint Commission on Accreditation of Healthcare Organizations pain guidelines	www.jcaho.org
10	American Academy of Hospice and Palliative Medicine Fellowship Directory	www.AAHPM.org/fellowship/directory.html
10	The Centre to Advance Palliative Care	www.capc.org
10	National Hospice and Palliative Care Organization	www.nhpco.org
10	Supplementary references relating to palliative care education in North America	www.cpsonline.info/content/resources/education.html
20	Accreditation Council for Graduate Medical Association, US	www.acgme.org/Outcome/assess/Toolbox.pdf
20	Higher Education Academy, UK–resources on assessment	www.heacademy.ac.uk/Assessmentoflearning.htm
24	Academy of Medical Royal Colleges–ten principles for CPD	www.aomrc.org.uk/documents/CPD10PrinciplesDocument-Dec05_000.pdf

Index

CPSIA information can be obtained at www.ICGtesting.com
Printed in the USA
BVOW07s0833060514

352688BV00005BA/23/P